ON DANGEROUS GROUND
A Memoir of the
Irish Revolution

ON DANGEROUS GROUND

A Memoir of the Irish Revolution

MÁIRE COMERFORD

Edited by **HILARY DULLY**

THE LILLIPUT PRESS
DUBLIN

First published 2021 by
THE LILLIPUT PRESS
62–63 Sitric Road, Arbour Hill
Dublin 7, Ireland
www.lilliputpress.ie

Paperback ISBN 9781843518198

10 9 8 7 6 5 4 3 2 1

The Lilliput Press gratefully acknowledges the financial
support of the Arts Council/An Chomhairle Ealaíon.

Set in 11pt on 16pt Baskerville
Printed in Kerry, Ireland, by Walsh Colour Print

Contents

PREFACE   vii

INTRODUCTION: Máire Comerford – an appreciation   xi

On Dangerous Ground   1

Avondale   3

Rathdrum   10

Ballycourcey   17

From School to Rotten Row   22

Home Rule   32

World War   40

Etchingham   47

Rising   52

The Risen People   59

Ashe   72

Sisters   76

Conscription   83

Women   88

1918 Election   93

The First Dáil   98

Living on the Green   105

My Half-Mile Radius   114

Inside Nos 6 and 76   118

Close Shaves, and Vigils   125

Raids, Escapades and Escapes   132

CONTENTS

Visits and Visitors   136

Bodenstown to Leitrim   144

Trips to Tipp   150

A Spy and a Mystery Man   158

Wicklow and Local Bodies   162

Unwelcome Visitors   166

1920–21   170

Arrests and Escapes   177

White Cross   183

Housekeepers   190

Thin Red Line   198

Truce   206

Beds   213

Dresses and Delegations   219

The Split   226

Flying the Flag   233

Making and Breaking Pacts   238

The '22 Election   243

Post-election '22   251

Inside the Courts   258

The Hotel   267

Driving and Dodging   275

The Final Chapter   283

EPILOGUE: What Máire Did Next   291

ACKNOWLEDGMENTS   297

APPENDIX: Newspaper Articles on Máire Comerford, 1923 299

INDEX   307

Illustrations between pages 78 and 79, 174 and 175, and 270 and 271.

PREFACE

When I first met my husband, Joe Comerford, in the mid-1980s, I also 'met' his much-loved aunt, Máire Comerford, although she had died a couple of years previously. Initially, I made Máire's acquaintance though her library of heavily thumbed and annotated Irish history books and pamphlets, in her collection of Republican memorabilia, in the boxes of her extensive archive – piled high in her former home, St Nessan's in Sandyford village, Dublin. But most of all I got to know Máire Comerford through the pages of her memoir of the Irish Revolution. When I read her account of that turbulent (and still strongly contested) period of Irish history, I was enthralled by her bravery, idealism and unbreakable commitment to fighting for an independent Irish Republic. I was also struck by the fact that she was, for all intents and purposes, a female combatant on a war footing in the Irish Revolution. In the 1980s, the role played by women during the revolutionary period, apart from figureheads such as Countess Markievicz and Maud Gonne McBride, was largely unknown. Máire's account not only focused on her story in the fight for independence from Britain, it also introduced a band of extraordinary women and men engaged in the same pursuit – some well-known, but many others virtually lost to history. This great citizen army, mobilized in common cause, is surely one of the most intriguing aspects of the War of Independence; *On Dangerous Ground* brings us closer to understanding how this worked on a day-to day basis. That their common goal was thwarted, at least in part, makes the tragedy of the Civil War all the more poignant.

My approach to editing the memoir was grounded in a simple methodology, or guiding principle – to preserve the authenticity of Máire's voice in the telling of her own story. I was determined to avoid any retrospective contextualization of her witness account. Máire believed, as I do, that the construction of history is rarely a neutral exercise; it is constantly evolving and changing through new research and interpretation, often in tune with the forces of present-day political realities and power struggles.

Máire Comerford deposited a version of her memoir with University College Dublin Archive in the 1970s, but this document was far from complete. An exploration of the contents of her archive revealed that there was additional memoir material available, including the concluding chapters of this edited version. I also discovered chapters and notes related to Máire's childhood and upbringing, and the social and political forces pre-1916, which began to shape and change the temper of the country. These forces, including the fight for Home Rule for Ireland, World War I and the rise of the Volunteers, combined to set in train the gradual politicization of a young woman, living on the fringes of the gentry in County Wexford. Máire was christened Mary by her parents and was known as Mary Comerford to most of her comrades during the revolutionary period, and by her wider family for the duration of her lifetime. This Mary/Máire identity is central to understanding her political awakening and subsequent life-long Republicanism. As such, throughout the memoir, she is occasionally Mary, but more often Máire.

Máire Comerford spent the latter years of her life writing, rewriting and editing her own narrative. My first job as editor was to gather together all this material and to begin the process of creating a broadly chronological narrative from the various versions of the available memoir chapters. I was always conscious that *On Dangerous Ground* was written to examine the revolutionary period from a Republican perspective. Máire made no apology for that, for this was exactly what she set out to do. She was clear that her memoir was not a historical account in the formal academic sense. Rather, *On Dangerous Ground* is a participatory witness account of the period, up to the sad conclusion in the bleak aftermath of the Civil War. It is a history told and examined by a woman who was present, on active service, her boots on the ground and moving all around the country. She had skin in the game, and her life on the line. And therein lies its unique historical value. I saw it as my job to find a framework that would allow her story to also tell the wider story of the period, without losing the resonance that comes from actually having been there, totally invested in the Cause; then subjected to a soul-crushing political and military defeat at the hands of former comrades.

Máire continued to write well into her old age with the intention that this memoir would be published in her lifetime – that *On Dangerous Ground* would find a place in the rich tapestry of the history of this fascinating time. Sadly, this was not to be. As editor of her memoir, I can only hope that almost forty years after her death, I have served her intentions well.

Hilary Dully

Máire Comerford – an appreciation

AS A YOUNG, eager graduate student, desperate to find out more about the activities of Ireland's revolutionary women, it was suggested to me that I should arrange to meet Máire Comerford. In my shy letter of introduction, I ended by saying that I would be in her debt forever. How true were those words. How much we are all in her debt becomes apparent on reading this wonderful account of her life and her participation in the Irish revolution. Her clear eye, extraordinary recall and attention to detail, coupled with an unerring ability to be at the heart of so much of the action, provides the reader with a witness account that rivals any of those produced by her male contemporaries. Her political acuity, evident in her growing understanding of the forces that were to create what she always termed the 'counter-revolution', generates an additional layer of complexity. There is real emotional punch not only in the fact that Máire witnessed the deaths of so many friends and comrades, but in the realization that their youthful dreams had met the brutal reality of an imperial power that knew how to manipulate to its own ends.

The organization she joined, Cumann na mBan, was the women's auxiliary to the male Volunteer movement. It began as a support organization, raising funds, learning first aid and making up field kits, but by the time of the War of Independence it was a highly militarized body, working closely with the men, moving armaments, scouting for operations, passing messages and finding shelter for those on the run. In the Civil War period, the women's role was even more vital, and almost 500 were imprisoned by their former comrades. The majority of female activists stayed in their local area, supporting the guerrilla war from their home base. After the 1920 local government elections a small proportion of women also gained experience of local politics as they worked to establish the administration of Dáil Éireann. What makes Máire Comerford's autobiographical account of those days so valuable is the fact that she did not remain with her Wexford branch of Cumann na mBan but became an activist in many different spheres. As she said to me in 1975, 'the work I got into independently [of Cumann na mBan] was much more interesting – it brought me out around the country'. Through the distinguished historian Alice Stopford Green she became acquainted with many influential figures. As worker for Sinn Féin, the Dáil and the White Cross, travelling throughout the country, her lively intelligence and powers of description make her an invaluable witness.

Even as a young child Máire's eye for a telling detail is remarkable. The Comerford family home in Rathdrum was close to Avondale, the Parnell estate. Her father James had been friendly with Parnell and after his death her redoubtable mother Eva would visit the ageing Delia, then living alone. When the contents of the house were auctioned, the ruined state of the Parnell billiard table made a deep impression; a small vignette, but an effective illustration of the sorry history of the Parnell split and the gradual demise of Irish parliamentarianism.

Although Catholic, the Comerfords were part of the gentry of Wexford. Eva was the daughter of Lieutenant Colonel Thomas Esmonde and a tennis champion, golfer and expert rider to hounds.

However, family finances declined as James Comerford resisted market demands to bleach his flour. After his death his widow brought her family back home to Wexford. As Máire's journey into political activism began, so too did her clashes with the wider family, who eventually sent her to a fashionable convent school in England. There are many echoes of Kate O'Brien. When she is taken to a debate on home rule by her cousin, Sir Thomas Esmonde MP, sitting alone in the 'ladies cage' as Anna Parnell did before her, her unease with British rule over Ireland intensifies. After attending a performance of *Cathleen Ni Houlihan* in the Royal Court Theatre, Sara Allgood in the leading role, Máire knew her course in life was settled: 'I wanted to win back the Four Green Fields.' Her secretarial school in London was run by a friend of her mother's, a 'furious Unionist of Anglo-Irish landlord stock', who gave her pupils the Ulster Covenant and speeches of Carson as exercises for shorthand and typing. Máire, picked on as the only Catholic, soon made up her mind: 'I would be nobody's secretary except on my own terms – in, and for, Ireland.'

She began by helping her cousin Ellice Pilkington, honorary secretary to the United Irishwomen, soon to rename itself the Irish Countrywomen's Association. It was Máire's first experience of a conscious policy of keeping women out of the political sphere. Her emerging feminism began to be articulated as she argued good decisions could only come from 'an equal partnership between the sexes'. She struggled to learn Irish but loved the Gaelic League, which gave them 'a classless society of idealists. It was not to last long, but it was lovely to be in it.'

Her ability to find herself in the heart of events begins in Easter 1916 when she stays with an invalid cousin in Rathgar. Returning from Blackrock on the Easter Monday she discovers she was now in the heart of the rebellion and her excitement is conveyed as she walks along the tramlines, crowds talking and wild rumours spreading. A sentry at the St Stephen's Green barricade would have brought her into Countess Markievicz but she returns to Rathgar, promising to come to the Green the next day. However, next morning she sees blood in the doorways around Harcourt Street but no sentry. It would be her only missed opportunity.

Her sympathies lay with Liberty Hall, which she had visited when she first came up to Dublin and went back to when her family arranged a shopping trip to Dublin. Máire (having secreted a few stone of Wexford potatoes as a present) met Markievicz and Marie Perolz (who offered to supply her with a .22 revolver). She becomes firm friends with the group of Wexford activists, Seán Etchingham, Father Sweetman and Aileen K'Eogh, matron at Father Sweetman's school. When Aileen is arrested Eva Comerford cycles the twenty miles to help at the school. Dulcibella Barton, sister of Robert Barton, part of the local gentry, is also strongly Republican. Máire ends up escorting many of those on the run to the Barton home, both in the Tan War and in the Civil War.

Appointed a Cumann na mBan organizer for North Wexford, helping with anti-war campaigns – 'with that soil under one's feet, and a job to be done, it was heaven to be young' – she finally gained her independence when Alice Stopford Green, a paying guest at her mother's home (together with Jack Yeats and others) invited her to live in her St Stephen's Green home and work as her secretary and researcher. Here she meets the famous and the influential. In late evening she also has 'three or four hours of glorious freedom' 'to see what one person could do for the Irish Republic'. There are fascinating snippets of social history: the small girls Mrs Green calls 'Dublin's little mothers' escorting toddlers and babies from the slums to the sandpit at the Green, and small boys pretending to shoot each other, 'Alan Bell – your time has come.' The apple and flower sellers with their 'capacious aprons' ever ready to help a Volunteer with a smoking revolver or undischarged bomb, 'Drop it here, son'. The half-mile radius of the Stopford Green house was a hive of Republican activity, with the Dáil, Sinn Féin and Cumann na mBan all having HQs nearby.

In October 1920 Stopford Green released Máire to work for the Dáil Publicity Department, reporting on the Tan reign of terror. In early 1921 she was working for the White Cross, reporting on the impact of the destruction of homes and factories and liaising with clergy as relief was paid through parish committees. She meets many of those working to maintain administrative structures, despite the dangers. Some were women – like Maria Curran, chair of Arklow Urban Council, whose services were never properly recognized. Throughout, Máire is alert to the contribution of women. A chapter, 'Women', pays tribute to the contribution of feminists like Hanna Sheehy Skeffington while also criticizing Cumann na mBan for letting down women at the end of the war: 'It never occurred to me to doubt that the Republican government, when we put it in power, would do justice to both sexes equally and, of course, to all of the people.' Another chapter, 'Housekeepers', includes Mrs Woods, 'when it came to hiding a hacksaw in a cake, Maa Woods was an artist'; the invalid Molly Childers, lying on her sofa, whom she believed had more backroom influence 'than any other woman in Irish history' and recognition of the homes where women took great risks in hiding armaments and providing safety to countless men on the run: 'It took a woman to hold her own floor and hope to be left behind on it after the raiders were finished.'

Máire gradually came to believe that Stopford Green and some of her close associates were pressing for a British compromise to bring an end to war. In Máire's eyes, victory could contain 'no compromise, blurred allegiance or any toleration of British rule'. Her worry was that the inexperience of the Irish leaders might lead them to accept joining the emerging Commonwealth. It was Máire and Liam Mellows who rushed to de Valera to tell him of rumours that a compromise solution without a republic had been advanced, and it was Máire, back in the Stopford Green house, who typed up the terms of the truce, given to her by Diarmuid O'hÉigeartuigh. Her misgivings grew. Young officers were now seen around Dublin in new uniforms 'plus the latest thing in green leather coats and fast cars'. By the time of the Treaty shops were selling 'Volunteer equipment' so 'the stage Irishman got a new uniform'. She now left the employment of Stopford Green and transferred to the Dáil lecture committee. Her friend Lily O'Brennan was over in Hans Place with the Irish delegation and rumours of too much alcohol circulating began to spread.

Unlike many, Máire devotes attention to the Northern counties and their abandonment. She was critical of the fact that the Dáil was not included in any discussion on partition or consulted on the content of the meeting between de Valera and Joe Devlin prior to the 1921 elections. She was an election organizer in Maghera, 'filled with both fear and fervour', and always believed that if those who had been elected to Northern constituencies had given up their Southern seats and insisted on representing Northern constituents in the Dáil, they could have posed a real challenge to the partition settlement.

Back to Wexford as an anti-Treaty election organizer with an inadequate £5 a week, the ever-resourceful Máire organized and led a raid on thirty post offices, netting £80 in stamps and a calling to Dublin, to be 'ticked off very severely' by Seán T. O'Kelly. Still not thirty and therefore ineligible for the vote, she was determined to have her say in the election. Someone found the name of a dead woman and let her cast her ballot.

As move and countermove towards a civil war begin, Eva Comerford comes to Charlotte Despard and Maud Gonne MacBride, helping the Belfast refugees sheltering in Roebuck House. Bored with gardening, Máire leaves Roebuck and volunteers at the Four Courts, remaining there throughout the bombardment. Refusing to surrender she slips away and offers her services to those in the Hamman Hotel. Markievicz is there on the roof, in her 'usual state of being alert with a rifle poised'. The descriptions of the Dublin resistance are memorable. There are vignettes of all the key figures and unforgettable images, like the pyramid of bath towels in the middle of the hotel foyer shielding Father Albert hearing confession, and the unending chain of men carrying filled sandbags to the roof. At the end she is a member of the Cumann na mBan guard of honour at Cathal Brugha's funeral, watching flies moving on his face. She joins the retreating forces, driving a Republican car and 'more in the IRA than out of it' and is eventually arrested, informed on by her former colleague Min Ryan, now married to Richard Mulcahy. Shot and wounded while in Mountjoy she is later transferred to the North Dublin Union, from where she escapes.

Another election, this time organizing in County Cork before being sent by de Valera on a propaganda mission to the USA. Smuggled over on a false passport as 'Edith Lewis' she is desperately homesick but home, when she returns, is no longer a place of comradeship and excited hopes. Now there are years of poverty and isolation as she tries to scrape a living as a poultry farmer in Wexford, with land loaned to her by her friend Father Sweetman. She remains a Cumann na mBan activist, suffering further imprisonment, but by the time of her expulsion from Sinn Féin in 1927 concludes that the Republican opposition is going nowhere. Ultimately, her hopes were with the younger generation that she befriended so generously.

I am delighted that, at long last, the manuscript Máire Comerford devoted the last years of her life to writing is now in print. To her and to all the women of that revolutionary generation, my deepest appreciation.

Margaret Ward

ON DANGEROUS GROUND

Avondale

WHEN I WAS a child it was a Sunday ritual in Rathdrum for people taking an after-dinner walk to stroll the mile or two to Avondale – the ancestral home of Charles Stewart Parnell. While travelling there and back before benediction, I came to know every stone of that road. I was born in 1893 and first travelled it by perambulator, but as I grew older, and began to eavesdrop on adult conversation, I do not recall any talk that the grown-up people must have had among themselves, remembering Parnell's glory, and his disgrace.* When later I was told about the fateful day of Parnell's final homecoming, from Brighton to Glasnevin, I imagined the ritual Sunday walk might be classed as a kind of permanent continuation of the funeral march for Parnell, who did great things for Ireland.

---

* Charles Stewart Parnell (1846–1891) began his political career as a land reform advocate and was first elected to the British parliament for the Irish Home Rule League (later the Irish Parliamentary Party) in 1875. Parnell employed obstructionist methods in parliament in order to bring Irish issues centre stage. His 'disgrace' was heralded by the divorce proceedings brought by fellow Irish politician William O'Shea, citing the adultery of his wife, Katherine, with Parnell. This led to a public scandal and a split in the Irish Parliamentary Party.

When we walked the avenue and reached the big house itself – long empty of human life – we took turns looking through a window into the square hall, where bundles of papers were piled along the walls. This was Avondale as it was before the auction; I recall the billiard table in the hall, the green baize risen up to form mountains and valleys, where moulds grew in more vivid colour, in the damp closeness of the house. At home I had been taught that our billiard table was sacred and that no child might put a finger on the green part of it; that Parnell's table should be in that condition made a deep impression on me. The house must have been closed for five or six years at the time of which I write.

My father, James Comerford, and Parnell were born about the same time – in the Famine years. One was Catholic and the other Protestant, but they both rode and drove the best horses to be had and liked to play cricket. I do not remember that my father ever mentioned Parnell until the time of the auction. Then, I heard the discussion between him and my mother about the book that must be bought. This book, *The Rise and Fall of the Irish Nation* by Jonah Barrington, really belonged to my father. Parnell had borrowed it and now we wanted it back to have in memory of him. As it turned out we did not retrieve our book because the library in its entirety was bought up beforehand. What we did manage to purchase was a Sheraton tea caddy on legs; I remember that coming home, and the polishing it got.

Long afterwards my mother told me the story. When my father and Parnell were both young men, and friendly neighbours, Parnell sometimes dropped in on my father to find him busy in his flourmill. Parnell was just home from Cambridge University and preparing to take up the reins of his ancestral estate. His mother, Delia Stewart, daughter of the famous American naval admiral, lived with him at Avondale. Charles was then unmarried.

Our mill in Rathdrum may well have been the most up to date of its time. The Comerford brothers and business partners, my father and Uncle Bill, had incorporated their own inventions in its works. The patents and pricelists for machines, which they built and sold both in England and Europe, still exist. My father was known for demonstrating the efficiency of the grindstones, balanced according to his particular invention; he liked to insert a visiting card, his own or his guests, to show how he could shear away the printed name without breaking the card itself. After some such occasion as this, Parnell lamented that he had nothing to do and they exchanged books; afterwards he told my father that *The Rise and Fall of the Irish Nation* had turned his thoughts to politics. In it Parnell read of the part played by his ancestor, Sir John Parnell, in the rise of the Volunteers[*] of 1782, and his opposition to the Act of Union[†] enacted in 1801.

Old Mrs Parnell continued to live in Avondale when Charles and his sister Fanny were both dead, and her other children absent. When she was newly married, my mother made regular visits to Mrs Parnell and afterwards told of her apprehension when she found the old lady, seated in the cane chair, which she continually drew nearer to the hearth, as she read a book by the light of a candle held in her hand. Mother recalled seeing some leaves of the book scorched where they had caught fire, and the old lady, patting it with her hand, had quenched the flame. She returned from Avondale frightened at the danger the elderly woman was in, but Mrs Parnell could not be persuaded to protect herself. As was inevitable, that brave and generous American lady died in a fire.

---

[*] The first Volunteers were enrolled in Ireland in 1778, following the outbreak of war between Britain and France and amidst rumours of the imminent invasion of Belfast by the French. The Volunteer movement grew to a membership of 80,000 men by 1782. The Volunteers of this period espoused loyalty to the Britain Crown, alongside a resolve to uphold a distinct Irish strategy.

[†] The Act of Union of 1801 rested on legislation, introduced in 1800, which effectively dissolved the Irish parliament that had existed since the thirteenth century, bringing Ireland into a legislative union with Great Britain. There was resistance to the proposed legislation in the Irish parliament but, through bribery or patronage, the government of William Pitt secured a majority in both houses of parliament and the Union came into effect in 1801.

In her day in Dublin, Delia Stewart Parnell held an open house for the Fenians.* When she toured the United States in the Irish cause Delia was acclaimed as the daughter of an American hero and in this role her popularity widened the Irish influence beyond the normal scope of the immigrants and their descendants. Mother was the only witness I ever knew to Delia Parnell's old age, which was sad, lonely, and I think by the standards of her class at the time, poverty-stricken.

Our Comerford branch came to Rathdrum from Ballinakill in County Offaly. Kilkenny, like Galway, had its 'Tribes'; but the Catholic Tribes like the Walshes and the Comerfords were evicted from the city of Kilkenny and ordered to live at Ballinakill. All this happened a very long time before our story began in Rathdrum. In a quiet way the Comerfords belonged to a class of Irish person who seemed relatively unaffected by the Penal Laws against Catholics; people engaged in primary industries – brewers, millers, wool merchants – who thrived relative to the many Irish people who depended for their livelihood on the land and nothing else. We were well enough off to enjoy life to the full and to be socially accepted as much, or almost as much, as other well-off Catholics of independent means at the beginning of the twentieth century. My mother, Eva Esmonde, was judged to have come down in the world when she married my father. On her equally Catholic but prouder side, there was a pedigree – supplied by request from the senior Esmonde family members to the editors of *Debrett*, and likewise to *Burke*.† I never knew anyone to buy either volume, but I held onto some proofs, which came every year until we were dropped.

---

* The Fenians were a nineteenth-century resistance organization, based in Ireland, the USA and Britain, who engaged in revolutionary activities, including a failed uprising against the British in 1867.

† *Debrett's Peerage and Baronetage* is a publication listing the titled aristocracy or British peerage, first published in London in 1802 by John Debrett as *Peerage of England, Scotland, and Ireland*. A similar publication – *Burke's Peerage*, first published in 1826, was a guide to the Peerage of Great Britain and Ireland.

But we, the younger branch, went even further to the right and were downright 'Castle Catholic'.[*] This happened when my grandfather won a Victoria Cross – for throwing himself on a shell in the Crimea and thereby quenching it. He came home from the Crimea and Burmese War and landed at Southampton. But the welcome there was too much for him and our family folklore tells of Queen Victoria giving him a day or two to sober up, before she could pin the Victoria Cross on his breast at a separate ceremony; this was followed in Ireland by a hero's wedding to my grandmother, who was a 'Castle' beauty of several seasons. When my grandparents married, my grandfather was given the job of Deputy Inspector in the Royal Irish Constabulary (RIC). Thomas Esmonde VC was a small man with a black beard, who enjoyed riding in races. He was in command of the RIC at the time of the Orange[†] riots in Belfast in 1867. His descriptions of action in the city included charging around on a horse, trying to provide protection for Catholic Mill girls, who were cut off by the mob from collecting their wages. In the end, when quiet was restored, Grandfather Esmonde had to send to Dublin for an implement to un-lead the police rifles. The usual way was to fire them off but he dared not do that, lest the sound of a thousand shots might cause the trouble to surge up again.

My grandfather had an accident to his eye in the hunting field and the family moved to Bruges in Belgium, where he died. They were living there at the time of the Franco-Prussian War. Mother's account of the enforcement of conscription, and their friendship with the people in the country place where they lived, was often repeated when we were children. Only a proportion of the young

---

* The derogatory term 'Castle Catholic' was applied to well-off Irish Catholics integrated into the pro-British establishment and administration in Dublin Castle.

† The Orange Order is an Irish Protestant, political and sectarian society, named for the Protestant William of Orange (King William III of Great Britain), who defeated the Catholic King James II at the Battle of the Boyne in 1690. The society was formed in 1795, arising out of local sectarian conflict in County Armagh, but over time increased its influence, becoming an important infrastructural element of political Unionism.

men had to go to war, and the fate of all was decided publicly by lot. The ceremony produced a gathering of the families of the youths. For them, the drawing of a conscript's lot was equivalent to a sentence of death; there was little or no hope that the unfortunate chosen would be seen alive in their native place ever again. Mother cannot have been more than ten years old when she witnessed these scenes, which undoubtedly made an enormous impact on her, and, in course of time, on me.

In contrast to this, it seemed to me that she was rather more reticent about the political events and the circumstances of their lives after they returned to Ireland. Granny was still beautiful and was welcomed back into the Castle set. When she took up residence in Kildare Street, lodging for the season of balls and receptions, my debutante aunts found their way somewhat obstructed at times by granny's elderly suitors plopping on their knees to propose marriage.

Of my three aunts, two, Zephie and Millie, were too loyal to their Church to marry the young Protestant officers with whom they fell in love, and from whom they parted in a firm spirit of resignation. My mother, Eva, never went to the Castle but this was not because she didn't like dancing. She often described how she and her sisters and brother hired a strange one-horse covered vehicle, travelling up a dozen rough and muddy miles each way to attend dances in what were certainly landlord-class houses. Mother told me how on one night of heavy frost, on their way to a ball at Mount Nebo near Gorey, they had to get out in all their finery and push the contraption up Hollyfort Hill. This was probably in the late 1880s – a time when blinds had to be drawn in landlords' and agents' houses before the oil lamp could be lit; this was in case some angry Land Leaguer* might shoot at an enemy of the people, unwary enough to show himself between a lighted lamp and an uncovered window.

---

* Land Leaguers were members or supporters of the Irish National Land League, founded in Castlebar, Mayo, in 1879, when Charles Stewart Parnell was elected president. The League worked to abolish landlordism in Ireland and to enable tenant farmers to own the land they worked.

In her sisters' view, when Mother married my father, she married the baker and therefore beneath her. I, it turned out, was only to be expected from such a union. But there was a very real affection between us and the aunts and it was proved on both sides. Later, in moments of pain and anguish to them, because of my politics or associations, I never heard them say anything stronger than, 'Of course you would not understand but this is what we think.'

If people concerned themselves with all their ancestors, instead of those they like best, it would be understood that if heredity does indeed influence actions it must in a very chancy and unpredictable way. For as well as being the daughter of an Empire soldier – perhaps to be classed a mercenary like more Irishmen of his kind – Mother was also a direct descendant of Doctor Esmonde, who sat in the Back Lane Parliament of 1792 in Tailors' Hall with Theobald Wolfe Tone,[*] and was afterwards hanged where O'Connell Bridge now stands.

---

[*] In 1792 Theobald Wolfe Tone (1763–1798) was appointed assistant secretary of the Catholic Committee, set up to improve the rights of Irish Catholics in Ireland. In December 1792 members of the committee met in Tailors' Hall in Back Lane, Dublin, subsequently known as the 'Back Lane Parliament'. Wolfe Tone was one of the founding members of the United Irishmen (1791) and a leader of the rebellion against the British in 1798. He was captured and sentenced to death by hanging in November 1798. Days after his sentencing Wolfe Tone died in prison from a self-inflicted wound to his throat.

Rathdrum

I DID NOT KNOW of it for many a year afterwards but Ardavon, the house where I was born and spent my childhood, was built a little bigger in all its dimensions than the limit that was permitted on the Meath Estates for Lord Meath's Catholic tenants. Ardavon was a beautifully placed house with a view of the Vale of Clara, overlooking the mill, which was my father's pride and joy.

The Lord Meath of my childhood was a venerable gentleman with a flowing white beard. He was then Lord Lieutenant of the county and the times had changed. It was the policy to appoint Catholic magistrates at that time. This was 'an honour', which my father had declined. Voices in the hall of Ardavon drew me from my bed one evening, probably around 1900. I watched through the bannisters, from the upstairs landing, a heated argument between the two, when my father refused to agree to whatever was under discussion. I found out later that Lord Meath had called to announce that he had put my father's name down as a magistrate, whether he liked it or not! I heard my father resist and repeatedly say no until the old gentleman gave up and went on his way.

The old mill was burned down in 1885, some years before my parents met and married; the grindstones were never to be set and balanced again. It was quickly rebuilt and equipped with the latest roller machinery, which was then making a revolution not only in the flour-milling industry but also, as happened eventually, in the diet of the people, as the craze developed for whiter and whiter flour. The new mill had only been up and running for three days when some hundred members attending the British and Irish Millers Convention, which was held in Dublin that year, visited it in 1886. The press account describes the mill and its machines, with mahogany furnishings, silk sifting, and the new dust-catcher – the last of the firm's inventions, which was sold all over the world. The quality of the flour was praised and mention was made of semolina, the new-fashioned product made from the germ of the wheat. The germ was now being taken from the flour, and therefore from the bread, in order to have flour that would last longer and make a whiter loaf.

I suppose things went well for the next ten or so years. My parents married in 1892. My father's wild oats were well sown. He handed the hunting hounds over to Lord Wicklow,* and gave up steeplechase riding, as an amateur jockey under the alias of 'Mr Thorne'. My parents met hunting and married when my father was forty-eight and my mother thirty-one. In those days the railway had important social significance and the hunting people engaged special carriages and horseboxes for their meets; then, in the evening, they held parties while waiting on railway sidings to be picked up by the returning train. My mother was Irish women's tennis champion for two years; she was also a hard and valiant rider in the hunting field, and a very good golfer. When their four children were old enough our parents gave us donkeys and ponies. I rode in a box saddle before I could walk, and don't remember having to walk anywhere until I was well into my teens.

I was the eldest and luckiest of the four children, and because of being older than my sister and two brothers, our wonderful

---

* Lord Wicklow, Ralph Francis Howard (1877–1946), was the 7th Earl of Wicklow, an Anglo-Irish peer with an estate at Shelton Abbey, near Arklow, County Wicklow.

childhood, up to the time we had to meet the real world, was best for me. Most children now seem to be taught to be afraid; we learned to fear nothing, and to perfect ourselves in dangerous country skills – with horses, with fire and water, and judgment of tides and river currents, with the behavior of cattle, rams and ganders, strange dogs, and boats; we learned to judge speed, if only of horse or bicycle. From the time our legs were firmly under us, our parents encouraged us in independence and widening adventures – climbing, rambling across country, exploring without let or hindrance.

There were, however, certain rules of expected conduct. If bucked by your pony, make no fuss, get up again, and again, no matter how often he bucks you, no matter how hurt; afterwards water and feed the pony before you eat yourself; never cheat at games; don't whinge. When there was an occasion for tears, I held them until I got to a warm, dark stable, where I could be nuzzled by a soft nose, and caressed by the warm breath of an animal; my tears may have startled the half curious, but wholly uncritical beasts.

My parents were musical and hoped for musical talent in the family. In this, I was the conspicuous disappointment. Coaxing, coercion, and even bribery to induce me to stay at the piano, all failed; instead, I developed tactics of passive resistance, which were to serve me well in other circumstances of life in later years. My mother and father never, in bad times or good, suggested or required from any of their children any compromise to expediency; that was the world into which we were born, and in which I participated with zest and vigour, until the times changed. I dimly recollect a point in time when our parents recognized that their girl children, as well as their boys, would have to earn a living. This registered for the first time on a Saturday night when I was called to the table to help count the takings, putting the money into little heaps. It was a task not destined to tax any of us much in the years ahead.

There was no love lost between my mother and my father's relations. Mother would have liked to have a family home of their own rather than living in the firm's house, with business intruding all the time. When Uncle Bill died, his nephew became the new partner in the firm and began to push relentlessly for the newer milling methods. I remember great arguments, elevated feeling in Ardavon, when my father refused to use artificial methods to whiten the flour. In the mill, men in white coats followed my father with samples of other people's flour, which he brushed aside in high temper. My father said that the business had become dishonest and dishonourable, and that he would not tamper with people's food. He would have nothing to do with bleached bread and resisted the new bleaching process to the point of ruin. Instead of being at the top of his profession, my father now had his back to the wall. Every Saturday when the travelling salesmen came in with money to be counted on the dining-room table, and with next week's orders, it was the same story – business was falling off. The mills we were in competition with were offering the whitest of white flour. The law is strict now regarding the use of 'conditioners' in the manufacture of flour but there was no such protection for the public when the battle was fought out in our home at the turn of the century.

Ardavon, so close to the mill, was a busy place and visitors came and went. 'Here comes the snipe,' my mother would say when we heard the clatter of horse's hooves trotting into the yard. This was her description of the Barton sisters, Daisy and Dulcibella from Annamoe, who often came in the hunting season, like the snipe to lowlands in wintertime. We enjoyed their cheery company while the horses rested, before they clattered off again. Dulcibella was destined to be the staunch little figure who surmounted many contingencies when she took charge for her brother Robert Barton at Glendalough House, Annamoe, when he was a Minister in the Government of the First Dáil; or away in prison in the stormy years that were still ahead of us then. Dulcibella was a light sleeper and very keen of hearing. During the War of Independence, and afterwards the Civil War, many a man on the run rested safely with her, relying on the fact that she heard the footsteps of raiders from the moment they touched the well-raked gravel paths approaching the hall and side doors of Glendalough House, which came to be known far and wide as 'glan' – a safe house.

Another visitor to Ardavon, who was to make a big impression on me, was Father Sweetman,* or The Very Rev. Dom J.F. Sweetman OSB – a great personality of his generation. A massive figure of a man, he was wearing white flannels when he walked up the little path from the station one summer day in 1905 or 1906. His blackthorn stick was easily the same thickness as my arm. He was looking for boys for his new school in Wexford and wanted my brothers, Tom and Sandy. Both went to his school near Enniscorthy; later the school, Mount St Benedict, moved to Mount Nebo, near Gorey. On that first occasion of our meeting, I distinctly remember standing jealously aside, furious that he paid no attention to me. He was, however, destined to be part of my story again and again.

Father Sweetman gloried in the fact that he was born on the slopes of Gibbet Hill at Clohamon in County Wexford. From the time he went to school at Downside in England he was determined to be a Benedictine monk, and to bring the order back to Ireland, from where it had been banished long before. It was to get money for that purpose that he volunteered to be a chaplain with the British army in Africa during the Boer War. The army pay supplemented his own family money that went into establishing his school. Other things that he brought back from Africa were good stories, great sympathy for the Boers, and a taste for their tobacco. To hundreds of people, he was simply known as 'the Reverend Man'.

When I first met Father Sweetman in the early years of the twentieth century, rural Ireland was undergoing great change. Tenants were buying land under the land acts, and men could acquire ownership of land as of right. In all Irish history there had probably not been so many who would become, as it seemed, their own masters in their own fields; men whose rent would never again be increased if

---

* Dom Francis Sweetman (1872–1953) was a Benedictine monk, Irish patriot and founder of Mount St Benedict, a school for boys in Gorey, County Wexford.

they made improvements; men who believed they had the chance to shape their lives and little knew of the odds against them. There was not a man at the fair at Rathdrum, or any other fair in Ireland, who experienced the delight of turning his first sod on his own land – or a woman who lit the oil lamp in her own home, knowing she could paint the door and pay for it out of her egg money – who could have conceived that great change was so close at hand.

Those were the days when people were only beginning to know the countryside outside the small circle where it was pleasant to drive a horse out and back in a day, from and to their homes; apart from that there was the train with the possibility it opened of travelling by sidecar in a similar circle from any of the stations where these cars lined up for hire. We were into the 1920s before taxis would challenge the sidecars.

I saw a motor car for the first time on a Sunday, when the people were walking to Avondale: the second time we were riding along and the horses were sent plunging and rearing. Not long afterwards Lord Wicklow appeared at the hunt meets in an enormous, pale yellow car, chauffeur-driven. I remember his anger one day when he learned that his English chauffeur had driven slowly behind our fleeing ponies, carrying us the whole way home from a meet at Churchmount, and caused us to miss the hunt. Until the motor car came, horses never encountered anything on the roads that could go faster than they could. Our well-fed hunters and trap horses could not bear to be passed, perspiring all over, even when they had ceased to be much afraid when a car overtook. Motorcars took the pride out of the harness horse.

I doubt that bicycles were common much before the time me and my elder brother got them at the age of about ten and twelve. I remember my mother and Aunt Millie learning to cycle at the same time. My bicycle opened Ireland to me. By the time I was twenty-five I had explored the coasts, riding every mile – Wexford, Waterford, Cork, Kerry; and Arklow, Wicklow, Dublin, Drogheda, Dundalk, Belfast, the Giant's Causeway, Derry and Donegal. I cycled to Kilkenny, and stood on the Hill of Uisneach* in Westmeath. At first it would be an absence from home for one or two nights. I packed food and carried small money, all that could be saved and enough to buy bed-and-breakfast once or twice. After that the holiday was by muscle power and cost little.

Travelling out from home, I struck across country, not by the biggest roads, which were liable to be very dusty in summer. Tar has taken the buoyancy out of the roads now, and widening has made them trap the winds, so that bicycling is more difficult. The narrow, winding roads of yore were fresh and beautiful, with ass cars meandering and people relaxed, shouting their greetings to one another as carts and traps met and passed, and no one in fear of imminent death.

Our bicycles were the fastest things, at least on down hills, where we let them rip, dodging potholes. History has happened on many of those roads I travelled since I first explored them. Now there are more stopping places, to read a name, say a prayer or learn a story at locations that have been added to the historical places of Ireland.

---

* The Hill of Uisneach in County Westmeath is the mythological centre of Ireland and an ancient ceremonial site. Spanning five millennia, Uisneach is considered to be one of the most sacred sites in Ireland.

Ballycourcey

MY FATHER had an accident while hunting; the muscle of his leg was severed when a horse jumped on it. As well as being angry about the flour situation, he was now crippled. I remember his hands, always very clean, his two sticks, his white overalls, his care and courtesy if he peeled an orange and handed it to me without his hands ever having touched the part I was to eat – so different was his from other people's way with us. I was thirteen when my father died after a long illness. He had only succeeded in delaying 'progress' for one small firm for a few years but his fight was an honourable one and a cause of pride, which we never regretted, although it left us poor.

After his death there was a big arbitration about the business and when this was complete my mother's capital was about the same as a few years income in the prosperous years. She had four of us to rear and educate and decided to leave Rathdrum and return to her own people. I can only remember the very few friendships that survived my father's death, our change of fortune and place of residence. Among these worthy exceptions were the Barton sisters of Annamoe, who mother loved dearly.

Mother brought us back to Wexford, her native county. My mother's brother, Uncle Tommy Esmonde, had established his mother and sisters in a pleasant Georgian farmhouse and a hundred-acre farm at Ballycourcey, Enniscorthy. This became the family headquarters until, a couple of years later, Mother rented Slaney Lodge, less than two miles away. Following his education by the Benedictines at Downside Abbey, Uncle Tommy went into the service of the Irish Land Commission. This was the agency that facilitated the transfer of a very great proportion of the agricultural lands of Ireland from the landlords to the people following the Land War, in which Parnell had been the leader. The time came when Uncle Tommy could afford to own a good-sized farm himself. He stood loyally between a multitude of his female relations and the collapse of their financial resources. While carrying everyone's burdens Uncle Tommy remained somewhat aloof and managed to keep us children a little afraid of him. He was an excellent farmer, and a public-spirited man, very serious-minded, always working, and one of the first to persuade famers to organize in their own interests. When he was drowned in the *Leinster** in 1918 the farmers of Wexford put a very fine monument on his grave in Glasnevin.

The Esmonde family was in essence West British. My mother, with her three sisters and only brother, had a happy, carefree childhood, but the letters that passed between their elders were full of anxieties occasioned by the poverty that crept on them slowly, but relentlessly. None of them had any training that would enable them to mend their fortunes; all had been brought up in a world of privilege and leisure. The family held themselves detached from the nationalist politics of Sir Thomas Henry Grattan Esmonde MP – the head of the extended family, who was Mother's first cousin. Sir Thomas, who often included 'Henry Grattan' in his name, was pleased as could be to be the grandson, through the female line, of the Irish patriot Henry Grattan – a

---

* RMS *Leinster* was an Irish ship operated by the City of Dublin Steam Packet Company, serving as the Kingstown (now Dun Laoghaire) to Holyhead mailboat. On 10 October, bound for Holyhead, the ship was torpedoed by a German submarine. The *Leinster* sank just outside Dublin Bay. There were 813 people on board and 569 were lost – the greatest ever loss of life in the Irish Sea.

distinguished Liberal in the old Protestant parliament (abolished by its own corrupt Act in 1801). Thomas Esmonde's career in the House of Commons started under Parnell and lasted until we, of Sinn Féin, defeated him in the election of 1918. When I remember him first, he was a member of the party that John Redmond[*] gathered together to heal the Parnell split. It was an oft-repeated family story that my grandmother wept with shame when Sir Thomas actively worked in favour of the tenants and against the interests of her friend and neighbour, the landlord George Brooke, during the No Rent campaign in the 1880s.

When we settled in Wexford, Granny was still mistress of Ballycourcey. She had retired to an armchair and put a lace cap on her thinning hair from the age of about fifty. Whatever current small dog dwelt in what must have been the supreme comfort of her floor-length skirts. She was attended by the two unmarried aunts, Millie and Zephie, and several maids. When granny went out it was always in the phaeton. This was a low, four-wheeled, open-sided carriage. The animal I remember her driving was Synx, an old racehorse retired from Ballinkeele Stables, owned by her cousins. Synx was so big and the phaeton so long that granny could not turn on ordinary country roads. It always exasperates me now to hear people talk about the dullness of country life!

The news came from *The Irish Times* in Dublin and from the local newspaper, and most memorably through the servants. 'Maggie Brady says, so it must be true' clinched many an argument. Maggie was pure gold and the talented wife of a farm labourer. There was no extra work she would not undertake if it would help to keep food on the table for her large family. Maggie was up to date in all things, trying out every new piece of advice offered by Miss Slattery – the poultry instructress who travelled the whole of North Wexford, driving her pony one day, and bicycling another. Maggie had honey, eggs and poultry in her ass car when she went to Enniscorthy every market day. In her spare time she came to help with our washing or butter-making, made cakes and

---

[*] John Redmond (1856–1918) was an Irish nationalist politician who, following the death of Charles Stewart Parnell in 1891, became leader of the Parnellite minority and subsequently, in 1900, leader of the reunited Irish Parliamentary Party.

brought us all the news. I never remember a time when she was not working. When rebellion arrived Maggie was devotedly Republican, and any matters or emergencies that came her way were certain to be handled with intelligence and without fear. But Maggie Brady had a bad old age. The Easter revolution of 1916 gave great joy and hope to the poor; afterwards, when there was no longer any need to stop for assistance, men in big motor cars went past those doors, except, perhaps, at election time.

In the long winter evenings in the drawing room at Ballycourcey we grouped around the little pools of light from two or three oil lamps. It seemed to me that we spent a great deal of time mending the woollen or lisle stockings, which made small resistance to our active toes and required much darning. By evening too, the elders of the family were finished with *The Irish Times* and our turn came to read it. I began to follow affairs outside the home.

We obtained most of our fun from riding and hunting. This was always supposed to pay for itself and my aunts tried their best to make pin money through occasional horse deals. This business was often spoiled by Uncle Tommy, who scorned the old established conventions, whereby it was 'up to' the buyer to carry his own share in valuing the beast, and bargaining about the price. Uncle Tommy always told the truth, and nothing but the truth. But this adherence to truthfulness only made the other side suspicious that some further defects, other than those that had been stated, were present. When Uncle Tommy pointed to the animal's hock and foretold the probability that a curb or a spavin might develop there, this was a thing the dealer had, of course, spotted from the first glance; reference to the weakness only made the buyer think that his attention was being diverted from the possibility that the horse was a windsucker or a whistler. Many good farmers were breeding half- or three-quarter bred hunters from their Irish draft mares. Some had thoroughbreds. My Aunt Zephie was a great judge of horses and always hoped to find an exceptional young horse. In one of her last bids for fortune, Zephie managed, with her last hundred pounds, to get 'on the turf' as an owner of two famishing grey racehorses. One broke its neck training and the other was placed in the Grand National more than once, and afterwards sold to the States – but all successful things happened after circumstances had compelled her to sell.

Aunt Millie was an artist with paint and brush but devastating with hammer and nails when she attempted to repair some shattered fragments of antique furniture, bought for shillings at auction. She drove a beautifully sprung low gig, painted blue and black, with bells on the pony's collar. Millie bred Pomeranians, or sometimes spaniels, for sale; but when the puppies were reared she was too kind-hearted to sell them, except to homes where she knew they would be well treated; but there, alas, the money would often be as scare as it was with us – so finances had a way of not working out. Millie was a wasted artist, who would certainly have developed her talent if she had ever in her life been able to support herself away from home. She was self-lessly generous – one lovable individual among the millions of good women who got no chance to blossom in life. Millie had a great sense of humour and had many a good story, which she told with an array of gesticulations. Her stories were always short and crisp, as were her comments when we came into the years when the Volunteers[*] began to organize. The fashion for brown suiting, something like the colour of shoe polish, seemed to be peculiar to the Volunteers. I remember Aunt Millie noted this, when she made a remark out of the blue one evening, as we were all gathered around the oil lamps in the dining room at the never-ending job of mending stockings. 'Tommy Brady is wearing a chocolate suit and he is walking very straight,' she said. Millie said no more but we all knew what she meant – that Tommy, who was Maggie Brady's son and one of my Uncle's trusted farm-hands, was now a member of the Volunteers.

---

[*] The Irish Volunteers, established in 1913 by Irish nationalists, was a military organization founded primarily as a response to the formation of the Ulster Volunteers in 1912 – an armed force in opposition to Home Rule for Ireland. The Irish Volunteers aimed to secure independence for the island of Ireland. The Volunteers included members of the Gaelic League, Sinn Féin and the Irish Republican Brotherhood (IRB).

From School to Rotten Row

WHILE WE WERE still living in Rathdrum, in about 1904 or 1905, the four of us Comerford children were sent to Our Lady's Bower in Athlone – a convent school for both girl and boy borders. I remember my mother's indignation at having to supply every item, down to the black kid gloves and umbrellas for each child, required by the nuns for their pupils. It was a sad day when we said goodbye to the horses and dogs before fitting ourselves into the new clothes from top to toe. At Our Lady's Bower Irish history and the Irish language were taught devotedly. Each of the subjects made an opposite impression on me. I was always to love history, particularly that of people, places and events nearest to me. I think we may have been withdrawn from the school in Athlone because my parents could not agree that we should be taught Irish. The trouble began when a teacher helped me to write a letter in Irish to Mother. This, of course, was totally unexpected at the receiving end; it did not occur to anybody that such a strangely addressed letter could be for the house at all. The postman took it away for further study, but eventually he convinced my mother that it was for her. Henceforth, I was ordered to the back of the class when the Irish lesson was on; I learnt what it meant to be a 'West Briton'.* Later, I came to realize the loss I suffered as a result of my failure to learn Irish at school, or to get more than a smattering in jail, or otherwise.

The question of learning Irish came into my life again, most earnestly when I went to Gaelic League classes in Dublin. I attended in body, giving allegiance to the idea but not to the task. It was in the years after 1916 when life was fast and adventurous. Observing my friends and acquaintances, who were devotees of Irish, I formed the impression that they revelled so much in the rich qualities of the language, they could not bring themselves to make it easy for beginners; the vast vocabulary, alliteration, subtleties of phrase and meaning, the syntax and prosody, which had survived in oral tradition and the old books since the time of the great schools – all this could not be absorbed by my willing but distracted mind. A further explanation was that a part of the great heritage of written literature in Irish had been translated and interpreted for us in English by the poets and writers of the period. The literature springing from the Celtic Renaissance† was in English. Delighting to this, I failed to go further.

I was enrolled in two further Irish convents after Our Lady's Bower. Shortly after my father's death, I ran away from the last of them. In my case the trouble arose because there were no games worth mentioning in girls' schools and the loss of freedom and activity became unbearable. My English school was at Farnborough, Hampshire. Over the low hedge from our hockey field the British army was learning to fly. There were monoplanes, and the dirigibles – engine-driven balloons and ordinary balloons. They had great work trying to fit the dirigibles into the shed. One of them burst in flames in the process. Another

---

* A West Briton, often abbreviated to West Brit, is a derogatory term applied to Irish people who reside in Ireland, but whose sympathies and cultural identity leans towards Great Britain. It can also apply to those whose lineage may be Anglo-Irish.

† The growing influence of the Gaelic League at the turn of the twentieth century resurrected a widespread interest in Gaelic culture in Ireland, inspiring a cultural revival often referred to as the Celtic Renaissance.

day when the school was out for a walk, in threes and always with a French girl in the middle – so that one or other of us, if we talked at all, would have to hear a language we were supposed to be learning – there was a plane crash very close to us on the common. How well I remember the nuns' outstretched arms, extending the whole width of their cloaks, in the effort to control us. But the ranks broke and we ran to reach the pilot after he left the plane, happily unhurt.

The school was a fashionable one, run by a French order. Many of the nuns were Irish, with a few French or Belgians. There were hot tempers among the Irish nuns: some did their best to suppress their native loyalties – for the sake of the 'high-class' Catholic education they provided in and for England. Although, at the end of every school year, there was general satisfaction in the school community when sometimes all three silver cups for good behaviour were carried home to Ireland, via 'Kingstown' or Rosslare. Even I, who had taken a lot of cornering before I was inducted to be an 'Aspirant to the Angles' – the lowest rank in school honour – carried home one of these cups on one memorable occasion. Over all this Mother Rowantree, the daughter of a doctor from Bray, presided with dignity and sound wisdom. However, the education, designed for ladies only, was fantastically out of date.

The history of England, and even that of Europe, was taught in a way to stir the imagination at Farnborough. My most vivid memory is of the newspaper descriptions of important events, which the teacher started reading to the history class during my last term in the school. There was a wonderful pen picture of the opening of the 'Mother of all parliaments' in London. I drank in every eloquent word of the description of the ceremonial, of the robes worn by the peers, and the gowns and the tiaras, the jewels that adorned the peeresses; the royal coach, the pink horses and the King and Queen: the ambassadors, representatives of the dominions and far-flung colonies of the Empire, on which the sun did not then set. How the senior girls in the class thrilled to all this, as I must have done too, or I would not have remembered it all my life since.

Excitement was high as we broke up for the final time. I was to go to London before travelling home. Our cousin Sir Thomas Esmonde MP had promised to bring me to see a debate on Home Rule* for Ireland in the House of Commons, where I had the Ladies' Gallery to myself; it was set over the Speaker's Chair in the old House of Commons, which was bombed in World War II. The light was very dim as I went to thick grating, which I recognized from the description in the newspapers. It had been put there not long before to prevent the suffragettes from throwing leaflets, or perhaps even throwing themselves, into the Chamber. I was an ex-schoolgirl now, glowing with a sense of the history of this impressive place.

It was with the most elated anticipation of the moment when I would behold the parliament that I peeped down through the haze. What I saw, of course, were two rows of legs, almost meeting down the centre of the big table; even the longest of these legs, which belonged to the government and opposition, did not meet in the middle of the vast table. The length of the table down each side was filled. I counted and identified them – everyone was present. It was a full dress debate. In the rest of the Chamber the seats were not full and those who sat were either sleeping, or, if awake, rustling papers. There was a good deal of walking in and out, and nearly always one or more men standing about halfway down in the centre passage. The MP who was addressing the house had very little life in him; anything in the nature of a cheer was coming from the Irish benches. It took me some time to understand why someone was nearly always saying 'baa baa'. Then, I realized that the men standing in the middle were generally on the far side of the line across the passage. Everyone in the place had at least one eye on this line and as soon as one of those standing put a foot on it without crossing over, the 'baa' started. What they were

---

* The Struggle for Home Rule began in 1870 when the Home Rule League, led by Isaac Butt, sought to bring about a limited form of self-government for Ireland. The cause of Home Rule was subsequently taken up by Charles Stewart Parnell and the Irish Parliamentary Party (IPP), albeit unsuccessfully. Finally, in 1912, the third (and final) Home Rule Bill was pushed forward by the then IPP leader, John Redmond, and debated in the House of Commons.

really saying, in the peculiar way they pronounce their own language, was 'bar, bar'. This apparently was a method whereby the members indicated their boredom, or worse, at the proceedings.

It was never again possible for me to think that any British government would ever rule Ireland for Ireland's good – or any part of Ireland either. I can understand very easily that many members of the House of Commons were very irked by the Irish at the time. This was because the Irish Party, led by John Redmond, with a strength of eighty-four members, held the balance of power between Liberals and Unionists; they were using this advantage to force the third Home Rule Bill for Ireland through parliament. Nonetheless, nothing that happened subsequently was to mitigate my disillusionment with the British parliament.

Within a night or two I was brought to see the Abbey Theatre Company; they were having a London season in the Court Theatre. It was my first time to be in a theatre for anything except the annual expedition to the Gaiety in Dublin for the Christmas pantomime. That night opened a new world to me, as I watched Sara Allgood in *Cathleen Ni Houlihan** by William Butler Yeats – one of the many writers and artists who creatively enhanced the cause of liberty at that time. Alas, that Yeats regretted writing *Cathleen Ni Houlihan*, for he need never have been under any illusion as to its effect on the young people who saw it! But neither did a great poet and writer ever have actors to interpret his work who were so involved personally as the women and girls of Inginidhe na hÉireann – Máire Nic Shiubhlaigh,†

---

* The nationalist play *Cathleen Ni Houlihan* (1902), written by W.B. Yeats and Lady Augusta Gregory, is set during the 1798 Rebellion and centres on the heroine of the play's title, an allegory for Mother Ireland. The play calls on young men to sacrifice their lives to save the 'four green fields', as representative of the four provinces of Ireland. Yeats subsequently regretted the strong nationalist tone and sentiment of the play.

† Máire Nic Shiubhlaigh (Mary Walker) (1883–1958), was a founding actress of the Abbey Theatre Company, who played the part of Cathleen Ni Houlihan on the opening night in 1904. Later, as a member of Cumann na mBan, she joined Thomas McDonagh's garrison at Jacob's biscuit factory during the Rising in 1916.

Máire T. Quinn,* Sara Allgood† and the incomparable Maud Gonne.‡ As I left the Court Theatre I knew my fate was sealed, my course in life was settled. I wanted to win back the Four Green Fields.

In the audience that same night, or during the season, there must have been men and women who would soon take part in the Irish revolution: Roger Casement might have been there, perhaps with the historian Alice Stopford Green, or Art O'Brien, future representative in London of the First Dáil Éireann; Sorcha McDermott and Cis Sheehan of London Cumann na mBan – my friends in jail afterwards; or Fintan Murphy, who helped with Éamon de Valera's escape from Lincoln Jail in 1919; in yet another group, Michael Collins with the young men of the Gaelic Athletic Association (GAA) or the Irish Republican Brotherhood (IRB), or both. How many were at that time as much strangers to one another as they all were to me, who had never even heard their names?

It was my mother's idea that I should train to be a private secretary and qualify for some interesting, adventurous or intellectual

---

* Máire T. Quinn (1872–1947) was a founding member of Inghinidhe na hÉireann, where she began her acting career. She was also a founding member of the Abbey Theatre Company.

† Sara Allgood (1880–1950) began her career as an actress with the Abbey Theatre and subsequently worked in British theatre. She toured Australia in 1918, starring in *Peg O' My Heart* by J. Harley Manners and in her first film, *Just Peggy*. Her most famous film role was as the matriarch of a Welsh mining family in *How Green Was My Valley* (1941), directed by John Ford, for which she received an Academy Award nomination for Best Supporting Actress.

‡ Maud Gonne MacBride (1866–1953) was born in Surrey, England. When she was sixteen, her father, a captain in the British army, was posted to Ireland and the family moved to Kilcare. In 1889 she met the man with whom she would be forever associated, the poet and writer W.B. Yeats. Maud Gonne founded Inghinidhe na hÉireann with the primary aim of securing independence for Ireland. Inghinidhe na hÉireann merged into the newly formed Cumann na mBan in 1914. Maud was living in France during the Easter Rising in 1916 but her estranged husband, Major John MacBride (who she married in 1903), was executed for his part in the insurrection. Maud returned to Ireland in 1917; she was arrested and imprisoned in Holloway prison the following year. After her release, and during the War of Independence, Maud worked to publicize atrocities carried out by the English forces. In 1938 she published her autobiography, *A Servant of the Queen* – an ironic title, one must presume.

job, in the service of some important personage or other. In this way, Mother imagined, I might see the world, and have an interesting life. I was entered into a secretarial school, run by a Miss Gradwell in Victoria Street, London. My new headquarters became a Ladies Club in Emperor's Gate, off the Brompton Road, recommended to Mother by the same Miss Gradwell, formerly from County Meath; somewhere, and from long before, Mother had known Miss Gradwell when they were both girls, hunting or playing tennis. It was represented as being a great compliment to us when I was elected as a member of this distinguished club. I found the members enormously interested in fortune-telling and table-turning. One of them started to read my hand, then threw it away. 'The most unlucky hand I have ever seen,' she moaned. I refused the request of another to pose in the nude for her. These were older people than I, and I found no interest whatever in their company.

I started my secretarial course in September 1912. The school was a sorry surprise to me. I was there at the time of the signing of the Ulster Covenant and Miss Gradwell was a most furious Unionist of Anglo-Irish landlord stock. She did all in her power to inflame her students against the majority in Ireland, and to get signatures. She knew the Covenant* by heart and dictated it to us for our shorthand and typing exercises – together with Edward Carson's† speeches,

---

* Commonly known as the Ulster Covenant, Ulster's Solemn League and Covenant was signed by nearly half a million people on or before September 1912. The chief architect of the Covenant was James Craig, MP for East Down, who had formed the Ulster Unionist Party in 1905, primarily to resist Home Rule. The Covenant was signed in protest against the third Home Rule Bill introduced by the British Government in 1912. Although largely a symbolic gesture of resistance, signatories were given a copy of their oath, which stated that their British citizenship would be defended by 'all means which may be found necessary'.

† Edward Carson (1854–1935) was the first person to sign the Ulster Covenant in 2012 and, in a series of huge rallies in Ulster, he built support for resistance to Home Rule. Carson studied law at Trinity College and became one of the most successful lawyers of his generation. He was elected as Unionist MP for Trinity College (1892–1918), and was appointed Solicitor-General for Ireland in 1892 and later filled the same role for England and Wales between 1900–5. In 1910 Carson became leader of the Irish Unionist Parliamentary Party, and in the following year, leader of the Ulster Unionists. During this period, his main political

which were reported at length, day by day in the newspaper. She picked on me, the only Catholic in the class: 'And what have you to say to that,' she demanded pointedly, leaving no time for a reply – which in any case I was inadequate to give because this was my first lesson in politics, and there was really no basis for argument at any level between us. Inexorably, I was being forced into the Irish struggle, and by the people in whose custody I had been placed to make what some Irish would have called a West Briton of me. Miss Gradwell drove me to my history books and to the decision by the end of my period there, that I would be nobody's secretary except on my own terms – in, and for, Ireland.

I had my bicycle and on Sundays explored London. The houses of people who were then in the news, and the mansions of those who had been absentee landlords of great areas of Ireland, fascinated me. I investigated Park Lane and the West End, to identify magnificent residences I surmised had likely been built from the proceeds of Irish rents. I mixed with the pedestrians and sightseers, who watched and named the riders enjoying themselves on Rotten Row, driving out in their carriages. Londonderry House in Park Lane, principal seat of the Marquis of Londonderry, was of the greatest interest because its owner was president of the Ulster Council,* which was then about to institute the Ulster provisional government. As I knew from my shorthand class, it was already replacing the wooden guns, used by the

---

objective was to preserve the union between Britain and Ireland. As the movement towards Home Rule for Ireland intensified in 1912–14, Carson worked to mobilize Ulster's resistance to any form of self-government for Ireland, where the majority Protestant population feared it was a first step to a fully independent Ireland.

* The Ulster Unionist Council was established in 1905 to bring together Unionist interests in the north of Ireland. The former Lord Lieutenant of Ireland, the 6th Marquess of Londonderry, Charles Vane-Tempest-Stewart (1852–1915), presided over its executive. A decision was taken by Unionists in September 1913 to form an Ulster provisional government, which would take effect if the Third Home Rule Bill was passed by the House of Commons. This gave full control of the provisional, or government in waiting, to the Ulster Unionist Council. Ulster Unionist resistance to Home Rule veered towards military resistance in early 1912, with the formation of the Ulster Volunteers. The following year they were established by the Ulster Council as the Ulster Volunteer Force (UVF) – a Unionist militia force.

Ulster Volunteers for drilling, with massive war equipment and every supplement, down to accident insurance.

About this time my cousin Maude Mansfield first spoke to me about Sinn Féin and its doctrine – that 'we ourselves' must save Ireland. She gave me a wonderful book – *Contemporary Ireland* by Paul-Dubois* – published in English, with an introduction by T.M. Kettle in 1908. This distinguished Frenchman had concluded that Ireland must get self-government or die. *Contemporary Ireland* brought me right up to date with both historical events and the people in Ireland who were then active in various spheres. The book explained the background to current affairs so comprehensively that a young person like me could turn from it to the daily newspapers, and be able to understand the news, and identify people in the current life of the Irish nation. Dubois explained that England had always maintained two races in Ireland and that it was an ongoing policy to keep them fighting one another. He foresaw the coming together of people, whose homes and hearts were in Ireland, but with their traditional loyalties then at variance.

Contemporary Ireland and other Irish history books were my consolation during lonely evenings spent in London, when I longed to be back in Ireland. The temper of the times influenced my history reading; I so delighted in the gallant stories of the Protestant patriots of the eighteenth and nineteenth centuries that I neglected to calculate that always they had been a minority, within a minority, and always quickly 'liquidated' by government. Like most of those who were young with me in three-quarters of Ireland in the coming decade, I found it impossible to take fervent Unionism seriously as an internal problem.

In fact, if one were to list the distinguished Irish scholars, writers, poets and patriots whose religion was that of the minority and whose talents found their inspiration in Irish national tradition, there would be the foundations for a united Ireland. It is hard to be sure that

---

* Louis Paul-Dubois (1864–1938) was a French sociologist, writer and essayist. His book *Contemporary Ireland* was closely read by the revolutionary generation in Ireland.

a nation would have survived in this island if it had not been for Protestant leadership, in rebellion, in politics and, to some degree, in scholarship.

But there never was a time in all Anglo-Irish history when an argument based on love of Ireland, or her democratic rights, could have been presented to people outside Ireland whose frame of mind was less receptive than in 1912–14. The external opposition to any extension of freedom to Ireland – by people who, for the most part, had never set foot there – was threefold. One section was engrossed in the party politics of Britain; the other side was outside politics, despised all politicians they could not use, and regarded the operation of democracy as a concept at the heart of the Empire. The third was Protestant fanatics.

Home Rule

WHEN I ARRIVED back home to Wexford, I began to follow the day-to-day newspaper reports on the controversy about Home Rule for Ireland. The crisis was presented to us, as to everyone possessing only surface knowledge, to suggest a clear-cut issue – 'Ulster versus Ireland', as if we were two races, and one held Ulster. The Third Home Rule Bill, which aroused so much fury, did eventually reach the English Statute Book; but that was as far as it got as a measure dealing with the whole of Ireland. If the bill had been implemented, adult male suffrage was certain to produce a government, which the 'establishment' in Dublin Castle – the seat of British power – and the surviving aristocracy of the plantation and 'Union' lords could not countenance. The time had come when the long domination of a class, or the values it imposed, would have to end, even in Ireland.

But in Wexford political controversy hardly touched us and, at the beginning of this period, we had many more Protestant than Catholic friends. As a family we were unaware of being in any sense less than equal to what used to be called 'the best in the land', or that the friendship between us was in any way conditional. I remember that when Lady Mary Lascelles, half sister-in-law to Princess Mary of England, married our neighbour Robert Doyne and came to live to in Wexford, she went to the school hockey parties like everybody else. Arriving in a donkey cart at our house shortly after she settled nearby, the newly married Mrs Doyne announced she was going to use our back door to come in and out, and we were to do the same at her house near Ballycanew. This neighbourly arrangement did not last for long.

One day, when the otter hounds had been hunting the Curavarragh and we were all at lunch at the Doynes, someone made a disparaging remark about John Redmond's Nationalist Volunteers, who had been reviewed in the district by, amongst others, my cousins Sir Thomas Esmonde MP, his brother Laurence and Colonel Maurice Moore. With perfect innocence, I said something to the effect that it was my under-standing that the people had elected Redmond and his party, drawing what turned out to be unwelcome attention to their legitimate right to organize politically, or parade publicly. A cold silence fell on the company. Believe it or not, things were never the same again; I don't remember being invited back there, or they coming to us. This was the beginning of the end of my social contacts in that sphere.

In my own community I was taking part in some of the integration forecast by Dubois. Our family members were all engaged energet-ically in the promotion of the co-operative movement, under the direction of Sir Horace Plunkett.* Its slogan was 'Better Farming, Better Business; Better Living.' What was preached was practised at home. The bull, Uncle Tommy's department, was in his high pen in the outer yard; Aunt Millie dispensed government-subsidized thoroughbred hatching eggs from her hatching station. She took a

---

* Sir Horace Plunkett (1854–1932) was a pioneer of the agricultural co-operative movement in Ireland, founding the Irish Agricultural Organisation Society in 1894; of Anglo-Irish stock, he was both a Unionist MP (1892–1900) and a sup-porter of Home Rule for Ireland. Sir Horace devoted his time to the development of agricultural co-operatives, first setting up creameries – perhaps the greatest and most enduring success of the movement in Ireland.

serious interest in 'Poultry Keeping on Modern Lines'. Millie tried every breed of fowl that was ever heard of: hens had a great fascination for many women at that time and they all, like my aunt, wanted to try every new breed that came along. During all of my youth, I was in touch with Millie's progress, from Brahmins to Andalusians, to Cochins to Sussex and Leghorns, and Rhodes and Wyandottes. The hen on the Irish penny is evidence that the original worst variety of mongrel continued to exist up to 1924; nevertheless, the poultry flocks of our countryside changed character as new breeds were taken up and interbred with their predecessors.

Thanks largely to my 'finishing course' – the shorthand and typewriting it was supposed I had learned in London – I was quickly made honorary assistant secretary to the 'United Irishwomen', helping my cousin Ellice Pilkington, who was the first National Honorary Secretary of the organization. The United Irishwomen were in close association with the co-operative movement, and Sir Horace Plunkett was only second in command to God Almighty in both organizations. Everybody in sight or hearing was full to overflowing with good will and determination to achieve the economic and cultural salvation of Ireland. Integration, as then understood – if indeed they used that word at all – meant fostering the material interests of the country, steadfastly apart from what they called 'politics'. Thus, Mrs Harold Lett, a hardworking member of the United Irishwomen, and a relative of Admiral Beatty of Britannia rules the waves,* could proudly fly a Union Jack on a post outside her house; but presently 'politics' came into it when someone stole and made off with the Union Jack, much to Mrs Lett's chagrin.

Years later the United Irishwomen changed their name to the Irish Countrywomen's Association (ICA). They must not have known their history very well when they took the original name. When they found out that the 'United Irishmen' of the eighteenth century had

---

* David Beatty (1871–1936) was British admiral of the fleet. In World War I he commanded Britain's battle cruisers, most famously for the Battle of Jutland in 1916. Admiral Beatty received the Order of Merit in 1919, when he became Earl Beatty.

aimed to cut the connection with England 'the source of all our evils', they quickly changed the name of their organization to the less 'political' Irish Countrywomen's Association. Throughout the years Republicans, like my mother and Dulcibella Barton, resigned from the ICA from time to time, but after they would go back again for the sake of all the good that was being done. It was, of course, desirable that every creed and class should try to work together for the betterment of the country; but now and again intolerable situations emerged when the West British among us argued that their point of view should be generally acceptable to all.

By holding women out of politics, the United Irishwomen, and their successor – the ICA – may have done far more harm than they did good in spite of all their other praiseworthy activities. It is my firm conviction that the public welfare can never be judged, or good decisions arrived at, except from the standpoint of an equal partnership between the sexes. These remarks are also addressed to organizations which give lip service to Women's rights, but fail in performance. Unfortunately, Cumann na mBan* also allowed itself to be pushed aside when the time came to implement the ideals for which we had been fighting – but that is another story!

My Uncle Tommy was not a Republican; nor was he a Nationalist Party man. Yet he loved Ireland and worked harder than most men for the betterment of his homeland. In addition to his interest in our local co-operative society, Tommy was helping to promote the meat industry. On his own farm he was trying out new methods of beef production and general farming. People were amazed when he brought his cattle into a big shed during the winter season, when the land was wet and cold. He was generous with his knowledge and played a worthy part in the establishment of a farmers' organization in Wexford. There was no such thing in our world as a labour organization. If this

---

* Cumann na mBan (the Women's League) was a female auxiliary organization founded in April 1914 to work alongside the Irish Volunteers. The primary aim of Cumann na mBan was to advance the cause of Irish liberty. The organization also worked to educate their members in first aid, drilling, signalling and rifle practice, and to assist the men of Ireland in their fight for freedom from British rule.

35

point had been raised it would have been met with the argument that the co-operative movement and the United Irishwomen were fostering the economic life of the country, and that better consumption of Irish goods would improve the demand for labour, bringing more money to every level of society. Everybody would be richer in body and mind as a result of their efforts.

The co-operative movement, Sinn Féin, the Gaelic League, the Volunteers and that section of the old landlords – whose members were beginning to recognize themselves as Irishmen – and the United Irishwomen, all believed ardently in supporting Irish manufacture. This belief came out in the clothes they wore. Irish tweed and home-spun fabric were heavily promoted but slow to catch on. There was considerable range in quality, starting from 5/- a yard or less, which stood plenty of wear but could get baggy at the knees. Home-spinning and weaving had ceased to be important in Wexford, and the public (outside the movements I have mentioned) was reacting against tradition in favour of mass-produced clothing and cheaper fabrics. The chemical dyes were crude and the colours liable to fade in patches; these were clothes with no quality of graceful weathering. It was a time when few could afford to be well tailored. The alternative, which emerged in the setting of the Gaelic Revival, was to be well tweeded. Homespuns began to distinguish men and women who were working for Ireland from those who were indifferent.

But that is not the full story. At the time of which I write, tweed was worn by the Sinn Féiners and Irish Irelanders on one side, and on the other by many of the native aristocracy, a few enlightened civil servants (when they visited the country), and all the Plunkett House people.* Thus, men whose politics never really coincided could find themselves wearing what almost looked like the same uniform. In Courtown Harbour for example, where we were soon to live, The Earl of Courtown and Volunteer Seán Etchingham both wore tweed; but the former was a harmless peer and the other soon

---

* 'Plunkett House people' was the collective term used to denote supporters of and organizers for the co-operative movement, led by Sir Horace Plunkett.

to be a convicted felon. At least they held it in common that Irish goods should be supported!

In 1913 Mother decided to start a girls' school. She left me free to make my plans as to whether I would teach in it, or follow my own fortunes into whatever secretarial or other job I could get. I stayed to help her and this involved no sacrifice whatever. The school, St Scholastica's, Courtown Harbour, was planned to take the sisters of the boys in Father Sweetman's school, Mount St Benedict in Gorey, where my two brothers were pupils. Mother's ideas about education met with high praise from the parents of our girls. She believed that she knew all about running an educational establishment, following her experiences with her own four children at boarding schools. Every child should have excellent food, she believed, and conditions generally. The pupils should also have the best teachers obtainable. Finally, every girl should be dead tired before the end of every day. Mother knew that idle children are naughty children. The girls in our school played vigorous games: they swam in the sea; some brought their ponies; all got a ride from time to time. As well as that our pupils had their music, painting and theatricals. Joseph O'Neill, then a school inspector, was highly pleased with us.[*]

The only thing wrong with the school was that it couldn't pay its way. The closing in 1919 was not, however, entirely due to poor financial management. The Benedictine Nuns, Irish Dames of Ypres, fleeing the war in Belgium, established a community at Macmine Castle in Country Wexford in 1915, and two years later opened a boarding school for young ladies. In this they had the wholehearted support of Father Sweetman, who sent carpenters and masons to convert an outbuilding for classrooms for the nuns' school. Some of the girls sent there might otherwise have come to our school, but The Reverend Man insisted to Mother that there was room for both schools. This

---

[*] Joseph O'Neill (1886–1952) was an Irish school inspector who subsequently became Secretary of the Department of Education in the Irish Free State. He was also a novelist: O'Neill's best-known work, *Land Under England* (1935), is a science-fiction account of an autocratic society controlled by telepathic mind control.

was not good advice. We held on until the school ruined us. The changing political scene in Ireland exacerbated our troubles. I had drawn official ire when I set up a tricolour on the school grounds at a time when the police were pulling the flag down all over the country.

As St Scholastica's went downhill, Father Sweetman's school was then at its zenith. It had about another decade to thrive. The large and highly respectable wealthy class known as Castle Catholics – meaning that they favoured, and fattened on, the British regime in Ireland – preferred the schools they selected for their children to meet with the approval of both Church and State. It began to be apparent that Father Sweetman, great man though he was, had no enthusiastic support from either. But unlike us, he was keenly aware of strengthening anti-British feeling in Dublin, from the time of the great strike of 1913 on.* He knew many of the men behind it all. Father Sweetman held it to be his special vocation and purpose in life to prepare future Irishmen to serve their country in times ahead, when it would be free. He had started his school when Home Rule seemed inevitable and his enthusiasm mounted with expanding national ambition. Many of his parents cooled off in the same proportion.

Father Sweetman brought me a present of a souvenir booklet from the public funeral of Jeremiah O'Donovan Rossa,† on 1 August

---

* The 1913 strike, or the Dublin Lockout, was a major dispute between approximately 20,000 workers and 300 employers in Dublin, lasting from August 1913 to January 1914. Central to the 1913 strike was the right for workers to unionize. This was opposed by many employers, who responded by locking out their workers, and bringing in blackleg labour from England and other parts of Ireland. The lockout finally ended when the Trade Union Congress (TUC) in Britain turned down a request from the Irish workers' representatives to engage in sympathetic strikes.

† Jeremiah O'Donovan Rossa (1831–1915) was a prominent Irish Fenian and member of the Irish Republican Brotherhood. Following six years in prison he went into exile in the United States (1871), and from there continued his revolutionary activity. He was the alleged mastermind behind the 'dynamite campaign' (1881–5) targeting British cities and infrastructure. He died aged eighty-three in New York, and his body was returned to Ireland. In Dublin 20,000 people formed the funeral cortège and hundreds of thousands stood on the streets to pay their respects. Padraig Pearse gave the graveside oration, which included the famous lines, 'They have left us our Fenian dead, and while Ireland holds these graves, Ireland unfree shall never be at peace.'

1915; Padraig Pearse's* speech over the Fenian's grave was the first bit of revolutionary literature to come my way. The achievement of the Irish Republican Brotherhood when they brought this funeral from the United States at the height of the World War I and carried it through Dublin is perhaps the best illustration of the feeling that existed in Ireland at that time. A year later, when the 1916 Rising was for the time being crushed, and the leaders were executed, the widows of some of the dead heroes – Tom Clarke, Éamonn Ceannt, Major John MacBride and The O'Rahilly – sent their sons to board at Mount St Benedict. Father Sweetman's school was their next choice for their son's education after the death of Padraig Pearse, founder of St Enda's School in Dublin.†

---

* Padraig Pearse (1879–1916) was an Irish revolutionary, poet and educator. He was Commander-in-Chief of the Irish forces in 1916 and the first president of the provisional government of the Irish Republic, proclaimed in Dublin on 24 April 1916. He was executed, along with fifteen of his revolutionary comrades, by the British.

† St Enda's School (Scoil Éanna), a school for boys, was set up by Padraig Pearse in 1905, firstly based in Cullenswood House in Ranelagh, Dublin, and later in Rathfarnham, County Dublin.

World War

THE GREAT WAR crashed into our lives when we were at a summer holiday camp on a beautiful day, 4 August 1914. A group of young people had gathered around Lord Dunsany (how or why he was there I do not remember).* A heron, flying high, passed overhead, across the Slaney and on towards the Blackstairs Mountains. Lord Dunsany had seen it and he asked us to show him, with our arms, the pace at which the bird was flying. We all started in flying motion, but found that none of us could keep pace with the speed with which the heron was using his wings. His flight looked effortless but he had covered miles in the minutes while we watched and tried to imitate him. So, too, peace went from our lives that afternoon. A telegram was handed to one of the company. 'It is war; I am mobilized,' he said and strode away. Others left too, in haste, to see if telegrams were waiting for them at home.

---

* Edward John Moreton Drax Plunkett or Lord Dunsany, 18th Baron of Dunsany (1878–1957), was a wealthy Anglo-Irish writer, with a family seat at Dunsany Castle and demesne in County Meath. Over his long career as an author Dunsany wrote close to a hundred books, including novels written in the fantasy genre.

Girls like me, who were left behind, collected sphagnum moss on the high mountains, dried and sorted it, and used it to prepare field dressings; we attended classes in home nursing and first aid. The ploughing of a certain proportion of the land was made compulsory and our hunting horses had to take collar, chains and swings, which they had never known before, and learn how to work.

Round about harvest time in 1915, when the field of oats in the marl-based field at the back of our house at Courtown was shoulder high, Sergeant Cullen of the RIC came to the door with an official order from the government, which he was delivering everywhere. This informed us that we must be ready to burn the crops, and everything else we could not carry. And then set out, driving the livestock before us, to Carlow. The notice would be short. If we failed to hurry when it came, the Germans would get us!

Mother, with a girls' school to protect, was very concerned about her responsibility until Father Sweetman told her to put the matter of the official order out of her head. If the Germans were invading, he argued, Wexford was not a likely place for them to come to; if they did come, the few miles she could walk with twenty girls, four cows, a couple of riding horses and the pony trap would not be much help. 'You are better with a roof over your head,' clinched the argument.

It would have broken my heart to burn those oats; so much labour had gone into the tilling of the field. But the Defence of the Realm Act (DORA) was not concerned with the technicalities of agriculture when it enforced compulsory tillage.[*] This Wexford incident was referred to in the report of the Inspector General RIC, and quoted at the Commission following the Rising in 1916, stating that – 'At certain places in County Wexford, after the promulgation of military order for the action of the inhabitants in the event of an invasion, counter notices were placarded calling on the people to disobey the

---

[*] The Defence of the Realm Act (DORA) afforded wartime emergency powers to the British government and was enacted three days after the start of World War I. In Ireland, the powers under DORA were used more extensively than in Britain and could be used to institute marital law. DORA continued to be applied in Ireland until 1921, when it was replaced by the Restoration of Order Ireland Act, 1920.

orders issued, and to welcome the German troops as friends'. I do not remember having seen such notices; but I heard of them.

During the war years I helped to welcome able-bodied refugees, who came with a sprinkling of women and children from the battle-fields in Flanders. I played the part of 'Belgium in Rags' in some performance or other, put on locally in aid of a British war charity. It is clear to me now that I took a long, long time before I understood the position in relation to freedom and war in my own country. Ireland was set on a path which, before the end, would cost her 35,000 lives, and partition.

Every man's attitude to the European War became known to everyone who knew him. I don't recall that, at the time, I knew anybody who stayed at home with an Irish patriotic motive, if he was an age to go. Some stayed to make money farming. Many thousands flocked to the English colours. Some of these belonged there; others went because of their sorrow for 'Little Belgium'; still more enlisted because of the hope for Ireland that was raised when the war aims were set out in huge posters on the walls, or because John Redmond had promised that 'Ireland would be the one bright spot'. The young, like my brother Tom, went adventurously, with a spring in their step. Old soldiers of the Reserve had feelings that were in accord either with their politics, Unionist or Redmondite, or with their foreboding as to what might be in store for them. Many would have welcomed an accident to incapacitate them – just enough. Within three weeks thousands of Reserve men were in the battle of Mons. By the end of October, the European front extended from Switzerland to the North Sea, with 57,000 casualties suffered; the names of the dead and wounded filled columns of newspaper space every morning.

There were many examples of men of my acquaintance with tangled military careers. Erskine Childers, who sailed his yacht, the *Asgard*, into Howth with rifles for the Irish Volunteers on 26 July 1914 was a British Reservist.* Like many others, Childers was called up and

---

* Weapons were smuggled into Howth Harbour near Dublin on board the *Asgard* in 1914. Erskine Childers (1870–1922), renowned spy novelist and Irish Republican,

was back in khaki within days. Later on, when he was in Dublin serving in the First Dáil Éireann, I heard him tell of military air missions over the western coasts of Europe. How strange to think that within a very short time of loading German guns into the *Asgard* from a ship in the North Sea, he may have been flying back over the same waters on a totally different mission.

I recall too that Peter Connolly of Gorey, who drilled the Volunteers, was called up on the Reserves, and was in a desperate fight on the Marne; he was captured, and was held prisoner in the German prison camp where Roger Casement went to recruit men for Ireland.* Peter did not think it was honourable to discard the British tunic he was wearing, so he said no to Casement on that occasion. But when he got back at the end of the war, Peter rejoined the Volunteers and became OC of the North Wexford column, fighting against the British.

David Robinson was another of my friends who managed to skirt both sides. He won the Distinguished Service Order (DSO) from the British, the Croix de Guerre from the French, and came home in time to qualify for the Black and Tan medal here. David didn't know fear and the men of the Irish Republican Army (IRA) loved him dearly. So too did his friends of the previous allegiance; when he was in Kilmainham Jail in 1922, gifts – silk pyjamas, records, high luxuries in food and drink, poured in from people like Lady Astor and other English and Irish notables: Lady Astor also sent him a blank cheque to buy a piano for the jail!

---

was at the helm of this daring mission. The weapons aboard the yacht, 900 Mauser rifles and ammunition, were bound for Irish Volunteers.

* Roger Casement (1864–1916) was an Irish patriot, a diplomat in the service of the British Realm and a leading figure of the 1916 Rising. Casement travelled widely for the British consular service and his report in 1904 on the brutal 'rubber terror' regime in the Congo was instrumental in ending an obscene abuse of human rights. Casement was subsequently knighted. He left the consular service in 1913 and turned his attention to the Republican movement in his native country. Casement actively pursued German support for an Irish Rising and in 1916 was discovered near Banna Strand in Kerry after a failed attempt to land German artillery for the Republican rebellion. Following a trial in London he was convicted of high treason. Roger Casement was hanged in Pentonville Jail on 3 August 1916.

The war brought with it a series of anomalies and contradictions. George Gilmore told me that his first political act was motivated by his awareness of the difference between the war propaganda near his parents' home in Dublin and what he saw in Portadown, when he visited his grandfather there.* He removed a recruiting poster at Amiens Street Station and stuck it up in Portadown. This poster depicted a Belgian church on fire. A Catholic priest, holding the crucifix aloft, stood in the porch among the flames. A German soldier was running his bayonet through the priest. Other recruiting posters, which George saw in the North, called on the Ulster men to fight against Austria – 'The Last Great Catholic power'.

My brother Tom, not yet seventeen, got a commission quickly after the start of the war. He was wounded at the Dardanelles while serving with the Munster Division. He was ready for active service again when recruiting and field statistics were manipulated to enhance the Empire loyalty and devotion of the 'Ulster Division'. During his whole service in Western Europe, Tom was attached to the Ulster Division. All his protests and efforts to get back to the Munsters were in vain. Poor chap! That was where the war for 'Small Nations and Democracy' had landed him. He was gentle, generous, brave and quiet, and he turned his back on Ireland. The British army caught him young.

Our family, like hundreds of others, split as the members went to one side or the other in the conflicts then developing. In a letter home from Tom dated 28 August 1917, he suggests that my humble political activities in Ireland were known and not much liked by his fellow soldiers in the British army. He wrote, 'I'm afraid Mary's frame of mind is better known than I expected. I have been spoken to by several people about it.' He did not reproach me about this. Thanks to the good God we maintained a reluctant respect for one another; at the end of our days this turned to friendship. Tom was always very good to our mother, although nothing could have been more different than his political views and hers.

---

* George Gilmore (1898–1985) was a Republican socialist and IRA Volunteer. He was active during the revolutionary period, firstly as a member of Na Fianna Éireann, and then as leader of the IRA South County Dublin Brigade.

In July 1914 the Home Rule Bill had passed all stages at Westminster, and in August it was entered on the Statue Book, together with an amending act, which ensured that it could be revised in the interest of the minority, after the end of the war. Inside the newly organized British army, divisions of Irish origin men were to fight the Germans for reasons that were utterly at variance. Edward Carson, now head of the Ulster provisional government, did not give the word for the Ulster Volunteers to recruit into the British forces until he was able to tell them precisely where they stood. His goal, to repeal the Home Rule Bill, was stated and was understood when he and 'The Galloper', Lord Birkenhead,* Englishman, were taken into the British War Cabinet in May 1915. The Germans were then near Paris.

I am compelled to conclude that this dark enigma was swept from our minds by the simple issues concerning liberty and freedom, which composed the stated war aims of Britain and her Allies. John Redmond was caught on this, and so too were thousands of men whose faith in the war aims were betrayed. Redmond died in his bed and they in mud and misery. For it was John Redmond who made the speech that eventually wrecked his career and the Irish Parliamentary Party. Speaking at Woodenbridge in County Wicklow, five days after Home Rule was put on the statute book, he said it would be a disgrace to Ireland if Irishmen refrained from fighting 'wherever the fighting extends in defence of right, freedom and religion'. We must have thought he was right. It was then little more than a month after the German invasion of Belgium. Redmond had been chosen as the Irish leader because he was Parnellite – and therefore might be

---

* Lord Birkenhead (1930–1972), formerly known as Frederick Edwin (F.E.) Smith, was a British Conservative politician and staunch advocate for the exclusion of Ulster from Irish Home Rule. His enthusiastic cheerleading for the Ulster Covenant campaign in 1912, led by Edward Carson, earned him the nickname 'Galloper' – as being Carson's galloper (army slang for an aide-de-camp or orderly officer). Under Liberal Prime Minister H.H. Asquith's wartime coalition (1915–16), Lord Birkenhead was appointed Solicitor General in June 1915, eventually succeeding his close associate – the self-same Edward Cason – to become British Attorney General in November of the same year. In this role he oversaw the conviction and hanging of Roger Casement. Lord Birkenhead was later centrally involved in the negotiation of the Anglo-Irish Treaty of 1921.

expected to take a strong hand in all his dealings on behalf of Ireland at Westminster. The opposite thing happened: he fell in love with the British Empire. John Redmond's faith in English promises was not unique in the history of the two countries. He had his forerunners, and, unfortunately, his successors.

Two weeks after the Woodenbridge meeting, it was announced that Redmond would 'bring Home Rule to Wexford' at a public meeting in the Bullring. Mother, my aunt and I decided to go. We squeezed into the packed Home Rule special train and after a time were placed in front seats on the right-hand side of the leader on his platform. The big majority was for Redmond, and they prevailed; the meeting was held successfully, but it was not unanimous.

Volunteers Seán T. O'Kelly,* Seán Etchingham, Greg Murphy† and others had made use of a Home Rule special train to bring arms to Wexford, part of a consignment, which had recently been landed in Kilcoole. The men also had a secondary mission – to distribute anti-recruiting literature and do whatever they could to warn the people against putting their faith in any promises made by the British government. It was Greg Murphy who told me, years later, how the Wexford Volunteers rescued them just in time, before the Redmonites could get their hands on them to pull them down. I did not know anything about this at the time; nor, of course, could I guess that the two individuals who had climbed the wall to distribute leaflets were to be the future Ambassador of Ireland to the Peace Conference, Minister of State, and eventually President of partitioned Ireland, Seán T. O'Kelly, and my great friend in later years, Seán Etchingham.

---

* Seán T. O'Kelly (Ó Ceallaigh) was a founding member of Sinn Féin and editor of *The Nation*, a Republican publication. He was elected in 1918 to the first Dáil Éireann, and became the first Speaker of the House.

† Greg Murphy was an Irish Volunteer and Secretary of the IRB for Leinster. He fought with the Four Courts garrison in 1916 and became a member of the Council of the IRB in 1917.

Etchingham

ONE DAY IN 1915 I took the old scattergun and two or three .22 rifles, belonging to my brothers, and I brought them down to Johnny Etchingham's shop and handed them to him, for the use of the Volunteers. I was welcomed with delight and the gift was accepted with thanks, far out of proportion to its value. I cannot now remember what event in the news of the day led me to this impulsive act. But wasn't I roasted when I got home! My defence was that if there was going to be war for Home Rule, it was desirable that those taking part in it should know something about arms. If they had not the means of instruction how could they learn? If later on they got arms and did not know how to use them, that would be very dangerous for everybody.

My mother had known Johnny Etchingham from her youth, when he had been employed in different stables in the area. She was a splendid rider and in the old days got loans of plenty of mounts from her friends for hunting. When she talked to Etchingham it was of favourite horses they both knew and their horsey chatter often went back to Friargate, the mare that won the Grand National for Mother's cousins, Matt and George Maher of Ballinkeele.

The Johnny Etchingham of those far-off days had now become Seán Etchingham – journalist, ballad-maker, Labour leader, and owner of an occasional racehorse. He was the author of a famous column in the *Enniscorthy Echo*, which came out every week under the name 'Patsy Patrick'. The *Echo* was far better than the English satirical *Punch* magazine to us, simply because of Etchingham's column; the humour was local and relevant to the times, and anyone in Wexford who did not follow the musings of Patsy Patrick was lost indeed. The *Echo* was an IRB paper but I expect we did not know that for I never heard it mentioned. What I do remember were the aunts coming in at teatime on a Friday and the one who opened the paper first being asked: 'What has Johnny Etchingham to say this week?' The interest was sometimes in his 'Personal Column', where he liked to follow local horse-trading. He made this particularly interesting by adding a nought to the prices, whether given or taken.

One of the early days after we Comerfords moved back to Wexford from Rathdrum, Mother bought a little pony for us. We were training him, and had put him in the trap. Shortly afterwards we felt competent to drive though Enniscorthy town. In the centre of the bridge we came face to face with Uncle Tommy, walking. He stopped, and we couldn't. The head of the pony went under his arm and stuck there until he ran out of breath, berating us and letting us know what he thought of our sense. Etchingham had turned our modest £5 paid for the pony into £25 and Uncle Tommy, knowing everything about our precarious finances, was hot from reading all about our reckless purchase in the *Echo* when we ran into him.

'Patsy Patrick' took the form of a conversation with 'Terry' and it went on for years until it got the *Echo* suppressed. This was not surprising with lines such as these by Patsy Patrick on the subject of 'diplomacy' in politics: 'The whole wisdom you want for politics is to have diplomacy: and diplomacy is the art of putting a passable face on the biggest divil of a lie … It's no use to say the divil goes round like a roarin' lion. He never did that since Cromwell's time. The divil goes round like a diplomat.'

Seán Etchingham was destined to be an Easter Week Volunteer, sentenced to death (and reprieved), a Teachta Dála in the First Dáil and Minister for Fisheries.* I didn't get to know Seán well until after 1916, when I started writing to him in jail. He was a wonderful person, more unselfish than any man I ever met; a wise judge of men and the person who was fondly remembered by many because of the little sparks of gaiety he could produce when despondency was everywhere else – in a prison, or in his own sickroom, for he was very delicate. He was among our elder revolutionaries. Seán once told me that he got practically no schooling but had learned to read somehow and found time to study by the light of a stable lamp, with the warmth of horses all around.

Stories about Etchingham were always cropping up. When he, and the other Enniscorthy men were court-martialled after the Rising, the officer read out their sentences, and then started at the top of the file again, commuting the death penalty to life imprisonment. Etchingham traversed the solemnity of the proceedings when he issued an intentionally audible aside to his neighbour: 'They will be letting us out under the First Offenders Act next time round.' Seán was a teetotaller but he did manage to make good use of a bar for his own purposes once. There were always complaints in Courtown about the need for more water in the harbour. It was customary to the extent of being a local joke for our cousin Sir Thomas Esmonde MP to promise to try and get something done about it. There were times when he succeeded in bringing some official (even on one occasion the Chief Secretary) to inspect, and to make more promises.

At last Dublin Castle decided to give Courtown an oyster bed. If you ever go there you will find it, still high and dry, to the south of the harbour. They say that the sea went properly into it for a while, at the beginning. At any rate the job was done under the direction

---

* A Teachta Dála, abbreviated as TD, is the title given to a member of Dáil Éireann, elected by the people to the Irish parliament.

of a retired RIC man, whose previous position had been to teach the people in Donegal how to pack eggs. When the oyster bed was finished and stocked with oysters, there was a celebratory official opening, attended by a band and the representatives of the local public bodies. Then, to cap it all, some misguided individual proposed that, in order to show their gratitude, they should arrange to present a barrel of oysters to their Gracious Majesties in London. To Etchingham's exasperation this was done; the oysters were picked with care and dispatched with all ceremony by the evening mail train connecting with the mailboat. When all was ended and those concerned were relaxing in the pub, one of Etchingham's men slinked in, ostensibly for a drink. Allowing time slip by as far as he dared, until the train would be well on its way, he chose his moment. ''Tis a pity Etchingham put a rat in them oysters,' he sighed. Consternation ensued. As the story spread around the country, it was related that the telegram from Gorey recalling the gift only caught up with it when the king was just about ready to sit down to his dinner! No doubt the oysters were packed up and sent back to where they had come from.

Seán knew all the legends of the countryside, as well as everything that was to be known about the people in it. When a skull with long golden hair was turned up in the old graveyard at Ardamine, he was able to supply the tragic story; his tale was of a beautiful young girl who was intercepted by the Yeos,* somewhere near Banogue Bridge, and her terrible death at their hands. Seán is buried in the same part of the same graveyard, to the north of the little Protestant church. Between the church and the road there is a section of a very ancient dyke or moat, which is said to mark the Bóthar Cualain, one of the five great roads that branched across the country from Tara in ancient times. Seán's monument, erected by his admirers, stands to the south near the tumulus, which, in tradition, marks the landing place of invaders to Ireland in mythical times.

---

* 'Yeo' is a shortened version for the force known as Yeomanry – a British militia force sent to quell potential revolution in Ireland in 1796, following the failed invasion of Ireland by French troops.

When the Civil War came, he had no doubt about his allegiance to the Republican cause; but Seán had no strength for another round, and such horror as then befell us. He died in the winter of 1922–3.

Rising

UP TO EASTER 1916 my visits to Dublin were always for family shopping or visiting expeditions. I had for a long time wanted to get away by myself in order to explore the treasures I had been reading about – the Cross of Cong,[*] the Ardagh Chalice,[†] the Book of Kells,[‡] the old house of Grattan's parliament. I wanted to visit the place where Shane O'Neill's[§] head was spiked on the Castle gate, and to stand

---

[*] The Cross of Cong is an ornamental processional cross, dating from the early twelfth century, presently housed in the National Museum of Ireland.

[†] The Ardagh Chalice, an eighth-century ecclesiastical object, is one of the greatest treasures of the early Irish Church. It was found in 1868 by a young man digging for potatoes near Ardagh in County Limerick, and can be seen in the National Museum of Ireland in Dublin.

[‡] The Book of Kells is a ninth-century manuscript featuring ornate Latin text and elaborate illuminations of the four gospels of the Christian scriptures, on display in Trinity College Dublin.

[§] Shane O'Neill (c.1530–1567) was an Irish chieftain of the O'Neill Dynasty of Ulster. He was assassinated by a rival clan, the MacDonnells, Scottish settlers in Antrim. In order to collect the bounty on O'Neill, his pickled head was sent to Dublin and displayed on the walls of Dublin Castle.

at Emmet's* execution place, outside St Catherine's Church on Thomas Street.

I went up alone on the Saturday, to spend Easter at Rathgar with our cousin Maude Mansfield, who was now infirm. The first Sunday mass in a Dublin church must always be memorable; I marvelled at the great numbers who went to the altar in the Church of the Three Patrons. The following day, walking down Grafton Street, unaccompanied, brought me to a collision with the new era of Irish history. I stood to watch a detachment of Volunteers marching up the street. They looked very well to me; many were in uniform. I had not gone much further on my way before a very smart Volunteer officer was driven hastily up the street on a sidecar. Having stared with admiration until he was out of sight, I boarded the tram on its way to Blackrock, where I had a luncheon engagement. About three hours later I discovered that I was in the middle of the Rising of Easter Week, 1916. When I looked for a tram to bring me back to town, there were none. Instead, people were walking and stopping, walking and stopping; wherever two heads were together on a pavement, a third and a fourth and a fifth head stuck itself into the party. I joined a group to find out what was agitating them all. We stood around a tram man, extravagant with words, 'The Shinners are up! The streets are runnin' with blood – up to yer knees.' The greatest news story in Dublin or Ireland for years was to be his for the next three days, and he was making the most of it; already he was a little drunk but too excited to be footsore, although he had tramped from Dublin, spreading the news as he went. He told us how he had seen the General Post Office (GPO) rushed and the windows broken with rifle butts; he had also witnessed the charge, and the defeat, of the Lancers in Sackville Street.

Having heard this much, and seeing the man stagger on, to be stopped soon by others, I started to follow the tramlines – the only way

---

* Robert Emmet (1778–1803) was an Irish nationalist patriot who led an abortive rebellion against the British in 1803. He was convicted on a charge of treason and executed in front of St Catherine's Church on Thomas Street, Dublin, where he was hanged and subsequently beheaded.

I knew back to Dublin. As I went, I met more and more people. The Castle was captured, according to one. Another said the Germans had landed; all agreed there had been fighting. I was advised not to go on: 'You won't be let in. Where do you live? Go home by Donnybrook; maybe you will get there and maybe you won't; anyhow it is shorter that way.' My only faith was in the tramlines; as long as I kept them in sight, I would find my way. I do not doubt that a spark of daring was in me too as I trudged forward. If going home the only way I knew was going to help me see a rebellion, that was a thing not to be missed. In my walks in Dublin that day, and the following early mornings, there was no steady walking on a settled course. Sometimes when the crowd ran, I ran with it; sometimes I stopped to talk; sometimes I stopped to help one of the women who were everywhere carrying loads too big for them.

The first sign that I was getting nearer on that first of my Dublin days was when I crossed Mount Street Bridge. A group of women shouted from the doorway at an unarmed soldier in British uniform, who was walking on the opposite footpath towards the bridge. 'Stop! Don't go there. You will be shot.' But the soldier did not pay the slightest attention, or even seem to hear. He just carried on until he went out of sight, around Clanwilliam House. Apart from the agitation of the women in Mount Street, everything was peaceful as I passed on my way. It was at Trinity College railings that the first sounds of battle reached me, and they were not much. It was getting dark. My way home led up Grafton Street and I hesitated before I took it; I knew by now that Trinity College was holding out against the Rising.

At the corner of Grafton Street and Wicklow Street a small party of British soldiers were flattened against the wall, while the man nearest to the corner was trying to see up the street with about half of one eye, the rest of him being under cover. I paused a while and waited very quietly until they withdrew back up Wicklow Street; then I walked on towards St Stephen's Green, following the route I had seen the Volunteers march earlier that day. I came to a barricade, which blocked the street on the west side of the Green. A man behind it waved me away; my road home, the only one I knew, was blocked. Then the man, the first armed Irish man in revolt I had ever encountered, told me to go around the Green and I would find my way.

I walked all around by the railings and I could see that there were men inside, but I remember nothing more until I came to the Russell Hotel corner. My road now turned up Harcourt Street. Before going that way, I hesitated again; then I crossed the road to the high iron gate of the Stephen's Green park. It was closed and a young sentry stood on duty outside. Unnecessarily, I asked what was happening. 'We are rising to free Ireland,' he told me. 'But I thought that was all settled,' said I. 'Home Rule will not satisfy us now. The Republic is proclaimed,' he replied.

I stood there, glued to the railing while the young Volunteer took up the thread of Ireland's history – from the Bridge of Athlone, Sarsfield, the broken Treaty of Limerick and the Wild Geese; he brought me to the United Irishmen, the Young Irelanders, the Famine, the Fenians, and the rebels of the hour, of which band he was one. He gestured into the darkness behind him: 'The Countess Markievicz is in there with us.' He would have brought me to her: I am nearly sure of that. But conscience hit me again, as it had done several times that afternoon. Poor Cousin Maude, in her bath chair, helpless, waiting for me. Bride, her daily maid, may well have been with her but I had not the heart to worry my cousin further. How could I leave her without a word? I thought about her frantic state of mind if I did not turn up by nightfall. I wavered, and then said to the young man: 'I'll be back in the morning, Will you let me in then?' 'I will,' he said.

In Harcourt Street I met a sidecar and the man undertook to bring me home, and did so. As we clattered over Portobello Bridge he pointed to a public house on the northeast side. 'There was fighting there, but it is over now.' Back in Rathgar Maude Mansfield tried to be firm. She forbade me to leave the house again. 'But I will have to go to mass,' I argued. 'Well, alright, you can go to mass,' she reluctantly agreed. Mass could be anywhere, said I to myself. Next morning, I was out bright and early, and straight back to the Green. But no encouraging young man was stationed there, with no sign of life until I got most of the way across the street from the hotel. Then a head popped out of a trench behind the railings and a fierce-looking old man with a white moustache shouted at me to 'Keep off.' I tried to explain but he would have none of it. He gestured with his rifle: 'Go away or you might get shot.'

The tricolour was flying from the College of Surgeons. This was the first time I saw it. I was pleased and proud to see it there. In the subsequent days, until I could not get past the canal bridges anymore, I always 'went to mass' far enough to see if it was flying still.

On the Tuesday morning after the rebuff I walked on around the Green and watched soldiers carrying a machine gun on a stretcher into the Shelbourne Hotel. I joined a small crowd at O'Connell Bridge and wavered forward through it, perhaps as far as Abbey Street. There was a good deal of movement in the street. Looters were about. The Volunteers wanted people to go away. An officer in uniform came from the direction of the GPO, and fired some shots in our direction from a revolver. I joined the crowd pelting back in flight across the bridge. On my way home I inspected a quantity of fine furniture, with plush red upholstery, outside a door in Nassau Street. The looters who were stripping somebody's home were people of discernment; this was a load of quality stuff, carefully chosen.

Next morning in Harcourt Street, blood pulled my shoe off. So keen had I been to see if the tricolour was still flying, I had not noticed a big red pool on the ground until my foot was held in it. There was more blood, mainly in doorways. In the street I met my literary cousin, Charlotte Dease. She was an author, of books and Catholic Truth booklets, and she knew people in Dublin more than most of the family. I found her, dressed in hat and veil, and nibbling at the veil in perplexity, drooping as usual. We stood in a doorway while she grieved for the poets and writers and gifted people for whom she had, at the same time, affection and profound disapproval. By this action, she said, they had spoiled everything. Pearses, McDonaghs,

Plunketts* became individuals to me, starting from what she told me about them in that moment of sadness and, for her, parting. On the Thursday, soldiers turned me back at the canal bridge and I did not get into Dublin again.

Food was now getting very short and I had to try and find some for the house. Having heard that Bewley's were selling butter at their farm at Orwell Road, I walked there with an ostrich-feathered Dublin lady, a crony of my cousin, who was as hungry as we were. Under the circumstances, with her sympathies and mine what they were, conversation was very difficult; besides my shoes were now worn through and I did not much want to waste what was left of them tramping after butter. Coming up the avenue I admired Bewley's herd of beautiful Jersey cows. 'My mother would love to have a few like those,' I said by way of conversation, and to change the subject from politics. Soon we came to a veranda where Mr Bewley in person, a tall old man, pink-faced through agitation, rage or perhaps naturally, was slamming pounds of butter onto butter paper, wrapping them and handing them out at full speed – four shillings a pound, if I remember correctly. I would have thought angels feared to tread in the presence of his poor mood and so when I heard my companion address him, and bring me into it, my heart stood still. 'This young lady wants to buy a cow,' she announced, as if I could buy Bewley's herd two or three times over. 'Just go round that way, please, I will send my herd to you,' Mr Bewley said quite calmly, business uppermost. We were shown around, accompanied by the lady's line of talk, to a herd. My face was burning. Thank God I had secured the butter before we got into this fix. I promised to describe the cows to my mother and that she would write if she thought one of them might suit her. Then we went; as far as I was concerned, never to return, no matter what butter was wanted.

Those last nights of the Rising countless eyes, like mine, gazed from behind the windows of dark houses circling the burning centre

---

* Leaders of the 1916 Rising: Padraig Pearse, Thomas McDonagh, Joseph Plunkett and their wider families, many of whom were also actively involved in the Rising.

of the city, back for mile on mile. None too far removed not to be held in fascinated vigil while fire, the last fatal weapon of war in those days, was used to burn out the dying throes of the rebellion.

The Risen People

SOME OF THE WOMEN I spoke with in the streets of Dublin during the Rising had first-hand information about events in North King Street, when British troops killed civilians in their homes, and, in some cases, buried the bodies in the cellars.* I spoke about this British atrocity when I arrived back in Wexford, travelling on the first available train out of Dublin; in my home county there was a very big demand for news from the capital. There was a scene in Main Street, Gorey, which I expect I set off, when talking about the people who had been murdered by British troops. There was, I recall, absolute fury when I mentioned this, and the group split up as if I had exploded a bomb among them. These people were not accustomed to have the British blamed – ever, or for anything. Lady Errington, wife of a former British envoy at the Vatican, had stopped to listen. Suddenly she started to shriek, 'They should all be hanged, they should all be hanged. Shooting is too good

---

* Towards the end of the Easter Rising one of the worst atrocities by British soldiers against civilians took place when fifteen men were shot or bayonetted to death in North King Street, an area close to the fighting in central Dublin.

for them.' She was not, of course, referring to British soldiers, but to Irish rebels. For me, as for so many others, the old world was shattered, former acquaintances turned into strangers, even into enemies; delicious new friendships began to form.

In Wexford I learned that three men and two women had marched on our former home, Ballycourcey, and bagged my Uncle Tommy's guns, but left his motor car, declaring it 'not good enough'. They or their comrades had made similar calls to other farmhouses in the county, collecting motors, petrol, guns and ammunition. The British commander against Enniscorthy was a friend of ours in the hunting field. Among ourselves we called Colonel French 'the Guardian Angel' as he was so kind when it came to stopping to help a fallen rider when the hounds were running, and would even delay to catch a loose horse. In his handling of the Rising in Enniscorthy he was as gentle as any soldier with such a duty could be. He had two field pieces and an armoured train carrying 'Enniscorthy Emily', a fifteen-pounder gun. Enniscorthy was more than grateful that he did not let any of this artillery off at the town. Instead, he waited until the fighting ended in Dublin and when the rebel leaders in Enniscorthy would not believe that Dublin had surrendered, Colonel French undertook to send two officers to Dublin so that they could get orders from their superiors. A truce was agreed, which was honoured with perfect correctness. Captain Seán Etchingham and Volunteer Seamus Doyle were brought to see Padraig Pearse in Arbour Hill Prison; they found him lying on the floor of a cell there. Pearse gave them their orders to surrender. 'What', said Etchingham, 'am I to bring that order to Wexford?' Then Pearse smiled and said 'surrender, or disperse'. And so, the two Wexford Volunteers decided that since they had not been directly ordered to lay down their guns on surrender, some of their poor equipment might be saved.

In Courtown our school resumed after the Easter holiday and life went on in the old pattern of society. But all my thoughts were away for good with excitement that old Ireland was alive again. There was hardly a day in the week when events of extreme newsworthiness to me might not be described in the evening paper; I rode on my bicycle three miles each way to get it in Gorey railway station, hot off the mail train from Dublin. There, the bundle had to be opened on the platform for messengers who, like me, had come from a distance and were in the mood of urgent dispatch carriers, spreading the news. By this time, we were exuberant rather than sad, delirious with joy and excitement.

Many historians subscribe to the view that my generation reacted to the Rising in the way we did because the English executed all the members of the provisional government of Ireland, which had been proclaimed in Dublin from the steps of the General Post Office on Easter Monday 1916. I contend that these historians are mistaken. It was not death but the call to freedom, and the new illustration of its meaning, which captured us; a flag on a pole, a proclamation that spoke the truth, and men deciding themselves how best to die, if die they must – these were the things that suddenly counted more than anything else in Ireland. The argument set out in the proclamation was unanswerable in the setting of the time.* Its theme was, and remains, that this whole island is the property of the Irish people; it is an assertion of their sovereignty in their own country, which denies the English any right of conquest. In the years after the Rising, it was widely understood that the self-respect of our ancient Nation, and of every individual in it, depended on some such action of our own, as the Rising had been. We were finished with being second-class citizens, with being insulted, and with being lied to. Our new proclamation promised to cherish all the children of the nation equally. And that was something new.

After the Easter Rising the members of the provisional government were shot and buried with contumely, un-coffined, out of a truck into a hole in the corner of a barracks yard. It was not only their brave deeds that made them heroes; for no enemy found anything to

---

* The Irish proclamation was the document issued by the Irish Volunteers and the Irish Citizen Army, in which the provisional government of the Irish Republic proclaimed Ireland's independence from British rule. Padraig Pearse read the 1916 proclamation outside the GPO, marking the start of the Rising.

defame the memory of the men themselves, except perhaps to call them foolish. In our eyes Padraig Pearse, James Connolly and their comrades certainly made no mistake in their timing of the Rising. The words read by Padraig Pearse outside the GPO in 1916 were accepted at face value, for every line was relevant to the life I saw all around me. The proclamation of the provisional government of the Irish Republic put the future of democracy in a setting, which was widely appreciated in Ireland. It was a supreme act of faith in the Irish people; and the people rose to meet it.

I cannot recall having contact with much national activity in the months following the Rising, beyond collecting money for 'National Aid'. I did this riding from farm to farm, and getting donations every-where. Years afterwards I was told that the majority of those from whom I obtained money had not the foggiest notion what it was all about. They might well have thought the cause to be some British army or navy welfare work. If this were so I had not the remotest suspicion of it! I began collecting after seeing Lily O'Brennan,* then Honorary Secretary of Cumann na mBan, at 25 Parnell Square. Lily was sister-in-law to 1916 leader Éamonn Ceannt and marched out to fight beside him in 1916. She was very small, very determined, always gay, and she worked endlessly to find places where men on the run could have shelter and hospitality. Later she was one of the staff brought to London for the negotiations with the British, which ended so disastrously in the 'Articles of Agreement'. On that first occasion when I met Lily, I asked to join Cumann na mBan, and to be notified in time if another Rising was planned!

---

* Elizabeth (Lily) O'Brennan (1878–1948) was an Irish Republican, writer and play-wright, who contributed to both Irish and American periodicals. Her sister Áine was married to Éamonn Ceannt, a prominent member of the IRB and one of the leaders of the Easter Rising in 1916. Lily reported for duty as the Rising began and was assigned to the Marrowbone Lane garrison under the command of her broth-er-in-law. After the Rising she was one of more than seventy-five women who were arrested and sent to Kilmainham Jail. In 1917 Lily O'Brennan joined the executive of both Cumann na mBan and Sinn Féin. She was one of the two delegation secre-taries for the 1921 Treaty, working from Hans Place in London for the duration of the negotiations.

Praying for the dead and collecting money for the support of the living dependants of men killed or in prison were the first concern of those Republicans who were at liberty after the Rising. In this work the widows of the National Leaders were the rallying point. Two outstanding women, Mrs Tom (Kathleen) Clarke* and Mrs Áine Ceannt,† were the two 1916 widows who had the best understanding of the plans of the insurgents, and of the duties that would have to be undertaken afterwards. Anna Rahilly,‡ Hanna Sheehy-Skeffington§ and

---

* Kathleen Clarke (1878–1972) was the wife of one of the leaders of the 1916 Rising, Thomas (Tom) Clarke, who she married in New York in 1901. They returned to live in Ireland in 1907 and opened a shop in Amiens Street in Dublin, which became a hive of Republican activity. Kathleen was a founder member of Cumann na mBan and before the Rising was sworn into the IRB, to enable her to continue the work of the Republican cause in the aftermath. Following the rebel surrender, Kathleen visited her husband in Kilmainham jail on the night before his execution. The next night she returned to visit her brother Ned, who was also executed for his part in the Rising on 4 May 1916. Kathleen then established a fund for Volunteer dependants. She was pregnant during this period but lost the baby. Kathleen Clarke remained active in the struggle for independence and the political life of the country, later becoming the first female Lord Mayor of Dublin in 1939. Details of her experiences in the revolutionary period were published posthumously in *Kathleen Clarke, Revolutionary Woman* (by Kathleen Clarke and Helen Litton).

† Mary Francis (Áine) Ceannt (1880–1954) was a founding member of Cumann na mBan, a Republican activist and the wife of 1916 leader Éamonn Ceannt. Her sister, Lily O'Brennan, was also a Cumann na mBan stalwart. The Ceannt home was a hotbed of Republican activity, both prior to the 1916 Rising and during the War of Independence. Áine wrote and delivered dispatches during the Rising while her husband fought in the South Dublin Union. After 1916, and following her husband's execution, Áine served as vice president of Cumann na mBan and was active in Sinn Féin, particularly in the Republican Courts.

‡ Anna Rahilly/O'Rahilly (1873–1958) was a Republican activist and a member of Cumann na mBan. Her brother, the 1916 leader The O' Rahilly, died from wounds sustained during fighting in the Rising in Dublin. Following the surrender Anna was arrested and detained and subsequently released in late 1916. She remained active during the War of Independence and the Civil War, taking the anti-Treaty side.

§ Hanna Sheehy-Skeffington (1877–1946) was a prominent Irish suffragette and political activist. She was a founding member of the Irish Women's Franchise League in 1908, along with her husband, Francis Sheehy-Skeffington, and Margaret Cousins. Her husband was shot and killed in detention following the 1916 Rising. Following this personal tragedy, Hanna embarked on a very successful speaking tour to the USA to raise awareness of the Irish Republican cause.

Helena Molony* head the women's roll of honour in the first years after the Rising, when they did more than most to tip the scales, which for a while were balanced fairly evenly between success and failure. In this period Irish women had the only chance they ever had to be important in the leadership of the nation. It lasted from the death of Pearse and Tom Clarke† to the release of Michael Collins‡ from internment at Christmas 1916. But an important extension beyond this time was the first Easter Week Commemoration, which was organized by the women of the Irish Citizen Army under Helena Molony.

The impact of the first Easter Commemoration of the Rising was all the more memorable for being unexpected. It far exceeded anything that had gone before. In Wexford we knew nothing of it until

---

* Helena Molony (1884–1967) was a political activist, teacher and actor who joined Inghinidhe na hÉireann in 1903 and later became the editor of *Bean na hÉireann* – the organization's publication. In 1913 she was active in the Lockout, when Dublin workers went on strike to achieve better pay and conditions. In 1914 Helena joined the Irish Citizen Army and Cumann mBan and during the 1916 Rising she was with the City Hall garrison. Following the surrender she was imprisoned until her release in December 1916.

† Thomas (Tom) Clarke (1858–1916) was an Irish Republican, a leading figure in the IRB and, it has been argued, the man most responsible for the 1916 Rising. Following his capture in connection with a bombing campaign in the UK in 1883, Clarke spent fifteen years doing hard labour in jail in Britain. His account of this imprisonment was published in *Irish Freedom* in 1912 and as *Glimpses of an Irish Felon's Prison Life* (1922). Clarke married Kathleen Daly in New York in 1901, returning to Ireland in 1907, where he opened a tobacconist's in Dublin and began to work to reform the IRB. He founded the organization's newspaper *Irish Freedom* and, along with his close associate Seán MacDermott, set up the IRB Military Committee in order to progress plans for the Rising. During Easter Week 1916 Clarke served in the GPO garrison and although he held no military rank he played a major part in directing military operations, particularly after James Connolly was badly wounded. Following the surrender, Tom Clarke was detained and executed by firing squad on 3 May 1916.

‡ Michael Collins (1890–1922) was a charismatic, brave and daring leader during the Irish revolutionary period. Collins fought in the GPO in 1916 and later became a pivotal figure and important military leader, directing strategy in the War of Independence. He was elected as a Sinn Féin TD for South Cork in 1918, and was appointed Minister for Finance in the First Dáil. He became Director of Intelligence for the Irish Republican Army and in 1920 established The Squad, colloquially known as the Twelve Apostles – a successful and ruthless counter-intelligence and assassination squad. Collins was a signatory to the Treaty in 1921, which he grimly equated to signing his own death warrant.

we read the newspapers. I still remember that when the postman came on the Tuesday, I brought the morning paper to Mother and we stood by the dining-room fire, reading together. The newspaper told of how the tricolour was set up about 9 am by a young man, who had climbed the perilous ruin of the GPO. Set first at half-mast, it remained so until the precise hour of the start of the Rising; then it was raised to full mast in the presence of many thousands of people. The police were there too, starting an endurance test, which was to send them in pursuit of flags up trees, telegraph poles, and on high and dangerous wires unable to take the weight of hefty policemen; on roofs, cliffs, and danger spots of all kinds in every part of the country. But the police had no one who could climb as well as Paddy Morrin, Derry man and Irish Citizen Army steeplejack, who travelled from Glasgow to do the job. The flag on the GPO stayed in place, flying over scenes of jubilation for five hours. When the post was eventually broken and the flag brought down, the police failed to get it. Young men carried it off, and raced away down Princes Street. Volleys of stones from the ruins halted the police giving chase but the official stewards of the ceremony, wearing tricolour armbands, rescued them from serious injury. The stone throwers were prevailed on to stop, and a day that was worth a major victory in the field came to a good-natured conclusion.

Years later, when I became a newspaper woman, I interviewed those still alive of the group of women who had largely planned and implemented the 1917 Easter Commemoration. As is well known, the 1916 proclamation was printed in two halves in Liberty Hall on the Sunday night before the Rising. James Connolly* borrowed the type from his English friend, Mr West. When the job was done, and the

---

* James Connolly (1868–1916) was a Scottish-born revolutionary socialist, a trade union leader, political thinker and author. Connolly came to believe in insurrection as the best means to achieve an independent Irish Republic, and using Liberty Hall in Dublin as his base, he began to prepare his Irish Citizen Army (ICA) for battle. He joined forces with the Irish Republican Brotherhood and during the Easter Rising in 1916 the ICA combatants fought alongside other Irish Volunteers. Connolly was injured in the fighting and following the surrender he, and the other leaders of the Rising, were executed by firing squad.

fight started, Liberty Hall was left undefended. Presently it was occupied by British military; they found the machinery with type standing.
After printing off some hard copies of the proclamation, which they
tried to sell for 2/6 each, the type was thrown around and the office
wrecked. It was nearly a year before the rightful owners were in a
position to tidy the place up. Helena Molony was the registered
owner of James Connolly's paper 'The Workers' Republic'. She got
the job, she told me, because it was desirable to have a 'man of straw'.
What use the Castle imposing fines upon a person who could not
pay? So, Helena was picked from the thousands in Dublin who had
no money. She became Connelly's lieutenant in running the Liberty
Hall co-operative and in other matters. The co-operative was founded
towards the end of the great strike of 1913 to provide employment
for some of the Citizen Army women in producing clothes, to be
sold as cheaply as possible to members of the union. The main team
members in the co-op were Rosie Hackett, Mrs Shannon and Brigid
Davis. But the soldiers who raided Liberty Hall had left all the sewing
machines smashed.

When Louie Bennett, founder of the Women's Workers Union,
visited Helena Molony in Aylesbury Prison after the Rising, Helena
begged her to do something to keep the women and girls of the
co-operative together. The Prisoners' Dependents' Fund gave a sum
of money, Dr Kathleen Lynn helped, [*] and Mrs George Bernard Shaw [†]
donated the price of one sewing machine. As quickly as possible the
team was at work again; soon there was such a demand for tricolour
flags they had no further worries about employment. Helena told me
that when she was in jail and heard so much about Ireland's 'loyal

---

[*] Dr Kathleen Lynn was a Republican activist, medical doctor and member of the
Irish Citizen Army. She became chief medical officer of the ICA during the 1916
Rising and tended to the wounded from her post at City Hall. Along with her life
companion, Madeleine ffrench-Mullen, Dr Lynn later founded and ran St Ultan's
Hospital for Infants on Charlemont Street in Dublin in 1919.

[†] Mrs George Bernard Shaw, formerly Charlotte Frances Payne-Townshend (1857–
1943), was an Irish political activist in Britain and the wife of author and playwright
George Bernard Shaw.

soldiers fighting in Flanders', she made up her mind 'to do it all over again'. The type of the proclamation was gathered up from the rubble and dust and sent back to Mr West, who undertook to help the plan for a reprint of the proclamation, as far as possible in facsimile. Helena told me that the IRB initially agreed to cooperate in what was planned. But at almost the last minute she learned that Mimi Plunkett, sister of Joseph Plunkett, had cancelled the printing job. When questioned, Mimi said she had been ordered to cancel for some unknown reason, and had also been told not to tell Helena about it. But, undeterred, the printing was done in Joe Stanley's works using the old type. The proclamation was posted again in Dublin, and the tricolour was raised once more on the GPO.

The first commemoration of the Easter Rising lifted the sacrifice of 1916 clear from sorrow and defeat, putting it into the context of the living present in a rebirth of national resolve. Tragedy was superseded by resurrection. Easter Sunday 1917 was on 8 April; on 10 April, immediately after the commemoration, the Lieutenant General, Sir Bryan Mahon, Commander-in-Chief of the British Forces in Ireland, finally woke up to the situation and issued his own proclamation. It banned all processions and meetings under DORA.

I was getting more determined to break away from all restrictions; to get to know the real people, the people who were doing things. One day when I was riding on my pony and thinking about this, I saw a familiar man standing outside Gorey town hall. Day after day I had hesitated, not knowing to whom I should apply. This time I turned in and asked if anyone could tell me how to join the Gaelic League.* Commandant W.J. Brennan Whitmore, an Easter Week veteran, introduced himself; he made me welcome and told me when to come back for classes. My cousin, Ellice Pilkington, came to the classes with me, until she discovered that at times the Irish language was used as a thin veil for other treasonable activities that might be afoot in the district.

---

* The Gaelic League was founded in 1893 by Irish writers and scholars interested in renewing Irish identity, primarily through the promotion of the Irish language and Irish culture.

Many people were influenced by the Gaelic League, which was born out of the Irish Revival, and was broad-based, including schoolteachers, farmers and country gentlemen, professors and wandering poets, Fenians and academics. But we know now what we did not know then – that it was not able to make a Republican whole. It is an ironic thought that we, who so loved the inheritance thus presented to us, went near to killing it as a nationwide influence with our love, and our efforts to translate it into an ideal State. In the small hall in Gorey, where Pearse once spoke, and in innumerable other places, I revelled in the chivalry of the sages, the wisdom of the Brehon Laws,* the history in place names from Gibbet Hill to Tara, the culture and traditions of ancient Ireland before the coming of the Danes or the English. The influence of the Gaelic League and the Volunteers had given us a classless society of idealists. It was not to last long, but it was lovely to be in it.

One thing that I noticed immediately in the Irish-Ireland Movement was that so many of my new friends had far more education than any of my old friends would have thought possible. Those who disparaged the Rising, and discounted the change in the temper of Ireland by saying that 'all the trouble was caused by ignorant people' would have fared very badly in any competitive test of general knowledge about the history, literature and present situation of our country. They might even have failed in a wider curriculum. More people than I ever knew before could write grammatical English, although few had been to school after the age of fourteen. Many had added to what the nuns, the Christian Brothers and the national schools gave them by home reading. Some had been through the university of the jails. A wealth of books and pamphlets were available after the Rising and these were distributed through the Gaelic League. We were constantly at the bottom of our pockets looking for the price of another book.

---

* The Irish Brehon Laws were comprised of statutes governing life in early medieval Ireland, operational in parts of Ireland until the English conquest of Ireland was completed at the beginning of the seventeenth century.

In the summer of 1917 the last of the Easter Week prisoners were released from prisons in England; they got a wonderful welcome home. Seán Etchingham arrived at Courtown Harbour with Seán McGarry (fated to be one of the bitter men of future years) and Charlie Murphy, one of the very best, who would be elected to the First Dáil and would continue to carry out its mission until the very end, with the remnant of the Second Dáil. Also in the party was James Joyce of the Irish Citizen Army. Dublin is better fed now, and you do not see many men much under five feet tall like James Joyce. The Citizen Army had plenty of them. Their souls were full-size, and Connolly and Larkin had nourished their spirit and capacity for bravery and fortitude; but those undernourished bodies could not be changed after a childhood spent in privation. In the fighting days ahead the little Citizen Army men flitted here and there. They had a way of turning up when there was a tight place, and disappearing before the net had closed, only to turn up again. I don't know anything bad about the Citizen Army; they held onto the democratic slogan – 'Each for All; All for Each' – long after it had been forgotten in other circles.

Seán Etchingham brought me a present, which I always treasured. It is an envelope with a spray of rough grass inside. On it he wrote: *From Roger Casement's Grave, Pentonville, June 1917*. I soon got to know these men better and remember a day when we drove a crowded pony trap out beyond Monaseed to the ruins of the house of Myles Byrne, the Wexford Rebel leader of 1798.* Something intangible lingers in my mind from that day. The countryside was part of where I lived, and the history and traditions, about which we spoke on our way, were not new to Etchingham, or the others; what overflowed to me was the joy in the recognition they felt that the nation now loved them. They were, at that time, the favourite sons of Cathleen Ni Houlihan. At every steep hill they sprang from the trap, but not only to lighten

---

* The 1798 rebellion was an insurrection launched by the United Irishmen (an underground Republican society) aimed at overthrowing British rule in Ireland and establishing an Irish republic based on the principles of the French Revolution. Following some initial successes, particularly in Wexford, the uprising was suppressed.

the pony's load. As they struggled between the fresh green hedges, talking or joking, light-hearted, frivolous or suddenly very serious, I realized that for them it was a most unusual experience to be relaxed and happy, in a holiday mood and at large in their own lovely country. All nature was clothed in their colours – the gorse and the grass and the flowering hawthorn.

The day came when I was summoned to the inaugural meeting of Courtown Harbour Sinn Féin Club. It was held in the small, windowless band room, and was strictly by invitation. There were more musical instruments than pieces of furniture. The papers were kept in a broken drum and the proceedings appeared in the following week's *Enniscorthy Echo*, to which Seán Etchingham was once again contributing. The Sinn Féin Club made a plan to hold an Aeriocht (open-air gathering) on the Burrow at Courtown, in aid of its own funds and for the nationwide movement. Seán T. O'Kelly and Eoin MacNeill* would be the speakers, with MacNeill staying at our house.

The Aeriocht was proclaimed (which really made us feel dangerous and important). District Inspector Lea Wilson took possession of the ground with a surprisingly large show of armed force. Fortunately, the skies opened and we had the pleasure of inspecting the enemy in his drenched misery while we sent a whisper round the people, 'Come instead to the pier this day next week.' The following Sunday

---

* Eoin MacNeill (1867–1945) was a Gaelic scholar and nationalist politician, a founding member of the Gaelic League and Chair of Early and Medieval Irish History at University College Dublin. In 1913 he took a lead in the formation of the Irish Volunteers, becoming Commander-in-Chief. In early April 1916 MacNeill was persuaded by what subsequently turned out to be an altered 'Castle document' as proof that action by the British against the Volunteers was imminent. He appeared to agree to a general mobilization of Volunteer forces for a Rising on Easter Sunday, but when he discovered that the Castle document was faked and that arms expected from Germany had been lost at sea, he ordered a demobilization of the Volunteers. MacNeill's countermand led to widespread confusion amongst the Volunteers and the Rising was primarily confined to Dublin, with reduced numbers of Volunteers. Despite his order for demobilization, MacNeill was nonetheless arrested by the British and court-martialled. He was released from prison in 1917. He became involved in the reconstituted Sinn Féin party and was elected in 1918 to the First Dáil (for two seats, in Derry City and for the National University of Ireland).

a British gunboat stood by off the pier, but the police did not risk the ducking which, they must have guessed, was planned for them had they decided to make arrests. We were delighted with ourselves because we had attracted so much attention and succeeded in doing what we planned; our hope was that when we put all the voice we could muster into 'Felons of our Land', in honour of the 500 prisoners then in jail – the sound would carry our tribute over the narrow expanse of water to the gunboat, silently stationed nearby.

Ashe

INSIDE THE DOOR of the Round Room in Dublin's Mansion House, I was introduced to Thomas Ashe* and Terence MacSwiney,† who were talking together at a *ceilidhe* in the spring of 1917. Ashe was a gallant figure in his kilts. The meeting had not long to stay in my

---

* Thomas Ashe (1885–1917) was President of the IRB and a founding member of the Irish Volunteers. He was heavily involved in Irish cultural and political life. Ashe led the Fingal battalion in the Rising of 1916 and, following his arrest and trial, was sentenced to death, commuted to penal servitude for life. He was released as part of the general amnesty in the summer of 1917. His freedom was, however, short-lived. A couple of months later Thomas Ashe was arrested again on the charge of inciting disaffection amongst the population and sentenced to two years' hard labour, before dying in prison. Ashe's body lay in state at Dublin City Hall. His large funeral procession was led by armed Volunteers through the streets of Dublin to Glasnevin Cemetery, where Michael Collins gave the graveside oration.

† Terence MacSwiney (1879–1920) was an Irish writer and politician. He was elected as Sinn Féin Lord Mayor of Cork in March 1920, following the assassination of his predecessor, Tomás MacCurtain. MacSwiney was arrested on charges of sedition in August 1920 and sentenced by a military tribunal to two years without hard labour. In response, he immediately went on hunger strike, which he endured for seventy-four days before he died, propelling the Irish Republican cause onto a global stage on the front pages of international newspapers.

mind before both men were dead following hunger strikes in widely separated prisons. There was enormous traffic of men to and from prisons, and women to prison gates. Men were court-martialled for singing 'The Soldier's Song' or 'Felons of our Land'. Everything that happened in prison leaked out and we knew about, and could follow, the fights inside, as well as those outside.

Thomas Ashe died on 25 September 1917, under forcible feeding officially administered in Mountjoy Prison. He had been arrested and sentenced by court martial to two years' hard labour for making a speech 'calculated to cause disaffection'.

I consulted with Aileen K'Eogh, who was matron at Father Sweetman's school, Mount St Benedict, about getting to the Ashe funeral in Dublin. By then both of our schools were beginning to feel the political draught. We decided that if we were to get to Dublin, we must bicycle there, leaving before dawn so that no one would miss us. Aileen K'Eogh always knew her own mind; her loyalty to her country was at white heat as long as she lived. She came from landlord stock at Kilbride, County Carlow and was then about fifty – a Catholic woman of magnificent physique, fair and grey-eyed. 'The Matron', as Aileen was widely known, could do manual work in farm or garden, level with any man; a powerful woman, who was very direct in her speech. Yet Aileen was so tender, she was miserable if doctor's orders compelled her to give an injection to some small schoolboy; but on the other hand, her anger could, and often did, make strong men quail. The Matron could get the wrong end of the stick more often than anybody else I ever met. The school and the care of school boys were her vocation, and for her the sun, moon and stars shone out of The Very Rev. Dom J.F. Sweetman OSB, whose educational mission was to produce good men for Ireland. Aileen K'Eogh was alight with patriotic fervour. I already knew from the many stories about her fortitude that when news of the 1916 Rising reached Aileen she set out immediately on her bicycle and scorched the sixty miles to Dublin. Aileen was pedalling, head bent for the GPO, when she was called to halt by the police at Trinity College. When she ignored them, they pulled her in, which must have taken some doing! To everyone's astonishment Aileen turned out to be cousin to the Provost, the illustrious Dr Mahaffy.[*]

On the morning of the Ashe funeral Aileen and I set out at 5 am; my brother Sandy came too. We rode the sixty miles to Dublin quick enough to be on time for 12 o'clock mass in the city. Then we queued to pass around Ashe's coffin, lying in state and guarded by Volunteers with Howth rifles in the rotunda of the City Hall. We marched in the funeral procession to Glasnevin Cemetery, which was one of the biggest to be held in Dublin since the death of Parnell – and for me the first in a very long, very sad procession of funerals stretching over the following decades.

The secrecy associated with the beginning of this expedition did not hold. Father Sweetman had attended and marched in the funeral in all publicity. He now ordered us to go home by train, like everybody else.

People who still belonged to the old world, including the more cautious of the parents who trusted us with the education of their children, thought that the clergy should keep out of politics. That was an argument that might well have started centuries or years earlier, before Orange and Green were heard of. For most of my generation the clergy were the only educated class. We found some among them who were ready to apply rather than conceal basic Christian principles in confrontation with the world. These reverend men were not exclusively Catholic, and I know of none who survived the 1920s in Ireland. Father Sweetman was to me the most important of these clergy. I can think of no other whose position was comparable. His young school at Mount St Benedict in Gorey, fondly known as the Mount, was tilling a new field in education, backed by 300 acres of indifferent land, which made him an employer and neighbour to other farmers. All the principles and problems of the new Ireland

---

[*] Dr John Pentland Mahaffy (1839–1919) was a distinguished academic and the Chair of Ancient History in Trinity College Dublin, becoming Provost in 1914. Mahaffy was a Unionist and supporter of the British regime in Ireland.

came together for discussion in his guest room, where I was often present, or in the grounds where he took a hand at reclamations using pick, shovel and axe.

It was a privilege to hear first principles expounded, and also applied, and to know a man to whom the image of God in man was ever present.

Sisters

I BECAME deeply interested in Liberty Hall in Dublin; there was no headquarters of Republicanism that was so eloquent of the past and so appealing to the present as Liberty Hall was at that time. The return of Countess Markievicz* from prison following the Rising, and her reception in Dublin, increased my determination to get in touch. When the family arranged a day trip to shop in Dublin, I took my opportunity. I knew that as well as being brave, as the women of Liberty Hall had shown at the Easter Commemoration, they were also trying to feed the hungry. I thought about this as I shoved a few stone of the potatoes under the seat of the dog car bringing us to the railway station. I paid

---

* Countess Constance Markievicz (1868–1927) was an Anglo-Irish revolutionary, a worker for the poor and underprivileged, a politician and an artist. The Countess, as she was widely known, embraced politics and public life at the relatively late age of forty, when she joined Inghinidhe na hÉireann (Daughters of Ireland) and Sinn Féin. She went on to found and head up Na Fianna Éireann, a Republican training organization for boys and young men, and fought in the Rising of 1916. She was the only woman to be sentenced to death, commuted to penal servitude for life. In 1917 she returned from her imprisonment in England to a tumultuous welcome home. She was the first woman elected to the Westminster Parliament in 1918, and served as Minister for Labour in the First Dáil.

a porter in Gorey, and another at Harcourt Street Station, and hired a sidecar to Liberty Hall to present the potatoes. It is evident from my recollection of this adventure that at the age of twenty-four, I had not the slightest idea of the value of either goods or money!

At Liberty Hall I was welcomed and brought to the dining room, where people were eating at long tables. It was here that I met Con Markievicz, full of work and enthusiasm. The ostrich-feathered hat, which she wore when she drove in triumph through the city, had been put aside; but there she was, a thin figure in the same cardigan suit. The Countess was working side by side with Marie Perolz* and soon I was gathered with them in a tight little group. Our talk must have been full of fire and fight because Marie offered to supply me a .22 revolver for £1. Alas I had not the money to buy, so the revolver had to be left behind.

My first letter from the Countess came after I got home, thanking me again for the lovely potatoes. When granny got to know that I had met Con she was in tears again and wrote a letter to Mother about 'that awful woman leading young girls to their destruction'. Poor Mother, who always had to bear the brunt, also received a letter on the subject from her brother, Uncle Tommy, declaring that 'unless you can control your children better than this, I shall have to change my will'. Our family became divided and we could no longer discuss national affairs; conversation between us became difficult.

The conflict of the time produced many family divisions, with brothers and sisters prominently on different sides. One such brother was Viscount French, Commander-in-Chief, Home Forces, and, at the time of which I write, soon to be Lord Lieutenant of Ireland; previously Chief of the Imperial General Staff and Commander-in-Chief of the British forces in France. As far as our information went, his office door, his club door, his back door and his main door at home were all closed against his sister, Mrs Charlotte Despard, when she wanted to

---

* Marie (also known as Mary or Máire) Perolz (1874–1950) was a member of Inghinidhe na hÉireann, which she joined in 1900, later becoming an active worker for Cumann na mBan. She was also a member of the Irish Citizen Army. Following the 1916 Rising, Perolz was interned without trial for her role in the insurrection.

talk to him about the wrongs that were being inflicted on India and on Ireland. Mrs Despard was a lover of justice for its own sake, and a great humanitarian. She was the widow of a colonel in the Indian army and gave away all she had. When Mrs Despard settled in Dublin she was old, frail, dauntless and a theosophist.[*] She carried herself straight as a soldier and the black lace veil, set with the point to the exact centre face, was on piled up white hair, adding height to her lined forehead. Her face was serene, commanding, ascetical and quite often humourless.

Her friend and companion in excursions all over Ireland, which demanded amazing resilience, was Maud Gonne MacBride. These women were no armchair critics of the administration. Instead, with enormous valour and devotion, they carried their protests against the actions of the government to the scene of every British atrocity, killing, burning, sacking or pogrom, from Cork to Belfast. They had great sympathy for the women, who often had to bear the brunt when houses and towns were wrecked. They were not doctrinaire Republicans but they selflessly helped their fellows and abhorred the British methods. These women brought great heart to people in tribulation.

The Earl of Midleton,[†] Conservative politician, Irish and English lord, ex-MP for Guildford, ex-Secretary of State for War, ex-Secretary for India, Leader of the South of Ireland Unionists in the Home Rule era and member of British Prime Minister Lloyd George's Irish Convention also had a sister who had formed her own opinions of current affairs. She was the Honourable Albinia Brodrick. Albinia was in her late forties when her father died and she finally got control of her own life, and of her affairs. She went at once to be trained as a nurse. This was a necessary part of her scheme to build a hospital

---

[*] A theosophist is a follower of theosophy, broadly understood to mean divine wisdom. Theosophists emphasize mystical experience or connection with a deeper spiritual reality and therefore practise methods that transcend human consciousness, such as meditation.

[†] William St John Fremantle Brodrick, 1st Earl of Midleton (1856–1942), styled as St John Brodrick until 1907 and as Viscount Midleton between 1907–20, was a British Conservative and Irish Unionist Alliance politician. He served as an MP from 1880–1906, as a government minister from 1886–92 and 1895–1900 and as a Cabinet minister from 1900–5.

*Ardaven c. 1900, where Máire Comerford was born
and lived until her early teenage years.*

*James Comerford, Máire's father,
c. 1890.*

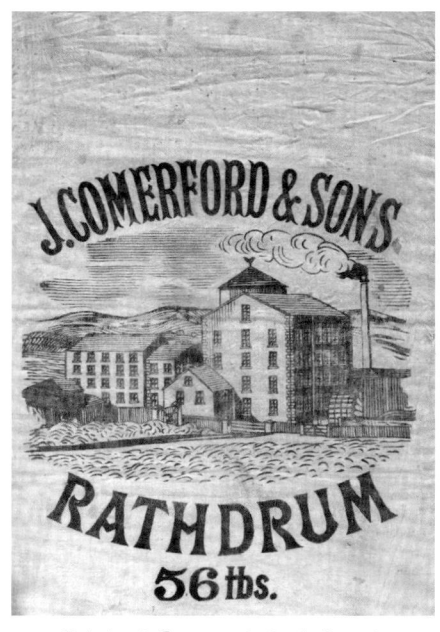

*Original flour sack depicting the
Comerford Mill, Rathdrum,
Co.Wicklow, c. 1880.*

Lieutenant Colonel Thomas Esmonde VC,
Máire's maternal grandfather, c. 1860.

Matilda Esmonde, Máire's maternal
grandmother, c. 1860.

Eva and Tommy Esmonde, Máire's
mother and uncle, c. 1870.

Milly and Eva Esmonde, Máire's aunt
and mother, c. 1875.

Eva Esmonde on horseback, c. 1890.

Máire Comerford aged four on horseback, 1897.

Eva Comerford (née Esmonde) with three of her four children: Tom, Dimpy and Máire, or Mary as she was then known, c. 1899. The fourth child, Alexander (Sandy), was born in 1900.

Ballycourcey House, Enniscorthy, Co. Wexford. Máire, her mother and siblings moved to Wexford and lived here with the extended Esmonde family following her father's death in 1907.

Aunt Milly Esmonde, Máire Comerford's maternal aunt, in her horse and trap, c. 1910.

Matilda (Granny) Esmonde, c. 1910.

[v]

Cricket game at Ballycourcey, c. 1900.

Tommy Esmonde, Máire's maternal uncle, training a horse at the Ballycourcey farm, c. 1910.

*The original Bailynastragh House, seat of the Esmonde Family,
c. 1920. The mansion was burnt down in 1923 by anti-Treaty
forces. In 1937 the house was rebuilt on a smaller scale.*

*Sir Thomas Henry Grattan Esmonde,
11th Baronet, c. 1902.*

St Scholastica's School, 1913. The girls' boarding school was opened by Eva Comerford in 1913 and closed in 1919. Máire Comerford also worked in the school.

Pupils at an outdoor art class on the grounds of St Scholastica's School, 1913.

in Kerry, where she planned to offer her life in a public display of amendment for the injustices done to the Irish by her family in their capacity as landlords of great estates in Cork.

When, after much pleading, I was allowed to go to an Irish summer school to learn the language, the family arranged that I would stay with Miss Brodrick and attend the Irish college at Caherdaniel, County Kerry. They knew who she was, but knew nothing of what she had become. I was soon to learn what Miss Brodrick's political views were, and where her allegiance lay.

I put a few clothes into the parcel post and started out pedalling by bicycle in eager haste for Kerry. There I found a small, laughing woman with bright eyes and a fresh complexion, who welcomed me in Gaelic. She wore glasses and the nearest approach to a nurse's uniform that could be made from the roughest Kerry homespun, dyed blue. Bustling ahead, she brought me to a stark little room, which she had prepared by, I found out later, bringing her own bed into the seclusion made by a ring of enormous, unopened packing cases of hospital equipment in the hall. Her small kitchen faced out over the wild sea line of Kenmare Bay. We were twenty-eight miles out from the town of Kenmare. The post came from Killarney, about forty miles, on a sidecar that was the only public transport.

The building was the shell, walls and roof of the hospital, intended to take about fifty beds. She had built it, largely from her own resources. The hospital stood on fifteen acres of wild, craggy land between the sea and the road and represented the fruits of her first ten years of personal freedom. Albinia had discarded her title – except on occasions when it might be useful for propaganda purposes – and wished to be known in the Irish form, Gobnait Ní Bruadair. Gobnait remained to the end of her days a regular and devoted member of the Church of Ireland, but her loyalty excluded the then head of that Church, the reigning monarch of Britain. As the thirty years of our friendship went past, we were thrown together in prison (after she was shot and captured), on committees, by firesides and in public places, I gradually came to learn of her story and that of the hospital.

Gobnait was brought up under the strict discipline of her parents in a great house in Yorkshire. Every night she and her sisters in turn read reports from the London *Times* about debates in the House of Lords and the Commons to their father. When they came to the name William Ewart Gladstone,* Prime Minister, they were not allowed to soil their lips with it. Instead, they were instructed to say: 'Then the gentleman whose name I cannot mention up and spoke.' When they went out it was always in the carriage, with menservants. Before the ladies emerged from their rooms every button down to their gloves had to be in place; otherwise, they were sent back to 'see to their toilet' and reproved for presenting themselves undressed before the servants. Once, when their butler's brother had returned from his sea voyages, they were allowed to go out in a small boat for a picnic on the lake in front of their grand house. 'He will see to it,' they were informed, for 'he is seaman and once sailed to China.'

The hospital was used in friendship's way for neighbours, and sometimes by people from afar needing rest and change. It was never staffed or accepted by the public authority – too inconveniently located, I imagine! Neither the British nor the Free State combatants during the Civil War would consent to honour the Red Cross flag when Gobnait raised it there to notify the presence of wounded. Instead, the hospital was raided and the purpose for which it was built was often obstructed.

On my first morning in Kerry in 1917, the smell of the ocean, the view of mountain and coast and the enchanting local sounds excluded every thought of past or future. I stopped beside a man who was digging a drain in the place Gobnait planned to have a garden. 'I don't know what will grow here,' he said to me, as he worked to dislodge a large rock. 'She has that much draught through the roots, the plants will be blown out of it.' One thing I noticed very quickly was that everyone in Kerry seemed to own at least some land. There was no labouring class,

---

* William Ewart Gladstone (1809–1898) was a British Liberal politician. In a career lasting over sixty years, Gladstone served for twelve years as Prime Minister over four terms, beginning in 1868 and ending in 1894. Gladstone campaigned for Home Rule for Ireland, an issue that dominated much of his third and fourth terms.

owning no property or land at all, such as we were accustomed to in County Wexford. If a man worked for Gobnait it was in the time he could spare from his own holding; poor, or in need of work as he may well have been, he had the status of a neighbour, not that of a servant.

I went faithfully every day to the Irish college but the part of my holiday that I remember most clearly was when I went sailing with the Reverend W.S. Green.* He, his wife and daughter were Gobnait's nearest neighbours and they were on what I judged to be good sparring terms. Rev. Green, with his long experience in the West, his concentrated interest in the fisheries and his background, was not likely to be swept off his feet in the revolution, whatever his sympathies might be. I fancy that he looked on rather quizzically at Gobnait's political conversation, and on her enthusiasms in the new life she was embarking on in late middle age. It was unbelievable good fortune to me when I discovered that my arrival was greeted with pleasure by the women of the Green family because I was willing to go yachting with Mr Green; they both preferred to get on with the jobs from which one of them was so often called to 'man' the boat. I got lessons in sailing from the master of the craft.

The family of Daniel O'Connell† in Derrynane, three or four miles away, might also have been reckoned as neighbours by Gobnait. Although she politely suggested that I might like to meet them, since

---

* Reverend W.S. Green (William Spotswood Green) (1847–1919), was a Cork-born naturalist and marine biologist. W.S. Green attended Trinity College Dublin and was ordained in 1873. He also achieved some fame as an explorer and mountain-climber, especially in New Zealand, where he attempted to reach the summit of Mount Cook in 1882. In the 1890s Rev. Green took up the post of Inspector of Fisheries and worked as a Commissioner on the Congested Districts Board, where he put his extensive knowledge of the West of Ireland to good use. He retired in 1914 and lived with his family in Westcove House in Kerry, where Máire Comerford met him in 1917.

† Daniel O'Connell, known as the Liberator (1775–1847), was a barrister and an Irish nationalist leader. After the Act of Union in 1801 O'Connell began to agitate for Catholic emancipation resulting in the Catholic Emancipation Act of 1829. O'Connell founded the Repeal Association in 1840 to agitate for legislative independence for Ireland under the British Crown. In October 1843 Dublin Castle banned a mass mobilization meeting organized by O'Connell in Clontarf. O'Connell's reaction, which was to cancel the meeting so as to avoid confrontation and possible violence, was seen by some followers as capitulation to British threats. After Clontarf, support ebbed away from O'Connell and the Repeal Movement.

they were very distant relatives, I knew that Gobnait had marked them off as being of little interest to her because she believed that the O'Connells had no modern Irish inspiration, and disapproved of the language revival. Gobnait had no use at all for social 'equals' as such. But Derrynane was part of the history of the place so I sped off there one day on my bicycle. My mind was on the Wild Geese* coming and going from this lonely sea shore; of countless young Catholics stealing away to Europe in search of the education denied to them at home in Ireland; of smugglers bringing in huge casks of wine, bales of contraband silk, anything and everything that was forbidden; on what history said about O'Connell's achievement and what we of the young generation thought of his failure to get more than he did. I thought too about O'Connell's lack of confidence and, like John Redmond, just at the point in both cases when there had been need for courage. We could not forgive O'Connell for shirking from possible bloodshed at Clontarf or for allowing the franchise to be restricted when Catholic Emancipation came. I remember being so critical of the great man that I evaded the old servant and guide when he extended his hand towards the Liberator's chair, inviting me to sit for a moment in it. The feeling of detached superiority, as one who now knows better, when I met Miss O'Connell and Mr John O'Connell and was invited to afternoon tea, is something I have seen on other young faces since, when they discuss the failures of our generation.

Nevertheless, giving justice where it was due, I also recall being very impressed when an excursion during that holiday brought me to Staigue Fort, to the old road, up and down, following the contours of the mountain; incredibly rough and rocky, the track straggled along the mountainside. I thought of poor old Dan, in his carriage or on horseback, travelling such rough ground when he set out on the people's business. There can have been very little comfort in politics in those times.

---

* The Flight of the Wild Geese is used to describe the departure of the Irish Jacobite army from Ireland to France following the Treaty of Limerick in October 1691. The Wild Geese believed that they had signed a treaty that would safeguard the rights of their people but what actually followed was the Penal Laws, which deprived Catholics of their land and other basic rights of citizenship.

Conscription

RECRUITING CLOCKS had been set up in the public view in Dublin. It was the last British effort to secure voluntary blood donors for the war in France. The Viceroy, Lord French, announced that if 150,000 men did not enlist before 1 October, steps would be taken to conscript three times that number. Recruiting meetings, held all over the country, were constantly interrupted and, at times, the speakers did not get a hearing. By October 1917 the clocks registered fewer than 8,000 recruits.

On our side in Wexford we had D.P. Walsh organizing the Volunteers, while Elizabeth Bloxham organized for Cumann na mBan. A parish committee was set up on orders from the Mansion House* to have everything ready in the event of conscription being imposed.

---

* On 18 April 1918 Laurence O' Neill, the Lord Mayor of Dublin, held a conference at the Mansion House during which the Irish Anti-Conscription Committee was formed in order to formulate plans to resist conscription. A memorandum to local defence committees (against conscription) was formulated and distributed. It is available at http://catalogue.nli.ie/Search/Results?lookfor=local+defence+committees+&type=AllFields&submit=FIND

Blacksmiths made pikes. There were said to be 150,000 men in the Volunteers. The police were very zealous – or very well rewarded – for their effort to make arrests and to pull down the Republican colours everywhere they were raised; the enormous men of the RIC were at great disadvantage in the climbing race to remove our flags, and all their misfortune, as when one of them came down through the roof of a school, were greeted with delirious joy. Prison sentences were savage but at the end of their imprisonment men were met with crowds, bands and torchlight processions, waiting to welcome them home again.

Miss Bloxham left me in charge, with instructions to get a branch of Cumann na mBan organized in every parish in North Wexford. Enniscorthy already had two branches of Veterans with pre-1916 records, both of them fully active. I enjoyed going to places like Killane – where 'Kelly the Boy from Killane'* came from. Evening and night hours were spent bicycling uncounted miles over the little roads where once the 1798 men had marched. With that soil under one's feet, and a job to be done, it was heaven to be young.

My most embarrassing military job was on a historic occasion for the people of Castletown, three miles from Arklow, when Father John O'Keefe had the whole place in a state o' chassis one Sunday morning. A statement had been issued laying out that priests would be conscripted, the same as any other young man in the proscribed age group. 'If they put Johnny O'Keefe in a military uniform it will be on his dead body,' he told us in his sermon. After mass all the men lined up on one side of the churchyard and all, or nearly all, the women on the other side facing them. It was now my turn to get the women on a war footing! I never felt more inadequate. In the years before us then, the men and the women of Castletown got lots to do for Ireland – and did it splendidly. But if they wanted to drill, they got little or none from me.

---

* 'Kelly the Boy from Killane' is a commemorative rebel song to remember John Kelly, a United Irishman, who fought in the 1798 Rebellion in Wexford. Kelly was one of the leaders who captured Wexford town during the rebellion and was subsequently sentenced to death. Along with seven other rebel leaders, he was hanged at Wexford Bridge, then decapitated and his head displayed on a spike in the town.

Memory dwells in particular on friends I met that Sunday: Mrs Margaret Kavanagh of Cronecribbon was a lion-hearted woman with sons and daughters as good as a regiment in any army; Mrs Lee in the post office and Hannah Shaughnessy, an indomitable cyclist dispatch carrier. She was thin as a rake, eager, cycling all over the place with dispatches, intercepted and hurt, but never daunted while she was on the job. I never really knew the names of the men, apart from Charlie Fogarty and the two Paddy Byrnes: one who danced in every Republican concert, his spine so long, his body so thin he could display a good-sized tricolour without it being folded; the other Paddy Byrne, short, thickset and earnest.

We must have got the girls of the countryside into some sort of shape for marching because my diary records that we paraded in the forbidden 'military formation' at the monster meeting against conscription, which was held in Gorey on 16 April 1918. I believe Father Sweetman drafted the resolution:

> That this representative meeting of the people of North Wexford calls upon the Irish leaders now about to assemble in Dublin to inform the British government that the passing into law of any Act claiming the right to impose conscription on Ireland will be accepted by this country as a declaration of war between Great Britain and Ireland, and will be acted upon as such.

Other places declared war too, but we always held that Gorey was first. The British had issued an order that all arms must be surrendered before a date around that time. I am sorry to have to relate that the four-wheeled gig, drawn by a chestnut horse, which deposited our cousin, Sir Thomas Esmonde MP – representing Redmond's party at our Gorey meeting – went on up the street to the police barracks to deliver a miscellaneous collection of elephant guns, as per British orders. We noted its progress as we sat on the platform.

A veritable arms race developed and funny situations arose, including the famous case of the Provost Marshal of Dublin, whose dilemma set all Ireland laughing. He had failed to surrender his arms, which were still in his house. One evening two men called to see him. They told him they were police officers charged with administering the Arms Order, and that they had not seen his name on the list of loyal men who had voluntarily disarmed themselves. This being so they thought it best, in view of his high and respected position in the city, to come to him in plain clothes and after dark, so that the matter could be straightened out without anything being known. If it did get out that he had arms and had not been prosecuted, there would surely be hell to pay. The Provost Marshal was deeply grateful. He brought his visitors to his study and treated them liberally; then he parcelled up his guns for them. At the end of the interview, he produced a 'tin hat', which he had brought from Flanders, and presented it to them as a small token of his gratitude. Then the two IRA men piled the collection into a waiting cab and drove off triumphantly!

The race to collect arms, of any sort, size or description, from those who owned them, continued at a pace. In many cases the guns were given willingly, with a heart and a half, but in other cases private houses were raided. In my opinion, some mistakes made at this time had very bad consequences for Ireland. Padraig Pearse, Eoin MacNeill and Roger Casement are only some of the people who publicly expressed hope that Irish Volunteers and the Ulster Volunteers would not come into conflict with one another. Conflict, even war, between the parties did develop later.

It is impossible for me to guess to what degree unnecessary and unwise raids on private houses contributed to this evil. The number of effective weapons collected was not in proportion to the trouble that was gathering. In saying this I do not intend to make any criticism of the Northern Divisions of the IRA, who were so often compelled to take action because of the plight of men, women and children, who were driven out of their homes in Belfast and other places in organized Orange pogroms, year after year. Men who suffered or lost their lives fighting for justice and human rights on that front, providing some protection when the law offered none, deserve far more credit than has ever been given to them by the nation as a whole. On the other hand, I find it impossible to believe that so many Ulster Protestants would have seemed to side with the pogromists, if they had not been frightened and driven in together by those unfortunate, blunderbuss raids.

Women

THE FIRST PERSON to attend an interview with US President Woodrow Wilson, and to present him with a copy of the Republican proclamation of 1916, was Hanna Sheehy-Skeffington. A report of this interview was given to the Ard Fheis of Sinn Féin in 1917, and was repeated at the Cumann na mBan convention in 1918. Captain Bowen Colthurst, a British soldier, murdered Hanna's husband, the journalist and pacifist Francis Sheehy-Skeffington, in Portobello Barracks in Dublin during Easter Week 1916. His widow, a woman endowed with intelligence, integrity, great fortitude and an unbreakable spirit of independence, carried the Republican message with her personal tragedy around the world. There was no paper wall Hanna could not break through. It is unlikely that there was another person in all Ireland at that time with the contacts she had abroad. Wherever in the world there were suffragettes, Hanna knew them, and she could rely on their help and their experience in politics to penetrate through to the central authority of power. When I was in America on Republican business at a later date, I too was helped by Mrs Skeffington's friends and was in a position to know the great esteem in which she was held outside, as well as inside, Ireland. Hanna made the British government regret the killing of her husband.

She was one of the early members of Cumann na mBan who did not stay with us. Along with Helena Molony, Mary Colum,* Rosamond Jacob† and some others, Hanna held us to be poor feminists – worse in fact, as being servile to the men. This was perhaps true enough during the War of Independence when, although men and women fought shoulder to shoulder for national freedom, it was the men who were doing the dying. But we were not servile in the sense that we kept our own organization intact. Cumann na mBan was part of the defence forces of the Republic. There was very little Republican work, military or civilian, we did not partake in. The same could be said of many other unaligned women, except that they left the care, protection and moving of arms to us. But it should never be forgotten either that the feminist group gave service of no less importance in their own field. These were women who could not be frightened, dominated or bribed.

I divided the men in the Republican movement into two main categories. There were those who worked easily and naturally with women, in full trust and confidence: and then there were the 'mystery men' who only wanted us to do what we were told and ask no questions. But even the IRB depended on Cumann na mBan extensively for their safety, night and day, their communications and sometimes for the holding and transport of their arms. They were only being childish when they held on to unnecessary remnants of mystery. It was not until much later, when splits came and arguments were bitter, that the IRB showed its hand; this helped me to analyse great and minor mysteries of the then recent past. One only has to read Charles Dalton's

---

* Mary Colum (née Maguire) (1884–1957) was a literary critic and author. She wrote for *The Irish Review* before emigrating to the USA in 1914. Her autobiography, *Life and Dreams*, was published in 1947.

† Rosamond Jacob (1888–1960) was an Irish writer, political activist and a lifelong activist for suffragist Republican and socialist causes.

book *With the Dublin Brigade (1917–21)* to understand the loneliness, strains, malnutrition and ugliness that were in the background of the men of the Special Squad – Collins's men, based in pubs not homes; men who were tragically young; the gun men, the hunters of spies, the hunted. They were the IRB and theirs was no woman's world. But why, oh why did Cumann na mBan let down the feminist cause when the war was over? Was it that individually the women were too tired, or too hard up? Was it that the leaders went into important and satisfying work in paid employment, which somehow curbed their social responsibility? Whatever the excuse, I feel sorry that we let the women of Ireland down. God knows they had been steadfast, as we too had been. It never occurred to me to doubt that the Republican government, when we put it in power, would do justice to both sexes equally and, of course, to all of the people.

The work of Cumann na mBan continued at a pace. Parcels of food in their thousands were sent from all over the country to political prisoners in jail. These included the 'German plot'[*] arrestees. Some prisoners were poor, others had no sympathetic relatives; some had everything, others nothing. The aim was to secure an even distribution of parcels to the prisons, and to see that no one was left out. Women attending the 1918 Cumann na mBan convention included Mrs Jenny Wyse Power who, as Jenny O'Toole, had been a member of the Ladies' Land League[†] in the days of Parnell. Her daughter

---

[*] The German plot was a fictitious conspiracy theory, promulgated in 1918 by Dublin Castle. The British alleged that a conspiracy existed between Sinn Féin and Germany to raise armed insurrection in Ireland while Britain was at war with Germany. The 'plot' began when a man called Dowling was landed from a German submarine and arrested by the RIC. Dowling had been recruited by Roger Casement at a prisoner-of-war camp prior to the Rising. Although Sinn Féin knew nothing of Dowling's arrival, the notion of a German plot was widely disseminated by the British. In May 1918 the British government ordered the arrests of a number of Sinn Féin members on the spurious grounds of this false conspiracy. Sixty-nine men and women were arrested in late May 1918.

[†] The Ladies' Land League (January 1881–August 1882) was a female auxiliary of the Irish National Land League. When the male leadership of the Land League, including Charles Stewart Parnell, were imprisoned, the Ladies' Land League took over the running of the organization under the spirted and able leadership of

Nancy Wyse Power took a prominent part in organizing Lá na mBan (Women's Day) * both in Dublin and in the provinces; throughout the country branches took part in the arrangements to oppose conscription. Subsequently a Flag Day was held in Dublin: 'Women won't Blackleg' was the slogan chosen for the flags.

The great influenza epidemic of 1918 took lives on every street and hundreds of people, often whole families, went down at the same time. At Cumann na mBan meetings we wondered what we could do to help. Dr Nolan, the dispensary doctor in Gorey, who had been giving us first-aid classes, told us what was really needed was a better town milk supply. He asked us to organize a milk depot – not as a charity, but because his patients simply could not obtain the extra milk he was ordering for them, to aid their recovery. One thing that lingers in my mind is how Dr Nolan expressed his concern about the extent of the housing shortage, and the living conditions for many families in the town of Gorey. Under normal circumstances, with only one person sick in a house at a time, overcrowding had not been so starkly evident. But during the flu epidemic whole families were sometimes sick together, and the real position – serious overcrowding – was laid bare. We formed a committee and asked for money to establish a milk depot and it rolled in from all sections of society. Farmers rose to the occasion and a depot was found and opened very quickly. Then it went around that we were an 'illegal organization' and 'the gentry' started asking for their money back. Poor Mother got involved in heated correspondence with some of her old friends in the neighbourhood about slights they seemed to put on my integrity. These people were accustomed to being boss and they saw their God-given right to command taken away from them. As a matter of

---

Parnell's sister Anna. In May 1881, when Parnell was released from jail, he turned his attention towards the Home Rule question and the National Land League was replaced by the broader-based Irish National League.

* Lá na mBan (Women's Day) refers to a series of large countrywide meetings organized by women on 9 June 1918 and on the following days, where Irish women gathered to sign a pledge to resist the conscription of Irishmen to the British army during World War I.

fact there was no charity aspect at all about the depot. People paid for their milk, which was ladled out into their jugs at the normal price. We were, as it turned out, able to fire back a good deal of the money. We had, of course, thought ourselves to be acting non-politically when in the first instance we asked for money that was needed, wherever we thought we would get it.

1918 Election

IRISH SUMMER SCHOOLS were crowded and Irish training colleges could not accommodate all the young enthusiasts who applied for admission. It was a crime to hold an Aeriocht – so one was held in every parish in Ireland on a given date. The Gaelic Athletic Association was declared an illegal organization, and hurling was banned; on one Sunday, fifteen hundred hurling matches were played in various parts of the country.* The old spirit of devotion and defiance had come back to Ireland. It was a time of danger, of dread, and of joy in Ireland unconquered.

Never was an election so long drawn out as that in 1918. On 12 October our Sinn Féin Election Manifesto appeared in the form passed by

---

* This became known as 'Gaelic Sunday'. No ban on hurling per se was imposed, but the introduction on 4 July 1918 of a proclamation prohibiting all 'meetings, assemblies, or processions in public places' without written authorization from the police had much the same effect as a ban, especially when the GAA refused to cooperate with the permit requirement. In response to the proclamation, the GAA made plans for 'Gaelic Sunday' on 4 August 1918, when throughout the country matches were openly played without the required permits. An estimated 54,000 GAA members turned out in defiance of the proclamation.

the censor; about half of the type was blacked out. Enough remained, however, to make it clear that we intended to establish the Republic proclaimed in 1916 as a functioning government in Ireland.

Before the campaign got much further, arrests had removed nearly all of our leaders and we found ourselves working under our fourth Director of Elections. Bob Brennan,* the first director, had left very precise instructions as to our duties before and during the campaign. These we observed in scrupulous detail. With patience and devotion we copied every name on the register into three different notebooks for each townland in every constituency. The attitude of voters, after each of the three canvasses, was recorded and sent to the constituency director. Absolutely no effort was spared to win the contest. The responsibility to vindicate the men of Easter Week was on our shoulders. Their pamphlets and writings were in our pockets, or under our pillows when we fell into bed at the end of work-packed evenings. I later heard rumours that that there was corruption in the 1918 election; if there was, I did not, and do not know of it. Our hard work counted.

Between the local children and our newly organized band, the election was a noisy one. Little girls marched in their own groups, or with the boys, cheering, chanting rhymes, calling for Sinn Féin leaflets to distribute. My cousin Ellice Pilkington, who was canvassing for her brother, Sir Thomas Esmonde MP and the Irish Parliamentary Party, suffered from this exuberance – driving in a phaeton drawn by a fat pony, which could not outpace the children. Ellice was not allowed to forget the guns that her brother handed over to the police several months earlier. 'Ould Esmonde is a hypocrite,' the children marching behind her chanted until, time after time, I went to my poor cousin's rescue. But nobody did Ellice any harm, and she held on her way with determination.

---

* Bob (Robert) Brennan (1881–1964) led the Wexford Brigade of the Volunteers in 1916 and was subsequently sentenced to death for his part in the Rising, later commuted. He was released in 1917 but was back in prison within months, this time in Cork Jail. He became Director of Elections for Sinn Féin in 1918. Robert Brennan also wrote many works of fiction, and his memoir of the revolutionary period, *Allegiance*, was published in 1950.

Father Michael Flanagan's* election meeting in Gorey stands out in my memory.

He reached us after dark on a wet winter night. A torchlight procession was waiting for him at the entrance to Gorey, with the Riverchapel and Camolin bands. All the cars and supporters we could muster walked behind him in the parade up the wide street of the town. Of all the orators I cheered in my time, there was none to match the range and the eloquence of Father Michael. There was no bombast; he could speak with the same reasoned conviction to men and women standing in a muddy field under the rain as he could in the hall of a great university. He based what he had to say on human rights and justice, and spoke with humour, directness, vehemence, metaphor, philosophy, Irishness. He was a man of the people.

Everyone knew that Father Michael had no permission from his bishop to lead the Sinn Féin election campaign, or from our bishop to speak in the Diocese of Ferns. On him, the clerical collar was an emblem of revolt. In his speeches during the campaign Father O'Flanagan was, as always, well aware of the presence of note-takers, police and spies. He mocked them from his podium, loving to have the audience on his side, pointedly asking the spies if they were noting a particular point, and, if so, to try and get it right. After the meeting he came to the Ram's Arms Hotel, at the top of the town, for some refreshment. I remember James Dillon,† then a schoolboy at Mount St Benedict, with us in the crowded room. James battled at all times

---

* Father Michael O'Flanagan (1876–1942) was Catholic priest, political activist, Irish-language teacher, scholar and historian. He was a prominent member of the Gaelic League and travelled to the USA as an envoy for the organization from 1910–12. He was an active participant in the reorganization of Sinn Féin after 1916 and was elected joint vice-president from 1917 to 1923 (and again from 1930 to 1931). During the 1918 election campaign Father O'Flanagan became the face of the Sinn Féin leadership in Ireland and was their primary election rally speaker during the campaign. Máire Comerford attended one such gathering in Wexford in 1918.

† James Dillon (1902–1986) was the son of the last leader of the Irish Parliamentary Party, John Dillon (1851–1927), and was educated at Mount St Benedict, in Gorey. James Dillon had a long political career as a Fine Gael politician: as a TD (1932–69), as Minister for Agriculture (1948–51) and as Leader of the Opposition and Leader of Fine Gael (1959–65).

with loyalty and devotion on the side of his father, John Dillon, leader of the Irish Parliamentary Party. This was the only time in my memory when young James was a silent spectator on any political occasion!

Father Sweetman had presided at the meeting. Outside in the rain people were dispersing, the bands playing them off the street. Suddenly someone rushed into the hotel to call Father Sweetman. 'Come quick, Father. The police are across the street to stop the band.' Out went His Reverence, the enormous blackthorn, which he always carried, in his hand. 'The Matron', Aileen K'Eogh, marched at one shoulder; at his other shoulder was a man we called 'Big Scanlon', who was rolling up his sleeves. 'I'm the man for you now Father,' he shouted, 'any little thing I can do for you now, Father.'

Outside rain was falling steadily. Two rows of police were drawn up across the street. In front of them stood the district inspector, Captain Lea Wilson, swaying on his feet and clearly drunk. Father Sweetman demanded to know what was happening. Lea Wilson, saluting, warbling, saluting again: 'We are protecting you, Father. We are keeping the peace.' Father Sweetman replied: 'If you are concerned with keeping the peace then take your men away,' Wilson, saluting again, looking sheepish and unsteady, gave the necessary orders and the cordon withdrew. His men looked depressed. I felt quite sorry for them having to obey an officer in such a condition!

For election day we were supplied with the seal bearing the letters 'I.R.' (Irish Republic) for every polling booth, and when the poll closed on 14 December we had our instructions to secure and seal every ballot box. This was in addition to the official sealing by the presiding officer. Orders were that no box was to be left out of the sight of the sentries appointed by Sinn Féin between the vote and the count. On the night of the poll I saw sleepy policemen and sleepy Republicans on hard benches, facing one another in Riverchapel Schoolhouse, the local boxes in between the two rows. Next day I rode with the bicycle escort to Gorey station to watch the police every second of the journey. I was there to witness our boxes handed into the train, where another Sinn Féin escort took over.

Our work well done, I went to Dublin for the results. For what seemed like endless wet winter days and nights – a strange and wonderful, and unusual Christmas season – I stood sometimes with hundreds, sometimes with thousands of people in the mud on Harcourt Street, outside Sinn Féin headquarters. The results were not declared until 28 December, two weeks after the casting of votes. It was agony to be idle for so long. Nationally Sinn Féin won 73 of the 105 seats, with the Irish Parliamentary Party only winning six seats and its leader, John Dillon, losing his seat to Éamon de Valera* in East Mayo.

Sinn Féin had aimed at contesting every seat where any opposition to the immediate ratification of the Republic was offered. Their intention was thwarted in Ulster, where candidates were chosen for the mainly Catholic constituencies in an election pact between Sinn Féin and the Irish Parliamentary Party. This was an attempt to avoid a split in the nationalist vote, or any three-cornered contests whereby a Unionist politician could be elected in constituencies with a Catholic majority. It would appear that Sinn Féin entered this electoral pact with the then much-maligned Irish Parliamentary Party, believing that all Protestants should be considered as enemies.

The blunder that Sinn Féin made when it shirked the electoral contest against the total forces of Orange and Green conservatism was devastating at the time, and into the future. The damage done by the 1918 electoral deal between Sinn Féin and the Irish Parliamentary Party in Ulster is still evident.

---

* Éamon de Valera (1882–1975) was born in New York and was returned to Ireland as a small child and reared by relatives in County Limerick. During the 1916 Rising he was commander of the 3rd Battalion of the Irish Volunteers at Boland's Mills in Dublin. Following his arrest, de Valera was sentenced to death but for a variety of reasons including his birth in America, his sentence was commuted to penal servitude for life. De Valera became president of Sinn Féin in 1917. In the same year he won a by-election in East Clare, and in the 1918 election he was once again returned for that seat, and for a second seat in East Mayo.

The First Dáil

NO DAY that ever dawned in Ireland had been waited for, worked for, suffered for like the Tuesday in January 1919 when the First Dáil Éireann met. In the queue that curled from the entrance to Dublin's Mansion House back to Kildare Street, men and women spoke softly of the dead, from the first coming of the English to Ireland, and who had given their lives to make our nation free. 'If Robert Emmet could be here with us,' I heard someone say; and the reply, 'Ah, he is not far away.' 'Did you ever think that you and I would live to see this day?' Never was the past so near, or the present so brave, or the future so full of hope.

A bazaar or some similar function in aid of British war charities had bundled up the last of its Union Jacks and, on the way out, more or less passed us on the steps as we waited to go in. We filed into the Round Room and pressed around until every inch of standing room was filled. I did not have a great view of Dáil Éireann, except for the heads of Cathal Brugha,[*] Count Plunkett[†] and Father O'Flanagan, and whoever else may have been on the platform, if they had occasion to stand. It was enough to be under the same roof and to be present with the elected representatives of the people, when the establishment of the Irish Republic was ratified and confirmed as the law of the land. The Ceann Comhairle asked us to pledge ourselves to finish the work that our generation had, by then, brought further than ever before. Cathal Brugha began by telling us that we were there to do the most important work that had been done in Ireland since the foreigners landed. He called on the most faithful priest, Father Michael O'Flanagan, to ask the blessing of the Holy Spirit on their work. We saw Father Michael's head and shoulders as he came forward, and our prayer went up with his. When the well-known picture of the First Dáil was taken from the balcony, the photographer's magnesium flare startled some of us country people; we took it for an explosion, just for a minute.

The name of every elected member for an Irish constituency was included in the roll call. All those elected were invited to attend. One

---

[*] Cathal Brugha (1874–1922) was an Irish revolutionary leader and politician, and member of the Gaelic League. In 1913 he was made a lieutenant in the Irish Volunteers and was also actively involved in the IRB (an organization he later saw as undermining the authority of Dáil Éireann). In 1914 Brugha led a group of Volunteers to the village of Howth in County Dublin to collect the smuggled arms for the use of the Irish Volunteers. Brugha fought in the 1916 Rising as second-in-command to Éamonn Ceannt at the South Dublin Union. Following the release of prisoners in 1917 Brugha, as a member of the Sinn Féin executive, took part in consolidating and expanding the organization. He also worked to bring the Volunteers and the Irish Citizen Army under the umbrella of the IRA, becoming Chief of Staff in 1917. In 1918 he was elected as a Sinn Féin MP for County Waterford and went on to play a prominent role in the first Dáil in 1919.

[†] Count Plunkett (1851–1948) was made a papal knight in 1884 by Pope Leo XIII and was a poet, journalist and politician. He was the Parnellite candidate for North Tyrone and the lone nationalist candidate for the Dublin electoral constituency in 1895. He was also head of a large family, many of whom were actively involved in revolutionary activities. Count Plunkett joined the IRB in 1916 at the behest of his son, Joseph Plunkett, who sent his father to seek both aid from Germany and a papal blessing for the Easter Rising in 1916. The count won the Roscommon North by-election in 1917 and presided at the first Dáil Éireann in January 1919. He was made foreign affairs minister by Cathal Brugha and subsequently served as Minister for Fine Arts (1921–2).

hundred and five names were called. No Unionists responded, nor any of the Irish Party's members. There was some laughter when the name of Sir Edward Carson was heard in its turn. Twenty-eight were present out of the seventy-three Republicans elected. Thirty-six were in jail. Some were on duty abroad. For obvious reasons a few key men were kept outside the Mansion House. Among those in jail were Arthur Griffith,* Éamon de Valera, Terence MacSwiney, Austin Stack,† Ernest Blythe‡ and Countess Markievicz. Deputies rose while the Declaration of Independence was read, followed by the message to the free nations of the world, and the Democratic Programme. Éamon de Valera, Count Plunkett and Arthur Griffith were appointed to represent Ireland at the Peace Conference in Paris;§ it was anticipated that the two internees would be released. We were prepared to believe a

---

* Arthur Griffith (1871–1922) was a nationalist, journalist and editor and principal founder of Sinn Féin. Griffith edited a number of political newspapers and journals, all with a strong nationalist slant. In 1919, following the decisive 1918 Sinn Féin electoral victory, Griffith became vice-president of the First Dáil Éireann.

† Austin Stack (1879–1929) was a Kerry Republican and politician who joined the IRB in 1908. He led the Kerry Brigade of the Volunteers, and prepared for the (failed) arms landing by Roger Casement in 1916. In 1917 Stack became an executive member of the Volunteers and was appointed joint Secretary of Sinn Féin the following year. While imprisoned in Belfast, he was elected for the Kerry West constituency in 1918.

‡ Ernest Blythe (1889–1975) was born and reared near Lisburn, Co. Down, in a Protestant household. When he moved to Dublin he became a member of the IRB; what was unknown at the time was that Blythe was also a member of Orange Order, which he left in 1912. He went on to organize the Volunteers in County Clare. Blythe, a generally contentious figure, was strongly pro-Treaty in 1922. He was appointed as finance minister in W.T. Cosgrave's Free State government of 1923 and is un-fondly remembered for his decision to cut a shilling from the old-age pension. He published three volumes of autobiography, all in Irish: *Trasna na Bóinne* (1957), *Slán le hUltaibh* (1969) and *Gaeil á Múscailt* (1973).

§ The Paris Peace Conference (1919–20) was the international gathering of statesmen to inaugurate a settlement in the aftermath of World War I. In February 1919 a letter was sent by the Irish Government of the First Dáil to the French premier, Georges Clemenceau, to request international recognition from the Peace Conference for the independence of Ireland – a strategy set out previously in the Sinn Féin 1918 election manifesto. As the wartime rhetoric centred on the rights of small nations, it was hoped that Ireland's case for independence would be heard at the conference. However, US president Woodrow Wilson accepted the British position, which argued that the affairs of Ireland were an internal British problem.

lot against the British government but I doubt whether it occurred to many that, in the spirit of the freedom of small nations, our delegates would be refused a hearing when the Peace Conference met in Versailles – let alone be left in prison, uncharged with any crime. The Dáil met at 3.30 pm; it rose at 5.30 pm, the day's work nobly done.

The Dáil's first social events took place that evening: a reception in the Oak Room and dinner in the Supper Room of the Mansion House. I am not sure now that Aileen K'Eogh and I did not gatecrash both. Anyhow, we were both present. I went home very thoughtfully. The 1916 proclamation required the establishment of a permanent national government, representative of the whole people of Ireland, and elected by the suffrage of all her men and women; that government had now been set up by twenty-eight men. It was not the fault of the twenty-eight that they stood alone, but of the English who held their comrades. Many – the more slave-minded, the more experienced and the more cautious – may have felt that we should wait to be given our freedom by the representatives of the nations, who were then assembling in the Hall of Mirrors for the Peace Conference. In their simplicity they imagined, as I did too, that a delegation of newly elected Irish MPs would be welcomed in Versailles, to present evidence that 'government by consent of the governed' was preparing to be established in Ireland. It was impossible for youth, my age group then, to see how our request could be refused in the atmosphere of the time, when we believed that tyranny had been roundly defeated by great and generous powers like the USA, fighting for small nations.

The experienced older men told us we were fools. Immediately after the first meeting of the Dáil, Harry Boland* and Michael Collins went to England to make arrangements for the escape of Éamon de Valera from Lincoln Jail. They must not have felt so confident as we did that the British government would release him.

The Dáil was proscribed by the British in September, and it met secretly after that. In January and June the municipal and local government elections were held. These confirmed the Irish people's will to govern themselves, in an election victory even more decisive than that of 1918. As we grew accustomed to having our own Dáil Éireann it became plain that we must change from destructive to constructive strategy. We could no longer pull down without creating. We had a government and it must serve the people. All Ireland was crying out for the performance of many promises. The minute books of the Dáil cabinet show that the task was tackled from the beginning. They set up committees to deal with consular services, a loan bank, Arbor Day, fisheries, courts, a national civil service, a commission into the Resources of Ireland, labour, local government, trade and commerce, agriculture, finance, foreign affairs and milk supplies in Dublin. All these were in planning, and some in operation, before the end of 1919. I believe we started with an all-Ireland Arbor Day in November.

Near the end of January Seán Etchingham, now a TD, was released in very bad health from prison, and came home. We met Seán in our thousands at Gorey railway station. He was barely able to stand, but he didn't have to try. Seán was taken from the train and put lying in the car. Then we all started off, marching the four miles to Courtown, while the Riverchapel band played:

---

* Harry Boland (1887–1922) was Leader of the IRB from 1919–20. Boland fought at the GPO during the Easter Rising of 1916 and was afterwards interned in Dartmoor and Lewes jails. He was elected for South Roscommon in the 1918 general election. Shortly afterwards Boland left for the US as a special envoy to propagate the Irish Republican case and to raise funds. From mid-1919 to 1922 Boland spent most of his time working with Éamon de Valera in the US. Harry Boland is associated with the love triangle involving himself, Michael Collins and Kitty Kiernan. Both men fell for Kitty and both proposed marriage, with Collins finally winning out.

Wrap the green flag around me, boys
To die t' were far more sweet
With Erin's noble emblem, boys,
To be my winding sheet.

I thought it most inappropriate to play that for a man who we wanted above all to keep alive; but when I suggested that he should hurry on to his house to be looked after following his long journey, his familiar voice came from the depths of the car. 'Leave them alone. I am enjoying every minute of this.' 'Wrap the Green Flag' was still coming on the breeze from Courtown five or six hours later.

Éamon de Valera made his escape, and we lit bonfires for him. No one knew where he might be – whether safely out of England or not, or perhaps even on the sea. Regardless, we helped to make sure he would not lay eyes on Ireland in the dark night without seeing the proof that he was welcome home. From Croghan Kinsella I helped to pick out the bonfires lit by our neighbours in Carlow, here and there through the night. These fires were signs of comradeship between the counties. From then on there was more and more activity by night – but fire ceased to be an emblem of joy. Instead, it became the weapon, one of many, of English terror.

Our thoughts at that time were never far from the prisoners. In January 1919 – while we were sure that the cause must almost be won and when Tipperary fired the first shot in the new revolt at Soloheadbeg – men lay in irons in Cork, Derry, Belfast and Mountjoy prisons.* Meanwhile, Cathal Brugha, acting First President, had to find the best men he could for the new ministries. Others were to follow the three TDs – Éamon de Valera, Seán McGarry and Seán Mulvoy – on the assisted escape routes. On 16 March Robert

---

* The First Dáil convened on 21 January 1919. On the same day members of 3rd Tipperary Brigade ambushed a party of RIC officers escorting a consignment of gelignite at Soloheadbeg in County Tipperary. Two members of the RIC were killed during the ambush, and weapons and explosives were seized by the Volunteers. This event is often cited as the first engagement in the War of Independence.

Barton* sawed through a bar in his cell window and climbed the wall of Mountjoy on a ladder provided from outside. Less than a fortnight later twenty Mountjoy prisoners, led by P.J. Fleming, left by the same route in broad daylight. They included two members of Dáil Éireann – Piaras Béaslaí and J.J. Walsh. Austin Stack and Piaras McCann may been the only TDs prevented by imprisonment from attending the April session of Dáil Éireann. McCann left Gloucester Jail in his coffin after he died there on 6 March; Stack and a hundred others in Belfast Jail were locked in their cells for five months, from February to June. But Austin Stack was needed for the Ministry of Home Affairs; he was actually nominated for that office in June 1919 by Arthur Griffith, Deputy President (de Valera, who became President following his escape from jail, appointed Griffith to deputize, while he was in the USA); this was four months before Stack's escape over the wall of Strangeways Jail, after his transfer to Manchester from Belfast in October. These rescues were the first official service performed by the Volunteers for the elected constitutional government.

My first participation in the annual tribute to Theobald Wolfe Tone, and his principles, at the grave in Bodenstown was in that June of glorious memory. It was the first, and last, year that we managed to parade there as people in proud possession of a legitimate parliament of the thirty-two counties, constituting the Irish Republic. We had come from Wexford in a trainload to meet other thousands, similarly carried, from the four provinces of Ireland. It became a unique Bodenstown Day for my group of Cumann na mBan when Countess Markievicz, miraculously recognizing me, waved us into a joining of picnics on a grass margin by the road.

---

* Robert Barton (1881–1975) was a nationalist politician, farmer and brother to the Barton sisters, Dulcibella and Daisy. At the outbreak of World War I, Robert Barton became an officer in Royal Dublin Fusiliers and was stationed in Dublin during the 1916 Rising. Following what he considered unnecessary force and suppression of the Rising, Barton resigned his British army commission and joined the Republican movement. He was elected as a Sinn Féin candidate for West Wicklow in the 1918 election, and later, in 1921, was re-elected for Kildare-Wicklow, when he was also appointed as Minister of Agriculture in the Second Dáil. Barton was first arrested for sedition in 1919, but within months had escaped from Mountjoy Prison. He was later a member of the delegation who travelled to London to negotiate the Treaty in late 1921.

Living on the Green

MRS ALICE STOPFORD GREEN, with the painter Jack Yeats, Mrs Yeats and Professor and Mrs Augustine Henry, came to stay, as paying guests, in our house in Courtown at the end of June 1919. Here were my first acquaintances among people who knew the wonderful world of the Irish renaissance, which I had been reading about. Mrs Green was a renowned historian and friend to Roger Casement, standing firmly by him during his lonely imprisonment and trial for treason. In her work she had challenged the prevailing conception of Irish history and Irish-English relations in a number of books and articles, then became entangled in fierce controversy, in defence of her writing. She was the author of meticulously researched history books including *The Making of Ireland and Its Undoing 1200–1600* (1908) and *Irish Nationality* (1911). Mrs Green had been married to the distinguished English historian John Richard Green (1837–1883), author of the *Short History of the English People* (1874) with its Epilogue that she, in her widowhood, had compiled.

Never were visitors more welcome in our home. Nor, I imagine, did a woman so learned and experienced as Mrs Green ever respond with more generous understanding and instant sympathy to the timid advances of as ignorant a young one as I was then! I was further encouraged when I found her ready to discuss and expand on questions of Irish history, or to look at the historical maps I had attempted to make. Mrs Green was eager to meet anyone who wanted to talk about rebel Ireland, past or present.

During the few years of our acquaintance, she trusted herself readily to my care on any excursions proposed to her. On holiday in Wexford in 1919 there were uneventful, fine summer days with local history discussed from the pony trap. But I cannot forget the evening when an offshore wind freshened after I took Mrs Green to sea in our rowboat. I was hard set to get us home again. I never found out whether she knew the trouble I was in, rowing with all my strength and barely able to hold my landmarks, while we viewed the old moat at Ardamine and talked of the early invasions of Ireland. Mrs Green continued to speak, and I tried very hard to listen; but at the same time my eye was on a certain tree in its relation to Croghan Mountain in the background, while my muscles (not inconsiderable at the time) strained at the oars during a very tough pull home. When the tide turned I stole into the harbour without having been noticed by James Redmond. He was our gardener and also coxswain of the lifeboat and would not have spared his criticism, either of my seamanship or my sense of responsibility, had his wide-ranging eye caught sight of the small rowboat in distress.

At the end of the holiday Mrs Green invited me to be her secretary. She explained that she needed somebody who would attend Professor MacNeill's history lectures in University College Dublin, make notes for her, conduct research for her writing in the libraries and live in her Dublin house at 90 St Stephen's Green. Mrs Green was then about seventy. She was a slightly built, white-haired woman; when her face was at rest it had a somewhat disdainful expression. She was always most handsomely dressed, with long, full skirts made of beautiful silk sweeping the ground in her own style, which had no regard whatever for the fashion of the moment. All her emotions showed. Most often she was generous, sympathetic, encouraging and very painstaking. But she also struggled valiantly against moods of deepest gloom, when she was hard to live with.

On the first day of my new employment Mrs Green brought me on an afternoon tour of the places she would soon send me to check material, or to work under her direction on details of historical research. She fired my imagination with descriptions of the vast materials of Irish history, in print or in manuscript, charted or uncharted, to be found in the Dublin collections.

We started with the National Library where we met Dr R.I. Best.[*] I stood by enraptured, there and later during the course of our tour to the Royal Irish Academy, the Library of Trinity College, Marsh's Library and the School of Irish Learning in York Street, where Colm Ó Murchada,[†] a scholar who later turned jailer, was at work. In each place we visited, the custodians of such vast erudition greeted my new employer warmly and with respect.

Dr Best of the National Library had in those days a most beautiful red-brown beard, as good as any Viking. Yet in terms of the world outside the library, where the War of Independence was hotting up, he was a timid and cautious man – although steadfast in duty. At the end of our visit, as he stood with us on the steps outside, Mrs Green offered my services to collect all the items of political propaganda and sedition I could find, and bring them to the National Library for its records. It was clear that Dr Best wanted the stuff, but he didn't want to be caught with it, or to put the library itself in any danger. Then he hit on the solution. Dr Best indicated to the letterbox in the outside wall of the Director's Office. Anything I could put in there,

---

[*] Richard Irvine (R.I.) Best (1872–1959) was a prolific writer on Celtic philology and literature and a librarian. Best began his career in the National Library of Ireland in 1904, and remained there until his retirement in 1940.

[†] Colm Ó Murchadha (1889–1939) was an Irish-language scholar and enthusiast and an Irish Volunteer. In 1916 he fought in the Four Courts and was afterwards imprisoned in Wales. Ó Murchadha took the pro-Treaty side in 1922. From July to September 1922 he served as a commandant in the new national army, while at the same time he was governor of Mountjoy Prison.

without name or address, would be very gratefully received for inclusion in the National Collection.

Not long afterwards Mrs Green and Desmond Fitzgerald,[*] TD and Director of Publicity for Dáil Éireann, arranged between them that two copies of each issue of *The Irish Bulletin*[†] would be posted into the letterbox at 90 St Stephen's Green; one of these I was then to drop into Dr Best's outside letterbox. Whether Dr Best knew that he had some very good patriots on the library staff, who were fully competent to collect the records of the time, I cannot say. In any event he deserves credit for putting duty to the Library before his own fears. The National Library has a splendid collection of seditious material of this kind, and a good deal of it may well have arrived through this very letterbox.

Dr Best belonged to Mrs Green's close circle of friends but that did not prevent her, in his absence, from delighting in a tale about him. This story was related with vivacity by Mrs Augustine Henry – small, light-footed, always full of fun – yet as scholarly, so it seemed to me, as her husband, a distinguished professor of forestry. Mrs Henry often told of how she ventured out for food during the battle of Mount Street Bridge in 1916. She was crossing, or attempting to cross the bridge when Dr Best dashed out in front of her; grasping her elbows with both his hands he exhorted her to 'Jump! Jump! Jump! Or they'll shoot us in the legs.' She used to illustrate this in jumping action saying, 'We jumped and jumped, and jumped, but nothing happened.'

---

[*] Desmond (born Thomas Joseph) Fitzgerald (1888–1947) was born in London to Irish parents. As a young man he wrote poetry and moved in literary circles. Fitzgerald joined the Irish Volunteers in 1914 and during the 1916 Rising he was in charge of rations. He was elected to the first Dáil Éireann and became Director of Publicity (1919–21). He took the pro-Treaty position in 1922 and subsequently joined Cumann na nGaedheal, later Fine Gael. He served in various government ministries, including Defence and External Affairs, until he became a senator in 1938, where he served until 1943.

[†] *The Irish Bulletin*, an information sheet published by Dáil Éireann from 1919 to 1921, was distributed to opinion-makers, journalists and other people of influence, to help publicize the brutal methods employed by Crown forces in Ireland.

In the Royal Irish Academy we came across Father Patrick Dineen MA,[*] best known as the author of the *Irish Dictionary*, published in 1904. He was at a crowded desk in the sunny window at the front of the building; a dilapidated and bent figure, grey-haired, and not striking at all until you saw his face and heard his voice. Mrs Green spoke to him with great deference. I was witness, for the first time, to her persistent regret and frustration in the presence of scholars of ancient, middle and modern Irish, whose literary sources were essential to her work and often quoted in her writing, but out of her reach at their source.

Many and many a girl in Cumann na mBan and outside it envied me such an interesting job. It had the incredible advantage of being based near the heart of the revolution. The College of Surgeons, where I had seen the tricolour aloft for the first time in 1916, was within sight of the window that was ours at the time. Soon I began to meet and recognize men and women attached to the Dáil or its army. Mrs Green seemed to be as interested in everything concerning the Republic as I was. History and the politics of the hour took turns on her desk. If she felt some doubt, not sharing my certainty that we were about to witness the end of the 750 years of occupation and finally get the English out, she did not reveal it to me until the great wave of idealism, which President Wilson set flowing into Europe, had ebbed. It is possible that, in the first six months of our acquaintance, Mrs Green also hoped that the history of Ireland would change character in our time, and that the long story of tragedy and defeat was over. In those days Ireland had no tears left in her eyes; they were wide open and they blazed.

Mrs Green liked men best. I do not know to what extent she was a suffragette, or a sympathizer with that cause. She had been President of London Cumann na mBan, and certainly helped to collect money for the Howth gun-running of 1914. When she came to Dublin Mrs Green did not transfer her membership; but sometimes she sent me

---

[*] Patrick Stephen Dineen (1860–1934) was an Irish lexicographer and historian, and a leading figure in the Gaelic Revival.

with a generous donation for the Republican Prisoners' Dependents' Fund. Socially and politically she had become famous in the role of hostess to the intellectuals. The people who gathered at her parties in St Stephen's Green 'knew the ropes'. They had many contacts at very different levels of society and in No. 90 they collected and exchanged knowledge. Her guests were all fifteen to fifty years older than I was. To them I was a sign of the times, and they were very interested in the times. They wanted the news just as much as I did. For the first time in my life important people took me seriously.

I found Mrs Green's handsome house uncomfortable, cold and austere. It was extraordinary to me to be put working in the small room beside the hall door, where there was neither blind nor curtain. Nowhere in the house was there a really comfy chair where a person could snuggle for a read. Mrs Green's study, on the first floor return, was lined on all its walls to the ceiling with books, and the bookshelves were edged at floor level with files of manuscripts and notes. Her table in the centre of the room was flanked with a chair. She had half a day's writing done by breakfast time, when I first appeared, and the whole day's writing ended at lunch. Her output was small and most carefully re-written over and over again, until each sentence was perfect and in the exact sequence she wanted. One good thing about my office was that the noises of the city came in and I could see every distracting stir on St Stephen's Green. With each sound of a bomb bursting, a shooting, or the shrill cry of barefooted children running past with a new 'stop press', I grabbed my ever-ready bicycle and rode out to investigate. For this my employer never reproved me. Mrs Green wanted to know the news just as much as I did; I would have failed her by not going.

Mrs Green's reception rooms occupied the whole first floor of the house; the front windows looked over St Stephen's Green, those behind over the Ardilaun Gardens, which subsequently were given to the National University. Mrs Green's guests were expected to keep awake and she made sure that they would do so. Most of the chairs were straight and no one was allowed to linger too long on the sofa.

Moving around herself, she kept them all alert and sharing in the good talk. There were two kinds of party, broadly speaking. Sometimes we were on ancient history and our host – more disciple than student – used all her social talent to draw out information from the professors – MacNeill, Osborn Bergin[*] and, on one memorable occasion, Robin Flower.[†] At that time Mrs Green was writing *The History of the Irish State to 1014* and we were deeply concentrated on the life and times of St Patrick. She had to depend on the leaned professors and on English translations of ancient Irish manuscripts – mainly the Annals of Ulster.[‡]

Her other kind of party was political, and here the tide flowed in the other direction. Mrs Green was the keenest, best-informed authority on English history and politics in Dublin at that time, outside the Castle. The great experience accumulated over fifty years from her London home by the Thames at Westminster, was now freely at the service of her own people. Mrs Green's political and professional friends, who attended her dinners and parties in the drawing room, included George Russell (Æ), Professor MacNeill TD, Mr and Mrs R.I. Best, James Douglas, Erskine and Molly Childers, James Stephens, P.S. O'Hegarty, Professor Augustine Henry and Mrs Henry. Members of Horace Plunkett's co-operative movement, most notably R.A. Anderson and Dr Henry Kennedy, were often guests of Mrs Green; I was witness to their distress in the following years when I brought first-hand accounts of Black and Tan destruction involving

---

[*] Osborn Bergin (1873–1950) was an Irish-language scholar who specialized in early Irish literature and was also a member of the Gaelic League. He is best known for his discovery of Bergin's Law – a grammatical law in Old Irish. In 1897 Bergin was appointed as a lecturer of Celtic studies at University College Cork.

[†] Robin Flower (1881–1946) was an English poet and scholar and a translator from the Irish language. He is perhaps best remembered as the translator of Tomás Ó Criomthain's classic memoir *The Islandman* (1934).

[‡] The Annals of Ulster are a historical account of Ireland from the first to the sixteenth century, compiled in the fifteenth century by Colm Maguire from Fermanagh, who was an ecclesiastical scholar and Dean of Clogher. After Maguire's death in 1498, Roderick O'Cassidy, Archdeacon of Clogher, continued the annals. Written in Irish and Latin, they are considered an authentic account of early Irish history.

their specialized interest – creameries and co-operatives. Shame on me that the parties held at No. 90 at least once a week have not left me with more memories of the literary and learned guests who attended them. Many a time I sat demurely at a dinner party when I was tingling with the desire to be away on my bicycle, to see how the war was proceeding in the city.

Those whom Mrs Green met individually in her study, morning or afternoon, included Michael Collins, Arthur Griffith, Desmond Fitzgerald, Frank Gallagher and Robert Brennan. She also held small lunch parties. I remember in particular Professor and Mrs Stockley from Cork and Mayor and Mrs O'Callaghan from Limerick, Lord and Lady ffrench, the Hon. Gordon Campbell (Lord Glenavy), and Mr Llewelyn Davies, who discussed his difficult position as a high civil servant in the London GPO; his wife, Moya,[*] had come to live in Dublin and was known to be a friend of Michael Collins'.

The contacts that Mrs Green most wanted to make when I first knew her were with the young people of the Irish revolution. For her, this was living history, evolving and carrying her forward with it towards 'The natural union of the Irish Nation – the union of all her children that are born under the breath of the skies, fed by the fat of her fields, nourished by the civilization of her dead.' (*Irish Nationality*, 1911)

This was grand! It had been grand in the moment when Mrs Green first set it down. It would have required infinitely more wisdom and foreknowledge than I possessed to perceive that a gaping difference of opinion, involving national principles, would arise in the interpretation, or rather the simultaneous application of benevolent

---

[*] Moya Llewelyn Davies formerly Mary Elizabeth O'Connor (1881–1943), was an Irish Republican activist. She married Compton Llewelyn Davies, a solicitor and friend of future Prime Minister David Lloyd George. They set up home in England but Moya took their two children to live in Ireland following the 1916 Rising, when she brought Furry Park, a decrepit mansion with land in Killester in Dublin. She was a friend of Michael Collins and Furry Park became one of his safe houses during the War of Independence. Following a raid by the Black and Tans, Moya was arrested at her home and imprisoned in 1920. In later life Moya Llewelyn Davies maintained that she and Michael Collins had been lovers, but this claim has never been definitively proved.

intentions and revolutionary ideals. I mistook Mrs Green, and most of her friends, for Irish Republicans, giving their allegiance to Dáil Éireann. It never dawned on me that there could possibly be two opinions regarding the absolute right of our new government to uphold the supremacy of the Irish people in Ireland. I had no eyes then, to see the wheels within wheels.

Dáil Éireann had vindicated the Republic of Pearse and Connolly but the party that created it, Sinn Féin, had been re-formed on a compromise between the old Sinn Féin and the new Republic.* These things were undoubtedly under discussion at after-dinner conferences in 90 St Stephen's Green – but by then I would be bicycle-borne, away into the night, to see what one person could do for the Irish Republic in three or four hours of glorious freedom.

---

* The original Sinn Féin Party was founded by Arthur Griffith in November 1905. Griffith espoused dual monarchy as a solution for Ireland, whereby Ireland would operate as a separate kingdom alongside Britain, sharing the monarch, but each with their own government. Griffith also argued for a policy of Irish abstentionism from the British parliament, and the establishment of an Irish parliament in Dublin. As support for Sinn Féin grew, many diverse people joined the party, including members of the IRB. The old Sinn Féin began to merge with the new and the Republican element grew in the leadership, and in the rank and file. This divergence in ideology between new members, led by Éamon de Valera, who wanted an independent Irish Republic, and those who followed Griffith, almost led to a split at the Sinn Féin Ard Fheis in 1917. Despite this tension the party won the overwhelming support of the Irish people in the 1918 election and Sinn Féin held together, albeit with the Republicans in the ascent.

My Half-Mile Radius

THE HALF-MILE RADIUS from St Stephen's Green, where I lived from 1919 to 1921, was a hive of Republican activity. Out of our five suppressed and illegal organizations – in the British government view – three, at least, had headquarters in the area. Dáil Éireann and Sinn Féin were at nos 76 and 6 Harcourt Street, around the corner from Mrs Green's, until the British closed both houses and nailed up the doors. Cumann na mBan was based in 26–27 Dawson Street. Opposite to that, a little up the street from the Mansion House, Eileen McGrane, a member of our executive, was sheltering one of Michael Collins's offices at No. 21. Mr F.T.F. Dumount, the United States Consul, flew his flag from the Shelbourne Hotel. As Mrs Green's secretary I was soon on visiting terms with him and his wife. I brought many messages there; we liked and trusted the Dumonts.

Parallel with Harcourt Street to the west was Wexford Street. It was called 'the Dardanelles' because of the volume of ambushes that took place in the narrow street. A saga could, and should, be written about Mrs Phelan's at No. 14. West again, my old friend, Seán Etchingham, then the Minister for Fisheries, was based at Lawlor's in Heytesbury Street and went by the name 'Mr Quinn'. Sometimes Seán gave me interesting news; he told me that money from the Dáil loan had been lent to the Russians, and that we held some of their jewellery as security! Almost a stone's throw from Mr Quinn, at the home of Michael Malone – killed in the battle of Mount Street Bridge in 1916 – Dan Breen* was to find shelter, and a wife. In this busy enclave – with its teeming side streets, and handsome hotel, office and professional residences – the national spirit was very strong, and the Republican army bravely supported.

In this period the Mansion House on Dawson Street attained an important national stature more than ever before, or since. It is a wonderful place, with underground passages, by which a person could go from one side of the building to the other without ever surfacing. All the public meetings of the First Dáil Éireann were held there, and many private ones too; people got there with enormous effort, some travelling from the far end of the country. But I was lucky and had only to run across the Green when the opportunity arose to demonstrate national solidarity with the independence movement in its various aspects. I discovered little shops selling ballads and broadsheets, and national papers – and not always from under the counter. Presently, I came to know some of the secret printers of all this delicious material.

I pedalled this way and that on errands around the city. I knocked on doors on my rounds to mobilize our girls and women, from all social classes and different kinds of streets.

---

* Dan Breen (1894–1969) from Co. Tipperary was sworn in to the IRB in 1912, and joined the Irish Volunteers in 1914. He is best known for his part in the Soloheadbeg Ambush, which took place on the same day as the first meeting of Dáil Éireann in January 1919, widely regarded as the first incident in the War of Independence. Breen was involved in several audacious attacks, ambushes and escapes and was badly wounded on a number of occasions. Breen met his wife, Cumann na mBan member Brigid Malone, when she helped with his recovery following a bullet wound. They married in June 1921. Breen's record of his life in the revolutionary period, *My Fight for Irish Freedom*, was published in 1924.

The War of Independence was, in many ways, a free-for-all, and so I make no apology for the word 'we' when I use it. It would have taken a very old inhabitant to know all the names of the local people, yet alone those of the new civil servants of Dáil Éireann, or the journalists and observers, who came to the small hotels in Harcourt Street to experience a grandstand view of the struggle at street level. They strolled around the Russell Hotel corner in a steady stream to interview Mrs Green.

'We' includes people I cannot name, like the women selling apples and flowers on the sidewalk, with their capricious aprons, ever ready to catch a smoking revolver, a packet, or an un-discharged bomb – 'Drop it here, son' – from a man in a tight corner. It includes people behind doors that opened at the crucial moment, and closed just as quietly. It includes the Phelan sisters and their Wexford-born mother in the fruit and vegetable business in the Dardanelles; and the coalman called 'Black Justice' who, when he presided over the Republican Court, fined a milkman £100 instead of the usual 10/- for watering milk sold to the poor.

'We' includes Joe Clarke, widely known as 'Duck the Bullet' of Mount Street Battle fame – the caretaker in No. 6 Harcourt Street; Miss Mary O'Sullivan, secretary to Larry O'Neill, the Lord Mayor; Dáithí Ó Donnchadha, secretary to the trustees of the Dáil Éireann loan;[*] and Charlie Murphy TD, manager of *Nationality*.[†] 'We' includes

---

[*] Funds for the fledgling Dáil Éireann and newly constituted governmental departments were raised by selling bonds during the War of Independence. The first Dáil loan was approved in June 1919, for internal and external (USA) subscriptions. Both were oversubscribed. A second Dáil loan was approved in August 1921, then suspended following the signing of the Treaty in December of the same year. Some of the money raised remained in the USA and, not surprisingly, following the Civil War, there were arguments and court cases about which side, Republicans or the Free State government, was entitled to the remaining bond money.

[†] *Nationality* was a radical nationalist newspaper, edited by Arthur Griffith and founded in 1915 following the suppression or collapse of a number of previously edited Griffith publications including *The United Irishman, Eire-Ireland, Scissors and Paste* and a publication with the simple title *Sinn Féin*.

Larry Nugent and the famous Mrs Nugent, a pair whose doings are set out in Larry's manuscript, which is beside me as I write.[*]

'We' is the word used in all cases where I have no right to put 'I' – although often I was somewhere in the assisting multitude; here it includes the known and the unknown comrades who carried on the fight in my square half mile, which is only half of one of the 52,000 square miles of Ireland.

---

[*] The Larry Nugent manuscript referred to by Máire Comerford was presumably on loan. An account of Larry Nugent's revolutionary activity, running to almost 200 pages, which may well be the same (or a similar) document, is available at https://www.militaryarchives.ie/collections/online-collections/bureau-of-military -history-1913-1921/reels/bmh/BMH.WS0907.pdf.

Inside Nos 6 and 76

JOE CLARKE told me how Arthur Griffith, the editor of the Republican newspaper *Nationality*, strode into the office at No. 6 Harcourt Street every morning until the place was closed. Griffith would throw his hat on a pile of papers and have a cheery word, or sometimes sweets, for the Clarke children to share, before he settled down to work. As caretaker, Joe had a simple device for preserving his own freedom and the general safety of the house. He lived with his family in the top flat in No. 6. Mrs Clarke did not have to decide if a caller was friend or foe. Whether it was a raiding party, a snooper or a friend who arrived at a dangerous moment, she had nothing to say but 'He is gone to Skerries.' Friends knew from this that business, if any, was transferred for the time being to the roof of Skerries College; enemies were welcome to look for Joe, fifteen miles away at the seaside.

Stories about the escapades of Michael Collins in Harcourt Street were repeated with delight, and a lot of what was believed was founded on fact. Collins was a daring and fearless man who might descend from the roofs without notice through selected skylights. It was rumoured that he hung from his hands from a back windowsill at No. 6 while a room there was being searched. Joe Clarke remembered him as being present but not taken when the house was raided. On that occasion 'a member of the staff' was sitting at a typewriter, neither hidden nor in any way attracting attention. Páidín O'Keefe, secretary to Sinn Féin, and Charlie Murphy had both been arrested and were sitting in a lorry outside. In the house the 'G Man' looked over the male typist's shoulder from behind. What he read was this: *The last man who did that was shot*. The raid went off without Collins being taken. Later, it became clear that the writing on the typewriter was no idle comment, for the G Man in question was shot dead.

The British government authorities proclaimed our national organizations, beginning with Dáil Éireann in September 1919. Nonetheless, their well-known headquarters were not closed down by the authorities. Harcourt Street was too convenient an observation post for the Castle for that to happen, at least before the supply of trained and useful detectives ran out. The G Men were the eyes and ears of Dublin Castle; they, individually, and in the service to which they belonged, had been the Irish forerunners of Quisling since the days of Peel. They were brave, unyielding men, faithful to the work they had undertaken and the ignoble wages of their profession. In the belief that their destruction was imperative to our survival as a revolutionary force, and carried out under government orders, my comrades and I stood over the shootings of these men. But in later days I was sorry for the Volunteers, who had taken life in the name of the Republic only to find that their trust had been abused by some important leaders; it turned out that these leaders shared neither the pure idealism of Easter Week nor the standards of honourable behaviour, which we believed was accepted generally in the movement.

No. 6 was the property of the Sinn Féin Bank, with the bank counter on the left as you entered the house. David Kelly, a disabled man, was manager. In the beginning the gold belonging to the Republican reserve was lodged in the bank. At a later time David Kelly carried what he had of it to his home each day. Then he brought it to a public house in Lincoln Place, where he dumped it for the night. The night David Kelly was killed, accidentally in an ambush on Pearse Street, he had no chance to save himself. When the British found the gold on him they thought they had got Michael Collins.

The permanent staff of No. 6 – in so far as they could at any time be called permanent – in addition to the chiefs already mentioned – were Brian Fagan, Anna Kelly, Brede Hegarty, Barney Mellows, Willie Murray and Seán Milroy. Máire Rigney was Honorary Secretary to the Ard Craobh of Sinn Féin, which also had headquarters at No. 6. I know from her about the brave dressmaker who lived opposite. She was Mrs White, the wife of an officer of the Dublin Metropolitan Police, and an important contact for information from the other side of the Castle wall. Dressmaking equipment, fashion magazines, patterns and tape measures made an impenetrable cover from raiders' eyes for the secrets that Mrs White guarded for Michael Collins. A dress, tacked and ready for fitting, was kept on the premises for Máire Rigney. If necessary, it would explain her presence in the shop if she happened to be caught in a raid, when she crossed the street to collect dispatches.

I was a little mystified by a quiet, middle-aged lady who never seemed to fit into No. 6 when I saw her there. She did not appear to have much spring in her step, or flash in the eye, and was usually dressed in brown or grey, always unobtrusively. I found out later that the mystery woman was Patricia Hoey, and that even her own mother knew nothing of what Miss Hoey, journalist, propagandist, suffragette, Republican activist, Cumann na mBan stalwart (and later Dublin correspondent of the New York Hearst papers), was really up to. Batt O'Connor had constructed a hiding place for documents at the back of the wooden stairs leading to the garden in No. 6. This was not found when the building was raided, and only Patricia Hoey was caught. Her account of her experience in custody in Dublin Castle was told many years ago to Piaras Béaslaí,[*] and published by him. Miss

---

[*] Piaras Béaslaí (1881–1965) was a writer and journalist. He joined the Irish Volunteers on their foundation in 1913 and was Deputy Commanding Officer of the 1st Dublin Battalion under Edward ('Ned') Daly during the 1916 Rising.

Hoey might not have had her freedom for years if a Dublin journalist had not confirmed her professional status. Then, the British dropped her like the hot potato she most certainly was!

It was the policy of Dáil Éireann from the beginning to press for the implementation of the victorious Allies' war aims, as stated by President Wilson. Our work would be conducted above ground – for as long as possible. The Dublin Mansion House was the first published postal address of Dáil Éireann. Business went ahead for eight months before the British decided, in September 1919, to suppress our parliament by force. Even after the suppression, private meetings of Dáil Éireann were held in the Oak Room. The courage and loyalty of the Lord Mayor, Larry O'Neill, was beyond praise. His secretary, Miss Mary O'Sullivan, had ample scope both for her ability and her patriotic devotion. She told me once about the day she went to No. 6 when the house had been raided and ransacked from top to bottom. She had a message for President de Valera – not long escaped from Lincoln Jail. Mary went through the whole building but met nobody, until she climbed to the very top. There she came across Michael Collins and asked him where she might find de Valera. 'I believe he is on the roof at the moment,' Collins nonchalantly replied.

We were quite ready to believe that Michael Collins, in his capacity as Director of Intelligence, had the mails so well under control that any letter sent to the Viceroy, General Lord French, through the ordinary post, would reach the Republican censor first. The Under Secretary, Dublin Castle, the Brigadier General, GHQ, Parkgate Street, and Col. W.E. Johnston, Head of the Dublin Metropolitan Police, all gave orders about censorship of certain mails in Dublin. Those referring to incoming post are recorded in the memo book that belonged to Peter Behan, Superintendent of the Sorting Office.

On his release from prison in 1917 Béaslaí was elected to the central committee of Sinn Féin, and was elected TD for Kerry East for the party in the 1918 election. During the War of Independence he worked as a publicity officer for Dáil Éireann and editor of *An tÓglach* (the IRA newspaper). He is probably best known as a biographer of *Michael Collins – Michael Collins and the Making of a New Ireland*, published in 1926.

The memo book is marked 'To be kept for 118.' '118' was Patrick Moynihan,* and he gave me the book in the 1940s, some time before his death. I subsequently gave the book to Kilmainham Jail.

The entries at the early stage explain in part why Dublin Castle was in no hurry to close the Harcourt Street houses: 'All correspondence addressed to No. 6 or 76 Harcourt Street should be detained and forwarded under confidential cover to the Under Secretary, Dublin Castle.'

And Dublin Castle was also keeping a close eye on the Mansion House: 'All correspondence addressed to the Mansion House, Dublin, with the exception of that for the Right Hon. Laurence O'Neill, Lord Mayor of Dublin, or members of his family, should be detained and sent to the Undersecretary, Dublin Castle.'

I was never in No. 76 that I can remember. That house had its great moments in 1919, before I got to Dublin, or when I was newly resident nearby. Dáithí Ó Donnchadha, Secretary to the Treasury, told me almost everything I know about what went on inside No. 76. The Finance Department was based there and the Minister's room was the one nearest to the roof. When Crown forces swooped on Armistice Day, 11 November 1919, Collins entered the Standard Hotel through the skylight, which was over the well of the house. He had to swing his body before he could make the spring to the banister of the upper landing. D.J. O'Donovan (afterwards Dublin City manager) stayed behind to save the records concerning the Dáil loan; he was successful but he was caught. But Dáithí O'Donnchadha – bowler-hatted, formally-dressed businessman – lit the cigar he kept for emergencies, then coolly joined other interested spectators of the raid, who dawdled in the street outside!

Dáithí told me that the money kept pouring in for the Dáil loan

---

* Patrick Moynihan (1867–1947) was a GPO employee who worked as a translator of Irish addresses and surreptitiously as IRA chief intelligence officer, known as '118'. Moynihan had eighty GPO workers working for IRA Intelligence under his direction, and engaged in a process of 're-directing' the British administration's post. This post was then passed on to Michael Collins for examination; 118 was a vital link in the formidable Republican intelligence chain.

and a receipt went out for every payment. No money was ever caught in a raid. Dáithí and his wife carried thousands of pounds to the banks, or to meet the weekly expenses of Dáil Éireann. Managers of banks bowed before Dáithí and he was ushered quickly into their private offices. The banks did their utmost to protect all of the money entrusted to them. Dáithí had to be ready at all times to be held up and searched so he kept his records in a form designed to mislead the enemy. The home affairs department (Austin Stack) was entered as 'Arthur Holmes'; The Belfast boycott (a source of revenue) was 'MacFarlands'; The department of defence was 'Mr Marshal'; The president was 'Mr Head'; propaganda was 'Mr Newsome'.

Seán McGrath was the official who brought money and wages to the government offices through the city. The staff nicknamed him 'Bainc ar Siubhall' – the Walking Bank. Staff, like Seán, were recruited for government and other Republican offices from the ranks of those who had been tried and found true – or from among the quiet sympathizers, people of any rank, gender or age who could go about their business unsuspected. While some 'wanted' men joined flying columns* in the country, others, who were unknown to the enemy, became civil servants. The IRA continued to be unpaid Volunteers but the Dáil took pride in paying excellent wages to the civil servants. Clerical workers were otherwise much exploited in those days.

The men and women in the new civil service gave example by their brave defiance of danger, which, to those who witnessed it in the circumstances of the time, was not less than the high soldierly standard of the Volunteers. When the split came there were many who disdained compromise and disappeared, for a time or forever, from the service they had helped to found.

But even the most efficient and high-ranking officers had their crusty moments. An English journalist calling to No. 6 met Kerryman

---

* Flying columns are compact, self-determining military units, which can operate with agility and the element of surprise. They are often employed as a guerrilla war tactic, when rebels are outnumbered by national or colonizing armies, in manpower and arms. The IRA fought the War of Independence very effectively using flying columns of Volunteers all over the country.

Páidín O'Keefe, Secretary to Sinn Féin, and asked him to define the objectives of the movement. 'Revenge be Jappers,' said Páidín and no more. Few minor stories of the time travelled further than this one! Páidín, small and dark, had beautiful eyes, and they missed nothing. His memory was such that it would hardly have mattered if the enemy had found the files of Sinn Féin. Not only did he know the principal men and women in the movement in every parish in Ireland, but Páidín also had his own ideas about their character, personality, achievement, the amount of Gaelic blood in the veins and the sins and services of their ancestors. A remarkable man, Páidín; I knew him from every angle.

If I was not at a Cumann na mBan meeting in Parnell Square, or at an Irish class, I was pretty sure to pick up a job at Heytesbury Street, or in Ranelagh from Mrs Éamonn Ceannt (Áine) or Lily O'Brennan, two sisters living at 44 Oakley Road. Lily was certain to have someone in immediate danger of arrest, and for whom a night's lodging in a safe place had to be found within the following hour. Lily's sister, Áine Ceannt, was a very able and steadfast woman, who was later chosen by the White Cross to be a second mother to the children who were made orphans in the fighting, or in the pogroms in Belfast. Before that, when I first started going to her house, she was a Justice in the Pembroke and Rathmines Republican Courts,* and official arbitrator in disputes for Countess Markievicz's Department of Labour.

I was never a cog in the official government machine of this period, or a candidate to be a cog. Ireland had thousands of girls and boys like me at that time. The most that I can claim is that I tried to be a drop of oil helping to make things work when the chance to do so arose, as it did in those times, daily and nightly.

---

* Republican Courts were the arbitration or judicial branch of the unilaterally-declared Irish Republic and were formally set up by the First Dáil in 1920 as a replacement for the ad hoc Arbitration Courts, already in operation. The justices of these courts were representative of local communities, and therefore far more accountable than resident magistrates of the British system. The Republican Courts were a direct challenge to British Rule in Ireland.

Close Shaves, and Vigils

ONE OF THE first jobs I got as a member of Central Branch, Cumann na mBan – with Headquarters at 25 Parnell Square – was to take a box for a Flag Day. I don't remember the purpose, or what our emblem was, only that both were seditious in the British view, and the police very active. My place of duty was supposed to be North William Street, a very populous area near the North Strand. I didn't know Dublin at the time, having only just arrived there to live; that is the reason I spent a completely uneventful morning collecting from the small trickle of people who use places like South William Street, a backwater near Grafton Street, on a Sunday morning. Things were very dull. But presently, someone told me that the girls were all arrested around the city and that I should look out for myself.

As it was now evident that I wouldn't be poaching another girl's territory if I moved to a better spot, I came down Suffolk Street to the bottom of Grafton Street; as soon as I showed my box there, I could not take on money fast enough from the people pressing around me to subscribe. Things were going along grandly until a newsboy shouted a warning and I saw a big hand across the people, a yard or so away, coming to swoop. It belonged to a policeman. I made a dive and started to run, although half spancelled by a foolish, fashionable tight skirt. In spite of the obstruction of the policeman by unknown friends, the odds were against me – that is until a milk car drove up beside me. 'Hold on,' the driver shouted; when I grabbed his dashboard, he whipped up his pony and went off at a pace which left my legs barely able to keep my feet on the ground as I was helped to the top of the street, and safety.

Dozens of Cumann na mBan women were arrested that day, and spent the night in the filthy, revolting abomination of a prison called the Bridewell. The City Courts were crowded the next day but by morning the women had changed and swapped their outer clothes to such good effect that the police were unable, perhaps, in some cases, unwilling, to identify any of them as members of an illegal organization. The proceeding ended in a big joke when all the women were released. Laughter can be a great tonic in revolutions! Now and again it even appeared from things that happened that the magistrates, under their skins, were Irishmen too. My experience in Grafton Street was typical of Dublin in those days. It was rare for an emergency to leave any Republican without help. Crowds would gather at the slightest hint of trouble and there was every evidence of popular support for the Republican government and cause.

The street light was shining through the rain of a winter night, falling onto the roadway loosely full of people, when Aonach na Nollag, the annual Christmas Fair of Irish goods and industries, was banned before Christmas in 1919. As the stallholders were ordered out of the Round Room and the Supper Room of the Mansion House, I noticed the small figure of Pádraic Ó Conaire* as he stood under a wall at the top of Dawson Street looking, as I was too, at

---

* Pádraic Ó Conaire (1882–1928) was an Irish-language writer and scholar from Galway, who was reared in Connemara. Ó Conaire is considered to be the most innovative Irish-language writer to emerge from the Gaelic Revival. His novella *Deoraíocht* (Exile) was published in 1910 and his collection of short stories *An Chéad Chloch* (*The First Stone*) in 1914, both to great acclaim.

the first tin-hatted English soldiers we had seen. The Aonach, sponsored by NAIDA (National Agricultural and Industrial Development Association) was a civilian event and had no way to hit back in the face of the bayonets. Most of the stallholders packed up their handmade jewellery, Christmas cards, knitted goods, tweeds, poplins, books and other wares scraped together to demonstrate the national industries of the period, and took their stalls away. But a few stood their ground and tried to carry on. One of these was offering Ballyowen tobacco, cigarettes and cheroots, grown and manufactured by Father Sweetman at Mount St Benedict in Gorey.

My heart nearly stopped when I heard 'The Matron', Aileen K'Eogh let out a sizable roar; she was furious that the promoters of the Aonach were not standing their ground. Cumann na mBan were dismantling their fine stall, over which they had a scroll representing their badge – a rifle with the initials of the organization superimposed on it. Then I heard Aileen's remonstration – 'You bundled up your rifles very quickly when the English came.' There was anger for a minute or two but the girls shrugged it off. I thought Aileen's comment unjust because the decision to go was not ours to make. There was no Aonach in 1920. When it was held successfully during the Truce in 1921, it was the last social event of importance before the great and terrible split when people who had been comrades parted after an argument and, sometimes, the parting was forever.

The Republican northside of Dublin had its heart in Parnell Square, where the IRB owned No. 41, while No. 44 had been taken over by majority vote from what was left of the National Volunteers. My Irish class was in No. 39 and Vaughan's Hotel, and the public houses, Devlin's and Kirwan's in Parnell Street, were Collins's territory. Central Branch Cumann na mBan met at No. 25 once a week. For me the warmest, most active house of friends on the northside was O'Donel's Home, Private Hospital and Nursing Home, all full of brave people, run by sisters Gerry, Joe and Lile.

The most infamous place on the northside was Mountjoy Prison, and the saddest Glasnevin Cemetery. Near the jail gates, on the road

127

from the city to the cemetery, the mother and three sisters of Michael O'Hanrahan (executed in 1916) had opened a shop selling papers, cigarettes and sweets. The rise and fall in their business often reflected the state of affairs inside the jail. Besides getting on with their day-to-day dealings, the women had opportunities to find out what was going on behind the high walls and iron gates on a secret line of communication with prisoners. The O'Hanrahan girls were my comrades in Cumann na mBan but their home life was so full of danger, excitement, service and financial sacrifice, they would probably have pleaded guilty to the charge that they came to us for relaxation!

I cannot now distinguish between the different occasions when immense crowds filled the North Circular Road outside Mountjoy Prison, extending to Cross Guns Bridge, and from there back around the northern side of the Mater Hospital to Eccles Street. Here the people gathered, hour after hour, while the rosary was repeated for the prisoners. I remember an armoured car on the scene, and that a tank arrived – the first we had seen. When the tank turned to go north, over Cross Guns Bridge, it skidded on the setts, and failed to proceed. Then, to our immense satisfaction, it began to smoke and the word went round that it was on fire – a delightful spectacle. Up dashed the fire brigade. When the brigade saw the tank on fire it turned away, leaving it there. And that was no surprise. Captain Connolly of the fire brigade was brother to Seán Connolly – killed in the attack on Dublin Castle in 1916. He and his men were popular idols, full of dash and gallantry. From the time Dublin Corporation gave its allegiance to Dáil Éireann, they were free to do the things they wanted to do anyway, within the limits of municipal green tape. After the failure of the tank, an aeroplane came overhead and continued to observe, perhaps threaten, the crowds. I was wedged beside a splendidly tall, immensely powerful and devout young woman, wearing a shawl and carrying a large basket in the crook of her arm, at about the height of my shoulder. We were all saying the rosary but she was rotating as she watched the plane. As the basket bruised its way across my back, I heard her prayer tangle with her imprecation against the aeroplane:

'Holy Mary, Mother of God – oh! May you fall down, you divil! May you fall down in the canal where you won't hurt anybody – and pray for us sinners now and at the moment of our death, amen.'

The prisoners we ardently prayed for in April 1920 were on hunger strike; the trouble was caused by their treatment – as common criminals. Sixty-four men, led by Peadar Clancy,[*] had started the strike after they had failed to get agreement about political treatment. Outside, we discussed the situation with anxiety, pity for the men involved, and mounting anger against enemy authorities. From the end of the first week every day made a new record of endurance and deaths were awaited hourly. On 12 April the workers of Dublin left their jobs in a sympathetic strike. When the prisoners were on their ninth or tenth day without food, and the workers three days on strike, the Castle weakened. The first sign of this to us, waiting outside, was the news, following a visit by the Lord Mayor, Larry O'Neill, that every prisoner might have a visit. Then, wonderful chance – I saw Anna Fitzsimmons (Fitz)[†] from Sinn Féin HQ coming into the space before the big black door. She looked around the crowd, recognized me, and beckoned. 'I'm going in to see Frank Gallagher.[‡] Would you like to come? We are

---

[*] Peadar Clancy (1888–1920) was a Clare-born Irish Volunteer who was in the Four Courts garrison during the 1916 Easter Rising. During the War of Independence Clancy was vice-commandant of the Dublin Brigade IRA. He specialized in prison escapes and was involved in the rescue of nineteen prisoners from Mountjoy Prison and five from Manchester Jail. He led the Mountjoy hunger strike of April 1920, tenaciously refusing all concessions except release, which was achieved after ten days. Peadar Clancy was shot dead by British Auxiliaries while under detention in Dublin Castle in November 1920.

[†] Anna Kelly (née Fitzsimmons) (1891–1958) was a member of Cumann na mBan and a journalist who served in the GPO during the Rising of 1916. In 1917 Anna worked in No. 6 Harcourt Street as secretary to Páidín O'Keefe, General Secretary of Sinn Féin. She later worked for Michael Collins and assisted in the publication of *The Irish Bulletin* from 1919–21. Known to her comrades as 'Miss Fitz' or 'Fitz', she later took the surname Kelly when she married a Sinn Féin colleague, Frank Kelly, during the Truce of 1921. When the *Irish Press* newspaper was launched in 1931 'Fitz', now known as Anna Kelly, became the first women's page editor in Ireland. (She was eventually dismissed from the *Irish Press* following the publication of an article critical of the Fianna Fáil government in the 1950s.)

[‡] Frank Gallagher (1893–1962) was a Republican, journalist and writer. He was an active member of Sinn Féin and strong campaigner during the 1918 elections.

cousins of course,' she added. So it was that I stepped into Mountjoy for the first time. Fitz and I, and all the others who managed to make entry, followed the crowd to the wings where the men were. The warders were thrown out of their normally inflexible routine, the keys at their belts swinging idle. The cell doors were open, the men lying on the floors. There was no furniture in the cells; they had been stripped, while the fight was on, of bed, table and stool, leaving only the fourth article of prison furniture – the chamber pot.

We sat on the floor beside Frank. Fitz kissed him, but I would not have known how to get myself that far. She did the talking. Frank was weak and looked ill – but he was not too sick to enjoy the victory. When we were called on to leave, Frank passed me a note. 'Bring this to the papers,' he ordered. I went hotfoot to the offices of the *Independent* and the *Freeman's Journal* and his message was in the stop-press edition, which the newsboys were shouting in the streets in a very short time. That evening I was back in Mountjoy when the big release came. Most men walked out but some were carried out on stretchers. The people waited to watch and cheer as ambulance after ambulance carried them away to the city hospitals. A woman from Cumann na mBan went in each ambulance to see that all was well.

On execution mornings too, a vast and sympathetic crowd gathered outside Mountjoy waiting there, singing hymns until the fateful notice that another man had died for Ireland was put on the prison door. I find it difficult to differentiate between vigils, when the people gathered, storming heaven. Sometimes Republican police or Volunteers were on duty but often we looked down the muzzles of British rifles; from time to time the bayonets moved with enough menace to demonstrate that we were at their wrong end. Although we were outside the walls, and at a distance of 100 yards or so, we hoped that our voices rose to the occasion and carried to within

---

He was an officer in the 3rd battalion of the Dublin Brigade of the IRA during the revolutionary period, while simultaneously working in propaganda for the Republican cause. He was imprisoned in 1919 and again in 1920, when he commenced a hunger strike, along with many other prisoners. His diary recollections of the hunger strike, *Days of Fear*, was published in 1929.

earshot when Kevin Barry* died in November 1920; and the same thing happened when Ellis – the English hangman – came again to send Thomas Traynor,† the father of ten children, to eternity. We hoped they heard our singing, and were helped by knowing that a great number of friends had come – waiting and praying until the fateful hour of their deaths.

---

* On 15 August 1920 medical student Kevin Barry (1902–1920) was part of a group of IRA Volunteers who attempted to ambush a British army vehicle in order to capture arms and ammunition. The group surrounded the vehicle and after a shot was fired and a gun battle ensued, three British soldiers were killed. Kevin Barry was the only Volunteer captured. He was eventually tried by court martial and found guilty. As the details of his case, and his young age, spread, there was considerable national and international sympathy for him. Nonetheless, he was hanged on 1 November 1920.

† Thomas Traynor (1882–1921) was a 38-year-old bootmaker and father of a large family who was hanged in Mountjoy Prison in April 1921. He was a member of the garrison at Boland's Mill in 1916 and was subsequently interned in Frongoch, Wakefield and Mountjoy jails. Thomas Traynor was captured during an IRA ambush in March 1921, when two members of the Crown forces and one Volunteer lost their lives.

Raids, Escapades and Escapes

WHEN MRS GREEN learned that Roger Casement's brother Tom was on his way home from South Africa, she became very worried. She knew of the great affection between the brothers, which had not been changed by the way Roger's life and career ended; but she knew too that Tom had lived in rough places. Tom Casement had a heart of gold, but he also had a temper, proud loyalty, and great pity for the weak. How, his friends asked one another, would Tom react when he arrived suddenly in the charged atmosphere of Dublin in those times? They feared lest he might, in hasty anger, pull a gun during some incident in the streets, and himself get shot. They also knew that he might get drunk and this would be unseemly in an Ireland where so many were reading the high-minded 'Ethics of Sinn Féin'.*

---

* This refers to *The Ethics of Sinn Féin*, as set out in a pamphlet issued by the National Council of Sinn Féin in 1917. The pamphlet explains how members should behave in their daily lives in order to project an image of the organization through their own exemplary behaviour, including temperance. The pamphlet argues for the principle that every Irishman and woman's own self is the Irish nation, or that each member of Sinn Féin is an ideal Irish nation in miniature.

After consultation, it was decided that Mrs Green would give Tom a good talking to, and I got the job of persuading him to give up his gun to the IRA.

Tom arrived at No. 90 and went into the drawing room with Mrs Green, where they sat down and spoke quietly together. Afterwards, he was ready to agree to give me his gun. We made an appointment and arranged that I would call to where Tom was staying – at the Gresham Hotel. This went off all right. He produced a .45 from behind a gilt mirror in his bedroom but then refused to give me his precious seven rounds. Eventually Tom promised that he would send the bullets separately. That night there was a ring at the doorbell. When I opened the front door the bullets were put into my hand by someone unknown, who went away immediately. The seven rounds were on my dressing table early next morning when we were raided. I was alerted by the noise a soldier made with his rifle and accoutrements, when he climbed the narrow stairs at the top of the house. There was barely time to drop Tom's seven rounds into my stocking. Throughout the raid, which was polite and harmless, the ammunition thankfully went unnoticed under my foot.

Two elderly ladies lived next door to us, in No. 91. They showed their intense disapproval of Mrs Green, and the times in general, by putting a Union Jack out of an upper window whenever the Crown forces raided us. This suited us very well because it made their place fairly safe. The ladies of No. 91 were no gardeners and their back region was a wilderness of many years growth. Little did they know what a grand cover the flying of their flag made for my dump on their side of the garden wall.

The Union Jack was the object of much derision at that time, and was often at the centre of a good story. I remember one instance in particular when there was a great big social occasion at the Liffey Dock Yard, with all manner of important people in attendance for the launching of a ship. When the champagne bottle was broken, and the ship slid towards the water, the Union Jack miraculously fell from the mast and a tricolour ran up in its place. This happened at the moment when 'The Quality' were absolutely powerless to do anything but gasp. Andy McDonnell[*] told me later that was an Oscar Traynor[†] job – as good a tonic as a successful ambush, and Oscar was a genius both ways.

Desmond Fitzgerald TD, Minister for Publicity, sometimes called in the evening to No. 90 to clear his pockets before going on somewhere else to sleep. Michael Collins's great friend, Batt O'Connor, made a secret place for me in the office where I worked. It often held Desmond's papers, and a good deal else besides. There were some very careful searches of No. 90, but nothing was ever found. I watched very carefully when soldiers did their searches and made some useful deductions from their behaviours. This helped me to be a very good hider.

Constance Markievicz TD was known to go about disguised as an old woman, popping up here and there on street corners. She would hold a brief meeting, then disappear; there were hundreds, perhaps thousands, in her own constituency – around St Patrick's Cathedral – to protect the Countess, always watching for her. The Chief Commissioner of the Police issued a special circular about the Countess to all stations in the Metropolitan District in January 1920; a sergeant gave his copy to Fergus O'Connor, who subsequently allowed me to copy it. In the circular the Chief Commissioner impresses on all superintendents the 'grave importance of securing this woman's arrest', who, he added, 'may possibly be heavily veiled and difficult to recognize'. He ordered his superintendents to have 'at least three

---

* Andrew (Andy) McDonnell was born in 1898 in Dublin, and enlisted in the Irish Volunteers in 1916, when he was seventeen years old. He was a member of B company of the third battalion in Boland Mills in 1916, and, following surrender, was held at Richmond Barracks for three weeks. He went on to become a lieutenant in the South Dublin Brigade of the IRA, rising to the rank of commanding officer.

† Oscar Traynor (1886–1963) was a member of the Irish Volunteers and the IRB. He took part in the Easter Rising, in charge of the Metropole Hotel garrison. Traynor was subsequently interned in Britain until his release in late 1916. He became vice-OC of the Dublin Brigade and was involved in the printing of *An tÓglach*, an IRA publication. He was commander of the attack on the Custom House in May 1921, which resulted in a high loss of life for the Dublin Brigade.

cyclists on duty' in every division to put a stop to these suddenly convened meetings.

The Darling of Ireland – only second to de Valera for a time – was Patrick J. Fleming, from the Swan, Athy. He led an escape of prisoners over the wall of Mountjoy Prison on 9 March 1919. Afterwards he came by arrangement to tell Mrs Green the inside story of prison conditions in Maryborough and Mountjoy jails. I was there to listen while his story, which we knew already in outline, was extracted from him.

He was a very tall young man, about twenty-six then, wasted and ill after a diet of much bread and water, and repeated experience of the full range of prison punishments and restraints. These were endured in Maryborough Jail after he was sentenced to five years' penal servitude, when he went on a lonely prison strike against being treated as a criminal. He had a big and strong body when first imprisoned and none of the ordinary devices for controlling unruly prisoners were able to hold him for long. Patrick Fleming could break handcuffs and work his way out of muffs and straitjackets. Confined in the soundproof 'tower' cell, he had somehow managed to break windows far overhead by kicking the chamber pot, even though his arms and the top part of this body were strapped. His resistance was suspended when he collapsed and was moved to hospital but was resumed immediately on each of the series of occasions he was judged fit to be brought back to the jail. Ultimately, they moved him to Mountjoy. I had my instruction; when the interview with Mrs Green was over I was to walk with Patrick Fleming to the canal bridge, then linger a little before parting, as if we were a couple spending an evening together in some more conventional way. This was my first assignment for the Volunteers in Dublin.

Visits and Visitors

PROFESSOR W.P. STOCKLEY and Mrs Stockley of Cork came to lunch with Mrs Green on a spring day in 1920. The talk was all the stranger in the setting of St Stephen's Green, which caused me to remember the beauty of the day as we sat around Mrs Green's elegant table, in the sun-drenched dining room overlooking the garden. The professor – a slight, middle-aged, spectacled figure – had recently been elected Alderman for Cork Corporation. He had come to Mrs Green's to talk about the murder of his friend Tomás MacCurtain,[*] Republican Lord Mayor of Cork, and also about the strange attempt on his own life as he was walking home to Tivoli, following a civic reception in the city centre in honour of St Patrick.

---

[*] Tomás MacCurtain (1884–1920) was an Irish Republican who commanded up to 1000 Volunteers, ready for action in Cork at the outset of the 1916 Rising. Due to conflicting orders from Dublin, the Cork men were not mobilized. MacCurtain was subsequently imprisoned in Britain. On his release he became a brigade commander of the IRA. In January 1920 he was elected as a Cork City councillor, and then Lord Mayor of Cork. Months later, on his thirty-sixth birthday, MacCurtain was gunned down at his home by men with blackened faces, in front of his wife and son. The men were later revealed as being members of the RIC.

A short time before our lunch party, Professor Stockley acted as chairman at the first meeting held by Cork Corporation following the murder of MacCurtain, when it had fallen to him to put the chain of office on the shoulders of the new Mayor – Terence MacSwiney. We knew as much or as little of all this as had been reported in the papers. Now we heard the full story in its setting of life in Cork, where the first of the new police reinforcements from Britain had begun to arrive in the month of March. The name 'Black and Tans', which had been coined for these unfamiliar arrivals, was new then, but was one that would become synonymous with brutality, murder and fear. They were brought in as reinforcements and wore a mixture of the police and British army uniform – khaki trousers and blue coat, or vice versa, and they never looked drilled in either. They were a mean, bad lot, without courage, boozers and looters. None of this was yet known to any of us when we sat down to lunch with the Stockleys. Nor, of course, did anyone present imagine that before many months had passed the Professor would stand by Terence MacSwiney's deathbed in Brixton Prison.

Germaine, Mrs Stockley, was alive to everything around her, an entirely devoted wife, yet with a strong mind of her own on all topics. From time to time, she cut across the professor incisively, to illustrate his accurate and scrupulous narrative with vivid and impetuous description of her own. Half German/half French, Germaine was a musician of distinction and a social leader in Cork – a brave and lovely woman and fast friend to Mary and Annie, the sisters of Terence MacSwiney. During all the years I was to know Germaine she never became accustomed to outrage and injustice. I cannot now discriminate between the facts regarding the MacCurtain murder, which had been widely disseminated publicly, and what we learned from the professor around the dining table that day. But I do have a lively recollection of Professor Stockley's description of his own shooting experience on the night before Tomás MacCurtain was shot dead in cold blood.

The professor told us that he was walking home to Tivoli when suddenly three men confronted him on the footpath, and one of them fired point blank at him. The professor was struck in the middle of his body; he doubled up, and almost fell. But then he straightened himself and addressed his assailant – 'If you were to do that again I should be compelled to ask you for your name and address.' The three gunmen turned to leave but suddenly wheeled around again and another shot was fired, which miraculously missed. The assailants ran away and Professor Stockley walked home, where his wife attended to him. Luckily for him, he had, earlier that morning, used a large safety pin to replace the top button of his trousers, and this pin deflected the bullet. The professor sustained no injury beyond bruising. Professor and Mrs Stockley possessed rare qualities of character and integrity; they were both very kind to me in later days, when they made their house my home and headquarters during post-Treaty election campaigns.

The Mayor of Limerick, Michael O'Callaghan, and his wife Kate had a similar mission to the Stockleys, when they came to lunch with Mrs Green, sometime in September 1920. The O'Callaghans were on their way to London and then further afield to Europe. They let no opportunity pass to publicize the state of Ireland under the reign of terror by the British government, and to give advance warning of the peril in which they, in common with the citizens of Limerick, lived every day and night of their lives. Mrs Green gave them some introductions and advice before their journey. The mission was urgent because by then Terence MacSwiney was in prison and suffering his long hunger strike. What I remember very clearly is that, for the second time, murder was the topic of conversation over lunch at No. 90. Michael O'Callaghan passed the death notices he had received across the dining-room table; he told us that the first of these was in his post when he returned from Cork, where he had attended the funeral of Tomás MacCurtain. He decided that the best course of action was to have the ostensible death threats published in the local Limerick press.

For nearly a year, everything that could be done by the Dáil Éireann Publicity Department, and by the O'Callaghans themselves, to halt the murder policy of the British government, was done in vain. Their visit to Mrs Green was part of this effort. Even after her long experience of British perfidy, starting with the Home Rule controversy, followed by the tactics employed against Casement, and now combined with renewed savagery in Ireland, Mrs Green found it very difficult to believe that the British government really knew about the things being done in their name. She persisted with her diligent and persistent letter writing to people of influence in London. After the O'Callaghans' visit Mrs Green wrote to Sir John Simon,* previously Attorney General, and to others of her acquaintance in political circles in London.

Michael O'Callaghan held his ground for almost a year until he was shot down inside his own hall door on 6 March 1921. I cannot recall if Kate O'Callaghan, when we met her, yet knew by sight or ill-fame the individual members of the Crown murder gang in Limerick, including the blue-eyed cadet whose glasses she tore off in the hall of her home, as they fired over her struggling shoulders and killed her husband.

Sometime later Dáithí O'Donnchadha, who was in Limerick on Dáil loan business, gave me an independent account of his experience of that fateful night. Dáithí was with the new Lord Mayor of Limerick, George Clancy, who had succeeded Michael O' Callaghan; Clancy was also an organizer for the Dáil loan in Limerick city and Liberties. Dáithí was in Clancy's house until shortly before curfew on 6 March. He was, of course, dressed in his usual dignified disguise. But none of this was much good to him when he set out with his bag of money to join the other 'commercials' in the Railway Hotel. The Crown forces were having things their own drunken and trigger-happy way. The

---

* John Simon (1873–1954) was an English barrister who was first elected to the British parliament in 1906. He was appointed Solicitor General in 1910 and Attorney General in 1913. He became Home Secretary in May 1915 but resigned some months later in protest against the introduction of military conscription for World War I. John Simon went on to have a long political career, holding a number of cabinet posts including Foreign Secretary and Chancellor of Exchequer. His autobiography, *Retrospect*, was published in 1952.

searchlights from their lorries probed the dark streets. Their bullets emptied those streets of life. It took Dáithí one and a half hours to make his short journey to the hotel. He hid in doorways, he ran for his life when he got the chance, he crawled over Sarsfield Bridge. Next morning Dáithí was in a first-class carriage on the early train to Dublin. He was seemingly calm, correct and outwardly indifferent when revolver-swinging soldiers rushed through the train – and missed him and his dispatch case. When his train met the down train from Dublin, Dáithí bought the morning papers and read about George Clancy's murder, and the murder of Michael O'Callaghan. There was a third murder – that of Joseph Donoghue, a Volunteer from Westmeath. Raiders at his home told him – 'You are the man we are looking for.' They apparently mistook his identity and killed him in error for Dáithí.

There is no way of knowing the degree, if any, to which the fears of people, whose nerve was broken by the murder gangs, may have contributed to the sad events, which put paid to our Republican dream later on in 1921, and subsequently.

Robert Brennan, Erskine Childers and Frank Gallagher – the men most responsible for the production of *The Bulletin* after the arrest of Desmond Fitzgerald, quite frequently arranged newspaper interviews with Mrs Green. Of course, every journalist wanted to interview Éamon de Valera or Michael Collins. Such occasions could be and were arranged, but rather rarely, for precautions had to be taken in the case of men who had a price on the heads. Erskine Childers himself, Mrs Green and Professor MacNeill were put forward as very good alternatives – people who could speak from the point of view of civilians and as democrats. Of all the journalists who came and went, I can only now remember two great English men – Henry Nevinson and Hugh Martin – the giants of the profession.* Martin, in particular,

---

* During the War of Independence journalists came to Ireland from all over the world to report on the conflict. Two of the most important of these were British journalists – Henry Nevinson and Hugh Martin – whose separate reports from Ireland had an important influence on British public opinion. Henry W. Nevinson was primarily a war correspondent who covered conflicts across the globe, working

refused to be frightened, or hunted away from his work reporting on the British terror campaign in the south and the west of the country. Journalists came from everywhere and from all sides. We set a particular value on the Europeans because they represented a part of the world where we hoped to get a hearing at international level – and where there were fewer other ways of making valuable contacts than, for example, the United States or Britain. We scanned newspapers for any indications of our success or failure in sending our message out to the world. When *Le Matin* (Paris) recorded that 'They (the British) are allowing the struggle between England and Ireland to transform itself into a moral conflict between England and civilization' (2 September 1920), this I remember as one of the signs that our efforts were bearing fruit.

Mr F.T.F. Dumont was the American consul in Dublin. He lived in the Shelbourne Hotel, in a suite overlooking St Stephen's Green. I frequently ran across the Green to Mr Dumont with every particle of news that came my way. He was significantly trusted and respected, a charming and hospitable man, who always included me when he asked Mrs Green to dine with him and his wife. Mrs Dumont went by the pet name 'Little Dear' and she invited me to use it; but the effort to do so made me very shy in her presence. Little Dear was as sensitive to Dublin fleas as the devil to holy water. She was the only person I knew in my life who could discuss these creatures with the whole world as her horizon. Dublin fleas, like Irish racehorses, were second to none, she exclaimed.

Another near neighbour on the Green was the writer and activist Dorothy Macardle, who lived in the top flat over Maud Gonne

---

for the leading liberal newspapers of the day, notably the *Daily Chronicle, Manchester Guardian* and *Daily News*. Hugh Martin worked mainly for *The Daily News*. In late 1920 he was reporting on the activities of the Black and Tans, travelling the country to investigate atrocities and writing articles, primarily using the testimony of local witnesses as source material, and rarely engaging with the official accounts. Martin was harassed and threatened by the Crown forces in Ireland, and denounced by some in Britain for his Irish reportage. His journalism played an important role in exposing British atrocities at this time. Hugh Martin gathered his reports from this period in Ireland into a book, *Insurrection in Ireland* (1921).

MacBride's house. One morning I saw a cloud of papers carried on the wind. The papers were all over the street after a Crown force raiding party threw Dorothy's manuscript out of her window. Her friends helped to recover as many pages as they could, but it was a muddy morning and soon there were wheel tracks across most of what we collected. Forever after, until she died, Dorothy lamented this particular literary work. She always thought of it as the best thing she had written. Nonetheless, she continued to write books, including *The Irish Republic* (1937), her classic history of the Irish revolution and her most famous work. Dorothy was an English teacher, always eager to help, very intelligent, courageous and sensitive. She could also be critical when it was called for, although this tendency was tempered by a fun-loving nature and a delightful laugh. Dorothy often accompanied Maud Gonne MacBride and Mrs Despard when they followed the Black and Tans, or soldiers, into towns where houses were burned down and people evicted. Dorothy was then about thirty-five, her companions in their fifties and seventies. The British dreaded their opinion and their pens as much, if not more, than an IRA column in the field.

In jail afterwards Dorothy told us about one of her missions. One day she found Maud Gonne MacBride (widely known as Madame) waiting for her return. Madame had an urgent job for Dorothy, and explained that she had been asked to intervene in an effort to save a young Irish man whose execution was imminent. This young man had been sentenced for a crime he had not committed and was not, to my recollection, even an IRA man. Madame thrust a number of documents into Dorothy's hands and told her – 'You have half an hour to catch the boat train. You will be in London in the morning. I have written to Mrs Asquith, to tell her to expect you.' Margo Asquith was the wife of H.H. Asquith, the Liberal politician and former PM of Great Britain. He was routed out in 1916 by David Lloyd George, who replaced him in the top job. Asquith and Lloyd George, although members of the same party, were bitter political rivals.

There was barely time to be briefed and to catch the boat. Next morning Dorothy arrived in London with the feeling that she had not had time to make the most of herself – her clothes were still those in which she had been bicycling the day before. She presented herself at the Asquith house and had scarcely time to prepare for the meeting when the famous Margo swept down a magnificent staircase to greet her. Margo's hands were clasped as she 'swam' towards Dorothy and took her hands in a gesture of sympathy. 'Are you the poor boy's mother,' she asked breathlessly, drawing Dorothy into an office. The ground had been very well prepared from Dublin and in the next few days Dorothy had a ringside seat to observe the brutal precision and effectiveness of top-level British scheming, when one politician gets a really good chance to attack and damage their political rival. The efficiency of Mrs Asquith's attack on Lloyd George amazed Dorothy. From the moment the campaign was launched until a couple of days later, when the young man was reprieved on the eve of this execution, Dorothy was a most interested spectator of the tactics used to cause trouble for Lloyd George.

When all was over, and her mission successful, Dorothy made a last call to thank Margo Asquith. They were saying farewell in the hall when Margot drew Dorothy to a corner and whispered to her – 'Now it is all over, the sentence reprieved and you have got what you wanted, just tell me one thing – was the young man really innocent?'

Bodenstown to Leitrim

THE NEW and terrible ruse in which the wings of freedom would soon be tangled was an unnoticed cloud on our horizon in June 1920, when all the young Republicans in the organized ranks set out on the annual pilgrimage to reassert the Republican principles of Wolfe Tone in Bodenstown Churchyard. It was a foolhardy undertaking to go marching heart and soul for the Republic, unarmed, in the middle of a long summer day, and into a position directly between the British military base at the Curragh and Macready's headquarters at Kingsbridge.* Dáil Éireann was proclaimed at the time and Dublin was under curfew; the Black and Tans had been rampant for three months; the Volunteers had burned several hundred police barracks. The way to prison might start around the next corner for any of us. That was the setting in which the special trains crowded up for

---

* Sir Cecil Frederick Nevil Macready (1862–1946), was a British army officer who was appointed general officer commanding in Ireland by the Prime Minister, Lloyd George, in 1920. He was the last British officer to hold this post. Macready superintended the evacuation of British forces, following the Anglo–Irish treaty in December 1921. He was made a baronet when he retired from the British army in 1923.

144

the journey from Dublin to Sallins, and from other places around the country. By the end of the day hundreds had reason to thank God because they were still free and that the high hedges and deep meadows of Kildare had provided salvation.

In spite of its serious national purpose Bodenstown always was, and remains, a recognized summer outing for anyone who wishes to attend. In our revolutionary times it had its own committee and semi-independent organization – backed by Sinn Féin and the Volunteers. The event followed a recognized routine – inherited from the 'old guard' of the Invincibles* by Arthur Griffith, Willie Rooney† and their contemporaries – who gave the event its present form at the end of the nineteenth century. The groups and individuals who went there were various, including family parties. Excursion trains and bicycles brought the crowds of long ago. Now the whole long street of Sallins fills with buses from north, south, east and west. The marching column can be up to two miles long, and many people will also stroll alongside, or take shortcuts, to the place where Wolfe Tone lies close under the wall of the ruined ancient church.

In 1920 I rode down with the Cumann na mBan cycling corps. It was our first big day out. We left our bicycles at Sallins and fell in for the march to the cemetery. The main body, where I was, never got there, and I am not aware that any graveside ceremony was held.

---

* The Irish National Invincibles were a secret society within the IRB between 1881–3, set up as an assassination squad, with a mission to kill the figureheads of the British establishment in Ireland. Their most notorious strike came to be known as the Phoenix Park killings. On 6 May 1882 Lord Frederick Cavendish, the newly arrived Chief Secretary for Ireland, and Thomas Burke, the Permanent Under Secretary, were walking in the Phoenix Park near the Viceregal Lodge when they were stabbed to death by members of the Invincibles.

† Willie Rooney (1873–1901) was a nationalist, journalist, political thinker and close associate of Arthur Griffith. Griffith was the editor of *The United Irishman*, launched in 1899, and Rooney – using up to twelve pseudonyms – wrote most of the paper's articles. The two men worked together to develop the basis of what would later become Sinn Féin policy. Willie Rooney died at the age of twenty-seven from tuberculosis. Arthur Griffith was deeply affected by the loss of his close intellectual associate and continued to pay homage to Rooney long after his untimely death. W.B. Yeats dedicated the 1908 edition of *Cathleen Ni Houlihan* to the memory of Willie Rooney.

Some scout or belated message must have reached the Curragh while we were on our way.

The first I knew of any departure from the usual programme was when our marching column wheeled left into a field, when its head was within 100 yards of the cemetery. We continued marching in formation until we were halted close beside a very high hedge, which ran down one side of a large field sloping downwards. Then an aeroplane, swooping low, roared down to disperse us with a sudden explosion of noise and wind. We were too proud to duck but I fully expected my head to go bouncing down the field in no time! When the plane came to the head of our column, on the lower ground, it was below my eye level, and the men threw themselves aside from its path. We went back to Dublin chastened, by the same route we had marched triumphantly earlier in the day. Things were very different for those who narrowly avoided being trapped in the graveyard. They had to filter back home as best they could, some journeys taking three or four days.

I got my first look at Belfast, and the people we in Bodenstown had hoped to conciliate, when I passed through very shortly afterwards. For her summer holiday in 1920 Mrs Green went in early July to stay with her friends Sydney and Gertrude Parry, at Cushendun, County Antrim. Mrs Parry was formerly Gertrude Bannister, cousin to Roger Casement. Mrs Green and Mrs Parry worked together to support Casement during his trial in London following the 1916 Rising and there was a very close friendship between them. For Tom Casement, who was with us, it was probably the first visit to Antrim for many years, when he had been living away in Africa. I was included in the house party because Mrs Green intended to continue her writing during July. Afterwards, I planned to go on holiday myself and leave her behind at Cushendun.

We came to lovely Cushendun by train from Dublin. Belfast was be-flagged for the Twelfth of July and in strange contrast to the atmosphere at Bodenstown, a fortnight earlier. While the train waited on the embankment, I observed a sea of Union Jacks flying over Sandy

Row. They were extended by a strong breeze and seemed nearly all to be the same size, on the same height of pole, flying from little chimneys on miserable, small houses. The flags were chosen for size so that each almost touched its neighbour. No demonstration by individual human beings could have produced such striking, and, it seemed it me, disconcerting unanimity.

The Twelfth that year passed off quietly. The short absence of fury may have been due to the municipal elections going on at the same time. It is believed that the dreadful pogrom – July 19 to 22 – was set off when the results of the election became known. It was the first proportional representation election,* and there were many Republican gains, including Derry. It was held that Edward Carson gave the hint for what was to come when he said at a meeting that he was 'sick of words without action'. The Parrys must have hidden the newspapers that recorded nineteen deaths, the burning of houses, and thousands of Catholic families driven from their homes. We were sixty or seventy miles away from Belfast and I presume the elders of the household must have decided not speak about the pogroms before either their maids, or before me. The Parry's maids and I were the only Catholics in the household, and the neighbours who came to visit were all, like the Parrys, liberally-minded Protestant Irish. It was touching, and a lovely experience for me to be among Roger Casement's friends. Not all of them went the whole way with him, to the point of insurrection. But they were a harmonious society; people who were Irish, talked about Ireland and continued to be, I believe, at least Home Rulers.

Something from that holiday that does stay in my mind is the Cushendall Regatta, and how the people of contrasting allegiance held onto their friendship. It was not in Tom Casement's nature to

---

* The Proportional Representation Society of Ireland was founded in Dublin on 20 April 1911. The electoral system endorsed by the Society was proportional representation (PR), combining the single transferable vote (STV), a quota-counting method and multi-member constituencies, as opposed to the 'first past the post' system. The PR system was promoted by Arthur Griffith and Sinn Féin adopted PR/STV as official policy. PR was first tested in a local election in Sligo in 1919 and introduced country-wide for the local elections in 1920.

stay quiet for long. One day he announced that we were all too dull and serious. He offered to train a ladies' rowing crew to represent Cushendun and suggested that we challenge the ladies of Cushendall to a boat race. Tom picked three local girls for our team and gave me the fourth oar. We did all the training we could in the Parrys' rowboat before the big day. Tom was our coxswain. My fellow team-mates were Antrim girls who had lived with the sea, and were as strongly Republican as I was myself. On the day of the regatta, we hoisted our tricolour and pulled out into the bay. Cushendall came out shortly afterwards with their Union Jack in the stern. I learned for the first time what really hard rowing can be like if one is determined to win or die. In the end we won easily. The nice Orange ladies caught crabs with shrieks of laughter and afterwards the day ended in good spirits with a pleasant tea party at the Parrys'.

In my plentiful free time, I was out and about in the Glens of Antrim. The Parrys' house was on a golden strand; the sea was the legendary Sea of Moyle, which seemed always restless. It was a glorious summer. The sun fell softly on Scotland or glittered hard on the narrow sea; it warmed us in the shelter of Mrs Parry's well-loved garden, and in the evenings sharp cut the outline of the mountains behind us. When my own holiday time came, I set out on my bicycle to ride the whole coast of the North, on my way ultimately to organize County Leitrim for Cumann na mBan. There was no sign of disturbance until I was in Derry for a night, when I walked about the city, and visited the walls. At one point I stopped by a small, intent crowd, gathered around a fire. I found they were burning Éamon de Valera in effigy, but without much exuberance. It was not, I deduced, a great or frenetic occasion – more like a street corner incident, which was not that unusual. As I went on towards the hotel something seemed to tell me that people were behind their doors, listening and observing. There was a distinct lack of well-being in the city. As the years went on I got to know Mr O'Kane, the proprietor of the hotel where I was staying on that occasion. He spoke to me that evening and I understood that he had been watching for my return with a little apprehension.

When I reached Leitrim I was soon very busy. It was easy in those days to recruit for Cumann na mBan. Branches were quickly started and arrangements made for first-aid classes, instructions for the care and safety of arms dumps, allocation of people for dispatch work, and intelligence – all these were routine. John Mitchell, in command of the Leitrim Volunteers, helped me with this work, but it was with some reserve in his mind. 'Do you expect me to trust these girls with the secrets of the IRA,' he asked. He then informed me that his men were very carefully sifted before they were accepted into the organization, and that they had to take a declaration. I brought this complaint back to Dublin. At the annual convention that autumn we ordered all of our members to take a declaration of secrecy regarding Cumann na mBan and IRA affairs. It read: 'I pledge myself to support, and to defend to the best of my ability, the Irish Republic, and to uphold the aims and objectives of Cumann na mBan, and to keep strictly secret all matters relating to Cumann na mBan and the IRA.'

Trips to Tipp

I HEARD SHOTS and looked over my shoulder, as I hurried on some afternoon business for my employer, moving northwards on Upper O'Connell Street. Shots were nothing strange in Dublin at the time; those I heard came from around the corner in Talbot Street. It was 14 October 1920 when Seán Treacy, ex-OC Third Tipperary Brigade, was shot and killed by British forces – the most important man on our side to fall in action since 1916. Treacy, along with Seán Hogan, Dan Breen and Seamus Robinson, were the men behind deeds that electrified the nation. On their own initiative they took military action at Soloheadbeg in Tipperary on the day Dáil Éireann met for the first time in 1919. Following on that they rescued Hogan, who had been captured, from a train at Knocklong. Seán Treacy took part in the attempt to shoot the Viceroy, Lord French, in November of the same year. On 11 October 1920 Treacy and Breen were holed up in a safe house in Drumcondra; they were discovered there by British forces and although the house was surrounded, they fought a gun battle and escaped from the home of Professor Carolan, who was sheltering them. The professor was put up against a wall and shot dead.

Seán Treacy's funeral in Kilfeacle Cemetery, County Tipperary was followed by the murder of the Dwyer boys at Ballydavid, and by an enhanced reign of terror by the British in County Tipperary. Mrs Green, I believe acting for the Dáil publicity department, released me to go and talk to the people on the spot, and report on what had happened. This was the first of many such assignments I conducted in the country. I set off, bringing my bicycle, and went by train to Limerick Junction. It was heartening to see the Galtee Mountains rise in the distance and, as we came closer, to watch out for the haunting Rock of Cashel, high up in the landscape.

In Tipperary town I called, following instructions, on Alice and Kate Ryan* of Cumann na mBan. I found myself disposed of quickly and went on my way, wondering why nobody wanted to chat. It was for my sake and their own, but I did not understand why until much later. These women were under siege and it would not be long before the Ryan sisters' café was closed by military order. In those days there were very few houses that were not friendly – but even friends can make mistakes. The Ryan sisters were paying the price for their close friendship with Seán Treacy; to go near them was akin to putting yourself almost in the firing line, and, in my case, your mission in jeopardy. Business had obviously receded from their counter; loss and gain were now reckoned in different values, those of life and liberty. A span of years would pass before a stranger could enter most country towns and knock at a Republican door, without being 'reported' by touts and sleuths. I took the road indicated by the Ryan sisters and rode on thoughtfully by the river to Bansha. The autumn sun was shining on a lovely scene – the dry road under a free bicycle, the streams and the woods – up to the moment when I turned right into the mouth of Aherlow. This was to be the last hour of my apprenticeship; at twenty-seven, I was clearly a slow developer.

---

* Further information regarding the activities of Kate Lynch (*née* Ryan) and Alice Ryan can be found in the Military Service Pensions Collection at MSP34REF64246 Kate Lynch.pdf and MSP34REF64207 Alice Ryan.pdf.

I found Ballydavid and Dwyer's small house – long, low, white-washed and old, with a thatch that might be suspected of holding pikes, or perhaps an old muzzleloader. The house was positioned on the far side of a very large, square haggard, with grass growing, free, fresh and peaceful; but places tell no tales, once the blood is soaked into the earth. Soon I was sitting by a wide hearth, talking with the mother and sister of Frank and Edward Dwyer – Volunteers who had closed the local school on the day of Seán Treacy's funeral. The women no longer had any secrets and they showed no fear. 'My two boys, who worked our farm, are gone without reason or cause. They were shot down before my eyes, but let it be so, we will bear it for Ireland,' said Mrs Dwyer. 'Tell me how it happened,' I asked, and wrote down the story as she and her daughter Kate told it to me.

On the night in question the father of the family, who was very old, blind and deaf, was in his deep feather bed in the room off the kitchen. The two Dwyer boys had gone to the room below the entrance door, and the women were barefooted and ready for bed. They were saying the rosary by the dying fire when shots crashed through the kitchen window. Although the women were unhurt, the house was divided by rifle fire, and they could not move from where they were. They heard the door burst in, the rush of soldiers to the boys' room, followed by a struggle. Then the soldiers came into the kitchen. They aimed their rifles through the dresser and the wooden wall of the lower room, but luckily the old man, deep in his bed, was unhurt. It is on the record that Frank and Edward Dwyer were bayonetted, beaten and shot dead in the presence of their sister Kate. But what stayed in my mind forever after was the mother's story, and I imagine for the rest of her life too. Mrs Dwyer ran first to the old man and found him unhurt. Then she hurried to the outside door to wave to her boys before they would be taken away as prisoners. She had her hands round her eyes to help her vision to the far side of the haggard, where she could see dim figures mounting the lorry. It was then that Mrs Dwyer felt warm blood under her foot and found Kate sobbing over the boys, dying and dead on the grass by the door.

The next time Mrs Green lent me out again to go back to Tipperary, the adventure started in Kingsbridge railway station. When I arrived there for the early morning train, the Auxiliaries, who arrived around the same time as the Black and Tans, were in possession of the platform. They were an ascendency corps – reckless, cruel and brave. I was pushed into a group of intending passengers and told to stay there. An officer, gesturing with his revolver, beckoned us two at a time towards window seats in the corridor train. His men then got in to fill the centre seats. We were placed to disguise the presence of the Auxiliaries, and to be their sand bags. I realized, with considerable satisfaction, that the Crown forces anticipated an ambush anywhere and at any time. It was their tribute to the fighting men of IRA. On the train journey I tried to follow what the Auxiliaries were saying; it was difficult initially to tune into their accents and quick speech. But after a while they seemed to forget that even sandbags, such as we were, sometimes have ears!

These ex-army officers, derelicts from the war for small nations, discussed the job in Ireland they had volunteered for; they compared to it to other employments that were open to men with their special talents. The oil industry in the Middle East offered opportunities – the working hours were regular, the danger less. But this Irish job was better paid than anything they could hope for outside it. On the other hand, they had no rest or quiet. They discussed the Republican censorship of letters. The soldiers could no longer use the normal post for fear that their people in England would be traced. Things happened, which disturbed and frightened their own families. A few of them produced home letters and spoke of threats of reprisals in England, against some among them whose detrimental conduct in Ireland had been noted. They complained too about questions and answers in Westminster regarding their behaviour, and reports in the newspapers. For me, listening quietly, it was all lovely evidence of the success of our publicity department.

When I left the train, I was bursting with news. I reported to Cumann na mBan in McCarthy's in Thurles. On this return trip to

Tipperary, I was to find out all I could about the Crown forces murder gang operating from Thurles. I pushed my bicycle into the highlands towards Upperchurch and came to Gleesons' of Moher – a small house, looking down from a height on the byroad. It was one of five homes raided by the same party of British forces on the night of 25 October 1920. The character I remember best from my investigations was Willie Gleeson, known locally as 'Black Willie'. He was the father in a family of Volunteers, with one daughter at home. Willie was a flaming, hot-spirited man – dark, thin, and straight as a ramrod but, to my eyes then, very old; Willie's wife, Mary, and their daughter, Mary Agnes, were staunch women, while the surviving boys of the house, John and Tom, were away with the IRA.

When Black Willie opened his door to the Black and Tans on the night of 25 October, the leader of the squad explained that they had come to shoot somebody, and if there was no young man at home, Black Willie would do. The soldiers laid hands on the old man to bring him out. But the two women, Mary and Mary Agnes, fought with them, trying to hold Black Willie within the house. All this was going on when young Willie, the third son of the house, who was a consumptive and very ill, came in from the back. 'If you must shoot somebody, take me and leave my father,' he told them. The Black and Tans readily agreed to that. But now the two women and the father put up a fight to hold young Willie. The pale and wasted youth put their hands away from his body and told his family to stand back. Young Willie left the house with the Tans, where they immediately shot him dead and left his body on the doorstep. In this house, the death of a son was in the inevitable setting of the long fight for freedom for the nation. The wrongs against Ireland burned in these people, unquenchably. And, there was never a week but the fire was re-fuelled in those days.

The next call that I made in connection with the events of 25 October was to Kinnanes' home. This house was well known to Dan Breen and his comrades; they had often found shelter there. Kinnanes' had a yard sloping down from the house, and a gate at the gable end that led to the farm. The Kinnane women showed me the spot in the yard where the sons of the house, James and Jerome, were put kneeling, to be shot by the Black and Tans. But the two lads made a burst for freedom and got away over the barred gate and into a field of turnips, which gave them some cover. Jerome was wounded but neither of the boys were caught. On the same night the Crown gang killed Michael Ryan of Curraghduff. He was a Justice of the Republican Court and was suffering from pneumonia. His sister told me that when she opened the door to Black and Tans, she tried to explain that her brother was very ill in bed. They assured her that they would not bring him outside. They went to his room and shot him dead where he lay, in his bed upstairs.

The next assignment that brought me back to Tipperary was when I was sent as a guide to Mrs Ethel Snowden, wife of the prominent British Labour politician. Mrs Snowden came to Ireland to find out for herself what was happening in the country. I was more than ready to show her. Ethel was a beautiful and charming woman, a pink and white blonde, then in her fortieth year. She was also a former actress, an executive member of the Fabian Society and a member of the National Union of Women's Suffrage Societies. I brought Ethel Snowden along to catch the morning train at Kingsbridge but this time, alas, there were no Auxiliaries there to make sand bags of us. That scenario would have been more eloquent than anything I could tell her. We travelled to Limerick Junction and onwards to Willie Gleeson's house. Black Willie opened the door and was looking down on us, ready to welcome, until I opened my mouth. 'I have brought an English woman …' I began, but was not allowed to finish my sentence. The old man started to curse the English, and I began to fear that he would never run out of words. Black Willie recounted their whole history in Ireland, never failing in his breath. His own experiences, and that of his people, seemed to take an eternity of time before it emptied the prodigious storehouse of his memory, and the history of over 700 years. Because Ethel Snowden was an innocent party, and in my care, I wanted to put a halt to Willie Gleeson's history lesson; but I never succeeded in finishing my first sentence! Apart from my concern for Mrs Snowden, I thoroughly enjoyed the spirit of Black Willie.

Ethel Snowden somehow managed to get past the door and into the house. When she was within distance of the kitchen, she hurled her arms on the table, and buried her head in them. There she lay in expressive silence until Black Willie finally ran out of words. When she got her chance to finally speak, Ethel told the old man about her purpose in coming to Ireland, of her horror of what had happened to his family and of her intention to do what she could to halt the British terror. She said that English people did not know of the things being done in their name and it was her intention to publicize the campaign of terror being waged in Ireland, when she returned to London. I cannot say that Black Willie believed what Ethel Snowden said but, nonetheless, we parted friends, I think in fair order, and perhaps with the beginning of mutual understanding. He was an unforgettable old man, and she a most remarkable lady.

In later days of trial and agony for the Republican cause, I often wished that our own leading men could have met Black Willie, or somehow gained an understanding of the spirit in which he, and men and women like him, stood for victory or death in Ireland. I have no doubt that he could have recited the chapters of Irish compromise as readily as those of English domination. I never met Black Willie Gleeson or Mrs Snowden again after that unforgettable day, but the encounter remains lodged as an extraordinary scene in my memory.

Grand and splendid people came to Dublin from America and England, to see what was going on. They came in a steady trickle and liked to stay at the Standard Hotel in Harcourt Street, or one of the cheaper hotels nearby. It was a place where leading Quakers, loyal Irish men and women, who stood apart from the fighting war, were available for discourse – J.H. Webb, H.C. Neil-Watson, James Douglas and Rose Jacob. Harcourt Street was within easy reach too, of Hanna Sheehy-Skeffington, Mrs Charlotte Despard and Molly Childers, who all had wide connections abroad.

Mrs Christy and Mrs Mary MacWhorter, representatives of the Women's Alliance of the Ancient Order of Hibernians of America – people of immense influence amongst Irish Americans – were welcome and cherished visitors, who came and stayed as long and as often as they could. I can see them both in my mind's eye still, standing together, when the steps of the Standard Hotel came direct to the street. These women missed nothing and the news they brought home went far and wide in the United States. I have warm memories too of the Women's League for Peace and Freedom – an English organization, which Mrs Despard inspired – although I did hear her complaining later that she found 'too much peace and too little freedom' in their attitudes towards us in their propaganda. This was intended to be kindly criticism. She liked and welcomed them, as we all did.

I have never ceased to admire the courage and integrity of men and women who are prepared to follow the soldiers of their own nation to the scenes of ugly deeds, in order to investigate for themselves at ground level. Ireland must never forget the English women and men, the churchmen and the journalists, who tried so hard to end the old conflict. It took a lot of strength of character and courage, when their own government was doing such things as the English were doing in Ireland, to follow the stories, report back and make trouble at home. These welcome visitors undoubtedly contributed to the creation of a formidable body of public opinion in England, calling for peace in Ireland.

A Spy and a Mystery Man

THE 1920 Cumann na mBan Convention was held in October in a hall lent to us in the Whitefriar Street of Dublin area, in utmost secrecy. Before we slipped away, in ones and twos at the end, an enquiry from the IRA was read out. They wanted to know the standing in our organization of a young woman wearing our uniform and circulating in the North Dublin-Meath area, who had turned up at some private IRA meetings. We were ordered to look out for this woman; our HQ wanted to know more about her. I had the answer they were looking for because I had met the lady in question, shortly after the sacking of Balbriggan on 20 September.*

---

* On the night of 20 September 1920, the town of Balbriggan, north of Dublin, was sacked by British forces. It started when an RIC District Inspector, Peter Burke from Galway and his brother (an RIC sergeant) were shot by members of the IRA. Peter Burke was killed. What followed proved to be disastrous for the town of Balbriggan, and for the British image internationally. Shortly after midnight lorries carrying Black and Tans and RIC men came from a nearby depot and began a frenzy of burning, looting, shooting and torture in the town. Four pubs, twenty houses and a large factory were destroyed. The British forces tortured known Republicans and murdered two of them. Images of the burnt-out town went around the world and caused international outrage.

Commandant Louie Kennedy* decided to investigate in person. She travelled in the sidecar of Doreen Synge's† motorbike, armed with a revolver. I was sent to scout separately, to locate the accused. Our mission failed that day, but I came on our suspect very soon afterwards. I invited her to meet me in Dublin – 'to discuss the distribution of relief after the Balbriggan disaster'. I guessed that would bring her in, and it did. On the evening of 30 October – when everyone in Ireland was following the tragic and eventful story of Terence MacSwiney's funeral – we pounced on our spy at Mrs Green's doorstep, and pushed her into a cab, provided for the purpose. I remember the long drive, and then being in the basement of Cullenswood House, Ranelagh, where St Enda's, Padraig Pearse's school, was originally located, before the move to Rathfarnham. The blindfolded prisoner was sitting on a bench. The person I remember best, as being present at the trial, was Paddy Sheehan, of Austin Stack's office. He ordered that the prisoner be put on the mailboat the next morning. Somebody produced 'civvies' in exchange for the uniform the spy was wearing. IRA Headquarters did not sanction the execution of female spies, as it did when male spies were uncovered.

Three months later, on a Sunday morning in January 1921, I was riding aimlessly on my bicycle when I came upon a small group of people who were looking through the closed gates of the same Cullenswood House. One or two military lorries were on the short avenue inside. I heard the crash of glass and, momentarily, saw rifle butts, which were being used from inside the house to knock out the

---

* Louie Kennedy, also known as Margaret or Lou Kennedy (1892–1966), was an officer in Cumann na mBan who served in the Jameson Distillery outpost in the Rising in 1916, and was afterwards detained in Kilmainham Jail and Richmond Barracks. She became a Cumann na mBan captain in 1920 and later rose to the rank of commandant. In later years she was appointed to Seanad Éireann and served as senator from 1938 to 1948.

† Doreen Hamilton Synge (1893–1988) (married name: Doreen Hamilton Farrington Synge) was the daughter of Alexander Hamilton Synge of Glanmore Castle, Wicklow. During World War I Doreen was an ambulance driver in the Women's Voluntary Aid detachment in France and on her return to Ireland she joined Cumann na mBan. Doreen owned a motorcycle and sidecar, which she used for her work with the Republican forces.

window frames. Soldiers on the roof used pickaxes to break the slates – sent scattering down to mix with glass and broken timber on the ground outside. They worked away soberly, solemnly and diligently under the morning sun, and to the sound of church bells across the otherwise normal city. Presently a soldier came out on the rafters with a red, white and blue flag, setting it up in some improvised way. A young man was beside me, pressing on the barred gate. 'I'll race you for that flag,' I said. 'Agreed,' said he.

The soldiers were now coming out of the house and settling themselves, each man with his rifle, on the benches in the lorry. At the first move to open the gates, we both squeezed through and ran into the house. We rushed past the last relics of Pearse's school to survive in the building. The mottoes of the ancient Fianna were painted around the top of the walls. *Purity in our hearts. Strength in our arms. Truth on our lips.*

We scrambled through, or over, plaster and rubble, which filled the whole hall. Where the stairs had been, we clambered up the jagged edges protruding from the wall. At the top of the house the landing remained. We hurled ourselves against a closed door until our shoulders burst it open. On the roof ridge outside, the pair of us had the flag down before the lorries moved away. It was, we discovered, in fact a French tricolour, which the raiding party had found in one of the flats in the house. The soldiers in the departing lorries only laughed at us; one or two raised their rifles, but they did so without anger. Their attitude was that of men who had carried out an order and had no further interest. My comrade on that occasion turned out to be Paddy McGrath.* Death by hanging was in store for him.

The surprising thing about Cullenswood house is not that it was wrecked in the end but that it had survived so long.

---

* Paddy McGrath (1894–1940) was a 1916 and War of Independence veteran who was involved in the IRA 1938–9 bombing campaign in England. In 1939, following his release from prison, he was a party to a shootout with the Irish Special Branch, when two members of the force were shot dead. McGrath and Thomas Harte were arrested, tried by a military court and sentenced to death. The executions of Paddy McGrath and his young comrade in September 1940 were the first carried out in the twenty-six counties, following the Civil War executions of the Free State government.

On the question of spies, suspected or otherwise, I also came to know a well-known Englishman, who came over to us from the other side. One evening in No. 90 Mrs Green called me to her study and introduced me to Mr John Chartres.* She told me that he was anxious to see something of life in Dublin and would be grateful if I could sometimes take him with me when I went out in the evenings. After that, John Chartres called for me whenever I was ready to take him on my adventures. He was an entertaining man, who expressed an enthusiastic and, to my mind then, a sincere Republicanism. Chartres had been a higher civil servant in London and was probably twice my age, but that did not interfere with his delight to be in Dublin instead of London, and to be in search of experience from the angle of the underdog. John Chartres spoke freely about himself and his wife, the writer Anna Vivanti, who was apparently as ardent in her support for our cause as he was. Prior to being a civil servant for the Crown, he worked in indexing and records for the London *Times*; this made him an extremely well-informed companion.

John Chartres has been described as 'the mystery man' on our side at the time of the London negotiations, which resulted in the infamous Treaty. He was greatly trusted by Michael Collins and was the legal advisor to our delegation on Constitutional Law. For some, a faint cloud of suspicion hangs over him. But so far as I am aware people always spoke well of him, and when I knew him, I was inclined to take him at face value. I recall too that John Chartres tried hard to reconcile the differences that arose in 1922, and that must always stand in his favour

---

* John Smith Chartres (1862–1927) was a lawyer, civil servant and diplomat. Born to Irish parents, he lived for periods in Ireland as a child but after his father's death the family settled in England. Chartres was the first head of *The Times*'s intelligence (news research, indexing and reference) department from 1904–14. Michael Collins recruited Chartres as an informer in 1918. To augment his role as a spy, Chartres obtained a transfer to Ireland as a section chief to the Ministry of Labour Irish branch. In 1921 he retired from the British civil service to become the Republican consul to Berlin. Just months later he was appointed second secretary to the Irish Treaty delegation. Accusations have been made that John Chartres was in fact a British agent. However, to date no definitive evidence has emerged to substantiate this allegation.

Wicklow and Local Bodies

REPUBLICAN IRELAND started in the rural districts to the north of Dublin, at the city boundary. The men of Swords and Ashford had set the standards there. But South County Dublin had traditionally returned a Unionist to parliament and Sinn Féin had to work very hard to win a seat there for George Gavan Duffy in 1918. East Wicklow was not much different. From the IRA point of view, it was not a suitable fighting area. The people in the mountains were too scattered and too poor to support a column of men. There were too many enemies on the richer lands, where the main road ran without so much as a trench until you got to Jack White's crossroads, about forty miles out from Dublin.

It may have been Seán Etchingham who asked me to find one or more houses in Wicklow, between Devereux at the Glen of the Downs and Christy Byrne's of Ballykillavane, Glenealy, where people might handle our dispatches going north and south on the main road. The weak point was around Newtownmountkennedy – a place that had been badly smashed in the 1798 Rebellion, and since then was well planted. The best of our dispatch work was done by Guard White on the Dublin–Wexford passenger train. The road system was only seen as supplementary to his excellent service; but in the event of a railway breakdown, we would need the alternative route.

Wicklow's two TDs were ministers in the government. One of these, Robert Barton, founder of the Land Bank, was sentenced to three years' penal servitude for a seditious speech in March 1920 and spent the rest of the period in Parkhurst prison. His sister, Dulcibella Barton, who I knew from childhood, was county secretary to Sinn Féin and she was punctilious and brave in the public duties that then fell to her. Their home, Glendalough House in Annamoe, was on the route from all parts of the south, which IRA officers took when travelling to Dublin. 'Daa', as Dulcibella was fondly known, made sure that the men who worked the farm, and the shepherd on the mountain behind, were vigilant in looking after the safety of 'visitors' passing through the house. The Bartons were among the very few of my comrades whose friendship dated from my childhood days. The duties that brought me to Glendalough House were always very welcome.

If Daa Barton had her way the Republic would have functioned far better than it did in Wicklow. I found her always very impatient with Christy Byrne, the then Chairman of the County Council. I never could help being fond of Christy, who was not made to be a soldier. Under the circumstances he was giving all he had. He started life, long before my time, with a good inheritance – a farm and auction-eering business – and a great love of reading and everything Irish. Mrs Byrne was of equal social standing and had the same tastes. But she had much more ability than her husband, with twice the fire in her belly. She was an old member of Cumann na mBan – a fine-looking, tall, dark and slender woman – with a soft voice and great charm. The Byrnes lived in a very old thatched cottage with large rooms and many, many books. Thistles and briars from their neglected farm pushed over the wall of the flower garden. The guard on the Wexford train threw out the morning papers as he passed. Ballykillavane had been a stopping place for the Gaels of Wicklow and Wexford for probably twenty years before I knew it. Between the newspapers and the constant traffic of people, there was nothing that Christy Byrne did not know about. Despite Dulcibella Barton's understandable irritation with Christy's working methods, in his own inimitable way he nurtured the revolution.

A favourite stop of mine in Wicklow was a corner shop in Arklow town, where the Wexford road turned up Main Street. There, an elderly woman, Maria Curran, and her silent brother John, sold everything that a fisherman or his family might want – from groceries to ropes, from rosary beads to ballads, from kettle and cans to plug tobacco and sweets. They always had the latest issue of seditious literature. When I called there, they loved to get all my news, and I loved to check up on theirs. Maria Curran and Mary Hoyne, of Hoyne's Hotel, were nominated by Sinn Féin and duly elected in the local government elections of 1920. It was difficult at that time for any courageous and public-spirited man to preserve his liberty while performing civic duties for the Republic. The good side of this was that hundreds of women had brief experience of public life in many parts of the county. This was not confined to Sinn Féin; various other interests nominated women for election in 1920. Arklow Urban Council was elected on 2 February and Maria Curran was made chairman. At the next meeting on 19 March, the council gave its allegiance to Dáil Éireann and broke the connection with the British Local Government Board. Arklow claimed to have been the first council to declare for the Republic.

Those were the days when it was an adventure to pay rates and taxes to the Republic. Although the money was not British money, having previously been extracted from the Irish people in taxation (and gross over-taxation), the British nonetheless withheld the grants for local government from rebel councils. That meant that the maintenance of hospitals, workhouses, poor law relief, roads, street lighting, drainage, and all the other social services – including the responsibility for the wages of council employees – were thrown back on the few elected representatives who were able to stand their ground. I had no knowledge of what it meant to be a public representative in that charged atmosphere until one day, when I was chatting in Curran's shop, I overheard part of a conversation, when Maria broke off to talk to a man. He handed her money and she put it down her neck. Later Maria explained that she had to keep the rates separately from the shop takings, for fear she might get the monies mixed up before she had time to enter the local government payment in her records. This was my first insight into the workings of William Cosgrave's local government department.

No one begrudges the Volunteers the credit and glory they earned by their bravery in the War of Independence, or the inadequate pensions that were later awarded to them. But let one small voice, my own, be raised now to claim for all the silent services provided by Irish women and men in those revolutionary times some proportionate share of recognition. The number of people who lost their lives while engaged on civilian duties has never, to my knowledge, been reckoned, or honoured.

When we buried Maria Curran in May 1945, her niece, Mrs Kenny, allowed me to help in the search for and safeguarding of her papers from the 1920–1 period. We found material in all sorts of hiding places around the shop; these were subsequently given to the National Museum.

Unwelcome Visitors

THE PRINTED FORM, on which I had signed my name to the Republican oath, was on the table one day in Mrs Green's office when I answered the door.* On this occasion the raiders were wearing sneakers, and so came noiselessly. They took the tablecloth by its four corners and went away with everything that had been lying there. A few days later Mrs Green's papers were returned, but I never saw my oath form again. Shortly after this, there was another raid at No. 90 late at night; this time by uniformed Auxiliaries. Once again, I opened the door, this time in my nightgown. I was pushed backwards by the leader of the raiding party until my head hurt, pressed hard against the wall. He forced his revolver into my mouth. He was a man we came to know as 'Taylors' nephew' because of what happened the next time we came into contact with him. Meanwhile, my mouth was full of steel. 'We

---

* There were a number of Republican oaths but the one Máire Comerford refers to may be the official IRA oath. Volunteers took an Oath of Allegiance to Dáil Éireann and the Republic from the autumn of 1919, which read: 'I will support and defend the Irish Republic and the Government of Ireland, which is Dáil Éireann, against all enemies, foreign and domestic.'

know you. Your mother kept a school in Wexford. You are the bad one of the family,' he said. After the first few minutes this turned into an ordinary raid, and the usual scenario of men searching for papers.

Another raid at No. 90 took the form of a manhunt. The Auxiliaries rushed in, with drawn revolvers, shouting that they had been fired on. They were careful not to have any lights behind them when they went upstairs or to the garden door – but not beyond it. The Iveagh Gardens were out there, and 76 Harcourt Street backed onto the gardens, and some hundreds of private houses and hotels, any of which might have been sinister to them. There was a night too when the house was full of Crown forces and Mrs Green stood disdainfully at the head of the stairs, outside her bedroom door. She was motionless, her proud face ringed with slightly dishevelled white hair, her brocade gown falling to her feet, with hands clasped low in front of her. The fullness of figure, from which I quickly turned my eyes, was not due to corpulence but to a whole file of *The Irish Bulletin*, which she saved from capture that night.

Not long after this raid we were at a meeting of the Dáil Éireann lecture committee in Erskine Childers's home in Bushy Park Road when the man whose revolver had been thrust into my mouth previously walked into the room at the head of his squad. He told us half mockingly that he had not needed to knock at the door because when he was a boy his uncle, by the name of Taylor, had lived in the Childers's house. It was then we christened him 'Taylor's nephew'. He asked for our names, which were not forthcoming, as his eyes travelled from one to the other around our group. 'I know you,' he said to Mrs Green, whereupon, directing her remarks to me, she retorted – 'He knows us, even when we are dressed,' referring to the previous raid in No. 90, when 'Taylor's nephew' stuck his gun into my mouth, and we were both in our night attire.

I noticed one evening that Robert (Bob) Brennan looked very serious when he called to No. 90. Presently Mrs Green called for me and hastily dictated a letter, which, she informed me, was to have no address, introduction or signature: I was instructed to post the letter but not in a nearby pillarbox. The letter was for Sir John Simon MP, ex-Home Secretary and ex-Attorney General of England. I fancy that Mrs Green also wrote him a personal letter under separate cover. She was acquainted with Sir John through his first wife, then deceased, who was Mrs Green's niece, and a sister of Dr Dorothy Stopford,* who was one of the doctors who assisted the IRA during the War of Independence and the Civil War.

The contents of the letter to Sir John concerned a man called Alan Bell. The time was early 1920 and Bell, as Bob Brennan had explained, was a new type of British intelligence man. Bell had arrived in Dublin with the rank of resident magistrate. Information leaking from the Castle revealed that it was Bell's special assignment to break the secrets between the Dáil trustees and the banks, and to discover where the Republican money was deposited. The 'Star Chamber' clause of the Crimes Act was put into operation and bank managers received a command to appear before a secret Commission of Enquiry set up by Dublin Castle.† This command document was signed by Alan Bell. A few days after I had posted the anonymous letter to Sir John Simon, Alan Bell was pulled off a Dublin tram and shot dead in the street. When Mrs Green read the news in the evening paper she became extremely uncomfortable.

It was her custom, and became mine, to watch the games the children were playing in the street in the vicinity of No. 90. Mrs Green liked to observe what she called 'Dublin's little mothers', often very

---

* Dorothy Stopford (later Stopford Price) (1890–1954) was the niece of Alice Stopford Green, Máire Comerford's employer. After graduating as a doctor in 1921, Dorothy worked in a dispensary in Cork, where she took on the role of medical officer for the local IRA brigade. She also provided first aid training for Cumann na mBan.

† The Star Chamber is a judicial court or executive body that meets privately and makes judgments. The original Star Chamber sat at the Palace of Westminster, from the fifteenth to the seventeenth century, its name coming from the gold stars painted on the blue ceiling of the chamber, where the court convened. The Star Chamber was established to ensure that the social and political elite of the time were treated the same as others under the law, but, over time, through arbitrary operation and the abuse of the power of the court, it became synonymous with oppression and persecution.

small girls, who escorted toddlers and babies from the slums of York Street and Cuffe Street every fine afternoon to the sandpit in St Stephen's Green. Mrs Green taught me to notice the seasonal changes in the street games, from lamp-post swinging to hopscotch, and variations inspired by the spirit of the country. I was near Kellet's shop windows on South Great George's Street one day when I noticed a group of little boys who trundled a butter box on wheels down the footpath. One boy was sitting in the box, carrying an open newspaper. When they came to the recessed window another group dashed out of their ambush position. 'Alan Bell – your time has come,' they shouted. The boy was pulled out. Imaginary triggers were squeezed. The boy pretended to die.

This nation, and some of its finest sons, was destined in the approaching years to pay dearly for the brutalization of men and the inevitable corruption of children which arose from the liquidation of enemy intelligence agents in this period in Ireland's fight for freedom.

1920-21

THE IRA IN DUBLIN was poorly armed. Even the short .32 revolver, which someone had given me, was called for on the night before Bloody Sunday, 21 November 1920.* After Bloody Sunday everybody important in public life, who recognized majority rule and the Dáil, was arrested, if they had not gone 'on the run'. Volunteer Frank Teeling was caught and arrested on the morning of Bloody Sunday. He was in Kilmainham Jail awaiting trial on a charge of murder when he, Ernie O'Malley and Simon Donnelly, Chief of the Republican

---

* Early on 21 November 1920 the men of Michael Collins's special squad killed twelve British intelligence officers in Dublin in a highly coordinated attack. Two Auxiliaries were also killed. The British authorities claimed that they suspected that the gunmen responsible may have disappeared into the crowd at Croke Park, where a Gaelic football match was taking place between Tipperary and Dublin. However, the police began to shoot indiscriminately into the panicked crowd. Fourteen men, women and children were killed. Later that evening Peadar Clancy and Dick McKee, two high-ranking IRA men, were arrested, along with Conor Clune, who seems to have been arrested in error. All three men died in custody. The official explanation is that the men were shot as they 'tried to escape'. This day of carnage came to be known as Bloody Sunday.

Police, escaped from the prison.* A big manhunt ensued. One of the many subsequent street hold-ups and house-to-house searches took place in Harcourt Street, around the corner from us in No. 90. As the raids progressed a young newspaper boy, who had the big voice of his profession, stood at the Harcourt Street corner of St Stephen's Green, advertising his wares. 'Photograph of Teeling, sixpence,' he boomed. An officer in charge of the searches tried to conceal his interest but eventually moved closer and paid his sixpence. The boy handed over an envelope, but it felt thin. Realizing that there was nothing in it, the officer turned back towards the boy, who was now at the corner, poised for flight. 'Did he escape again, sir,' came back on the wind.

About a week after Bloody Sunday, I had collected the morning papers from the hall of No. 90 when Mrs Green appeared and asked me to read out the headlines in *The Irish Times*. I read the biggest one: 'Machine Guns in Action in Cork; Seventeen Auxiliaries Reported Dead.'†

I never did get the chance to read any more of that newspaper. Mrs Green crossed the hall and seized it from me. She glared at the headline intemperately, tore the newspaper in two and then threw it to the floor, stamping on it. After this outburst, my employer fell into one of

---

* Ernie O'Malley (Earnán Ó Maille) (1897–1957) was a member of the Irish Volunteers who took part in the 1916 Rising and was imprisoned in the aftermath. During the War of Independence O'Malley was staff captain of the IRA and attached to the 3rd Tipperary Brigade. O'Malley took part in a number of attacks on RIC barracks. He was captured and imprisoned (under a false name), while organizing for the IRA in Kilkenny. He escaped in February 1921 and took command of the 2nd Southern Division. Committed to the Republican ideal, Ernie O'Malley took the anti-Treaty side in 1922; he was OC HQ section in the Four Courts in June–July 1922, but, following the surrender, managed to avoid detention by escaping his Free State captors. He was appointed to the IRA army council in October 1922, becoming chief of staff of the anti-Treaty IRA. O'Malley left Ireland soon after to travel and to fulfil his ambition to become a writer. He wrote two acclaimed memoirs of his experiences in revolutionary Ireland: *On Another Man's Wound* (1936) and *The Singing Flame* (published posthumously in 1978).

† The Kilmichael ambush was an audacious attack by an IRA battalion of thirty-six men, led by Tom Barry, on a convoy of Auxiliaries. It was the largest ambush carried out by the IRA in the War of Independence. The attack took place near the village of Kilmichael in West Cork on 28 November 1920. Seventeen Auxiliaries and three IRA men were killed.

those dark silences of hers. I was affronted by her behaviour and may, in that moment, have mistaken its cause. At the time I wondered if the agitation that Mrs Green exhibited when she read of Tom Barry's victory in Cork arose from remorse, because she had helped to arm the Irish in 1914 – to confront the might of Carson and defend Home Rule. But I later came to believe that this accounted only in part for her reaction to the news. For Mrs Green must have known about the mounting pressure on the British government from their own citizens, and about the tentative negotiations beginning in England. She had helped to inform investigators from all over the world, who travelled to Ireland to learn the truth; and, of course, she must have been in touch with the British coterie when they were home again. Then, from the perspective of my youth, this was old people's work, which did not register as having much importance. But I have no difficulty under-standing now what I did not appreciate then, that Mrs Green was working steadfastly and hoping for peace based on justice in Ireland.

The problem was that her line of thought ran counter to the Irish experience. For is it not a well-known fact that concession has never been won from the English except as a result of violence? Against this fact, Mrs Green was pitting her faith, where her late English husband's had rested too, in the inherent greatness and exceptionalism of the British. That faith may have faltered, but it had always refused to die. Mrs Green did not at any time deny the right of Ireland to determine her own destiny; but, as her letters, * which later became available, show, she was troubled about the competence of our untrained and inexperienced leaders to confront national problems of the utmost difficulty. She had great faith in the emerging Commonwealth and knew much more than we did about the workings of the British Empire. In her view, the Irish were arousing every evil and arrogant spirit from the wrong side of the English character. And this, I now believe, was the feeling that caused her to react as she did when she tore up *The Irish Times.* Mrs Green, more than most, knew the ruthless

---

* A collection of Alice Stopford Green's letters, which may be the collection of letters Máire Comerford refers to, are housed at the National Library of Ireland.

ferocity a thwarted British government was capable of, with her finger on the pulse of history when British arms were still conquering the people of Africa, still triumphant in India, dominating China, expanding Empire, amassing stupendous wealth. Against this aggressive and mercenary imperialism, on which we all deemed ourselves authorities, Mrs Green set the other side of the British conundrum, which had produced the democratic revolution, and, after her time, the welfare state.

Perchance, Mrs Green was indignant because Tom Barry, for one, did not share her faith in the British coming good. From then on there was a certain gulf between us. The victory for which I and my comrades battled could contain no compromise, blurred allegiance or any toleration of British rule.

President Éamon de Valera came home from America two days before Christmas in 1920. Michael Collins had been Acting President for six weeks, following the arrest of Arthur Griffith. At one stage negotiations with the British came to a point where there might have been an unconditional truce. Archbishop Clune, coming onto prepared ground, very nearly did bring about a truce. If this had happened before, instead of after, the passing of the Partition Act into British law, it would have had obvious advantages.* At the last minute British Prime Minister Lloyd George changed his mind and made peace impossible by demanding a surrender of arms.† The Tories

---

* Máire Comerford writes of the 'Partition Act', which refers to the Government of Ireland Act (1920) passed by the British parliament in 1920. While many people assume that the Anglo-Irish Treaty of 1921 created partition in Ireland, in fact it is the earlier Government of Ireland Act that introduced partition, by creating two separate parliaments on the island of Ireland: one parliament for Northern Ireland and a separate one for Southern Ireland. The act was drafted to accommodate the demands of Ulster Unionists. Many decades later the ramifications of the Government of Ireland Act still resonate politically on the island of Ireland and in Britain.

† David Lloyd George (1863–1945) was Prime Minister of Britain from 1916–22 and a central figure at the post-World War I peace conference held in Paris in 1919. His policy on Ireland at that time adopted a dual approach – reform and coercion, including the sanctioning of official reprisals against Irish citizens, which, perhaps predictably, resulted in an escalation of resistance to British rule in Ireland. By mid-1921 Lloyd George was in favour of a truce in Ireland.

had triumphed again, but it was one of their narrowest escapes from having to recognize the Irish nation.

Earlier in 1920 both Éamon de Valera and Arthur Griffith made public announcements stating that when the freedom of Ireland was won, it would not imperil the security of Britain, or the safety of our native West British. Michael Collins was more direct. In an interview, he repudiated the suggestion of a Republic within the British Commonwealth. He told the American journalist Carl Ackerman that the same effort that would achieve dominion Home Rule would secure an Irish Republic. Collins stated that the objective was not that Lloyd George would put 'a little red spot on the map of one corner of Ireland and call it a part of Britain, as he does in Gibraltar. We want a united Ireland.' Collins added that Ulster would be given every guarantee. If there was a suspicion that the leaders showed signs of going further than guaranteeing the safety and security of the minority religion, as I believe there was among ardent Republicans of rank and file throughout the country, we contented ourselves with the belief that we were a democratic organization; these matters would eventually have to be put to a vote. My own attitude in every argument was that we served the Republic, but not any individual man or men in deviations. If that faith had not been general who would have been prepared to die for the cause?

On his return from the States Éamon de Valera took up the reins decisively, asserting his authority as president of the Republic and president of the Volunteers. He tried to impose discipline on all the busy peacemakers, running back and forth to London. A very far-reaching decision that he made was to draw a firm line between those who were, or were not, to be regarded as ministers of government. An inner cabinet came into being and the majority of those excluded were intransigent Republicans – Count Plunkett, Constance Markievicz, J.J. O'Kelly (Scelig), Art O'Connor, Joseph McDonagh and Seán Etchingham. I do not know if this cabinet change was known about in the movement generally. No public notification was made and, so far as I know, the ministry set up by the Dáil, in open

House destroyed by British forces in Wexford, 1921.
(Photograph by Eva Comerford)

Seán Ethchingham's shop and homestead, Courtown, Co. Wexford,
destroyed by British forces in 1921. (Photograph by Eva Comerford)

A page from Eva Comerford's 1921 diary, depicting destroyed houses in Wexford, and with reference to the burning of the Custom House, Dublin, 25 May 1921.

Mount St Benedict school building, Mount Nebo, Gorey, Co. Wexford.

Father Francis Sweetman OSB, founder
of Mount St Benedict School, 1938.

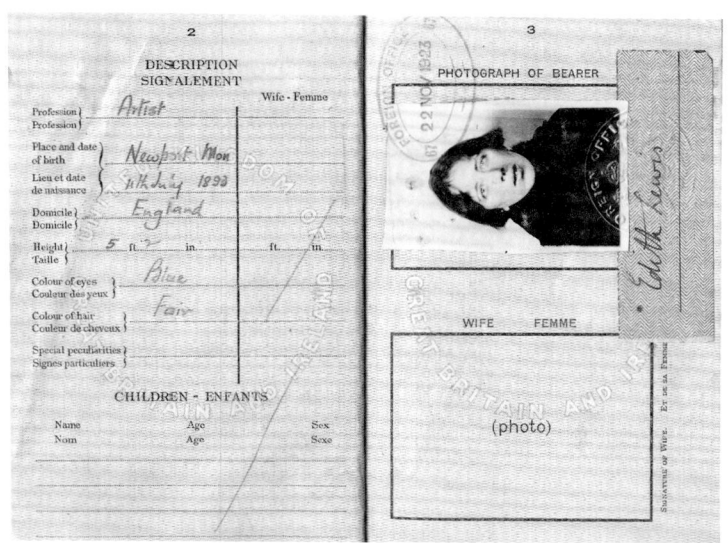

Interior page from the false passport in the name of 'Edith Lewis',
artist, used by Máire Comerford to travel to the US in late 1923.

*The exterior of the cottage on the grounds of Mount St Benedict
where Máire lived in 1925–34.*

Máire with her donkey outside the cottage at Mount St Benedict, c. 1930.

St Nessans, Sandyford Village, Dublin, c. 1948. Máire lived here from c.1940 to her death in 1982.

Eva and Máire Comerford in the garden at St Nessans in 1948, shortly before Eva's death in 1949.

Máire Comerford (centre) *with Cumann na mBan comrades at a commemorative march in the 1940s. Credit: RTÉ Archives.*

Máire working as a journalist for the Irish Press, *c. 1950.*

Máire with her nephew Joe Comerford in 1955.

Máire fishing with her maternal aunt, Zephie Dawson
(née Esmonde), c. 1950.

Máire at home in St Nessans, shortly before her death in 1982.

session in April 1919, was still the government of the Republic. We relied on these men, and Countess Markievicz (or Joe McDonagh, her substitute while she was in prison). I do not doubt that the demoted ministers – Count Plunkett, Etchingham and Joe McDonagh, who were still around Dublin – were pestered with the very questions that they themselves would have liked to see answered. Count Plunkett, a modest and straightforward man, was always kind and sympathetic to the anxieties of youth on these matters. This consideration, I remember as carried in his smile, and in the turn and toss of his head when he had no answer to give. He was a very splendid old man. But one man who always produced an answer was Frank Gallagher, one of the mainstays of the Dáil publicity department. Frank was a very brave man, with a lifelong and unshakeable devotion to Éamon de Valera. 'Dev,' Frank told us, was 'codding Lloyd George.' He told us not to be worrying ourselves.

None of us danced foreign dances, or would enter any un-Irish environment for pleasure. I, for one, had no money for the cinema, and the Abbey Theatre hardly knew me – but I do remember going over and over again to *A Serious Thing*, written by Oliver St John Gogarty under the pseudonym Gideon Ousley. This play depicted the Romans in Palestine at the tomb of Lazarus; however, the lines of the play seemed, word for word, to come straight from current editorials about law and order, and the duty of governments to suppress crime. In the last scene of the play a Roman soldier, spear in hand, cries out – 'What can we do when even the dead rise up against us?' When the play came around again British Tommies, with rifles and tin hats, had taken the place of the Romans.

In the houses I visited, where visitors were welcome on off-duty evenings – Mrs Ceannt's, the Woods', Madame MacBride's, Louise Gavan Duffy's, O'Donels', Plunketts', Phelans' and Childers's – we hung on to the lips of anyone present who might have fresh knowledge to help us in forecasting the future. It was wonderful to feel certain that the rebuilding of Ireland was at hand, and that we could help. This hopeful anticipation was probably in contrast with the perplexities confronting the Republican government – unemployment, land hunger and the Belfast rebellion; Dáil Éireann had set reports of many kinds in motion, and some of these issues now demanded decisions.

No man who was as actively and as variously engaged as I was in the national struggle could have moved around the country as freely as I did, merely because I was a woman. The leaders of the nation, and the army headquarters, were in Dublin and the men involved all lived in hiding and in great personal danger. But events proved that they underestimated the courage of their own people at this stage. Every government, everywhere, is certain to feel mounting pressure as they hear the voices of dissatisfied people, usually in organized groups. Owners of burned-out factories; employers of labour, Southern Unionists, all had the means and the motive to come to Dublin to press their case. The arguments for compromise must have haunted our leaders morning, noon and night. They held on bravely but none measured accurately the will to victory, which was in the country. No conclusion short of victory was open to them without coercion of their own people. The Oath to the Republic, and to Dáil Éireann, was taken very seriously.

Our leaders were very different from one another, but Éamon de Valera and Michael Collins had this in common: each believed that he alone could interpret the inspiration that had swept Ireland in the wake of Pearse and Connolly and 1916, and that they could guide it, without defilement, through compromise, to the best attainable solution. When I ponder on these gifted men now, I wonder at the length of time during which they held together as a team, more than I do that they split in the end. Their friendship, and with it the hopes of Ireland in their generation, was destined to be destroyed in the analysis of the meaning of freedom, in definitions of democracy and characterizations about the true nature of an oath.

Arrests and Escapes

AFTER MOTHER CLOSED her school in 1919 she lived mainly with her mother, Grannie Esmonde, and her sisters, Millie and Zephie, at Ballycourcey, Enniscorthy. She kept a spare and cautious diary, which she illustrated from time to time with her own snapshots. Mother made frequent trips to Dublin – she records lunch and tea parties with Mrs Green, the Childers and Mr and Mrs Dumont in her diary. Apart from Mother, my grandmother's household had not moved with the times. For peace's sake, I kept away from it.

Mother had a talent for finding people in misfortune and she gave great help to Mary Moran of Cumann na mBan in solving some of the local problems that arose around Enniscorthy. We had two branches of Cumann na mBan in the town, both fully active. Mary Moran was a born leader and, given the times, it was the Republic's misfortune that she was not a man. She lived with her parents in their small tailor's shop in Church Street, where she dealt with every crisis that came her way with resourcefulness and instant good judgment. She was a very able intelligence officer too. There were times when I got off the train from Dublin with some job that had to be done and always made my way directly to Mary Moran. She knew every resource that we had and how best to use it quickly.

Wexford earned no great reputation as a fighting county, but there was enough potential rebellion there to have it included in the areas put under martial law by the British in early 1921.The detachment of the Dorset Regiment, under Captain Yeo, earned an evil reputation in Enniscorthy, mainly because of their treatment of a large number of prisoners held in the courthouse. Not only was the building unsuitable but also the handling of the men was violent, degrading and aimed at breaking their spirit. The men were stripped naked in the yard and assaulted with yard brushes. National organizations were of long standing in Enniscorthy and this left it that, even in 1916, the men connected were well past their youth. The effort of the Dorsets was directed to cow the town, more than to search out and destroy the Republican army.

Aileen K'Eogh, the Matron, was arrested in the course of a raid on Mount St Benedict when a tin canister with a small amount of explosive, which she had confiscated from a schoolboy, was found in her room. In Aileen's absence Mother cycled the twenty miles from Enniscorthy to help Father Sweetman. She stayed at the Mount, carrying out the duties of the matron; Mother's first photograph in her 1921 diary is of the Matron's lonely Kerry Blue. She came across the dog outside a window where the Crown forces had posted their large divisional proclamation, by order of the General Officer and Military Governor. It was a fairly familiar feature on wrecked and raided houses at that time. The penalties threatened against anyone who ventured to remove the proclamation were drastic in print, and outrageous when uttered by Crown forces on the spot.

In the martial law areas, the Crown authorities required that a list would be compiled in every house, naming those sleeping there, and then hung on the inside of the hall door each night. This was for the convenience of official raiders, who might call after nightfall. In theory then, they only had to check the list, comparing it with the number and genders of the members of the household. This would give them a good starting point if they were on a manhunt. Under the circumstances of the time – so many men having been shot dead when they opened the door to the Crown forces – it took courage to neglect the making of the list. Nonetheless, in thousands of houses it was never made. I remember no list at the back of Mrs Green's door or in any house that I visited. But Father Sweetman, with a boarding school on his hands, had little alternative but to comply. The manner in which he tackled the task was very characteristic of him. He started by entering 'Mary Kavanagh, Rangefinder' and went on down the official paper, filling in the duties of his staff according to his own idiosyncratic device. He said that he started with Mary Kavanagh because she was the person who had to get up first in the morning, and then grope her way to the big kitchen range, which had to be lit before anyone in the house could get their breakfast. Mary, stone deaf and intensely loyal, was delighted with her promotion. When a raid came, she could be relied upon to see that, from the raiders' point of view, the scrutiny of the list was not going to speed anything up!

Following her arrest, Aileen K'Eogh was brought to Waterford and charged before a court martial with the illegal possession of ammunition and seditious documents. She refused to recognize the authority of the court, and was reported in the papers as saying – 'Unless orders come to me from the Republican government that I am not to have ammunition and explosives, I consider that I have a perfect right to have them.' She was sentenced to two years' imprisonment. During her incarceration in Mountjoy her fellow prisoners included Countess Markievicz, Máire Rigney and Eithne Coyle from Donegal, who was arrested in Roscommon with a sketched plan of a military barracks. Their number also included Eileen McGrane[*] and Linda Kearns[†] from Sligo. Linda was arrested while driving her car,

---

[*] Eileen McGrane (1895–1984) was a university teacher and a senior member of Cumann na mBan. She also worked as secretary to Michael Collins, and during this time her flat in Dawson Street was frequently used to hide arms and documents. Eventually Eileen's flat was raided and she was sentenced to four years' penal servitude and imprisoned in Waltham, Liverpool and Mountjoy jails.

[†] Linda Kearns (later Kearns-MacWhinney) (1888–1951) was a nurse, a member of Cumann na mBan and a dispatch carrier and driver who was active in 1916. After

and when she took responsibility for its contents to save the men with her – who otherwise would have been involved in a capital charge – she received a sentence of ten years' penal servitude. Also imprisoned at the time in Mountjoy were three very young 'lifers' – Kate Crowley and Madge and Lily Cotter from Glanmire, County Cork. The three girls were arrested and tried because they were working in a field nearby a road when it was blown up before a Black and Tan lorry. The girls were convicted of attempted murder and were sentenced to penal servitude for life.

Then, and later on when I was there myself, the visiting justices to Mountjoy Prison included a well-meaning and dignified lady, Miss Angela Boland, who dressed from head to foot in black and confined her attention to the women's section of the prison. Her concern was primarily for the spiritual rather than the bodily welfare of the prisoners. Miss Boland had only one line of thought about why pretty little girls would be in prison. One day Kate, Madge and Lily were together on the exercise ground when Miss Boland met them and asked what had they done 'to your poor little babies'. The girls, in chorus, replied – 'Oh no, Mam! 'Tis for killing Black and Tans we are here.' The justices must have been almost equally surprised when they asked Con Markievicz whether she had any complaints and the Countess replied that she could do with a load of dung for her garden. Máire Rigney told how when one of the justices arrived back with a sack full of cow manure, Con slung it over her shoulder and carried it to her plot of earth beside the exercise yard. The Countess and Aileen K'Eogh were often busy gardening and produced a miracle from their efforts – an orange, white and green cross of flowers for Easter Monday 1921.

---

the Rising she returned to nursing, helping to fight the flu epidemic on Achill Island in 1918 and opening a nursing home in Dublin in 1919. She remained an active Republican, sometimes sheltered men on the run and also owned a car, which she used for dispatch missions and to move arms. In November 1920, on one such mission, she was arrested in Sligo (along with her male accomplices) and was sentenced to ten years' penal servitude. She served her time in British jails and Mountjoy, from where she and three other women prisoners escaped in 1921.

Arthur Griffith and Eoin MacNeill were among the prisoners in Mountjoy at the same time as Aileen. Archbishop Clune, of Perth, Australia, first visited them there on 3 December 1920. Prior to this, the archbishop had been to see Lloyd George in London, and was authorized by him to propose a truce, which subsequently came unstuck. The terms were drafted within the jail. As all this went on for a considerable amount of time, Archbishop Clune must have visited the prison with some regularity.

In the ordinary way when you visited a prisoner in Mountjoy, you knocked at a great big door and spoke to a warder through the little grille. Then, after you stated your business and all was deemed to be in order, he let you into a room, which was in the space between the outer door and the equally formidable iron-barred gate. You sat, in the presence of God only knows what agony or trouble, among women, and perhaps a few men, who were waiting to visit prisoners. I think that we 'political' friends and relations, who shared the bench and the few chairs in that normally sad waiting place, often saw real human trouble and suffering there. But it was also true that we undoubtedly listened with sorrow and sympathy to some very tall stories indeed! Meantime, deep in the jail the prisoners' iron-plated door was unlocked, or in the case of a civil inmate he was called from a working party and escorted, stage by stage, lock by lock, to the visiting box, where he was locked in. Then you, seated in the waiting room, heard the clang of the keys on the bars of the inside gate and a name was called.

If it was your name, you were let through a narrow trap in the gate, and escorted to the visitor side of the line of boxes. The door was unlocked for you, and, finally, you saw your prisoner. The prisoner was seated on the other side of the counter, perhaps behind two sets of wire mesh, with a warder pacing between – and with other prisoners having visits, crying, shouting and trying to discuss intimate things in the midst of bedlam.

But when priests, or even an archbishop visited, the parties met informally, usually in the governor's office. When Father Sweetman went to see the Matron, he was brought to the office and soon afterwards Aileen was brought there too. When she saw where she was, her reaction was instant. She strode over to where a picture was hanging on the wall, pushed it swiftly aside and drove her clenched fist, with all her strength, through the wallpaper and into the space behind. Aileen knew via the jail underground that Archbishop Clune's interviews with Griffith and MacNeill had been spied upon. Having explained her action to a startled Father Sweetman, Aileen settled down and the visit proceeded as normal.

Aileen K'Eogh remained in jail until she was one of the four women prisoners who climbed a rope ladder, thrown over from the outside, and escaped.* It was no small feat, for she was last to climb the rope ladder with no one to hold it for her, as she had held it for the others.

---

* Four Republican woman prisoners: Linda Kearns, 'the Matron' Aileen K'Eogh, Mae Burke and Eithne Coyle, escaped from Mountjoy Prison in October 1921.

White Cross

I DID NOT directly experience the fury of the English terror campaign. I merely followed some of its tracks – within days, weeks or sometimes months, and mostly in daylight. I was not involved in the sense of having anything to lose except, perhaps, my own life or liberty. It was not my woman's lot to have those nearest to me killed, imprisoned, with or without trial, 'on their keeping', or away with the trench-coated, disciplined guerrilla units of the IRA. No home was burned over my head. No children in my care depended on income or wages, which a soldier of Ireland or a prisoner had ceased to earn, or a worker left high and dry following the destruction of a creamery or factory. I was not one of the 10,000 victims of the Belfast pogroms. This left me available when I was nominated to be a member of the General Council of the Irish White Cross, which was formally launched at a meeting in the Round Room of the Mansion House in January 1921. The White Cross was founded when the Red Cross in Geneva turned down our appeals for help. The service of the Red Cross is to established nations; the rules for 'Civilized War' extended no protection or agreed standards to restrain the behaviour of strong nations against rebels, irregulars, conscientious objectors or revolutionaries.

According to Mother's diary I went off on tour for the White Cross on 2 March 1921. I had a new Wexford-made Pierce bicycle and set out by train for Connaught, carrying a letter for Mrs Geraldine (Gerry) Dillon, sister of Joseph Plunkett – executed in 1916 – and wife of Professor Tommy Dillon of Galway University. I must have been tracked from Galway railway station because I was hardly inside the Dillons' house when the raiders came. Gerry Dillon only had time to glance briefly at her letter before the ominous knock came to the door, and she quickly thrust it down the front of her blouse. Unfortunately, the blouse was made of lacy material and the letter showed through. Gerry was arrested on the spot and spent the rest of the War of Independence in Galway Jail. I blamed myself for Gerry's arrest; I should have had the wit to know that anyone on the Dublin train arriving in Galway was bound to be followed.

The raiders had paid little attention to me and, later that evening, I was guided by friends across the railway lines, then helped into the train on the wrong side. I had business to attend to in Loughrea with the Bishop of Cloyne, Dr Robert Browne, and also with Seamus Murphy of the IRA.* I spent the night in the workhouse, where Seamus's mother was matron. She was a very fine woman, always ready to help wandering Republicans on their way.

I called to the Bishop's Palace next morning – the greatest wet day in my memory; the water from my coat made embarrassing pools all around me on Bishop Browne's nice polished floor. The bishop was friendly though, and blessed my efforts in his diocese. He advised me that I should see His Grace of Tuam, the archbishop. In Tuam Dr Gilmartin questioned me very closely about my work for the White

---

* Seamus Murphy was a veteran of the 1916 Rising and OC of the Galway IRA from 1917–20. He was involved in many operations during this time while also working for *The Galway Express*. The premises of the newspaper were burnt down in September 1920 in one of a series of reprisal attacks by Crown forces following an incident on 8 September when a member of the Black and Tans and two IRA Volunteers died in a shootout in Galway railway station.

Cross, but nonetheless gave me his approval. These visits were necessary because personal relief had to be distributed through parish committees, acting for the White Cross. My instructions were that the clergy must always supervise the collection of funds for the society, and the awarding of relief to those who qualified to receive it; it was my job to organize committees everywhere, according to these rules.

Although the religions existing in Ireland at that time were mostly represented on the governing body of the White Cross, the calls I remember making were invariably on Roman Catholic archbishops, bishops and clergy They all consented to the establishment of White Cross committees, and although most were very cordial, I found that every parish priest was a personality in his own right, and at that level my progress was very uneven. Some of the elder clergy had been supporters of the Irish Parliamentary Party – perhaps, in their youth, they were fiery curates, who denounced Parnell. There were priests amongst them who were as strongly opposed to the Republican cause as anyone could be, who at the same time believed that Ireland should have Home Rule. Included in the clergy of every rank I met, there were some who would have preferred not to engage with the work of the White Cross, even if it provided for the relief of distress. They did not want to work with us because they believed that the financial relief would help to prolong resistance to the British. Others were simply grieving that young men were losing their lives and the people suffering so much. Less than a year later, after the Treaty, many Catholic priests made haste to show where their sympathies had been all the time, when they denounced Republicans in no uncertain terms.

Experience taught me to learn all the local facts in each parish and to have my list of those who needed to be helped before I approached the parish priest. Destitution was a new and terrible condition frequently experienced by proud women. I found that those in most distress were often the least likely to advertise their predicament. The bravest people can be too thin-skinned to face a parish committee, or submit to questioning about their means. My calls at the houses of fighting men, or dead men, were homes where wives or widows were learning hard lessons, which, too often, are the consequences of wars of resistance. It was in their blood and tradition to suffer in the causes of national, religious and personal freedom. In many homes, where children stood around silently, the issues at stake were clear enough. Mothers would face hardship if only we could together win our present battle. The thought that they were rearing the first generation of children who would live their lives in a free country was enough to support the mothers. There the issue lay.

On another occasion I had some White Cross business that brought me, on my bicycle, from Limerick Junction through the martial law area around Oola in County Limerick. On the night in question I had delayed too long in a hospitable presbytery. On the way out I passed through a military post where sandbags had been placed to narrow the road sufficiently, so that a Tan with a bayonet could menace with ease. It was after the curfew hour. The dusty road was white under the moonlight and seemed strange to me. No other soul was abroad. My good bike was running very silently – or the sentry sleeping very soundly – as I sped through the narrow opening made by the sandbags and away, without word or sound. Then, before I had time to count my blessings, out of nowhere an enormous dog dashed from a roadside farmyard and began his attack. I could see the black patches on his body, and the flash where the moonlight caught his eyes, as he sprang for my throat. His jaw snapped by my shoulder before he fell back, to spring again. When I got past the place, the dog did not persist. Between one thing and another, that was a night I was grateful that my trusty bike was carrying me. My legs would have been hard set to do so.

My next job for the White Cross was as a member of a commission of three – formed to work through parts of Tipperary and North Cork and to report on the destruction to homes and factories, perpetrated by the Black and Tans. Most of the detail of these cases is blurred in my mind now but I do remember a tour of Mallow with Frank Dempsey, Chairman of the Urban Council and member of the Railway Men's Union. We walked through the battered town and saw the wrecked factory; I took down the details concerning the plight of the unemployed workers and the extent of the damage. Some weeks previously, at the end of September 1920, lorry-loads of Crown troops had arrived in Mallow from Fermoy and Buttevant Barracks with supplies of petrol or oil, which were used in a night of incendiarism, terror and destruction. This was in reprisal for a successful arms raid by the IRA on Mallow Military Barracks, carried out the day before the burning of the town; a sergeant based in the barracks was killed during the operation.

On another occasion our arrival at a home on the Cork–Tipperary border coincided with the hurried return from England of the daughters of the house, where they had been teaching in a convent school. We came on them, still wearing their city clothes and with suitcases and umbrellas scattered around, grouped together in a ruin. Their mother was boiling a kettle on a primus stove and hunting around to see if she had enough unbroken cups for everyone present, after they invited us to join their family group. I sat on the remains of the house wall, which had been lowered that far. The women didn't want any compensation money – they made that clear to us, but they were happy to compile the account of their loss for us to collate and bring back to Dublin. The discussion, I remember, was spirited, very angry and completely uncompromising.

The fishing villages and towns of Donegal traded with Glasgow for flour and Indian meal, and other merchandise. It is not difficult to surmise that during the War of Independence the last category was liable to include more than domestic goods or hardware. At any rate the Crown government stopped the traffic of the little trade ships and soon the newspaper headlines were predicting 'Famine in Donegal'. I was sent to investigate, in May or June 1921. Riding the ring of Donegal, I encountered road trenches, which would only have been wise, from the Irish viewpoint, if the sea were ours. The IRA had taken chunks, each one the size of a house, out of the roads here and there. Two or three times a day I had to drop to waist or shoulder depth, then carry my bicycle across the stepping stones to the other side.

It was clear that the shops would not be restocked easily over land. I reported back that supply was low and would not be replenished without difficulty.

So far as I know work for the White Cross was carried out voluntarily by a great number of people. Mrs Green continued to pay my salary and lent me to go to the country on research trips, as I had gone on previous occasions for the Dáil publicity department. The White Cross reported that during this reign of terror by British forces at least 2000 houses, farmsteads and shops were utterly destroyed, with 1500 partially demolished and 3000 families made homeless. Forty co-operative creameries were totally ruined and their machinery reduced to scrap iron. In the course of the struggle some 7000 people were arrested and confined to prisons and internment camps.

In September 1920, by way of reprisal for the killing of a police officer in a drunken brawl, twenty-five dwelling houses and the famous Balbriggan hosiery factory were burned down. The burning of Cork in December caused damage assessed at two million pounds and close on 4000 people received relief from the White Cross. Relief was given in personal payments at the maximum rate of ten shillings for an adult and five shillings for a child per week. Reconstruction grants were provided to cover some of the cost of immediate repairs, following the destruction of factories and dwelling houses. Finally, £150,000 was given to a special committee charged with the care of orphans. Reports of the White Cross record that, notwithstanding the extent of havoc and ruin wrought in the south and west of the country, the situation in Belfast was the most serious task that confronted the society. In a three-week period nearly 10,000 Catholics were prevented from earning a living and their 20,000 dependants became reliant on charity.

Mrs Green never suggested going to the country on White Cross business with me. But I knew she was longing to expand her personal experience of what was happening. Once, when I thought I could do so without involving her in undue fatigue or danger, I invited her to come with me to Nenagh. I had a job to do there and would be away only for the night. Mrs Green and I were in a hotel dining room when a sergeant of the RIC arrived and began questioning us. I hadn't anything much to hide but with another man, that might not have mattered if suspicions were aggravating a bad mood. He started truculently enough, then, when he was sure no one was listening, his voice dropped. He told us that our presence in the town had been reported to the barracks. The sergeant had, he informed us, sent the Tans up the street to the wrong hotel and had come himself to help us out of their way. I met the same man later, when he had thrown off the uniform. He was Sergeant Flannery, cousin to that wonderful Republican woman – Maa Woods of Donnybrook, who 'kept house' for the cause.

Housekeepers

LILY O'BRENNAN HEARD of 'a grand house' that would suit Seán Etchingham because the Bean an Tí (woman of the house) was warm-hearted, brave and skilled in nursing – a woman who would look after a delicate man, past his youth. Seán had dozens of friends around Dublin and was never short of a meal, or a place for the night, but pressure on reliable safe houses was intense. Seán had stayed with Mrs Kilkelly – a most kind hostess in Fitzwilliam Square – but Richard Mulcahy, IRA chief of staff, was protective about the security of 'his houses' and wanted that one for himself. Lily directed me to 131 Morehampton Road, and to the home of Mrs Woods, who later came to be affectionately known as 'Maa Woods of Donnybrook'. If God created another Irish woman to match her it would be my urgent aim to get acquainted, and as soon as possible. She had the best little man who declared that he was 'no Republican' for a husband, and three boys and girls, beginning with Tony, who was, when I first met him, a very young Volunteer.

On this first meeting Maa Woods answered her door and led me into her parlour. Then, the brightest eyes examined me through spectacles and we got to know each other very quickly. Mrs Woods was a little stout, her hair always pinned back tightly in a bun at the back of her head. She was a Sligo / Roscommon woman, a lover of tradition, of poetry and literature and a council member of the National Literary Society. I soon got to know that Mrs Woods extended her sympathy and hospitality to students from India and Egypt, whose countries were also struggling against British rule. It was in Morehampton Road that some of us listened to first-hand accounts of poverty and degradation in India under Crown rule, and of the leadership role played by Mahatma Gandhi in their struggle for freedom.

There was no household task that Mrs Woods could not do; she was a splendid cook and there was always a spare place laid at her generous table. And, when it came to hiding a hacksaw in a cake, Maa Woods was an artist. Her delicious cakes played a part in two escapes from Mountjoy Prison, in 1918 and 1920. I was behind her in the hall when, one evening, she opened her door to find men, who had been caught up in an explosion, supporting a badly injured comrade. Maa wanted to send at once for an ambulance but at the same time, she assumed control and made the men welcome in her home. Men on the run were always sure of help and food from Mrs Woods, and even, on occasion, the use of one of her husband's suits to facilitate escape. Mr Woods was a member of a wholesale grocery firm whose butter boxes were transported by rail to numerous destinations. These boxes did not always contain only butter in their comings and goings.

There was a famous story that on one particular day Mrs Woods had a big cooking job to do; she decided that along with her normal gas cooker, she would also bake in the range, which was rarely used. Maa had just lit the range when she heard a ring at the front door. On the doorstep she found a strange woman, who began to introduce herself. As the women spoke a loud explosion came from the house. Mrs Woods, with her usual grace, smiling and eyes twinkling, moved out onto the doorstep, closing the door gently behind her. She began to hastily cover up a situation that she herself did not understand. It turned out that Volunteer Noel Lemass[*] had hidden some ammunition in the little used range, and once the fire took off the bullets exploded. Life in Morehampton Road was anything but dull, so it was no surprise that from the minute Seán Etchingham crossed the threshold of No. 131, it became his second home.

At the end of 1920, I was visiting Louise Gavan Duffy's home in St Stephen's Green.[†] There were several people there, most of whom I knew well. But I noted the presence of one stranger in the group; I remember wondering why no one addressed him by name. It was my habit then to watch for any hesitation when men were leaving a house at the end of an evening, looking out for indecision as to the direction a man might take when he reached the street. Those with no homes to go to could be detected at that moment. On the night in question the stranger looked firstly one way and then the other. 'Are you alright for a stop,' I whispered. 'Would you know where Seán Etchingham is,' the stranger asked. I led him to Maa Woods's house in Morehampton Road. By all the rules this was not a good thing – to bring a stranger to one of our secret places was forbidden, yet instinct resisted all the set rules. It was late night when we got there and I did not go into the house, but did wait anxiously while the stranger was admitted, and then proceeded through the house to Seán Etchingham's room. Then to my relief, I heard a gregarious

---

[*] Noel Lemass (1897–1923) was a member of the 3rd Battalion, Dublin Brigade. Alongside his brother Seán (in later years Taoiseach of Ireland 1959–66), Noel fought in the GPO in 1916. The brothers again fought side by side as anti-Treaty insurgents in the Four Courts in 1922. Noel was imprisoned, but escaped to England, finally returning to Ireland in 1923. In July of that year he was abducted by agents of the Free State. Some months later his mutilated body was found on Featherbed Mountain, near the Wicklow–Dublin border.

[†] Louise Gavan Duffy (1884–1969) was an Irish nationalist, suffragist, educator and Irish cultural enthusiast. Louise was born in France and only came to Ireland as a young woman, where she became one of the first females to graduate from University College Dublin in 1911. She was a founding member of Cumann na mBan and was present in the GPO in 1916. A year later Louise co-founded the first Gaelscoil in Ireland, Scoil Bhríde in Dublin, which was covertly used to store seditious material during the War of Independence. In 1918 Louise was elected to the executive of Cumann na mBan, but as a supporter of the Treaty she left the organization in 1922.

shout, and laughter and greetings, and all was well. Liam Mellows,* home from the States after many adventures since the Rising, had reached his old friend and his band of comrades, who were destined to serve and help him during his few remaining years.

Liam's alias was 'Mr Nolan', a commercial traveller. He was fitted out to the smallest detail with pricelists, notebooks and trade papers. 'Mr Nolan' was uncommonly fair-haired – the palest gold. Mrs Woods was tasked with the job of dying his hair, and there was much fun and quizzing as we sat around to watch while she worked to make his moustache match the rest of his hair. It was certainly our opinion that her decision to make his hair only some shades darker than natural was a much better option than to dye him black or brown. William Cosgrave was the same kind of blond as Liam but he used a very dark dye. Those of us who got the chance to study the question at close quarters decided that Maa Woods's job was the better one!

Seán Etchingham went by 'Mr Quinn', a journalist in the racing world. He had a line of racing talk, starting in the most casual way, which made raiding parties lay their guns aside and forget why they had come. It began when Seán wondered whether he might be detained so long as to prevent him being able to put his 2/6 on a certain horse. From that, a situation generally developed and wide-eyed Black and Tans sat on Seán's bed eagerly awaiting every

---

* Liam Mellows (1892–1922) was born in Lancaster but spent much of his youth in Ireland. A nationalist from an early age, Mellows approached Thomas Clarke, who recruited him to Na Fianna Éireann. He later joined the IRB and the Irish Volunteers and was arrested and jailed on several occasions. In 1916 Mellows escaped from Reading Jail, returning to Ireland to command the Western Division of the IRA during the Easter Rising of 1916. After the insurrection failed Mellows escaped arrest, and made his way to New York, where he was detained without trial on a charge of attempting to aid the German side in World War I. Following his release in 1918 he helped to organize Éamon de Valera's fundraising tour of America in 1919–20. While still in New York, Mellows was elected to the First Dáil. He returned to Ireland in 1920 and became the IRA Director of Purchases, importing arms for the War of Independence. Mellows was a strong opponent of the Anglo-Irish Treaty. On 28 June 1922 the Free State army attacked the anti-Treaty force, including Liam Mellows, in occupation of the Four Courts in Dublin, since April of that year. After sixty hours of fighting the Four Courts garrison surrendered. Imprisoned in Mountjoy, Mellows and three other Republican prisoners were executed by firing squad on 8 December 1922.

each-way betting tip that came from his lips. This happened once, early in the morning, when a raid on 131 Morehampton Road started viciously. While a tea cosy in the middle of the breakfast table covered a revolver, and danger was in every corner, 'Mr Quinn' and 'Mr Nolan', in the same big bed, drew the raiding party into a discussion of the racing column in the morning newspaper, and all ended in civility, with no prisoners taken.

I happened to be at No.131 on a day when Mrs Woods was talking about a house on St Mary's Road, Ballsbridge, which she had secured on behalf of the government for the particular use of Michael Collins. It was her job to make all the arrangements so that Collins could live like a young man with elderly relatives. 'Who will we get to go in there and pretend to be Mick's aunt,' she asked. 'I'm sure that Mother will do that for you,' I replied without thinking. Mother was in Ballycourcey so I sent a telegram asking her to come to Dublin. I met her off the train from Wexford and then by appointment we met somebody else, and Mother was taken away. I was warned not to go near the house in St Mary's Road and not to try and see Mother. In her brief sojourn as 'Mick's Aunt' Mother was impressed with his indifference to the curfew law. The strong likelihood that he might be caught abroad in some volley-racked street did not prevent Michael Collins from burning the candle at both ends. When his escorts left him at his door, they went on their dangerous way, and certainly not to homes of their own.

Mother's time as Mick's aunt did not last long because she had been given a false name to cover her new identity. Quite quickly she discovered that the lady living next door was a fellow member of Greystones Golf Club, where Mother had once been Lady Captain. There were also other old acquaintances living in the vicinity of St Mary's Road. The result was that Mrs Comerford was somebody else to the milkman and others associated with her new 'auntie' role, but was herself when she went out, or inevitably had to offer her old acquaintances a cup of tea. The complications became too great and after about three weeks an alternative arrangement was made.

Another house that was constantly abuzz with revolutionary activity was the home of Molly and Erskine Childers. Molly, an American, was in the public spotlight for one brief hour during her forty years of political activity in Ireland. Despite physical challenges (she was unable to sit or walk without pain) it was Molly who steered the yacht, the *Asgard*, into Howth Harbour carrying arms for the Volunteers in 1914. Her name slipped back into obscurity until Éamon de Valera paid tribute to her on the fiftieth anniversary of the Howth gun-running. I was brought one day to the Childers Home in Bushy Park by my old friend Daa Barton, a cousin of Molly's husband Ernest. Molly Childers was crippled and although she went upstairs to bed, and to the dining room for meals, she spent the rest of her time on a couch in the drawing room. This was a tastefully furnished room, which extended from the front of the house to the back; the predominant colour was crimson, lined with books in beautifully fresh condition, with coverings on the couch of the loveliest silken materials. On this first visit, neither Daa nor I were quite at home in this plush setting. I in tweed, jumper and thick shoes, my everlasting mackintosh and bicycle; Daa in tailor-mades, well broken-in and hefty country shoes.

Over the years I was often in and out of the Childers house on different errands. Molly suffered a lot but she was always smiling and, in her own way, humorous. She lay there all day, seeing people, acquiring nuances in the information or current affairs of the time, being a bit mysterious, making never-ending cuttings from a host of newspapers – always somewhat fathomless. Occasionally, Ernest came in from his study and took a cup of tea. He stood with it in his hand to the back of our chairs, courteous to everyone present, responding a little to what they said, but keeping his own thoughts together during a short break from work, which, it always seemed, he intended to resume immediately.

Molly Childers followed the battles and the deeds of the Republican army with the most excited interest, and she always knew more about what was happening behind the scenes than I did. I gathered that she was in touch with Volunteers all the time, and that men from the flying columns came to visit her. To my mind, Molly really knew a lot more than she understood. Using her mystery technique to absorb the news we brought her, for consideration at levels over our head – in short, not discussing things she shouldn't, while also being a very expert conversationalist.

It is my belief that Molly had more influence in the background of the events of that time than any other woman in Irish history. It was not, to my mind, a revolutionary influence in the spirit of Pearse and Connolly, but I am sure that it began as such.

She knew Michael Collins from his early days in London and had recognized his genius, advising him as to the books he should read. It is certain that Molly held money for Collins from time to time, which belonged to Dáil Éireann. How and when she broke with Michael Collins I do not know, but the fact of the friendship makes it all the more difficult to understand the enmity Collins had for her husband, Erskine Childers. I was in the Childers house on the night before, and on the morning when Molly's husband Erskine was executed before a Free State firing squad (November 1922). I know that Molly was in spiritual and political harmony with Erskine up to and on the day of his death. Molly also had a long friendship with Éamon de Valera. Many years were to pass before I gave up trying to understand her unwavering support for Dev's policies, which must have broken everything except the memory of past friendship between them.

'Houses' were all important in the revolution, but the word had a different meaning from the usual one. A hunted man's 'house' was not his home. It was a place where he could count on a bed and food, and perhaps the news and some interesting conversation. A man's 'house' (or houses) changed as the enemy found them out, and he had to move on. Often a man and his 'house' were complete strangers when they first met. Townspeople met country people; rich met poor in this business of 'houses'. Many a man got his first sight of a comfortable home when he woke up in a strange place, and stepped out onto a Dun Emer carpet.* For some, the houses they had known

---

* Dun Emer Guild was the textile-producing arm of Dun Emer Industries, founded

'on the run' were the first stage on a journey towards material betterment; for others the experience was a passing one in a life filled with
tragedy and hardship. Among the latter however, were many who
would retain through life warm-hearted memories of gracious living
and generous people, whose world was that of the professions or of
the universities, of art, of literature or even of good-natured leisure,
accompanied by sufficient means to support it.

It was only natural that some of the hosts and hostesses had their
own reasons for doing what they did; but so far as I know, they were
overwhelmingly well and kindly intentioned. And very little was given
to the IRA that had not been well earned. This provision of 'houses'
was primarily woman's work. It took a woman to hold her own floor
and hope to be left behind on it after the raiders were finished.

in 1902 by Evelyn Gleeson and sisters Elizabeth and Susan Yeats, known as Lolly
and Lilly. Their more famous brothers were the poet W.B. and the artist Jack Yeats.
Dun Emer made hand-woven carpets, rugs and tapestries, incorporating Celtic
designs into the fabric.

Thin Red Line

MARTIAL LAW for Munster and parts of Leinster came into effect in the same fortnight as the 'Better Government of Ireland Act' in December 1920. The issue was now clear and straight. It was a question of freedom or submission. In the last half of 1920 I heard no talk of the latter. From slum to mansion, men were minded and fed and sheltered, and scouts put out while they slept. Their dependants were looked after. Parcels were sent to prisons. Arms dumps were moved where necessary. I learned from experience that the Lee Enfield service rifle could be carried under my coat without showing at the bottom, with my head in a big hat. With a concealed rifle each company of Cumann na mBan could infiltrate the streets, moving from one dump to another – all thanks to the long skirt!

In the lower ranks we were all keeping secrets. Even while we were living in a flat together, I did not know that my brother, Sandy, a student in an agricultural college, was an active Volunteer. It was only in the course of long years afterwards that friends, acquaintances and neighbours discovered that they had all the time been working shoulder to shoulder. Yet, in moments of trouble, friends were near and brave, and always vigilant. Throughout Ireland there are still tracks left by the fighting men of those days, now known only to the few. From time to time in subsequent years, I inspected 'Courtney's Anvil' where it lay on the grass outside a collapsed granite worker's shed, by the mountain path on Kilmashogue. It marks the site where Jack Courtney and his brothers repaired arms for Andy MacDonnell's column, undisturbed by raids for many months. They worked away there, with the whole city of Dublin spread at their feet and Dublin Castle only six miles away, as the crow flies.

The Crown terror campaign – one arm of their pincer – was stepped up with the announcement of an official reprisals policy. The Black and Tans and the Auxiliaries both drove around in fast lorries; it was hard to distinguish between the backfiring of their engines and shooting, often going on at the same time. In the beginning the lorries were open. I remember that the 'Auxies' sat back to back, facing to the sides, and to the rear. It was normal for each man to have one or more drawn revolvers on his knee. You would not know if they were drunk or sober when the lorries were on some special harassment, dashing here and there on the streets, right side, wrong side, swerving, turning, up on footpaths, making people jump out of their way. Our men fought them with homemade bombs. In response the Auxies put a cage of wire netting over their lorries, and set a post with handcuffs in the centre. Soon we saw bound hostages in these military vehicles, the victim strapped to the central pole. TDs were 'deterred' from any further effort to stand their ground in public when Michael Colivet[*] TD of Limerick was carried as a hostage in his own constituency. That was to teach him, and other

[*] Michael Colivet (1882–1955) was a Sinn Féin politician, leader of the Volunteers in Limerick City during the 1916 Rising and Commander of the Volunteers in Limerick and East Clare. He was elected to the First Dáil in 1918, while interned in a British prison. The hostage incident that Máire Comerford refers to was debated in the British House of Commons in April 1921, when questions were asked about the conditions at Rathkeale Jail, where Michael Colivet was held awaiting trial and paraded as a hostage in a Crown forces vehicle. He was elected unopposed in the 1921 election for Limerick City / Limerick East.

members of Dáil Éireann, that the British were intent on the alternative two-parliament arrangement, instead of one parliament to represent all Ireland.

The new imperial dispensation, cooked up in London, became law on 20 December 1920; this gave the British government power to carry out two elections in Ireland – one for the twenty-six counties of all four provinces, and a second for six of Ulster's nine counties. It created two subservient states with limited functions on paper and enacted that the two parliaments of these two states might, if they so wished, set up an all-Ireland parliament, also subservient to London. The minority in Ireland was thus given a veto on Irish Independence. It amuses me still that Britain then, and ever since, pretended to the world that the settlement of Irish affairs was entirely in the hands of the Irish. A 'benign' Britain was presented as being prepared to accept the decision of the Irish people. TDs, interned or imprisoned or on the run, were kept where they were until a thin red line had been drawn by the military and by the 'Specials' (a partisan police force, organized from the more belligerent elements of Carson's army). The aim was to cut off the largest area possible to create a region where the Belfast-based pro-British minority could be turned into a local majority. Then they would be free to operate the Parliament of Northern Ireland – flying the Union Jack behind artillery pointing southwards. The principle of majority rule was to be overturned in two elections.

The success of the British trap was dependent on what the Catholics and Protestants of Ireland would now do. If they lined up under their religious banners then Lloyd George might emerge as the statesman who settled the Irish question. Our side walked into the trap. What had happened in 1917, when the executive of Sinn Féin stooped to bargain with the Irish Parliamentary Party for the Catholic vote in the north-east, happened again. The leaders, who pledged themselves time and time again at Bodenstown to the principles of Wolfe Tone and the United Irishmen, went after the Catholic vote; another bargain was struck, this time between Éamon de Valera and Joseph Devlin.* There was no prior consultation with the Dáil, and any questions put there got no straight answers. The Dáil had not been called from September 1920 to January 1921; it met in the house of Alderman Cole on Mountjoy Square on 21 January to celebrate the third birthday of our own Dáil Éireann. But the Republican government allotted no Dáil time for any discussion of the proposed partition of Ireland. On 11 March, at a private session of the Dáil, Piaras Béaslaí TD complained because there was nothing on the agenda about the election. He felt that the subject should not be passed without full consideration. The president responded by stating that Sinn Féin, who had decided in favour of a contest, had considered the whole matter. And that apparently was that.

Elections for the two new states ordained in London were to be held on 24 May, and the speeches of enemy leaders made it clear that the elected representatives of the Irish people were, and would be, under duress. Michael Collins reported to President de Valera that the proclamation extending martial law from Munster and parts of Leinster to the whole twenty-six counties was already in print in Dublin Castle. The alternative to acceptance of partition would be Crown colony government. This, as Lloyd George might have said, depended on the decision of the Irish themselves. The Republican government's determination to recognize the election in order to secure a further mandate for Dáil Éireann to carry on as it had been doing, met with no dissent I ever heard of from our side. The issue in the forthcoming election was now clear. The candidates put forward by Sinn Féin were pledged to refuse attendance at the parliaments of Northern or Southern Ireland, and to refuse the Oath of Allegiance to the King of England.

---

* Joseph (Joe) Devlin (1871–1934) was a nationalist politician, MP for the Irish Parliamentary Party in Westminster and later a nationalist representative in the Northern Ireland parliament. 'Wee Joe' as he was known, was renowned for his oratorial and organizational skills. The period from 1905–16 was the most productive of Devlin's political career, when the Irish Parliamentary Party were key players in the fight for Irish Home Rule. However, the ongoing debate about the exclusion of Ulster from an all-Irish settlement diminished Devlin's authority in nationalist politics, and in the years after 1916 his political influence gradually declined.

The strategy that nominated the national leaders for constituencies along the border looked like genius, and a demonstration of the daring courage we believed our heroes possessed. Questions and doubt were swept away by enthusiasm in favour of the move. They were certain of election – Michael Collins for Armagh, Éamon de Valera for Down, Arthur Griffith and Seán Milroy for Fermanagh and Tyrone, O'Mahony also for Fermanagh / Tyrone, and MacNeill for Derry; let Lloyd George put that in his pipe and smoke it! Soon he would find half of the total area he tried to separate represented in Dáil Éireann and refusing British allegiance; if he wanted to talk about Ireland, he would have to talk with TDs firmly established in the place where he least wanted to have them. It seemed obvious that, having been elected to stand in the 'Gap of Danger',* the leaders would resign their other constituencies within the twenty-six counties.

What all this amounted to was a castle in Spain, which was nonetheless very stimulating to morale in the lower ranks of the movement. Many years later, it is almost impossible for me to believe, what subsequent facts assert, that this was no more than a gambit in the election game, to be forgotten when the polling booths closed. This is the point from which ruin followed; for this let no one blame the Irish people, or their army, or the backbenchers of Dáil Éireann, or the junior ministers. The failure was in political leadership, and it is unlikely that it went unnoticed in Downing Street, or Conservative Party Headquarters, or anywhere cute men worked to negate and defeat the long fight for the freedom of the Irish people. Whatever the original plan for the election was, or why it might have been abandoned, I do not know, but its failure had sad results for the people in the six counties; this applies whether they were the dominant Unionist majority – guilty of setting aside human rights – or part of that substantial, and henceforth friendless, nationalist minority.

But in May 1921 there were no clouds that we could see on the political horizon. Indeed, we may have been discussing impending

---

* A place that is hard to defend, in this case territory where there is a danger of losing an election.

victory in the election in Mrs Ceannt's house in Ranelagh when Páidín O'Keeffe TD, Secretary to Sinn Féin, joined us. He looked around the company and then his finger shot out, pointing in turn to perhaps a half dozen of those present. He told us to be at Amiens Street Station for the early train north the following morning. Then Páidín, who was 'on the run', disappeared as quickly as he had arrived.

Early next morning I joined about 150 other election speakers in the train that carried us across the newborn border. I was filled with both fear and fervour. Early on the Sunday morning, before we separated to cover the dozens of election meetings planned for that day, Father Michael O'Flanagan joined us. I remember the effect of his presence, his leadership and his kindness, as he quelled our concerns and sent us off braced to make the best we could of the job in hand. Soon I was standing on a grass bank with a congregation of people, who had just attended an early mass, grouped on the road before me. I had the experience, often repeated in subsequent years, of listening with interest and sometimes with astonishment to the speech that I was making. It was as if my mouth and my ears belonged to different people. When I finished speaking and came down from the grassy bank, my hands were bleeding; in my great nervousness I had grasped a branch of the prickly hawthorn hedge behind me.

Sinn Féin did well at that meeting because the crowd waited until we had finished, instead of melting away towards their breakfasts. I knew little then about the problems of the men and women in the chapel gate audience in Maghera, and other places where I later spoke. There would certainly have been soldiers of the Republic and women of Cumann na mBan amongst them, whose local problems were far more complicated than any known to me. They lived and worked in a territory torn apart and devastated by the older, more organized, religious Civil War, which no longer survived outside Ulster to any important degree, but remained indigenous there. Edward Carson, in his day, had merely fanned it. But I believe too that some among them would have been hard set to determine whether their worst enemies were in the Catholic or the Protestant camp. In our election addresses we tried to promulgate the doctrine of Wolfe Tone, hoping that our voices would carry from chapel gate to Orange Hall.*

All over the country military and police pressure was intense against us; the IRA were fighting back on fronts that had been extended as far as possible from counties where resistance to the British had, up to then, been strongest. It was impossible to think of anything except fighting. The Dublin Castle statement on casualties during the week ending 16 May 1921 made them the highest since 1916. Although I was well occupied in Dublin, Wexford was never far from my mind and I travelled there on average about once every month. On Empire Day† the British military blew up Seán Etchingham's house, the family home of Charlotte Veney of Gorey Cumann na mBan and Kenny's homestead, where two of the boys were Volunteers. This was in my own North Wexford, so it stands out amongst similar incidents in other places. Mother cycled to two or three of the houses with her camera and took pictures of the ruins, with martial law proclamations pasted on them. By the time I arrived at Veneys' to commiserate, they had already spent a night or two in the stables. Nonetheless, Mrs Veney made tea while we worked on our report for the White Cross.

Peg Cuffe and a friend ran a small Irish-speaking school three or four miles outside Bunclody, on the hilly road to Killane and Ross, where some of the pupils were boarders. She was a very small young woman, full of life and fun with lovely brown, curly hair. Whether the Tans knew there were about ten sleeping children in Peg's school the night they set it on fire I cannot say. Perhaps they thought only Peg was there, and that is quite bad enough. Fortunately, no one was killed; all the children were taken out without injury. When I got to the school, a few weeks later, I inspected the burnt-out building; I saw what everyone who went there also saw, the statue of Our Lady still

---

* Members of the Orange Order join lodges, equivalent to branches. The meetings of the various lodges take place in individual Orange halls.

† In 1903, following the death of Queen Victoria in 1901, the celebration of the queen's birthday on 24 May was renamed Empire Day and celebrated throughout the British Empire until 1958, when it was rechristened British Commonwealth Day. In 1966 the title was simplified to Commonwealth Day.

standing in its place at the head of the damaged stairs. It was held by all that divine providence had saved them from being burnt to death.

Such incidences close to home may have pushed important national operations, such as the Custom House action, out of my mind at that time. But events in Dublin were much more dangerous. We lost men – killed, wounded and taken prisoner – in retreat after British forces rushed up in time to surround our fighting men, who were delayed because of a wrong whistle signal inside the Custom House. Two out of every three men engaged on our side were casualties. Oscar Traynor, Dublin Brigade Commandant, was saved when Dan Head, a young Volunteer, threw himself into the line of fire from a lorry, at point-blank range from Oscar, under the Loop Line Bridge. Before his death Dan Head put a bomb into the lorry. The dockers and the women of the locality gave great help to our men in the Custom House. Commandant Tom Ennis, in charge inside the building, was badly wounded; he was carried out in a railway lorry. Captain Paddy Flanagan of the Active Service Unit (ASU) dropped a great height, and then lay flat on the donkey cart while he was brought clear to have wounds, which shortened his life, attended to. Ned Dorrins was still wearing bandages from another engagement when he was killed, with fellow Volunteers Patrick and Stephen O'Reilly. Seamus Doyle, ASU, fought his way to Store Street where he collapsed and was saved by women. Before he died in the Mater Hospital that same night, Seamus heard the sound of gunfire, and was happy to know the fight was still on.

In the May election of 1921, Ireland as a whole rejected partition, and the Better Government of Ireland Act, by 136 to 44 (including University seats in Dublin and Belfast). Our leaders – Éamon de Valera and his fellow candidates – were successful along the border and in Derry; but except for O'Mahony for Fermanagh and South Tyrone, the 'Gap of Danger' waited in vain for any personal leadership from those supposedly representing them. The time would come, within the year, when the blind eye of Nelson on his pillar in Dublin was no more purposefully blind than those of Michael Collins and Arthur Griffith telling us that Ireland was now free.

Truce

FOLLOWING THE ELECTION all kinds of rumours were circulating but there was no hard news. In mid-June I was on some forgotten errand in Limerick or Tipperary when I became embroiled in an argument with a man in the hotel at Limerick Junction. I was told by this stranger that a compromise solution for Ireland was far advanced, and a settlement that would not recognize the Republic was imminent. On my arrival in Dublin, I raced to find Liam Mellows and told him my story in the Woods's dining room. He said that Éamon de Valera should hear this news and we took our bicycles, riding the back way and avoiding Donnybrook Road, until we arrived at a house in Blackrock (the whole of Ireland knew about this house four days later when de Valera was arrested there). I had met President de Valera before, but that had happened in the middle of a crowd; I was enthralled to be in his company on national business. It was a short, very formal interview. Liam explained our business and I told my story. Éamon de Valera thanked us gravely and I left alone, cycling on air.

The annual Bodenstown ceremony was due to take place on Sunday 19 June, but it had been decided to take no risks this time. Seán O'Murthuile, top-ranking IRB man, and a member of the Commemoration Committee, sent a note to Eilís Ní Riain, Captain, Central Branch, Cumann na mBan and 1916 Veteran:

> Eilís, The Big Fellow says you are to lay a wreath at Bodenstown Sunday next. There will be a taxi at 41 Parnell Sq. at 10.30. There is seating accommodation for five people and you can bring who you wish.

Eilís decided to bring her four section commanders – Fiona Plunkett,[*] Emily Valentine,[†] Margaret McElroy[‡] and myself. For those few hours, we became the representations of the Republic. The British were in occupation in Bodenstown but we passed through them, without comment on either side. Eilís unlocked the gates of the cemetery and placed the wreath in position. Then we left and made our return trip to Dublin. From the Republican perspective this must have been the smallest Bodenstown on record!

Three days earlier on 16 June Michael Collins reported to Éamon de Valera that the proclamation of martial law for the whole country was ready for implementation on 29 June. Whether the order would be issued or not depended on what happened on the 28th.

---

[*] Fiona Plunkett (1896–1977) was one of four daughters of Count and Josephine Plunkett. Her brother Joseph was executed for his role as a leader in the Rising. Fiona took the anti-Treaty side in the Civil War and continued to be a staunch Republican, and friend and comrade of Máire Comerford for the remainder of her life. In 1976 the two elderly women were prosecuted for their participation in a banned commemoration of the 1916 Rising at the GPO, but avoided prison on that occasion!

[†] Emily Valentine (1895–1969) joined Cumann na mBan in late 1916 in Dublin and was based in Belfast from 1917, mainly visiting Irish Volunteers prisoners, moving and storing arms and hiding men on the run. Later, Emily was in charge of collecting and distributing the Prisoners' Dependents' Fund in the North Dublin City area. She was on duty at Croke Park on Bloody Sunday 1920 and rendered first aid.

[‡] Margaret (Mairéad) McElroy (1886–1974) took part in the 1916 Rebellion as a member of Cumann na mBan and served in the GPO, where she provided first aid and remained at her post even after Pearse had asked the members of Cumann na mBan if they wished to leave on the Friday, when fighting had become intense and the building was on fire.

This was the appointed day for the first meeting of the 'Parliament of Southern Ireland'. King George travelled in person to officially open the 'Parliament of Northern Ireland' in Belfast. Men who were in action when one of King George's troop trains was ambushed at Adavoyle on 24 June told me later that they hated the appalling carnage that ensued. Cavalrymen and horses, returning from ceremonies connected with the royal opening, were hurled off the high railway embankment. This was the first significant 'border incident'[*]

On this day too Mr Lloyd George, Prime Minister, invited Éamon de Valera 'as the chosen leader of the majority in Southern Ireland' and Sir James Craig 'the Premier of Northern Ireland' to attend together at a conference in London. The president in reply stated that he was in consultation 'with such of the principal representatives of our nation as are available'. De Valera saw no avenue by which peace could be reached – 'if you (Lloyd George) deny Ireland's essential unity'.

I was in Wexford the weekend after Lloyd George wrote to Éamon de Valera inviting him to discuss peace in London. People would not understand now what it was like to have your heart and soul in agony for news. That was the way I was, and the way I found my friends. I set out to find out what Father Sweetman was thinking about the situation, and arrived at Mount St Benedict before dinner time on Sunday. As we talked in company of about five or six other people, quite suddenly Father Sweetman decided that he could not stand the tension any longer, and suggested that all of us present should set out straight away for Dublin to discover what news we could there. This plan involved catching the Sunday train at Woodenbridge, a journey of about thirteen miles, on the far side of the Wicklow Gap.

---

[*] In June 1921 the 10th Royal Hussars travelled by train from the Curragh military camp in County Kildare to Belfast in order to escort King George V to the opening of the first parliament of Northern Ireland on 22 June. On the return journey to Dublin on 24 June, the third of three specially commissioned trains was derailed by a mine planted by the IRA. The derailment led to the deaths of three members of the machine-gun troop and a railway guard at the scene. Two further soldiers died later of their injuries, and two railway officials were seriously injured. The incident also led to the death of some forty horses, many of whom had recently been through, and survived, World War I.

Father Sweetman's departures for Dublin were always exciting. His pony, Jacob, was so 'hot' he could hardly be kept on the road. Together they would canter the first half-mile down the grass verge of the avenue and pull up at the station when the guard had his watch out and the train already moving. But this departure for Dublin was exceptional. Father Sweetman shouted to John Corcoran, a worker at the Mount, to yoke Dandy, the white Connemara; he then signed to Mary Kavanagh to pack food, and told the rest of us to eat while we could, for there would be nothing on the train. Within half an hour the walkers were on their way. The trap, when it overtook us, facilitated short lifts. In that way every walker would be rested and our miles per hour increased. The train had steam up and the guard's flag was raised when, after crashing downhill in a shortcut through Glenart Wood, we hurled ourselves into the last carriage. At Wicklow, Seán MacBride*joined us. The train was moving again when he told us that he suspected that the lines ahead were up; something had happened in the town that made it necessary to stop Crown forces from getting there quickly. It stood as evidence, duplicated country-wide, that as the Tan War[†] drew to its close, the IRA were visibly in control of wide areas of the country.

I have to attempt an assessment of the position between Ireland and England at the time of the Truce. This is still very difficult. Fear – of raids and house burnings, of torture and of death – this was the experience of every intelligent Irish citizen. Bravery nestled in their hearts too. Fear and bravery fought a battle, with no outsider knowing afterwards whether a man's actions were understandable in the light of his honourable conviction, or his hidden terror. This

* Seán MacBride (1904–1988) was the son of Maud Gonne and Major John MacBride, who was executed in 1916 for his part in the Easter Rising. He joined the IRA during the War of Independence and took the anti-Treaty side in 1922. MacBride remained active during and after the Civil War, becoming IRA chief of staff in 1936–7. Following a distinguished career in human rights, Seán MacBride was awarded the Nobel Peace Prize in 1974.

† The Irish War of Independence is sometimes referred to as the 'Tan War', a term often preferred by those who took an anti-Treaty position during and after the Civil War.

was particularly the case in cities and towns, and among men, who if caught, would likely be tortured because of what they knew, or what the enemy knew about them. There was only the thickness of a wall, at best, between these men and capture at night, and the risks they ran when they walked or cycled about their business in the streets are terrifying to imagine even now.

The Truce was negotiated by Lord Middleton, at Lloyd George's bidding. This was the point at which people with a social outlook far removed from Republican entered Irish politics. Lord Middleton was an important man in the British establishment – a past Secretary of State for War in the British government; his Irish record was that of an enemy. Gobnait Ní Bhuadair (aka the Hon. Albinia Brodrick), Lord Middleton's sister, had warned us that her brother was a dangerous foe. But the situation in which Middleton and the governing class of England went to work for a cessation of hostilities was one where many English people had turned against their government's policy of violence in Ireland; many Britons were sympathetic, and totally opposed to the Black and Tan regime.

On the morning of 8 July, Kate, the parlour maid at No. 90 who knew everything, left Mrs Green's hall door unlatched. Shortly afterwards from my office I heard men arrive. Soon the hall was full of bicycles. I saw Bob (Robert) Barton TD arrive in a side car; this may have been the first I knew of his release from Portland Convict Prison. Presently the dividing door between the rooms opened and Diarmuid O'hÉigeartuigh, Secretary to the Dáil and IRB man, requested the use of the typewriter. Then, he changed his mind and asked me to type a copy of the document in his hand. What I typed were the terms of the Truce. Bob Barton, in a hurry, jumped into his waiting side car. The jarvey drove off with all the dash and importance that Cuchulainn's charioteer might have shown on a day of battle. The other men melted away one by one.

Under the terms of the Truce, British forces were to cease 'pursuit of Irish officers and men, or war materials or military stores', while the IRA was to cease 'attacks on Crown forces and civilians ... [and] British government and private property'. That evening, for the first time in my life, I was unsuccessful in my attempt to get into the Mansion House on a great occasion. The Republican police never failed to recognize their friends, and even while they struggled with great crowds, I had always before managed to squeeze past. The space in front of the Lord Mayor's steps was open then. But there was no such thing as a hollow square, or that kind of formality, when Richard (Dick) Mulcahy, IRA Chief of Staff, and General Macready, Commander-in-Chief, Crown forces, joined the Mansion House conference at about 6 pm. Mulcahy stopped to respond to the cheers but Macready did not turn his head before the door closed on them. Later, after Macready's departure, I was still wedged in the same place in the crowd when Eamonn Duggan TD read the official announcement of the Truce from the Mansion House steps, which was to come into force on Monday 11 July.

Dublin had never known such a moment before. This was the fitting sequel to the struggle of centuries, the justification of Easter Week, the fulfilment of Dáil Éireann, which had first assembled in the same place thirty months before. No wonder countless parties, like ours from Wexford, came together in the rejoicing city. An evening or two later I was with the Woods family on the platform at Harcourt Street station to see Seán Etchingham, Liam Mellows and Cathal Brugha off on the evening train to Wexford. They were like schoolboys going home, with laughter and larks and hand-waving. Seán went to his mother, sister and nephews in the wrecked house near Courtown; Liam to his mother and aunts near Castletown, and Cathal to his wife and children at a summer cottage by the sea in Ballymoney. For two of them it was no more than a joyful break of a few days away from the city; but Seán Etchingham, in bad health, needed a longer break. Arrangements were made in Gorey to ensure that all three men could be quickly collected and brought back to Dublin, if they were needed.

People only laughed bitterly when Seán T. O'Kelly – almost twenty years later – told us that 'We had whipped John Bull.'* But truth be told what he said was true for a week or so. What really whipped 'John Bull' though was the bravery of our fight and the intransigent idealism, which led men from Pearse and Connolly, Terence MacSwiney, Kevin Barry, and many less well-known men and women, to face impossible odds for the freedom of our small nation – a principle consistent with what most of the world had believed it was at war for in 1914–18. And, for a short moment in history, world opinion gave us their accusing fingers all pointed decisively at the big bad bully in London.

But in 1921, between the anniversaries of Easter Week and the death of Tone, the executive of Sinn Féin and the cabinet of Dáil Éireann adopted the path of conservatism. They had been deflected from the cause of human justice by, amongst other things, an intense and worldwide propaganda campaign against the Russian Revolution (1917–22).

---

* In 1938 Ireland negotiated the Anglo-Irish trade agreement with Britain. In a memorable speech in Dáil Éireann, Seán T. O'Kelly, then Tánaiste, and later the second President of Ireland, bragged about whipping 'John Bull right, left and centre' in the terms of the trade agreement. John Bull is a political caricature, laid out as the personification of the English character or nation. John Bull first appeared as a caricature in 1712 but became more widely known in the latter end of the nineteenth century in cartoon form, especially through the influential periodical *Punch*.

Beds

AFTER THE TRUCE seemed to be effective all the important people on our side could sleep in their own beds and keep important papers in their pockets, or in offices. They did not need our help to keep clear of prison, or the grave. To that extent women like me were out of a job. Technically the Dáil was still proclaimed. There was no mention of it in the published terms of the Truce. Neither had there been any meeting of the Second Dáil. But in the atmosphere of victory no one was in the mood to search for clouds. The government functioned openly and President Éamon de Valera's office was located in the Lord Mayor's drawing room in the Mansion House. The place was besieged. I remember sitting back to back on a table in the hall with William Cosgrave, Minister for Local Government – his hair now back to blond again.

Rather suddenly it seemed a long time ago since evening fell on Lily O'Brennan, or on Mrs Nell Humphreys,[*] Mrs Gordon[†] and other members of Cumann na mBan, before they found the beds they needed, where wanted men could sleep with some degree of safety. Now everyone you met claimed they had been 'putting up' wanted men. And some of them had; but there were many, whose nerve had not lasted, who often talked loudly before those of us who knew the parts of the story which they might prefer to forget. But in Cumann na mBan we would not forget the wonderful people who never failed to say – 'Let him come anyhow. We do not know whether this place is safe or not, but we will do our best.' The most committed Republicans – and these were not only of the rank and file – were now handicapped in their understanding of the situation because of their steadfast faith in the Cause and its leaders, and in every line of reassuring propaganda emanating from our own headquarters. Any day when the newspapers did not produce a stop-press edition – which might come from 11 am onwards – the newsboys invented one. Barefooted, fleet as the wind, shrill-voiced, they sped through the streets, sometimes with two or three sensations a day.

---

[*] Mary Ellen (Nell) Humphreys (*née* O'Rahilly) (1871–1939) was born in County Kerry. Following her husband's death in 1903 she moved from Limerick to live in Dublin. In 1916 her teenage son Dick fought alongside Nell's brother, The O'Rahilly, in the GPO. The O'Rahilly was shot and died during the fighting. Nell was arrested and was taken to the RDS in Ballsbridge, where she was held in a horsebox for the remainder of Easter Week, then removed to Richmond Barracks. Following her release Nell joined the Ranelagh Branch of Cumann na mBan in 1919. She was elected as a Republican member of Pembroke Urban District Council in 1920. Her home became a centre of Republican activities, and was frequently used as a safe house during the War of Independence.

[†] Winnifred (Una) Gordon (*née* Cassidy), later Stack (1878–1950), an Irish Republican activist, was born in Enniskillen, County Fermanagh. She married Patrick Gordon, a district inspector of the RIC in 1901, who died in 1912. Una was a friend of Countess Markievicz and her house in Dublin became a safe haven for Republican men during the revolutionary period. She had a hideout closet built in the bathroom of her home, which reputedly could hold up to eight men at any one time, and was never discovered by the authorities. Una married Irish Republican Austin Stack in 1925.

The daily papers operating from Dublin showed as much courage now as they had during the war, despite the censorship. After the Truce they gave prominence to rumours and speculation about what was to come. We were not slow to call this treason, and to accuse them of disloyalty to the established Republic. My subsequent career in journalism enabled me to see what happened in a different light. We played into the hands of our critics and were furious when they were given a great deal of space to hit back, and to draw us out. The art of glorious pretend, which had used the flag of the Republic to cover partition, drift, betrayal of social principles, incompetence and cowardice, assumed its fatal role to cover the Mansion House Peace Conference in July 1921. The grim fact was that James Craig had gone to London, where he was received as the representative of the 'six counties'. The expedition to London of our president, Éamon de Valera, members of his cabinet and private individuals, was legally and from the British perspective, a delegation from Southern Ireland. The position could have been corrected if de Valera made it clear that his mandate was from County Down, as well as from County Clare. Instead, it seemed that a secret policy had been adopted – under certain conditions the functioning of a six-county state in the North would be recognized.

The space outside the Mansion House was rarely without crowds, watching the comings and goings; I was there when Éamon de Valera made his first speech from the steps, following his return from London. He told us that it was not a time for talk, and that if Ireland had learned one lesson it was that acts, and not talk, would achieve freedom for the nation. He lifted the crowd by declaring – 'If we act as we have acted for the last couple of years we will never have to talk about freedom, for we will have won it.' Cheers, and more cheers, greeted this. Everyone happy! Many years later Éamon de Valera put the truth in a nutshell for me when he said, 'The people believed our propaganda.'* I belonged to that credulous multitude.

---

* This quotation from Éamon de Valera comes from a phone interview conducted by Marie Comerford in 1969. Contemporaneous notes from the interview (uncatalogued) are in the Máire Comerford Archive Collection.

Dáil Éireann met secretly most of the time during the War of Independence. When the Second Dáil did finally meet, the public sessions were held in a general atmosphere of perfect comradely love and defiant repudiation of the dominion proposals of the British government. The British and Irish Truce offices were set up in rooms beside one another in the Gresham Hotel. Here the Crown installed one of their cleverest men, Alfred Cope, as undersecretary. I believe that Cope was the civil servant who, more than anyone else, brought about the downfall of the Irish Republic. Next door, the Republican army placed one of our few trained and professional officers, Emmet Dalton, formerly a captain in the British army, who had also served with distinction on Collins's staff. But in the wider context of this arrangement, responsibilities, for which they had no training, were now placed on the shoulders of young officers. These men had proved themselves in the flying columns, but had not established the ability to keep their heads when flattered, or to hold their drinks. The more exuberant of these officers were soon to be seen around Dublin in their new uniforms, plus the latest thing in green leather coats and fast cars.

The IRA men in general were kept under discipline. All ranks were called out again to attend special training courses, which were severe. But organizers of training camps in the 'six counties' soon found that the Truce did not count where they were concerned. The camps were broken up and the men arrested. The general assumption that the IRA had been 'recognized' in the Truce negotiations, and that the Truce itself was between nations, quickly dissolved in the minds of those involved in these clashes north of 'the border'. The oppression of centuries continued unabated in half of Ulster. The President of the Republic, Éamon de Valera, washed his hands of the people who had elected him in Down, as did his colleagues, including Collins, Griffith and MacNeill, who won seats in 'The Gap of Danger'. While Dublin relaxed – or schemed – Belfast bled under renewed pogroms. Catholics were now held to be 'Shinners'* and therefore

---

* 'Shinners' was a pejorative term used for supporters of Sinn Féin, or sometimes used erroneously for Irish Volunteers. The term is widely used nowadays for

'disloyal'. Whether they all quite liked it or not, that was the position into which they were driven – where they could best be debarred from full citizenship of the newly-formed state, itself carved out of Ireland.

Special trains unloaded hundreds of refugees from the Belfast pogrom into Dublin. The IRA commandeered the premises of the Kildare Street Club, and those of the Masonic Order in Molesworth Street, to accommodate these poor people with nothing left but the children in their arms and the clothes they stood up in. I have vivid memories of those days, and especially of the cluster of women and children, who were to be seen on the steps of the Kildare Street Club on fine days. When the Belfast women brought their children into the fresh air and sunshine, the scene must have been so different from that they were accustomed to, outside the mean little slum houses of factory workers, in the back streets of the Falls Road district.

As for the members of the Kildare Street Club – the most exclusive male sanctuary belonging to the Ascendancy class – my information, and even more that coming from my mother, indicated that the IRA had made a deep impression on some, or many of its members. This came through personal contacts, and mainly in country districts. Our fighting columns behaved very correctly when they were sometimes billeted in castles and mansions. The owners of these splendid, but now near landless properties – some with an evil history – had moved at least a little with the times, and were not always unwilling to adjust themselves. Even if they could not have their own way about every-thing, they still wanted to chase the fox across the fields of Ireland, to fish its waters, drive its roads, live with its beauty. The sight of the poor victims of the Belfast pogrom in their club, and on its exclusive doorstep, must have provided food for thought, even for the most hard-headed and intransigent ex-landlords.

Life at No. 90 St Stephen's Green lost a lot of its interest for me when the Truce threw us back on history and the parties carried on, but where the hostess and guests seemed to have stopped enquiring.

members or supporters of the present-day Sinn Féin. Máire Comerford named her beloved dog 'Shinner' in the 1970s.

I could not forget the incident with the newspaper headline, when Mrs Green seemed to grieve more over our victory in Cork than she did over what the Black and Tans were doing, reprisal after reprisal. The writers Æ Russell and James Douglas, Professor MacNeill and P.S. O'Hegarty began to look like other old people; I did not want to hear any more forecasting from Mrs Green about whether we would be made to suffer as much as the Boers* in South Africa had, before we would learn sense, as they had had to learn it. Her talk to me was of barbed-wire entanglements from one end of the country to the other, and all disloyal men, women and children captive in vast internment camps, where many hundreds would die as the result of hunger, disease, or imperial policy. I did not wish to be present or to hear any talk, which put less value than I did on our independence and sovereign status.

I had Mrs Green's goodwill for my transfer from her employment to that of the Dáil. We had both been committee members of Cumann Leigheacht an Phobail – the lecture committee grant aided by the Dáil to prepare adult educational material in the form of lectures, for the use of clubs and discussion groups. When the first secretary, Eithne Kelly, resigned, they gave me her place. This meant that I could continue to work for the Republic, except when I was asleep.

---

* The term Boer is derived from the Afrikaans word for farmer and was used to describe people who traced their ancestry to Dutch, German and French Huguenot settlers to the Cape of Good Hope in South Africa from around 1652, the first white settlers in the region. The Boer War started in October 1899, arising from conflict with British settlers, who took possession of the Dutch Cape colony in 1806. In response the Boers moved into African tribal territory, setting up two new republics: the Orange Free State and the Transvaal. However, in 1867, gold and diamonds were discovered in the region and conflict again arose, leading to war between the Boers and the English in 1899. The Boers employed guerrilla tactics and the English responded by detaining the families of Boer soldiers in concentration camps. The war ended in May 1902, when the Boers ceded control of Transvaal and the Orange Free State to the British military administration.

Dresses and Delegations

ONE EVENING in September 1921 I turned up at Áine Ceannt's house in Oakley Road, as was my wont, in search of a job to do. Lo and behold! When I got inside, the sisters and some friends were contemplating dresses – spread out on the table and draped on the chairs. 'I'll be going to London for the negotiations and I have nothing to wear,' said Lily O'Brennan, who was Áine's sister and secretary to Arthur Griffith. 'You will not be there long enough to wear more than you stand up in. Anyhow why dress up for London,' I said somewhat archly, for Lily's enthusiasm for London fashion had put me in a very bad humour. 'You are all wrong. We will be there a long time,' Lily countered. 'If they must have King and Empire and six counties, and we stand for an all-Ireland Republic, there is not enough in common between us for it to be worth sitting down with that.' I replied. Lily told me that I didn't know what I was talking about. She reiterated that the delegates were going to be a long time in London, and she was sure they would succeed there. Lily had complete confidence in the Republican proposals and, when they were published, I would find myself agreeing with her. Meantime, I could take it that Lily was as good a Republican as I was. The last sentence at least was proved true. A year later she got jail without court or trial, before I did.

It had been proclaimed from thousands of platforms that John Redmond's mistake in trusting an English government would never be repeated. Now, it seemed, all that was discarded. We would enter a war of diplomacy and negotiation where there were neither rules – such as existed in my time for 'civilized' war – nor any clear code of conduct. Was it possible to succeed in London where so many had failed? Of course, it was encouraging that England was a fading power, and in difficulties at home and abroad. Our relentless exposure of the brutal Black-and-Tan methods had hurt British prestige, particularly in the United States; it was a cheering thought for us that world power had changed hands, and the old tyrant might have to mend his ways.

Nonetheless, I found that I could not cheer when the Irish delegation left for London by the morning boat from Dun Laoghaire on 9 October. I stood instead in a group of silent people who watched them go. Some may have wondered whether we had another Parnell among them, who would know how to talk to the English (we hadn't). Nor would it transpire that England had a Gladstone either.* We did not spot Michael Collins in the considerable party, which gathered around or behind Arthur Griffith. Robert Barton arrived late. I thought of his long ordeal in penal servitude, and the sudden change for him from the institutional discipline of life for an unrepentant convict, to the dangerous situation now facing him, and Ireland. I was too uneasy to wish to speak to him, or to Erskine, or Lily. I stayed in the crowd, on my own side of a gulf.

---

* In 1886 Charles Stewart Parnell joined with the British Liberals to defeat the sitting Conservative government in London, and William Ewart Gladstone became Prime Minister. Gladstone was impressed by Parnell and was committed to granting Home Rule for Ireland. However, in 1886, his first attempt to introduce Home Rule split the Liberal Party. The bill was defeated in the House of Commons by thirty votes and Gladstone temporarily lost power. Following Parnell's death and his return to power in 1892, Gladstone attempted to introduce Home Rule for Ireland for a second time. On this occasion the bill was defeated in the House of Lords.

Before departure, as the delegates gathered together to be photographed, someone stepped forward and presented the group with a small tricolour. The flag was accepted, but then quickly disappeared. If the donor hoped that the delegates would hold the tricolour for the photograph, or in London, he or she was to be disappointed. One can say now that they were a brave little party, as they turned their faces across the sea, to secure victory for Ireland by peaceful means. Preparation for this moment, when our issues with England would come to the table, was considerable, and the pressure immense. From the Rising of Easter Week to the defence of the established government of the Republic against the Black and Tans, the effort and the sacrifices of our people had secured a great deal of world publicity. Our foreign representatives, successful in most fields of propaganda, had nevertheless failed to get a hearing at the Peace Conference in Versailles, or in the capitals of other nations. Appearances at the time when our plenipotentiaries went to London would emerge as being far different from the reality. On the British side their massive propaganda effort of the previous months was working; creating a growing consensus that Ireland did not need a World Court, for she had already won her case. The expedition to London was represented as a kind of prize-giving, with Michael Collins cast as the hero of the day. That was all very well except in Downing Street, where Lloyd George's team avoided having to shake hands with him, or his colleagues. Nor did they provide an opportunity for the formal presentation of credentials carried by the 'Envoys Plenipotentiary of the Republic of Ireland'.

Our plenipotentiaries were already in London when an English bishop persuaded Pope Benedict to congratulate King George on the resumption of Anglo-Irish negotiations. This brought a quick reaction from President de Valera. He cabled the Pope and pointed out that the British had, by brutal force, robbed the Irish nation of their ancient right to liberty. De Valera's response lifted our hearts at home, and removed any misgivings. There was, however, disagreement in Hans Place – our London headquarters for the period of the negotiations – concerning the wisdom of making such a statement. Our delegation was already showing the signs of being infused with a fatal overconfidence. This was displayed every time they called themselves a 'peace mission'.

In October eight hundred branches of Cumann na mBan were represented at our convention in Dublin. Following her release from Mountjoy Prison, Countess Markievicz, presiding, told us: 'This is a time for action not talk, but we must think about the future. Don't think it is going to be peace. Go out and work as if the war was going to break out again next week.' In the convention we asserted the right of all citizens over eighteen years of age to vote in any plebiscite or election where the honour and fate of Ireland might be at stake. We declared that any appeal to the country on any other basis would be unjust, and its decision not binding.

My happiest memory of that period is of tea breaks during meetings and conventions, when friendships between people who did not ordinarily meet deepened. Country representatives and delegates to the Dáil or national organizations were constantly in Dublin. It was a pleasure to encounter them on the streets and in restaurants. Two women stand out in my memory from the time: Mrs Kate O'Callaghan TD, who I met previously in Mrs Green's when her widowhood was not yet fact, and Mary MacSwiney TD,[*] sister of Terence, also recently dead. These were women of great ability, steadfast and courageous; they were always keenly interested in any news we might have about the spirit of the country. Mary MacSwiney had considerable prior experience of public affairs through her Dáil work, and through her contacts at home and wider afield. She was strongly connected to political and social life in Cork, engaging with the pupils and parents of her school (Scoil Íte) and as an active member of Cumann na mBan. Her experience abroad was also exceptional, following a successful tour to the US in early 1921, to promote the cause of Ireland. She

---

[*] Mary MacSwiney (Máire Nic Suibhne) (1872–1942) was elected as a TD for Cork city in 1921. She took the anti-Treaty side and made a long speech during the Treaty debate, which was uncompromisingly Republican.

was one of the finest people I ever knew, straight, incorruptible, kind and just, very brave, soft when it was right to be soft, clear-headed and intelligent.

At the Sinn Féin Ard Fheis in late October, the president told us that Ireland's representatives would never call on the people to swear allegiance to the English King, but they would, perhaps, be forced to call upon them to face 'an abomination of persecution' again. I was there in the cheering crowd. While negotiations continued in London, Dublin was full of rumours, which centred on the lack of dignity on display, as a false sense of confidence went to the heads of some members of our delegation; eye witnesses coming home were grieved because they had seen too much alcohol circulating in Hans Place, or in Cadogan Gardens, where Collins had set up his IRB headquarters. Mrs Áine Ceannt, interpreting from her sister Lily's silence, and Mrs Nell Humphreys, who had seen for herself, were among those who appealed to Éamon de Valera to take control of the situation. The president had remained in Ireland and was not part of the Irish delegation.

The varied dangers in the streets and houses of Ireland, which our men had survived, were as nothing compared with the pressure, and the traps being baited for them in London. Lily O'Brennan was often present to take notes at full sessions of negotiation in Downing Street. She later recalled how one day, quite suddenly, Michael Collins reversed his chair, and sat astride on it. She observed the effect with dismay. English ministers, who at first avoided having to shake hands – men who waged war and murder against us – came round the table to pat Collins on the back and to call him 'Michael'. He had breached the formality of the occasion and the English were swift to take every advantage until, after a few weeks, they had divided the Irish delegation and there were no more plenary sessions. This was the turning point towards which, undoubtedly, the English team had been directed from the time of the opening of the 'six-county' parliament by King George in June. The King's speech on that occasion was used, disastrously for us, in worldwide propaganda, and especially in

Britain itself. In his speech King George declared that the future lay in the hands of the Irish people themselves; that the six-county parliament would be a prelude to a day when north and south, under one parliament or two, would work together 'in common love' for Ireland.

It was folly indeed for any Irishman, influenced by the tone of this speech and judging by appearances in London, to conclude that the British government was only deterred from surrendering all the rights of Ireland by the perverseness of the Orange men. Yet, that was the way it was, for a while. As to the issue of the unity of Ireland, the Irish team was instructed to 'break' if England would not drop her policy to divide and conquer. Indeed, Arthur Griffith and Michael Collins wore the idea of national unity like a lifebelt in a stormy sea. Perfidy was the whirlpool that caught and held the Irish, and both men died the following year without knowing the full extent of the deception.

The signing of the Treaty on 6 December 1921 coincided with the coming into force of the government of Ireland (Partition) Act, in the Northern six counties. The local majorities inside the 'six counties', whose councils and public bodies had given allegiance to Dáil Éireann, had anticipated the latter event with anger and dread. Numerous deputations, intent on pressing their claim to be counted as part of the nation in whatever settlement might be reached, sustained contact with the Dáil up to the very last moment. Then, after the Treaty was signed, another successful propaganda campaign began to convince the Republicans in the six counties that their wishes would be heard in the proposed Boundary Commission. It was even stated, with all the appearance of authority, that the diminished area surrounding Belfast could not survive as a separate entity without the support of arms and money, which the British government pledged not to give.

It is accepted, admittedly sometimes with difficulty, that none of the men involved on the Irish side doubted that they had, at least, secured the eventual unity of Ireland. The leaders of the delegation would not have forced their views on the whole country if this had not been their absolute conviction. Lloyd George survived long enough as prime minister to prove that many such conceptions of what the Treaty actually meant were wrong. In September 1922 he imposed a constitution on our Dáil whereby no representative of a 'six-county' constituency could be admitted, nor anyone who was not prepared to take the oath of allegiance to King George. In October of that year Bonnar Law* and the Conservatives threw Lloyd George out. He had served his purpose.

---

* Andrew Bonar Law (1858–1923) was a Conservative politician and Prime Minister of Britain from 1922–3. Bonar Law was born in Canada, of Scottish and Ulster-Scots descent, and moved to Scotland in 1870. First elected to the British parliament in 1900, he became leader of the Conservative Party in 1911 and, in this role, worked in favour of tariff reform and against Irish Home Rule. From mid-1915 to the end of 1916 Bonar Law served as Secretary of State for the Colonies, as a member of H.H. Asquith's coalition, and subsequently as Chancellor of the Exchequer in Lloyd George's government. Bonar Law and the Conservatives won a majority in the 1922 election in Britain, but due to ill health he resigned in May 1923, serving only 211 days in office before dying later that year.

The Split

THE DAYS of the sad wake started with a small paragraph in the morning papers of 6 December, which announced the signing of an agreement in London at 2.30 am. Dublin would not have been Dublin at the time if rumours and hints of the news had not come in stop-press editions during the day. At afternoon teatime I was with Molly Childers in Bushy Park Road when the evening paper came, and we read the hateful facts. She may have been a little bit more prepared for them than I was; Molly was not a person who ever gave much secret information away. My heart was too full to discuss what had been done; I fancy hers was too. I went home and, so my sister Dimpy told me, I cried on my bed. Under the Treaty Ireland was required to bow to the sovereignty of England. She must abandon the Republic. Any servant of the Republic must now consent to an oath to the British King George. Men who had been elected to the second Dáil with the one and only mandate – to maintain the legitimacy of the Republic – would, if this was accepted, set up the Free State designed in England, and swear a contrary allegiance to that under which we had all worked together.

Mine were not the only red eyes in the Mansion House that night. Aonach na Nollag (Christmas Fair) was taking place in the Supper Room and an official commemoration of the Italian poet Dante was in the Round Room. The commemoration had been organized by Count Plunkett, Minister for Fine Arts, with Éamon de Valera presiding. The room was filled with tension as the count mounted the platform and introduced the president. I waited long enough to make up my mind that there would be no pronouncement from de Valera that night before I went to the Aonach, where I could talk about the only thing that now mattered. I passed around between friends and acquaintances and eavesdropped the conversations of identified and unidentified strangers. Some comradeships were strengthened and others broken. I do not recall any individual waverers, only some of those, like myself, whose minds were made up. In the days that followed the cabinet doors flew open to reveal enormous disagreement. We knew nothing then about the proposals and counterproposals put forward in London. All we knew was that the Republic of Easter Week and of the First Dáil was betrayed.

I do not recall that I then knew Rory O'Connor *more than grew out of very occasional meetings, yet when I met him in Fitzwilliam Street on 8 December, not far from the Plunketts' hospitable door, his anger and his misery over the treason committed in London communicated with my similar emotions; we stopped a while, talking to one another.

Each having confirmed the other's loyalty to the Republic in the new circumstances, Rory referred to the Treaty-signers, who had delayed in London until President Éamon de Valera summoned them home. They were expected at Dun Laoghaire by the evening boat to attend the cabinet meeting arranged for that night. I agreed with

---

* Rory O'Connor (1883–1922) was an Irish Volunteer and later prominent leader in the emergent IRA. As a young man he trained and worked as an engineer and emigrated for a period to Canada. O'Connor returned to Ireland in 1915, when he joined the IRB. He fought and was wounded in the 1916 Rising and, following arrest, was imprisoned then released under the general amnesty in 1917. O'Connor was director of engineering for the IRA.

Rory that they should be put on trial for treason. Then he said that he was thinking of arresting them when they landed. He wanted them impeached. What did I think of that? he asked. I was silent. Even at that early stage I sensed the impending division enough to know that any such action would start a gun battle on the spot.

We learned that a destroyer, full-steaming through the night of 5–6 December, had carried the Treaty to Belfast. By this time the nationalist-controlled local government bodies, representing the majority of people in half the total area of the six counties, had sent delegations to Dublin to give allegiance to Dáil Éireann. At that very moment Crown forces were in forcible possession of the county council offices in Omagh, County Tyrone, from where the representatives of the people had been evicted, after passing a resolution of loyalty to Ireland.

Later, Mrs Clarke TD, widow of the Easter Rising leader Tom Clarke, told me that she went to ask Éamon de Valera for an explanation. She met Mary MacSwiney on the steps of the Mansion House on the same errand. The president was in the Lord Mayor's drawing room. He handed the two women a copy of a document and asked for their opinion of the contents. Both women promised to read it and to see him again. This was the first time, Mrs Clarke later told me, that either of them set eyes on, or indeed heard of Document No. 2 * – de Valera's alternative proposal to the Treaty. Not long afterwards Mrs Clarke met Michael Collins, for whom she had great affection. Michael told her that the Treaty would give us more power than we ever had before. We will work it out eventually, he said, just like South Africa!

In the North things went on as before. Irrespective of the Truce the old rumpus was worked up again, with meetings of Carson's army and Church meetings; behind it all and helping was Mr Bonar Law, who would shortly succeed Lloyd George as British Prime Minister. As

* Éamon de Valera's Document No. 2, circulated during the Treaty debates, was presented as an alternative to the Treaty signed in London in December 1921. De Valera included the idea of External Association in the document whereby Ireland would be associated with, but not a full member of the British Commonwealth. De Valera's alternative proposal was not successful as a compromise solution.

Dáil Éireann debated the Treaty, Belfast suffered pogrom and partial curfew. The IRA was involved, trying, against great odds, to protect the nationally-minded people from eviction. Some men, who had given very good service to the Republic, demeaned themselves when, in their support of Michael Collins, they turned bitter; out of this, lies became current in the propaganda against President de Valera personally, and against the intransigents, such as myself. I write this book with the hope that it may one day stand beside P.S. O'Hegarty's *Victory of Sinn Féin* (1924) in libraries and bookshelves, where he has misrepresented me for decades, producing this flight of fancy: 'Nobody loved the Treaty; everybody objected to partition; but everybody felt that the Treaty was a tremendous achievement, and wanted it accepted'.

O'Hegarty goes on to comment on Éamon de Valera's rejection of it, and brings me into it, in a most disingenuous way. He writes:

> As an instance of the effect his (de Valera's) pronouncement had, I may say this. On the morning of the publication of the news of the signature of the Treaty I met Mary Comerford, one of the most prominent of the Cumann na mBan workers. 'Have you seen the papers?' said she. 'Yes.' 'Do you believe it?' 'Of course I believe it; I told you weeks ago that something like this was coming.' She stopped for a moment, shrugged her shoulders, then turned away. 'Ah well, all for the best. No more war.' In the afternoon Mr de Valera's Pronouncement came out and Miss Comerford promptly embraced it. Left to herself, she would have given the Treaty a trial …

I did meet O'Hegarty as he states, and it was in St Stephen's Green, where I may well have said what he reports me as saying; but the terms of the Treaty had not been published then. When I saw the evening paper in the Childers's house, I formed my own opinion. Éamon de Valera made no statement for two days; it finally came after the cabinet meeting on 8 December. P.S. O'Hegarty was known to be an IRB man at Supreme Council level. When I first read this paragraph in his book, which twists the facts to misrepresent me, I was angry; but my justifiable offence had to be content with calling him a liar, and leaving it at that. Neither I, nor Mary MacSwiney, who was more seriously libelled than I was, could do a thing about it. So O'Hegarty got away with it; he was high in the order of mudslingers in his time. Were it not for the fact that some of O'Hegarty's bitterest and most unjust allusions about the period were made with specific reference to the women of the revolution, I would not have referred to him at all, or at least not at such length.

More than forty years later when I read O'Hegarty's reference to me again, I recognized the significance of his quotation of his own words to me: 'I told you weeks ago that something like this was coming.' There spoke the IRB man, giving a strong hint in advance about the organization's secret decision, in the summer of 1921, to compromise with the English, even to the extent of betraying the Republic. Collins, presenting his dominion plan to Mr Chamberlain in November, acted in what was held by the IRB to be his capacity as their head centre, rather than as a member of President de Valera's cabinet.

I, and those like me, who had been totally absorbed in the promotion of the Republic at ground level, were at vast disadvantage in the new situation. So convinced had we been of our strength as a team, of our support in the allegiance and bravery of the people, and above all in the integrity of our leaders; so accustomed and trained to discount every criticism, dispraise or political rumour appearing in print, we were totally unprepared for the disaster that then befell us. For the domestic enemies, the go-betweens, the saboteurs, who now disclosed themselves, the opposite was the case. They were on their toes, poised for counter-revolution. Arthur Griffith and Michael Collins were their idols. Both men accepted the laurels that came their way from the strangest quarters. Griffith was in conference with the Southern Unionists before he left London and before communicating to the home cabinet about the document that had been signed.

Griffith and Collins erred in their estimate of Éamon de Valera at that time – but not by any means to the extent we thought, because events proved all three to be counter-revolutionaries. Since there was basic agreement between them on the need to parley with the English, it must have seemed reasonably to be expected that de Valera would come down on their side, and against the intransigents. This was what he did not do, at least not until Griffith and Collins were both dead. Then, Éamon de Valera did it with a vengeance. Jealousy and recrimination and argument about the difference, or lack of any great difference, between the Treaty and Document No. 2 mounted, until each of the three men – de Valera, Collins and Griffith – had their own faction. Thus, the organizers of 'victory-through-peace' were split amongst themselves. As for the intransigents, the old lesson, which came down to us from past generations, was once more proved true: nothing good ever did, or ever would, come to Ireland through compromise with the English. Disaster this time had befallen us almost at the moment of victory.

There was always a crowd outside University College Dublin, gathered on the street for every night of Dáil Éireann's long debate on the Treaty. After working hours, Earlsfort Terrace was blocked with people; I can't remember any of them apart from their umbrellas in the pouring rain, and the dim lights glancing off wet faces. The entrance to the university building was kept clear with difficulty by Republican police, assisted by the DMP.[*] The cheers that greeted the leaders, and those who became prominent on either side, changed from the kind we knew previously into those of partisans in the developing argument. When the Dáil was in private session, or had risen in order to eat, the doors of the Convocation Room were closed. Visitors, who did not want to miss the next session, sat on the stairs. There were poignant moments when lovers of the Republic of Ireland arrived from distant places, at home or abroad, fearing, as if coming to a deathbed. One man I do remember came down the steps for the very last time; I believe he was crying as he went out. He was a priest, who had been ordered to Australia by his superiors and was to leave

---

[*] The Dublin Metropolitan Police (DMP) was the unarmed police force for the city of Dublin. The DMP was in existence from 1836 until 1925, when the force was merged with An Garda Síochana in the new Irish Free State.

that night. This first political exile of the new era was to be followed later by others – Father Dominic, Chaplain to the Lord Mayor of Cork, who had attended Terence MacSwiney to his death, and Father Albert, who attended some of the 1916 men at their executions.

The press and the politicians at the head of the counter-revolution called every word we uttered 'Rattling the bones of the dead.' We learnt only gradually, on some points over many years, that the leaders had long ago decided between themselves that an independent Irish republic was unattainable. The war of words that ensued was between men who were, to some degree, on the slippery slope of compromise. No clear issue was ever put directly to the people.

There was room for only a small number of visitors in the Convocation Room at UCD, where I had a ringside seat, squashed together with others along benches down the side wall – we just sat there all day. It was an agonizing experience: my intense excitement, anger and fear probably stopped memory from functioning, and only a few things stand out; the blue lips of Cathal Brugha when we met face to face on the passage outside after he made his speech defending Document No. 2. Others congratulated him but I could find no truthful words to convey the mixture of sorrow and sympathy in my mind. I was beside Gobnait Ní Bruadair when she shouted 'No' to a Kerry TD, who, in his speech declared that his people supported the Treaty – 'With,' he retorted, 'the exception of one, an Englishwoman.'

Flying the Flag

SOME LARGE and fashionable shops, and practically all the banks in Dublin city centre had availed of the Truce to fly Union Jacks on 11 November. These were the people who five or six years earlier had urged, and even coerced, their staff to serve in the British army 'for the duration' of the War for Small Nations. It was certain that even more flags would greet the passing of the Treaty by Dáil Éireann. We had flown our tricolour from trees, from telegraph wires and chimneys; but now we feared our West Britons would stage their own display of triumph. Not if we could help it!

I was one of a group of Cumann na mBan members attending the debate on the Treaty in Earlsfort Terrace who decided (in the spirit of satire) that the Union Jack might now be given superior status in public view, over our own tricolour. We saw the chance to demonstrate to the Dáil, and to the public, that, for the first time in our history, there was danger that the British conquest might actually be legalized by an Irish vote. We planned to raise the Union Jack at University College Dublin to shame the men who supported the Commonwealth settlement, and to demonstrate the extent of the British triumph. The first thing necessary was to get a really big flag. The thought that followed was to corner all the Union Jacks in Dublin. We stole headed notepaper from the Sinn Féin offices and delivered individual letters to every shop and bank on our list, asking for the loan of a flag. Comdt. Louie Kennedy approved and took part in this operation.

> Dear Sir,
>
> We have found that it will not be possible for us to obtain a Union Jack of sufficient size in the event of it being necessary for us to display one at the end of the session of Dáil Éireann when the Treaty will, in all probability, have been ratified. We are anxious to comply with all the necessary courtesies, and propose to hoist the Union Jack beside the green flag on the University building as soon as the result of the discussion is known. We would be grateful if you would give the bearer your largest flag. We will, of course, return it to you as soon as the one which we have ordered arrives,

I was the messenger who 'did' the Bank of Ireland. The kind gentleman in charge there ordered his staff to spread three enormous flags out on the ground before me, and invited me to select whichever one I wished. I decided with regret that I could not hope to take all three. I picked one and walked out with it past a group of smiling bank officials.

In those days the Brown Bread Shop, run by the Fitzgerald family, was a Republican haunt. We made this our headquarters for the flag collection. Seán Etchingham and Brian O'Higgins* lingered over pro-

---

* Brian O'Higgins, also known as Brian na Banban (1882–1963) was a poet, writer, Gaelic Revivalist and politician. He joined the Gaelic League in Dublin in 1901 and later became a múinteoir taistil (travelling teacher) of Irish for the league. O'Higgins served in the GPO in the 1916 Rising, and was subsequently imprisoned, then released in 1917. He was arrested again in 1918 and served time in Birmingham Jail but was elected as a Sinn Féin candidate in the 1918 election for West Clare, holding his seat in the 1921, '22 and '23 elections. O'Higgins also operated as a justice of the Republican Courts in West Clare. Later, in 1938, he was one of a group of seven, previously elected to the second Dáil in 1921, who signed over the authority of Dáil Éireann to the IRA army council.

longed cups of tea while the floor space under their table filled with large brown paper parcels, carried in by 'messengers' from the various establishments. I do not recall that there were any refusals. According to the rumour of the time, Mrs Cosgrave (wife of William) went for a fitting in a Grafton Street shop, where she was welcomed by the staff member who had given us their flag, and who expressed their delight that the Union Jack would be flown officially. Mrs Cosgrave carried this quite astonishing news home to her husband. But sadly, this stunt did not get to the point of raising the Union Jack over, or even near, Dáil Éireann. The Volunteers took the flags and they were used for burning at public meetings afterwards.

Those who peruse the official Dáil reports concerning the Treaty debate are often surprised because so little was said, on either side, about the boundary clause. The existing partition of Ireland was hardly mentioned; the Belfast parliament might not have existed; no clear authoritative picture was presented to show what would come of this in the areas from Derry to Downpatrick. Yet some of the last words spoken before the vote were about the North-border seats, whose six representatives in the Dáil were now divided 4–2 in favour of the Treaty. The whispers, the propaganda, the word from the 'Organization' had convinced us all, including the six constituencies, that the Boundary Commission would extend the area to be governed from Dublin to all the areas where the inhabitants showed by major-ity vote that was what they wanted. Even to the most intransigent of us, the boundary clause seemed to be one of the least objectionable sections of the Treaty.

Michael Collins and Arthur Griffith carried the Treaty by the strength of their personalities, and because of the respect due to them for their great services in the past. They were sincere men hoping to avert what they thought of as worse evils for the country. They both died very soon after – prevented by their obstinacy, self-confidence and trusting natures from a full understanding of what they had done. In their last dreadful course, they were impelled by the belief that when Lloyd George got over his own urgent political problems across the water, the terms of the Treaty would be interpreted according to his agreement with them. I find it difficult to believe that the heads of our politicians were supporting their hearts at that stage. The Boundary Commission* has since been represented as the cruellest swindle ever perpetrated against us and against the Northern nationalists from London. But what secret Irish policies led the blindfold Dáil from election victory mandate against partition to the final scene? 'The Speaker: The result of the poll is sixty-four for approval and fifty-seven against. That is a majority of seven in favour of approval of the Treaty.'

Éamon de Valera spoke and offered his resignation as president. He went on to say that the Irish people had established a republic and therefore the Republic could only be disestablished by them. As such, the Republic would go on. The Civil War could have started at that moment. Among the spectators, or in the background, Michael Collins's men – the Special Squad, nicknamed 'the Twelve Apostles' – had their trigger fingers engaged to triggers. Each man had been allotted another man to shoot. This was one of the things discussed between old comrades in after years, when some of the blood had

---

* The Boundary Commission (1924–5) was established under Article XII of the 1921 Anglo-Irish Treaty as a way to determine the extent of the border between Northern and Southern Ireland 'in accordance with the wishes of the inhabitants, so far as may be compatible with economic and geographic conditions'. The loose wording of the article allowed Unionists to believe that economic arguments would prevail in their favour, while nationalists put their faith on 'the wishes of inhabitants' as being paramount. The commission was to be made up of three representatives – one each from Southern and Northern Ireland, and a third as 'neutral chairman'. However, Northern Ireland refused to appoint a commissioner and Britain appointed J.R. Fisher to represent Northern Ireland, with Richard Feetham as chairman. The Free State appointed Eoin MacNeill, Minister for Education. In November 1925 the British *Morning Post* reported that the Boundary Commission was to recommend only minor changes to the pre-existing border, which came as an apparent shock to the Free State government, under William Cosgrave. Although Eoin MacNeill had appeared supportive of the commission up to this point, he resigned as commissioner following the newspaper revelation, and some days later as Minister for Education. In December 1925 the Boundary Commission was revoked and the report set aside, only becoming publicly available in 1968. The border on the island of Ireland, created by partition in 1920, has remained in place.

cleared from their eyes. I heard it at Andy MacDonnell's fireside. He was one of the anti-Treaty men present, and they were armed too. It is likely that Éamon de Valera's words averted an instant gun battle

Making and Breaking Pacts

ÉAMON DE VALERA'S government had fallen; Arthur Griffith was the new President of the Republic. Griffith gave his word that the Republic would be preserved in the old sense, until the Irish people disestablished it.

Restlessness and anger led me to resign my nice Dáil Éireann job. I was far too perturbed to be able to do an honest day's work on anything apart from the rights and wrongs of the current dispute. I told Molly Childers that I intended to give my entire time to maintaining the Republic. Loyalty and treason were as white and black. We agreed between friends that our allegiance was to the Republic proclaimed in Easter Week, and to the elected, constitutional Dáil of all Ireland. Any leader we would follow must conform to that. This opinion was widespread and Éamon de Valera adjusted himself to our viewpoint in his speeches. Had he not done so, he could not have regained his mastery of the anti-Treaty forces. He did not regain it quickly.

A decision was made at a meeting of Cumann na mBan in January 1922 to picket and protest outside the meeting of MPs (the official British title) called by Arthur Griffith in his capacity as first signature of the Treaty, to arrange for the provisional administration of 'Southern Ireland' and for the purpose of constituting a provisional government. In Cumann na mBan we agreed that this meeting could not be allowed to pass off without dissent. Our chosen slogan for the protest banners was 'Thou are not conquered yet, Dear Land', a quotation from Thomas Davis (first used in the demonstration against a British Royal visit in 1911).* While our protest was very tame under the circumstances, it was still impossible for us to believe that old comrades who supported the Treaty would actually attend and subscribe to the oath of allegiance to the Crown. Our intention was to ensure that any press photographs taken of members assembling or leaving the event would include evidence of our dissent and protest. If memory serves me correctly, only four of the men who had voted for the Treaty failed to pass our picket. Some of the 'MPs' pretended to never have seen or known us before; others kept their eyes down; a few men smiled apologetically, but they walked past too.

A number of our executive members, who had not been attending meetings, came to our next one to denounce the protest. A few of these women resigned without waiting for our convention, due to take place in the following month. Of all the great Republican organizations one at least, Cumann na mBan, made up its mind definitively about the Treaty and stuck with it. We held the convention on 5 February and divided 419 to 63 in favour of maintaining the Republic. Of the 63 against, we lost some very fine members including Jenny Wyse Power, Min Mulcahy, Chrissie Doyle, Mrs O'Shea-Leamy, Mabel Fitzgerald, Máire Rigney and Louise Gavan Duffy. Some were married to Free Staters; others were foundation or executive members, who

---

* British King George V visited Ireland in 1911, his coronation year. The king and Queen Mary drove in an open carriage through Dublin as well as attending official ceremonies. There were some objectors to the visit. While the royal guests were welcomed by the Lord Mayor of Dublin, the nationalist-dominated Dublin Corporation refused to take part in the festivities. James Connolly wrote of 'parading royalties' and 'insolent aristocracy' welcomed by 'grovelling, dirt-eating capitalist traitors'. George V was the last monarch to visit the south of Ireland until the elderly Queen Elizabeth II came, one hundred years later, in 2011.

had helped to guide us through the war years; all had proved themselves. Mabel Fitzgerald crossed the bridge very reluctantly and, despite now being on different sides, she and I continued to meet as friends over cups of coffee in Bewley's Café.

In the same month I attended the Sinn Féin Ard Fheis, when three thousand delegates refused to split on the Treaty; there were urgent voices, raised arms, and heads bobbing up and down from the floor. The leaders were asked to retire and work out an agreement among themselves. When they emerged and said that unity would be preserved there was a great cheer. The Ard Fheis adjourned for three months. Many delegates were happier going home, sometimes on long journeys deep into country places, than they had been, gathered in twos and threes at little railway stations, on their way to Dublin.

As soon as the MPPs (members of the provisional parliament) appointed the provisional government, Michael Collins was 'received' by his Majesty's Lord Lieutenant in Dublin Castle. When the formalities were concluded, Lord FitzAlan – the first Catholic Viceroy – transferred roughly three-quarters of each department of State to the provisional government of Southern Ireland. At the transfer of Dublin Castle, and other barracks throughout the twenty-six counties, the British flag was lowered with respect and ceremony; enemy troops marched out to the sound of bands playing; the IRA (or the minority still controlled by Michael Collins) marched in and raised the tricolour. We resented this, holding that the provisional dominion government should have invented a flag of their own, or adopted the harp surmounted with crown.

The lie, gross as a mountain, prevailed; the news was carried to every home in the country, and across the world, that the British army had evacuated Ireland. Our Cumann na mBan publicity department had been loaned a small office in Dame Street in Dublin. From there we heard and saw the British march out to the strains of 'Let Erin remember the days of yore. 'Ere her faithless sons betrayed her.' This rendition gave us the idea for our first issue of *Heads Up*, a news leaflet we published and pasted to walls in the city every weekday for a couple of months. We also tried, without much success, to remove the tricolour from pro-Treaty platforms.

It was impossible to estimate whether Michael Collins or Éamon de Valera had the larger meetings in College Green. The crowd extended most of the way to O'Connell Bridge, filling up Westmoreland Street, the whole of College Street, Lower Grafton Street and well into Dame Street. There were usually two platforms, one at each side of the Old Parliament House in College Green. At a Collins-Griffith meeting in early March we captured the tricolour at Foster Place, while Michael Collins was speaking. As we ran with the flag, we were mobbed by a large group of British ex-service women shouting 'tear the clothes off them'. The most welcome sight of my long life was the party of Republican police, who extricated us from very serious trouble. I believe that we heeded their warning not to repeat the effort. The following issue of *Heads Up* on 7 March gave vent to the issue of the tricolour:

> The use of the Republican flag by those who urge us to enter the British Empire and take an oath to its king must be resisted, for that flag has been sanctified by those through whose hands it had passed until it came to be in our keeping, and we must at least pass it on un-smirched.

On 2 March 1922 the Dáil rejected a motion, introduced by Kate O'Callaghan, asking for the admission of Irish women to the parliamentary franchise on the same terms as men. The question was discussed and dismissed, by 88 to 47 votes. The reasons given by Arthur Griffith, William Cosgrave (Minister for Local Government) and others for refusing to bring the electoral register up to date were that it was contrary to the Truce, and that only the provisional government had the power and authority to change the franchise, or to update it. Another reason proffered was that the motion was a dishonest attempt to thwart and postpone the upcoming election. President Griffith made an interesting observation in the course of his speech against the motion. After saying that he had always been in favour of equal rights for women, Griffith proclaimed that, in the past, the Dáil had not made an effort to enforce Franchise Law:

> The fact that I am sitting here for two seats, Mr Collins for two seats, Mr de Valera, Messrs Milroy and MacNeill for two seats each, means that we disenfranchised these constituencies because we had no power to deal with the matter except by applying to the English Parliament for resignation, which we would not do ... We were cribbed, cabined and confined by the fact that we were elected under a British Act of Parliament. The only body which can pass such an act as this is the legislative body which can be set up under the Treaty.

There were shops engaged in a new trade of manly adornments, advertised as 'Volunteer' equipment – new and second-hand: pistol holsters, 12/6; green ties; green collars; green putties; and officers' ready-for-service breeches at a handy 19/6. The stage Irishman got a new uniform. Every thief, crook and shaper could now dress as a patriot. The enemies of Ireland did their utmost to shift every blame and every disgraceful criminal act to the shoulders of the IRA.

The '22 Election

TWO SINN FÉIN party headquarters were set up in preparation for the inevitable election, which would bring the war of principles and policies back to the nation. A Republican organization was established at 23 Suffolk Street in Dublin, staffed by some of the girls who had been dismissed, or had resigned, from government offices under the Dáil. It was a place of good will, and a place to talk of their misfortunes, where people drifted in and out, including Liam Mellows and Rory O'Connor, over from their occupation of the Four Courts. [*]

I was sent to Wexford as an anti-Treaty election organizer. I had £5 a week and my bicycle. We also had one T-Model Ford for election work, christened 'Tin Lizzie'. I could buy enough petrol out of my £5 to keep Tin Lizzie going for two days a week. After that we had to bicycle or walk. The funds of Sinn Féin had been tied up, and their

---

[*] On 7 January 1922 Dáil Éireann passed the Irish Treaty by 64 votes to 57, dividing the Sinn Féin party and the country. In response, armed groups of pro- and anti-Treaty forces began to occupy strategic positions. In April anti-Treaty forces, led by Rory O'Connor, occupied the Four Courts, along with several other buildings in Dublin.

great election machine closed down. Men who knew the ropes at Sinn Féin HQ were now rivals, divided in their allegiance. Dan McCarthy, previous Director of Elections, and Páidín O'Keefe, secretary of Sinn Féin, were against us. Our team included, Robert (Bob) Brennan and Eamon Donnelly.* By agreement Sinn Féin remained as one organization. It took artillery to split that, in the end.

Every constituency was expected to finance its own activities. This proved impossible by ordinary methods. The wealthy people who normally supported party funds were often not ready to show their hand in any public way. The less well-off no longer had any money to give. Among them were many who had kept open house for the lads, and who could still not bear to lock their doors at night; they were often on their way to private calamity.

That large and respectable section of the community – the men and women of no property – are given honourable place in revolutionary folklore. I, and thousands like me, would soon know more about it. The financial slump set in, and those who came out of the War of Independence without private means, or even owing money, were now in a sorry plight. Many tried to keep their troubles to themselves. No one likes to admit that they are down while their situation can still be concealed, and false pride maintained. Republicans could still give their lives, or spend long years in jail, or experience the desolation of being rootless, on the run.

All our efforts to collect money for the election had failed. Eamon Donnelly and his team at anti-Treaty HQ were in a tight place themselves. I was too thin-skinned to take my share of the letters of reprimand and abuse, which flowed from them to the constituencies. I grappled with the situation and finally organized and led a raid on

---

* Eamon Donnelly (1877–1944), was a politician, a member of the Gaelic League and of Sinn Féin and one of the Northern Irish Volunteers who mobilized at Coalisland, County Tyrone during the Easter Rising of 1916. Although not actively involved in the fighting, Donnelly was arrested and imprisoned in England. He worked to organize the Sinn Féin party in the North and was director of elections for the north-east of Ulster for the party in the 1918 election. Eamon Donnelly remained active during the War of Independence and took the anti-Treaty side during the Civil War.

about thirty post offices on the same day. We took a few pounds' worth of stamps from each office and left a receipt for the amount involved. The receipt was to distinguish our raids from others of a different sort. We got enough stamps (about £80 worth) to send unlimited telegrams during the rest of the campaign; the stamps were accepted too in lieu of cash for payment of some of our bills. In the same spirit, I took down the shutters from a closed shop in Market Street, Enniscorthy, and made the premises an election headquarters. I was called up to Dublin, and ticked off very severely by, if memory serves me correctly, Seán T. O'Kelly, over the post office raids. My defence was that all the stamps we had taken had King George's head on them, over-stamped with *Rialtas Sealadach na hÉireann*, and that there was nothing wrong in making the English pay for some of our troubles. He did not accept my argument and warned me that raids must never happen without authority, and never from the political side of the movement.

A stone rolled slowly at my heels on a day when I was walking in Irish Street, Enniscorthy, and 'to hell with the Republic' shouted after me by a group of budding Free Staters – very young ones. In the constituencies it became a weary fight to hold the ground that had been won since 1918. I can still picture the scene, as I spoke from a four-wheeled dray under the 1798 monument in the town, when Mary MacSwiney came to help the campaign. The meeting was all right by the more recent standards, but it was not up to the old style. As I spoke my eyes were on the little boys who were at our feet, this growing generation, who might still have been the first to live in freedom in their own land.

It was better for those in Dublin at that time than for us in the rural constituencies. Efforts to restore the old harmony, from the best elements of the IRA and the IRB, were underway in the capital. Young soldiers in politics are blamed by particular Republicans for providing the pro-Treaty majority in January 1922; but it should be said for some, or even for many of them, that they were active in a sincere effort to restore the national position in April, May and June, when the real nature of the Treaty began to be understood in IRB circles. I leave it to students of the period to pinpoint the dishonourable exceptions.

What came to be known as the Executive Forces – the anti-Treaty men, who had occupied the Four Courts – included men I greatly admired; they held that any abandonment of the all-Ireland Republic severed their contract of service, as defined in the Oath for the Republic. But, for the time being, TDs from both pro- and anti-Treaty factions of the IRA made an important and responsible contribution to the business of Dáil Éireann. A Peace Committee was appointed by the Dáil in early May, with the aim of finding common ground between the pro-Treaty and anti-Treaty parties. Harry Boland was the outstanding man on the Republican side; the leader of the Treaty men was Seamus O'Dwyer.* The Dáil followed the work of the Peace Committee with close attention. However, its prospect of success was made much more difficult by the misconceptions held by some important people. For example, Arthur Griffith believed, and stated in the Dáil, that 98 per cent of the people would vote for the Treaty as soon as they got a chance to do so. Patrick Hogan, Minister for Agriculture and big shot in the pro-Treaty hierarchy, stated that the Irish Free State, brought into existence by the Treaty, comprised the whole of Ireland! He went on to say that 'a certain concession – a very small measure of autonomy, of self-government – has been given to certain counties in the North'.

Agreement reached on 20 May secured the election of the Third Dáil in the twenty-six counties, and provided that constituencies where an election was not held would continue to be represented by their present deputies. This in practice gave John O'Mahony his seat in Fermanagh, and in theory still left it open for Éamon de Valera,

---

* Seamus (James) O'Dwyer (1886–1922) was an Irish Volunteer, politician and Dublin businessman. He served as an intelligence officer for the IRA Dublin Brigade and was arrested and imprisoned during the War of Independence. O'Dwyer became a TD in the second Dáil and took the pro-Treaty side in 1922. He was appointed to the Peace Committee following the Treaty, leading to the formulation of the Pact and agreement for the 1922 election. On 20 December 1922 Seamus O'Dwyer was shot dead in his business premises, presumably a reprisal killing by the anti-Treaty forces, a day after the execution of seven Republican prisoners by the Free State.

Arthur Griffith, Michael Collins and Eoin MacNeill to refrain from going forward in the South, and thus take their stand as representing constituencies in Down, Fermanagh/Tyrone, Armagh and Derry. It was further agreed that the pro- and anti-Treaty factions of Sinn Féin would fight the election jointly, and then form a coalition government. They also decided that sitting members of the Second Dáil would not be opposed by the other faction, be they pro- or anti-Treaty. This arrangement became known as the Pact.*

Michael Collins and Éamon de Valera issued a joint appeal for the 125 Sinn Féin candidates going forward for the Third Dáil. Nomination day was 6 June; on the 9th they spoke from the same platform at the Mansion House. Collins's good will for peace had survived many pressures since the Sinn Féin Ard Fheis in February. But the Pact challenged all the sacred cows of the British Empire; if it came to pass, a united Irish cabinet in a Third Dáil might choose to test the meaning of the Treaty and thus the very fabric of Empire – the nature of the 'free' dominions of the British Commonwealth. What if the Republic decided to push the boundaries created by the British?

It was necessary for the rising reactionaries of England to break Michael Collins. They could not afford to allow the working of the Empire to be tried and tested in Ireland. Michael Collins went to London. Be sorry for Collins, or be savage with him – it matters not which. But, in the spirit of justice, try to put yourself in his position as he prepared to cross the sea back to Ireland, ordered, under another threat of immediate and terrible war, to implement the British conception of the Treaty, which he had signed. You can imagine how his world was in ruins. Whatever his state of mind, of one thing he would make sure; whoever marched south over the border it would not be the much-despised Field Marshal Sir Henry Wilson.†

---

* 'The Pact' was an agreement between pro- and anti-Treaty Sinn Féin, with provision for a panel of candidates for the 1922 election. Panels were formed according to the numbers of sitting TDs for both factions, ensuring that a sitting TD would not be opposed by the other faction.

† Sir Henry Wilson (1864–1922) was a staunch Unionist and senior British army officer during World War I. In early 1914 he worked behind the scenes to support

Having relieved himself on that score, Michael Collins returned to Ireland.* Two days before the election Collins broke the Pact at a public meeting in Cork, when he told the people to vote for the candidate they thought best of:

> When I spoke in Dublin I put it as gravely as I could that the country was facing a very serious situation. If the situation is to be met as it should be met, the country must have the representatives it wants. You understand what you have to do, and I depend upon you to do it.†

'Serious situation' here meant that the British government was backing down from its promises. Neither the signatories of the Treaty, nor their masters – the Irish people – would be allowed to test it. The reason is that it would not stand the test. The British government and all the armed forces at its disposal stood between us and dominion status, or a boundary adjustment based on the will of the people concerned. Michael Collins was not the first or the last Irish leader to be broken in London, but he was the most important of the great failures of the twentieth century. His restless ghost is abroad still in Ireland. It is important to note that IRA men, like Harry Boland and Liam Mellows, on the anti-Treaty side, who took so much part in formulating the Pact, were outrageously misrepresented afterwards. There should be a code of conduct for historians.

British soldiers who refused to stand against Ulster Unionists, widely known as the 'Curragh Incident'. He was a military adviser to the new government of Northern Ireland, when the notorious B Specials was set up. He retired from the British army and became a Unionist MP for North Down in 1922, shortly before he was assassinated outside his home in London in June of that year.

* There is no definitive answer to the question of whether Michael Collins ordered the killing of Sir Henry Wilson. While it was not in the interest of the new provisional government of the Free State, some historians suggest that the assassination may have been ordered prior to the Truce by Collins, who then forgot to rescind the order. It may also have been that the two IRA men who shot Wilson, Reggie Dunne and Joe O'Sullivan, acted of their own volition. Sir Henry Wilson was certainly a much-hated figure in nationalist and Republican circles. Máire Comerford seems to be in no doubt that Michael Collins ordered the killing and that it was not an old or forgotten order.

† The intention behind the Collins speech in Cork, so close to polling day, is still a matter of debate.

I was in Wexford during this whole period; I remember standing sad and lonely at the outskirts of a Labour Party meeting on a Sunday morning, outside the church at Ballygarrett. It was painful to be denounced from their platform and to be told that Labour, which played its full part in the revolution in the spirit of Connolly and Pearse, had now lost faith and were determined to look after their own interests.

On election day I did a ring of the county on my bicycle and was returning to Enniscorthy when I came upon old Jack Breen, a lifelong Fenian, at the side of the road. He had taken up position on the large stone near his premises – his favourite seat when the sun was shining. Old Jack was settled in to spend the day canvassing all who passed to give their number one vote to 'poor old Seán Etchingham – for old times' sake'. For many voters it was their first lesson on proportional representation. I left him explaining to voters how, after Etchingham, they should distribute their preferences to uphold the Republic. I passed over the bridge and was heading for the office in Market Square when I met the morning papers, hot off the train. People opened their copies and read the headlines outlining the proposed new Constitution.* All I needed to see was the Oath to King George, which came like a bomb, bursting and scattering all the illusions built up during the peace talks. We were only about eighty miles from Dublin, and I knew that other parts of the country would receive this news correspondingly later, or perhaps not at all until the following day.

I toured the polling booths with fellow election workers Tom Dwyer and Paddy Tobin. In most places we were in front of the news. But in one polling station it was there before us and voting had ceased, the people turned back. We met the local Volunteer officer, very flushed and angry. 'Why go on with this farce,' he asked. 'I put a sniper to turn them back from voting. There was no other way to warn the people that things had gone wrong.' His point was that preference given to all candidates of the Pact would, after publication

---

* The draft Constitution of the Irish Free State was first published on 15 June 1922; it was unacceptable to Republicans.

of the Constitution, be taken as endorsing the Treaty, and now the Constitution in the form just published. In any case, we would not now get reciprocal preferences from the other side. He thought it better to invalidate the election, than to let it proceed. As far as I know this did not happen in any other part of the constituency.

I was not old enough to have a vote, not yet being thirty and female. But I knew that I had earned the right to vote, and was determined to have my say. In a far part of the constituency – somewhere around Screen – I thought that I could chance impersonation. Someone found the name of a dead woman for me and I stepped into the voting booth. I knew that there were men from the Labour Party there, but no bitter enemies. Unfortunately, notoriety had preceded me; 'Hello Miss Comerford, what can I do for you?' I stood my ground. 'I only want one vote. I think I am entitled to that.' The small group of officials conferred and thankfully they found justice in my case, and allowed me my vote.

At the end of that long day our party was rebuffed with physical violence when we tried to put our own seal on some of the ballot boxes, and to guard them in the interval between closure of the polls and the start of counting the votes. I was pushed back from the guard's van of the train at Gorey station, and not by railway officials. All we had tried to do was to follow the routine devised and successfully operated by Sinn Féin in 1918. It was poor consolation to be told that the boxes would be 'well minded'.

Post-election '22

A UNANIMOUS DÁIL had adjourned before the election, in which pro-Treaty Sinn Féin, led by Michael Collins, secured fifty-eight seats, while our anti-Treaty faction emerged with thirty-six seats. The return of seventeen Labour members need not have made much difference to the Republican character of the Third Dáil, all of whose members were men under comparable pledges, apart from the few businessmen of unknown allegiance. Therefore, the new House should have been no weaker than the old one. This is the salient fact that led to the coup d'état of 28 June. Our election results in Wexford disclosed a swing from Sinn Féin to Labour, and constituted a rebuke to both parties in the old Dáil – directed as much against Arthur Griffith's conservatism as our Republican zeal. Two out of three Easter Week veterans were defeated, including Seán Etchingham. There were four seats available and Labour won two; Seamus Doyle, Republican, got one and the fourth went to an Independent. I do not remember his politics sufficiently to state with certainty whether there was 75 or 100 per cent vote in our constituency in favour of the Third Dáil Éireann – government for the Irish by the Irish in Ireland. One thing absolutely clear was that neither of our two Labour men consented to the dreadful deceit that tried to cover succeeding events with a cloak of democracy.

When I got back to Dublin I found Mother very busily engaged with Mrs Despard and Maud Gonne MacBride helping refugees from Belfast at their home in Clonskeagh. A maimed child was trying to use her crutches in the driveway; adults and children were sitting around, playing or involved in hand crafts. It was a busy, self-contained place, with a splendid garden and plenty of room. Madame had started a jam-making industry using home produce and her French recipes. Mrs Despard, tense, active and generous, tried hard to make wise decisions between schemes for help and employment, whose implementation was only possible if she could find the money, which she did, over and over again.

I stayed with them to help but it didn't take long for me to get bored with gardening. I slipped away on my bike and went to the Four Courts; it was my first visit there. I told the sentry on the eastern gate that I wanted to see Liam Mellows, and was brought to him. Liam was sitting on a bench with a busy-looking table before him. Margaret Skinnider, Cumann na mBan veteran since 1916, had arrived before me. Liam asked if I would like to volunteer for ambulance work in Ulster. He was sending a party of Cumann na mBan to the Donegal border on the first train out on Wednesday morning, 28 June. I agreed to go, wondering what kind of twenty-ninth birthday I would have the following day.

It was a very quiet time for the public and for politics; in fact, you could have heard a pin drop in all political circles outside Sandy Row. The election results showed that no party, except Sinn Féin, had a clear verdict but that there was approximately a 90 per cent majority in favour of cautious progress in the direction of national independence, national unity and social reform. The Dáil had adjourned on 8 June without making any decision to change its address before the meetings of a new assembly scheduled for 30 June and 1 July. There were arguments in Oakley Road – Mrs Ceannt's – as we debated the question of whether Arthur Griffith would take over the old Parliament House in College Green, and what his plans would be if he did so. On 29 May Lord FitzAlan – the newly-styled Governor General – had called 'a parliament to be known as the provisional parliament' for the Theatre of the Royal Dublin Society* for 1 July. Our opinion of the Treaty Party was pretty low at the time, but we did not go so far as to think them capable of going in behind all those railings to join with the Trinity men† to enact Lloyd George's Irish Constitution. Winston Churchill, the British Secretary of State for War, who had sent the Black and Tans and the Auxiliaries into Ireland in March 1920, now informed his government colleagues that 'the Irish ministers wished to avoid setting up a provisional government and a parliament for Southern Ireland by Act of the Imperial Parliament'; they wanted instead to act through Dáil Éireann. If we study that piece of information, giving the Treaty men credit for the best possible intentions in their increasingly terrible predicament, we find ourselves switching a new beam of light on the facts leading to the Civil War.

Perhaps there were men in the pro-Treaty faction who wished to avoid setting up 'a parliament for Southern Ireland'; men who hoped to work Dáil Éireann and who, although they had perforce agreed to the Oath of Allegiance in order to get the British out in January, were not willing to make it permanent; men who were not prepared to operate from Leinster House, and at least one man, Michael Collins, who, one likes to think, would never have agreed to do so. I set that

---

* Máire Comerford refers here to the old RDS premises, which was Leinster House in Kildare Street. In 1731 a group of men of learning and leisure formed what is now called the Royal Dublin Society, to advance knowledge of agriculture, industry and the arts. The society began in Trinity College, then moved to Leinster House in 1814, and later to a larger site in Ballsbridge in 1923. The Free State government then took over Leinster House, which houses the Irish legislature to the present day.

† The Dublin University / Trinity College constituency was represented by two MPs in the British parliament until 1922 (hence 'Trinity Men'), electing Conservative and Unionist candidates including Edward Carson. The constituency was decidedly Unionist – so much so that Sinn Féin did not put forward any candidate there in the 1918 election. The nationalist candidate who did run in that election only received a 9 per cent share of the vote.

down because I think you ought to know about it; but lack of full conviction drives me to alternative thoughts, which may have influenced the joint meeting of the government of Dáil Éireann and the provisional government on 26 July.

Did they imagine, and maybe even worry, that Mary MacSwiney and the rest of us might disgrace them publicly by turning out in a poster parade outside their 'parliament for Southern Ireland', had it been held in Leinster House? If that had transpired, it would not have been the first time women were forced to chain themselves to railings in protest. Or did any thought crop up in the minds of the Treaty ministers that the Second Dáil would find a last way out before it died? Was it not conceivable that Harry Boland would go on fighting for peace and national unity? What might Éamon de Valera have done in the face of the oath – put in the Free State Constitution for the purpose of keeping him out of parliament? So, bearing these potential difficulties in mind, we can understand why Lloyd George did not succeed in forcing Arthur Griffith and his group to hold the provisional parliament of Southern Ireland. What passes understanding is to explain how they got away with starting the Civil War in the name of the Irish people, without the sanction of any Irish parliament at all.

Kevin O'Higgins,* intelligent and nearly as conservative in his outlook as Arthur Griffith, now had plenty of experience in high-level negotiation. He understood the hopelessness of the Treaty position, owing to the English retreat from their earlier promises. O'Higgins was a friend of Rory O'Connor and recognized, then and after, the sincerity of the young Republicans. He wrote a memorandum on the

---

* Kevin O'Higgins (1892–1927) was an Irish Volunteer and politician; he joined Sinn Féin after the 1916 Rising and won a seat for the party in the 1918 election. O'Higgins was assistant to William Cosgrave, Minister for Local Government, in the First Dáil. He supported the Treaty in 1922 and became Minister for Home Affairs (later renamed Justice). Between 1922 and 1923 O'Higgins was responsible for ordering the execution of seventy-seven Republican prisoners. He was assassinated by anti-Treaty men, who apparently came upon O'Higgins by accident on his way to mass in July 1927. His killing was predominately in retaliation for the execution of four Republicans in December 1922, including O'Higgins's former friend Rory O'Connor who, somewhat poignantly, had been best man at O'Higgins's wedding the previous year.

position for his pro-Treaty colleagues; in it he warned that the British intended to dominate the home policy of the Irish parliament.

One would like to know the identities of the army chiefs who cast a vote for Civil War, and whether Michael Collins was present – perhaps evading questions to which he had no answer, or intended to give none. Historians tell us now that Winston Churchill and Lloyd George both staked their careers on the Irish 'settlement'. For them, as for us, as for Arthur Griffith and Kevin O'Higgins; for Ireland, and for the hold England still had on the restless people of her old Empire; for all these Michael Collins was the axis on which future events would now to a greater or lesser degree turn. If he had owned up to ordering the killing of Sir Henry Wilson and faced the consequences – as we had to do – such action would have been consistent with his record before the split. The shooting of the Tory general gave Lloyd George and Winston Churchill the pretext they sorely needed if they were to prolong their tenancies in Downing Street as members of a British government. They were under heavy pressure from the Unionist friends of Carson. The British navy might be delimited; but there still remained to Britain Winston Churchill's tongue. Had it not been for the murder of Field Marshal Sir Henry Wilson, even he would have been hard set to work up the hysteria of abuse and blame against the men in the Four Courts, who were now accused of the assassination. Winston Churchill ordered the British General Macready – still in the Phoenix Park – to attack them. But Macready said 'wait and see', for Arthur Griffith, with Emmet Dalton and Alfred Cope, had already visited his encampment in the Park to enquire about the loan of artillery.

What should have been one of the final meetings of the outgoing cabinet of Arthur Griffith took place in what we now call Government Buildings; Michael Collins's provisional government, functioning legally – even in English eyes – for only another four days, joined it. The political future was now a dismal prospect for these men, whose absolute majority had gone in the election. Michael Collins had received letters both from Winston Churchill and Lloyd George. What these can have contained more than the threats that were in the newspapers for everyone to read, it would be difficult to imagine. The English required action against the Four Courts as the price for implementing the Boundary Commission, and the rest of the Treaty. Possibly, the personal letters merely stressed the reasons why Collins and Griffith could not afford but to save Lloyd George's government from defeat by the Unionist extremists, under Bonar Law. No evidence suggests that Michael Collins owned up to Arthur Griffith, Kevin O'Higgins and their group, that he was responsible for the shooting of Sir Henry Wilson, or that he was actively engaged on a joint operation to rescue the perpetrators, Reggie Dunne and Joe O'Sullivan.[*]

Some un-named friend sent the information, while it was hot, to the Executive in the Four Courts, warning them that an attack on them was imminent. A conference was held and Paddy O'Brien, OC Barracks, gave his opinion that they should evacuate quickly rather than wait to be surrounded. But he did not doubt that the building could be held. Their informant had not known of the intent to borrow the English guns, so Paddy O'Brien had no suspicion that they would be shelled at point-blank range across the Liffey. The men occupying the Four Courts decided to make their protest from the ground then under their feet. Lorries had been loaded and stood in the centre court ready for Peadar O'Donnell and a party of comrades to go north with him in the morning.[†]

They were left there; no effort was made to set them out. An armoured car was sent out to scout for signs of military activity. Maa

---

[*] Reginald (Reggie) Dunne was Commandant of the London Battalion IRA who previously served in the Irish Guards of the British army in World War I. Joseph (Joe) O'Sullivan was also a World War I veteran, serving in the Royal Munster Fusiliers. Joe O'Sullivan was injured during the war and lost a leg in 1917. O'Sullivan fired the shots that killed Henry Wilson on his own doorstep at Eaton Place in London. After the shooting Reggie Dunne could have escaped but chose to stay with the one-legged O'Sullivan; they were captured by policemen, aided by an angry crowd. Both men were hanged for the murder on 10 August 1922 at Wandsworth Prison.

[†] Peadar O'Donnell (1893–1986) was a teacher, writer, socialist and IRA Volunteer. At the beginning of his teaching career, he taught on Aranmore Island in County Donegal. O'Donnell was active in the IRA in Derry and Donegal during the War of Independence. After 1922 he took the anti-Treaty side. His experiences of the revolutionary period are recorded in his memoir, *The Gates Flew Open* (1922).

Woods's son, Volunteer Tony Woods, was the driver and he returned shortly after midnight, with nothing to report. It was 3.40 am before the place was fully surrounded and the ultimatum received;

> To the Officers in Charge, Four Courts.
>
> I acting under the order of the government, hereby order you to evacuate the building of the Four Courts and to parade your men under arrest, without arms, on that portion of the Quays immediately in front of the Four Courts by 4 a.m.
>
> Failing compliance with this Order, the building will be taken by force and you and all concerned with you will be held responsible for any life lost or damage done.
>
> By Order.
>
> (Signed) Thomas Ennis
>
> C/C 2nd Eastern Division.

The order was signed by poor, brave Tom Ennis, who had led the attack on the Custom House only thirteen months before.

Excitement had overflowed into 131 Morehampton Road on the Tuesday evening when I was there – perhaps telling Mrs Woods that I did not expect to see her for a while, as I was catching the first train north out of Broadstone next morning. What I do remember is that we were both aware that 'our man' Leo Henderson had been sent to Mountjoy Prison and that the Four Courts men had captured 'their man' Ginger O'Connell,* and were holding him for exchange.

Two and two made four very quickly in the early morning, when the bombardment of the Four Courts woke me at Clonskeagh. To the sound of bangs from the city quays, I was away on my bicycle, and making for the Four Courts to see what was happening. When I arrived a big vehicle was across the side gate, but somebody opened the small door to my knock. It was then that I met Paddy O'Brien OC, and offered my services. Life had taken a strange new turn.

---

* IRA Volunteer Leo Henderson and a group of fellow insurgents commandeered about fifteen cars from a garage in Dublin; Henderson was captured by the Free State army. In reprisal, the IRA decided to kidnap Ginger (Jeremiah Joseph or 'J.J.') O'Connell, who was deputy chief of staff of the Free State army.

Inside the Courts

NOW I WAS in a place where there was no need for argument, and among people whose unanimity was like a distilled spirit of highest concentration. We were all too young, too involved in the job in hand, to realize that as we reached the next and the next age groups, we too would fall apart, seeing the nation's problems differently, one from the other. For the moment we were comrades of one allegiance only. The men there were facing death or great hardships, and much prison; what was worse was that their motives were misrepresented and their characters aspersed. It would be a long time before tributes would be raised to their memory.

I may have been the first reinforcement to arrive that early morning but I had no weight to carry. Gerry O'Donel and her nurses were soon there, and began to set up a hospital on the floor of a big room. Presently I heard Madge Clifford of Central Branch Cumann na mBan discussing arrangements for baking bread – for 180. However did she do it? Leitrim woman and Cumann na mBan stalwart Bridie Clyne arrived to offer her services. My job was mainly doing messages and jobs outside and it was only at intervals that I met these women over the next few days. Dick Barrett, Quartermaster (QM) Cork, had called in for the night, breaking his journey to London, where he was to take part in the rescue of Dunne and O'Sullivan, who had assassinated Sir Henry Wilson. Now, he decided he had better stay with us.

It has been suggested that 'the last straw' argument explanation offered by pro-Treaty advocate and politician Professor Michael Hayes[*] of UCD and others, and Kevin O'Higgins's 'desperate bid', were advanced in the expectation that the attack on the Four Courts would lead to a quick victory. The facts do not support this theory because no guns were needed to secure a meeting of the Dáil, and there could be no acceptance of anything else. *Poblacht na hÉireann* (War News), ran a typed stop-press edition carrying the proclamation issued from the Four Courts – 'Our righteous cause is being treacherously assailed' – and also Éamon de Valera's statement to the press where he said: 'At the last meeting of Dáil Éireann an agreement was ratified which, if faithfully observed, would have given us an opportunity of working for internal peace and of taking steps which would make this nation strong against the only enemy it has to fear – the enemy from outside.'

The Four Courts had no arrangements for efficient defence. We had revolver ammunition, which the brigade soon needed outside, together with detonators. The rifles were inside, but the .303 ammunition outside. No tunnel had been made. We were not a threat to

---

[*] Professor Michael Hayes was a founder member of the Irish Volunteers in 1913. He took part in the 1916 Rising and escaped imprisonment, but was later arrested during the War of Independence and interned. He was elected for the National University of Ireland for Sinn Féin in the 1921 election, while still imprisoned. Hayes took the pro-Treaty side and was Minister for Foreign Affairs and Education for periods in 1922; in the 1923 election he was elected for Cumann nGaedheal, serving as Ceann Comhairle from 1923 to 1932. Michael Hayes lost his Dáil seat in 1933. He was a Fine Gael senator from 1933–8. Hayes was also a UCD professor from 1951 and a public commentator on revolutionary-period history during his lifetime. Máire Comerford took issue with the professor concerning differences in their interpretations of the history and events of the period, as ascertained from correspondence (uncatalogued) in the Máire Comerford Archive Collection.

anyone. Liam Mellows was one of the signatories to the Pact. There was no need or excuse to attack us. We were what we had always been, citizen soldiers, who pledged our faith, and were waiting for a government that would respect our oath and their flag.

The state of tension in which the British cabinet awaited our fate is shown clearly in their minutes. They did not expect us to hold out over the first day; they discussed whether or not to take over the attack, should the provisional government fail in it, or abandon it; they considered the use of aeroplanes to carry more ammunition to Dublin, or for dropping bombs; they rejected the use of ship's guns and wondered whether the provisional government possessed bayonets. After midday on 29 June, they sent a message to the provisional government to use the 300 18-pounder high-explosive shells with heavier guns, and also to take the 60-pounder, its gunners and ammunition and to use the 6-inch howitzers: aeroplanes were available. We still had more than a day to go.

The big guns seemed then to speak only with the voices of Arthur Griffith and Michael Collins, of Lloyd George and Churchill, of Orangemen and of lords; but they spoke for more than these because they were also part of the great Red Scare, which was worldwide following the Russian Revolution. The violence and hate, the shame of the Civil War were not ours only: the same words of condemnation after the event suit the world experience, from the United States to India. Only one man knew how to meet it and he was Mahatma Gandhi. It is possible that Christian Ireland was recognized, in some millionaire enclave, as presenting an even more difficult revolutionary problem than they had on the hands already.

Part of the reason for the length of the Battle of the Four Courts is that the shells did not always explode; I leaned this at some point during the first day when I was told there was little danger except from a direct hit. It was not known whether a friend was managing things this way, or if the Free State gunners did not know how to use their weapons effectively; I like the first explanation best. Bob

Dixon's[*] driving lessons of a year before in Gorey came in conveniently when Gerry O'Donel wanted some more medical supplies for her wounded, before the attack was many hours old. At Barry's Hotel on Great Denmark Street I said 'yes' when asked if I could drive, and a van was commandeered for me. Within a short while everything we had requested was loaded into the vehicle. A Fianna scout came too. We hoisted the Red Cross and set off. The streets were empty of people and traffic and I managed to steer around fallen cables, but encountered no other obstruction until the Free State held us up on the Quays. They found cigarettes in the van, and told me that this was a contravention of regulations, which deprived me of any right to fly the Red Cross.

The Free State officer put a soldier into the rear of the van, and arranged the soldier's rifle so that it was pointed against the middle of my back; the officer told me to drive as directed by the soldier. I asked the officer for his name, and got it. I was feeling very correct, quite prepared to argue my case anywhere. I did not object to being ordered to drive to the Four Courts Hotel, their headquarters. My soldier was a countryman and did not know the streets around the Dublin markets. I was obeying him when the van bumped against the back wall of the Four Courts. The engine stopped, and Bob Dixon had given me no lessons on reversing. The soldier was now convinced that if he showed himself my crowd might shoot him. I did not let the soldier down, and he in turn, helped me with driving advice. The soldier stayed under cover in the back of the van and instructed me how to crank the engine – without getting my arm broken by a backfire – and how to reverse back to the street. We reached the Four

---

[*] Robert (Bob) Dixon, a Wexford hackney-car driver, often drove Máire Comerford and Seán Etchingham to various engagements in Wexford, separately and together, in the autumn of 1921. On one of those journeys Máire asked Bob Dixon if he would mind if she 'took a run behind the wheel'. Bob Dixon later told Máire that, in view of her later escapades, he was 'very proud' to have been her first driving instructor. He recalled that on that first occasion Máire drove around the Mount Road and then up to the Mount School, and that she was most pleased with herself! And that, Máire recalled, was the beginning of her driving; her next run behind the wheel was during the Battle of the Four Courts in the summer of 1922.

Courts Hotel. My protest there was countered when I was told I had no right to have cigarettes. They held the van but allowed me the supplies. The next thing I can remember is bringing poor Ginger O'Connell, still held as our hostage, a share of the smokes. He was under guard in the basement and he came to the door of his room to accept them; the gift of cigarettes, however, did not seem to relieve his gloom, and this disappointed me a little.

Liam Mellows stopped for a word, and I took the opportunity to ask what he thought might happen next. He said that the people were not prepared to make further effort; the old spirit was burning low and it would not revive for a long time. 'A year?' I asked, and Liam shook his head. 'Five years? Ten years? Thirty years?' He remained doubtful. 'It will come back again with a new generation, but not in our time. We can do no more than hand on the torch.'

That evening, after the fall of dark, I was asked to make contact with the Free State post opposite in the Mechanics Institute Building, and to arrange a ceasefire in order to discuss the safety of our hospital. I was to tell them that the place had been made untenable by rifle fire and that we had been forced to move the wounded to the basement, where the floor was stone and there was no light. I had already seen the conditions under which Gerry and her nurses were working, with no space at all between the mattresses on the floor. I needed no urging on this. There was no sign of life in the Mechanics Institute, nor any answering shout to mine. An open door led to a stairs, and a passage; I was at the end of it before they heard my approach. A door opened. I explained what business had brought me there. The officer in charge assigned two privates to escort me to his superiors in the Four Courts Hotel, which involved travelling through the little streets. My two escorts were fighting their own war, verbally. Unfortunately, the Republican-minded solider did not know his case, while the other had all the arguments that carried the Treaty in the Dáil. Whenever I came in to help my friend, he passed me a handful of .303 ammunition – he must have known we were short of it!

By the time we got to the hotel and met Paddy Daly* my skirt pocket was over-weighted to the extent that I feared a break down in the stitching, which would scatter the bullets all around the floor. Daly was attended by another officer – a dark, low-sized, angry man – who looked as if he might strike me. He was very offensive. Daly ignored him and quickly agreed to the ceasefire. We went through all the signals I had been instructed to tell him and understood what needed to be done.

Daly came out with me onto the Quays; he shouted across to the gunners, telling them to cease fire. Then he signalled with his torch to our men and we started to walk together past the front of the Four Courts. I was on the riverside, and seeing that Daly was interested in making the most of his chance to see the damage done by his guns, I tried to make my conversation so interesting that he would turn his head my way. With this job in hand, I could not allow myself to make my own assessment of the exterior of the building. When we reached the eastern side door, six or eight of our men came out to talk. The atmosphere was informal; the voices did not sound angry, and none was raised. It seemed to me that they had the attitude of men who had already said everything that could be said, many times before. Daly disclaimed all intent to hurt our hospital and told the men to put it back where it had been; it was agreed between the two sides that we would put out certain lantern signals from the Four Courts. The ceasefire was extended to allow this to be done, and the hospital to be reinstated. But when the battle recommenced our lanterns were quickly shot up and the unfortunate wounded had to be brought back down to the basement again.

---

* Paddy Daly (aka O'Daly) (1888–1957) fought in the 1916 Rising in Dublin and was interned in Frongoch camp. A leader of Michael Collins's squad, he was involved in the assassinations of British secret-service officers and DMP detectives during the War of Independence. He took the pro-Treaty side and was commandant of the Free State troops in Dublin, then took charge of landing 450 Free State soldiers in Kerry. Daly and the men under his command became synonymous with violence and atrocities, including the infamous killing of eight IRA men blown up by mines at Ballyseedy. Several acts of violence ordered by Daly, involving the killing of IRA anti-Treaty men, followed. In 1923 Daly and two junior officers violently assaulted two sisters, the daughters of a doctor in Kenmare. The women had their hair smeared with axle grease and were whipped with Sam Browne belts.

When this was all over, Liam Mellows, looking very determined, called Bridie Clyne and me into a great big room where there were two beds in the inside corner, and told us to sleep. He forbad us from leaving that corner of the room because the rest of it was dangerous. The moon gave light enough to show fragments of glass, hanging from the tall window. I was still too agitated to sleep. But I lay there obediently and watched Liam's small figure ignoring the other noises, as he moved on tiptoe. He changed the position of a table, and other things, to bring all the amenities he could provide for us into the safety zone. If anybody came to the door, he behaved like a nurse guarding a sick room, shooing them away. But a moment came when he was not on the spot. Then the door flew open before Seán Nolan's* shoulder and he made straight for our corner, obviously coming off duty and expecting a bed. He didn't see us. Seán humped his rifle on top of me and sat down heavily on Bridie. After that, Liam Mellows gave up and we talked the night away. Outside on a marble floor, under a marble pillar, I saw Rory O'Connor; he was curled up and fast to sleep. It was not hard to guess who should have been in one of the beds given over to us.

There was a job outside for me first thing in the morning, but, when I wheeled my bike to the guardroom door, I found the whole floor full of men asleep – in every kind of attitude; some lying on top of the others. The sun was coming through a deep and narrow hole where a shell had taken part of the corner of the building, without bursting. Liam took my bicycle and told me to follow him. He held it high over his head, and we walked across the room through sleeping bodies to the side exit.

On my second day in the Courts there was a stir of hasty activity and I saw the men preparing to go out. Imitating them I packed my pockets and tied important things on to my belt. Obviously, it was important to keep our hands free. I broke up parcels of bandages

---

* Seán Nolan was an anti-Treaty insurgent and a Sinn Féin TD for Cork in the Second Dáil. In the 1922 election he stood as an anti-Treaty candidate, but failed to be elected.

and divided them between the men. I remember handing Ginger O'Connell his share, and the dumb look he gave me. I know now that Ernie O'Malley was to lead the breakout, which did not come off. By then to emerge would have been suicide. Nobody called off the operation, and I do not know when it was abandoned. Our belts were closed and coats still buttoned as night fell. I remember leaning against sacks in a small place that was crowded, and that George Plunkett[*] came over several times to tuck a coat, his own, around my legs. At 3 am Madge Clifford was still doing her rounds, with her bucket of tea and dry bread, which she baked in one of the ovens in the Courts. She told me afterwards that she found Liam Mellows standing guard over his men while they slept, with his rifle in his hand – certainly looking very sad. That was, she was sure, 'the last bit' he had until he reached Mountjoy Prison.

When the bombardment intensified I gripped the back of a balcony, or circular seating, and I had my head as low as it would go between my arms, and so stood all, or most of the Volunteers, with backs to the wall in the centre of the Four Courts. The leaders had arranged us there, and they were in a mood that answered no questions, and invited no argument. The orders, sterner than I had heard before, or since, held us in position. I recall no announcement that the big explosion was coming but nobody could have been in much doubt. The shock blew me back, the full length of my arms, then forward again, while dust and fragments scattered everywhere, including something light that slid down my back. As far as I know our OC Paddy O'Brien was the only man on our side hurt; he had been minding us all so well, he did not mind himself enough.

After the explosion we were all crowded closely together, near the eastern side gate. The fire brigade came to take Paddy O'Brien

---

[*] George (Seoirse) Plunkett (1894–1944), was the son of Count Plunkett and brother of 1916 Leader Joseph Plunkett. George fought alongside Joseph and another brother, John, in the GPO, and although all three were sentenced to death, George and John had their sentences commuted. Following his release, George was active during the War of Independence and the Civil War, and remained a committed Republican throughout his life.

and perhaps other wounded, if they had not already gone. We had to squash together in a ring around the discussion between Paddy and the others, for he did not want to go. He argued that he was OC but I believe that it was Liam Mellows who told him that because he was wounded, and unable to command any more, he had to be replaced; Paddy must accept the decision to send him out. It was an order. It could not have been a more distressful, affectionate parting if Rory, Liam and Paddy had known at the time that they would not meet again in this life. The fire brigade took Paddy away from the Courts. Presently, he escaped from hospital, only to later bleed slowly to death from a sniper's bullet in Enniscorthy.

Now came the time of surrender. Father Albert put a Red Cross band on my arm but I had not been all the time on Red Cross duty, so I had a scruple; it was not, I believed, the time to show false colours, so I tore it off and marched out with the men, wheeling my bicycle. Lorries were waiting for us on Bachelors Walk, but I managed not to go, and instead made my way to the Hamman Hotel in nearby Sackville Street.

The Hotel

THERE WAS a great crowd of people in the Hamman Hotel when I arrived there. Éamon de Valera was sitting in conference, and all wall seats were occupied. Hundreds of bath towels made a pyramid in the centre of the foyer and this, being the only place out of earshot, had been chosen by Father Albert to hear confessions. As long as he sat there, men came to him. There was an unending chain of men moving up the stairs with filled sandbags. I saw one man suddenly collapse to the ground; but the next man stepped over him, and the work went on. The victim was dragged out and somebody told me there was nothing wrong except that he was dead tired.

The hospital was in the billiard room. I was sent in there for a rest, which I now needed. The seats were recessed all around the room, and very comfortable. The roof was glass. Doctor Joseph Brennan was in charge. I noticed that his billycock was hanging nearby and, remembering from my hunting days that hats can save heads, I asked him why he was not wearing his. The doctor just shrugged and asked, why should he? 'It would be nice for you to have it on when this roof comes down,' I replied. He put it on rather quickly then! I drifted into a doze, but was shaken awake when I heard the word 'fire'. I saw Cathal Brugha, framed in the door beside me. His parabellum, butt to the ground, was against his knee. Cathal held it carefully that way, and looked down to his feet, adjusting them to the outer doorway. In this way he made absolutely certain that neither his person nor his weapon would infringe on the hospital. He told us that the place was on fire and that we should be ready to obey all orders; but meanwhile to stay where we were. While waiting I fell asleep again. When I woke up the fire alarm was over.

Oscar Traynor, that very kind and gallant man, who had been OC Dublin Brigade since the death of Dick McKee,[*] gave me some instructions on how to use motor gears. He demonstrated with ball change and gate change, at the rear of the Hamman. After that I drove a Corporation ambulance from Stanley Street back to HQ. My next job was to visit our posts in Parnell Square, Barry's Hotel and Moran's to see if they had wounded. The men in Parnell Square tricked me with a drunken stranger, who had been troubling their post. Now they pushed him into my ambulance. Not knowing the nature of the case, I asked where I should bring him. 'Anywhere you like except here,' came back, as I moved off. The 'patient' was behaving like an earthquake in the locked ambulance. I was afraid to open the door and unwilling to keep driving until he sobered, I drove up with a sweep to the front of the Mater Hospital; instantly their white-coated team, with stretchers, ran down the steps. My drunk fell into their arms and I left him there, ignoring their protests, which followed me. On this trip I got my first sight of the petrol-can mines our side used to prevent traffic on the streets we were holding. Sometimes the can on the road was no more than an empty one, with the cord attached to resemble electric cable; but it could be, and sometimes was, the real thing.

---

[*] Dick McKee was a leading member of the IRA. He was killed, along with two others, Peadar Clancy and Conor Clune, by his British captors, while in custody in Dublin Castle on Bloody Sunday, 21 November 1921.

Every time I woke up after a sleep, or returned from some duty, the interior of the Hamman and the neighbouring buildings looked different, as the men burrowed from house to house to make new ways in and out, or facilitate for defence. Once I could not find my bicycle until I saw it in the latest street barricade. Cathal Brugha went out himself to bring it in and when I examined the frame it had several bullet holes – which did not seem to weaken it at all because it was a good old Pierce from Wexford. The *Daily Mail* described me as cycling down Sackville Street to the chagrin of a cinematographer operator, who at some personal risk was filming amidst the shooting. 'That girl,' he declared, 'has ruined my picture. I've risked my life for nothing for no one will believe that serious fighting is taking place if a girl cycles through the thick of it.' I would like to think that his 'ruined' shot lies still in some forgotten vault of rejected out-takes![*]

We began to have far too many prisoners as Garry Houlihan's party, of the 2nd Battalion, captured Free State posts, which, only a short time before, had been established near our position. Cathal Brugha was worried about the safety of these harmless and puzzled men, recruited under false pretences, and who did not want to fight us. He asked me and my comrade, Muriel MacSwiney, wife of the late Terence, to escort them to their own line. By then it was dark – perhaps the Sunday night – and we set off at the head of 120 men marching towards Parnell Street from the rear of the Hamman.

As we walked, I could hear the uneasy speculations of the prisoners. Finally, some of them asked us where we were taking them; we replied that we had to treat them strictly as prisoners of war, according to the rules. The prisoners expressed anxiety and said that they did not want to be given back. I told them that we had our orders but that we had no power to make anyone follow us if they did not want to. The men were worried that they were in uniform and did

---

[*] As reported in *The Daily Mail*, 10 January 1923: 'Women Republicans; The exploits of Mary Comerford'. Original cutting in the Máire Comerford Archive Collection. For full article, see Appendix.

not know the city. It would be difficult for them to get away. I had to admit it was beyond my power to help them. In Parnell Street, and in Hill Street, I continued to shout, 'Any Free Staters here?' – as it would have been flat against Cathal's orders to put the prisoners in danger of being fired upon by their own side. At last, an angry voice answered, 'No, only Republicans.' I told them that Cathal Brugha was sending prisoners to safety, and asked if they could help. Some officers came out onto the street and we handed the soldiers to their care. As we went away their remarks to the prisoners were anything but kind.

Our main force was withdrawing from O'Connell Street. Someone asked me to guide a man, under doctor's orders to be evacuated, but who did not know the latest way out.

We exchanged greetings with a very dishevelled Seán McEntee,[*] who seemed to be in charge of the building on the other side of the lane. He waved us through a hole into another street. Here we had to jump in and out through somebody's cab in the centre of the barricade. As we reached the next street corner a file of Free State soldiers were just appearing, perhaps a hundred yards away. The leader, a decent man, waved us a signal to take cover quickly. In next to no time we were at the top of a tenement building looking for the way onto the roof. All the people there seemed anxious to help our escape. A point of significant importance now was that the man in my charge was dressed, from head to floor, in new clothes – his own having been spoiled, he was authorized to replace them from one of the shops under our control. Now this new raiment might very soon cost him, at least, his liberty. Quickly an action by barter got underway, and his coat, hat and trousers, even his shoes, were exchanged for the well-worn working clothes common to the area. Our friends completed

---

* Seán McEntee (1889–1984) was a trade unionist and Irish Volunteer, who fought in the GPO in 1916 and later had his death sentence commuted. Following his release in 1917 he was elected to the National Executive of Sinn Féin, becoming a Sinn Féin TD in the First Dáil. McEntee was anti-Treaty and anti-partition. He later became a Fianna Fáil politician and minister for a number of departments, including Finance (1932–9 and 1951–4) and Tánaiste (1959–69).

19 Thursday—262—103

From the grave of Wolf Tone Bodenstown

This flower fell beside the grave of T. Ashe from the wreath placed thereon by Mrs Pearse Glasnevin Sept 30th 1917

Page detail from Máire Comerford's 1916–19 scrapbook/diary depicting Thomas Ashe, following her attendance at his funeral, which was held on 30 September 1917.

8 HEADS UP! 8

No. 8.   FEBRUARY 2, 1922.   PRICE 1d.

IN INDIA Connacht Rangers revolted to show sympathy with their kin at home. They refused to represent Ireland in the slaughter of Indians.

ONE WAS EXECUTED.

The rest are now in Penal Servitude.

IN ENGLAND members of the Irish Republican Army on active service were captured by the enemy and are STILL PRISONERS OF WAR.

IN DERRY GAOL the Scaffold is being raised on which MESSRS. JOHNSTONE, MACSHEA, AND LEONARD ARE TO BE HANGED WITHIN A MONTH.

What do these men think of Common Citizenship in the British Empire?

ORDERS AND SUBSCRIPTIONS MAY BE SENT TO CAIT NI DUIBHIR, G.P.O., DUBLIN.

---

21 HEADS UP! 21

No. 21.   FEBRUARY 17, 1922.   PRICE 1d.

BOYCOTTED

NOT ENGLISH GOODS, WHICH ARE POURING INTO IRELAND TO KILL IRISH INDUSTRY.

NOT BELFAST, WHERE OUR PEOPLE ARE BEING SLAUGHTERED.

BUT

THE TRUTH

THE SUPPORTERS OF THE TREATY DARE NOT FACE BOB BARTON'S ACCOUNT OF

WHAT HAPPENED IN LONDON.

THEREFORE IT IS BOYCOTTED IN THE PRESS.

AND NO WONDER

---

26 HEADS UP! 26

No. 26.   FEBRUARY 24, 1922.   PRICE 1d.

WHEN ON NOVEMBER THE FIRST 1920, KEVIN BARRY MARCHED WITH HIS HEAD UP FROM HIS PRISON CELL, WAS IT INTO THE BRITISH EMPIRE OR OUT OF IT?

MANY IRISHMEN HAVE LEFT THAT EMPIRE WITH THEIR HEADS UP— SWINGING.

SHALL WE NOW SUBMIT TO GUILE WHERE FORCE AND TORTURE COULD NOT CONQUER THEM?

ISSUED DAILY

---

36 HEADS UP! 36

REPUBLICANS!

Boycott Belfast.

The "Imperial" Provisional Government, masquerading as the Cabinet of the Republican Government, have seen fit to grant complete freedom to the Orange mobs in Belfast, to murder our fellow-countrymen and women.

It is up to you to stop this.

Boycott Belfast.

Samples of HEADS UP propaganda posters, which were posted around Dublin by anti-Treaty members of Cumann na mBan during spring–autumn 1922. Máire wrote the text for many of these.

27-VI-23

a chara,

I have not written to you hoping that from day to day Mary would be released and that I would be able to send a note of congratulation instead of one of sympathy.

I know how much you are suffering — I have no doubt whatever Mary will win. There is no fear of the future when we have such brave girls.

As soon as ever she is released and gets convalescent we must get her away where she will not run the risk of being caught again. It was so unfortunate the last time that she had not gone.

The awful thing in these hunger strikes is that we can do nothing once they have begun.

I pray that the Almighty may soon turn your sorrow into joy.

le meas mór,
É. de Valera

Handwritten note sent by Éamon de Valera to Eva Comerford on 27 June 1923, expressing sympathy following Máire's capture and her subsequent hunger strike. (De Valera refers to 'Mary', as Máire was known to her family and many of her comrades at that time.)

a chara,   29-VI-23.

I received your note. We all here
Share your joy.

Tell mary that she is badly needed
for certain work, and so, that she must
not run any risks either to delay her
getting well or to give the F.S. another
chance to take her.

I am sure she is very weak but
there is no tonic like the prospect of
useful work.

Mrs Childers + miss B. will be
delighted ~~to see~~ to see her.

                                        le meas mór

                                        E deV.

*Dated 29 June 1923, this note, signed 'Edev' (Éamon de Valera), was delivered
to Eva Comerford following Máire's release from jail in late June 1923.
'Miss B' most likely refers to Albinia Brodrick, Republican activist and sister of
St John Midleton, 1st Earl of Midleton.*

DAIL EIREANN
[GOVERNMENT OF THE REPUBLIC OF IRELAND]

OIFIG AN UACHTARAIN

BAILE ATHA CLIATH

May 16th, 1923.

Miss Mary Comerford,

A Chara:-

I want to send a special messenger to the U.S. as soon as possible. I wonder could you manage to get over the passport difficulty without much delay. I would like you to go. When there you could also do work for the Prisoners Dependents Fund.

Le meas mor,
Mise,

Edev.

Memo sent by Éamon de Valera to Máire Comerford in May 1923, requesting that she travel to the US as a special messenger. Máire eventually set sail for America in late 1923, following her arrest, detention, hunger strike and release in the summer of 1923.

Irish Republican Army

Headquarters,

Ref. No, ...

First Southern Division

Dept. Adr.

........8/.8/............ .....1923.

To :
o/c.
"Each Brigade"

1. Miss Comerford (bearer) has been appointed to organise work bands on behalf of Sinn Féin.

2. You will facilitate her in every way by giving her names of persons willing to assist, & putting her in touch with them.

A/Adjutant

Memo from the Irish Republican Army introducing Miss Comerford as the Sinn Féin (anti-Treaty) election organizer for Co. Cork for the 1923 election campaign.

[xxi]

56 Grand Parade.
Cork,
Wednesday,

My dear Mother.

I just got your note per Annie MacSwiney, I was delighted to hear your news. We have been very busy here so you must exuse me for not being a better correspondent. I have been all over the place by bike and car, and we are at it night and day. If we had the time we could lick them to a cocked hat. As it is we epect to do very well indeed. Someone said to me yesterday that the swing is better than in 1918 but it remains to be seem whether that is true or not. Anyhow we are going on grandly. I have been dragged into a good deal of speechmaking at which I feel epremely foolish but Thabk Goodness Mary MacS. is down for these few days and I am getting a rest from that particular work. I felt so desperate that I wired for Victor Collins and he has gone off with her in the car for his first effort this election just now. I took a beautiful header off the bike yesterday but it didnt hurt either of us. This I suppose is as necessary as the three falls peope have to take off a horse and it has made me careful on corners. I showed Dorothy s paper round and everyone praises it. We have nothing so good our side though they are getting out a Munster editiono of Sinn Fein every day. Dorothy should not mind doing such great work even though she likes the other better. If she is in town when you get this and could get away for a day will you go to Suffolk St. and insist on her coming here for net Sunday as we are being badly treated in the matter of speakers. They seem to treat Cork as if it were the same size as any other county instead of being five constituencies.

There is no chance at all I think of my getting back to vote on Monday. I do not know if I will be put on for the count or not and on this will depend whether or not I see you on Tuesday or Wed.

Dev s arrest makes a great difference, and his name invariably is received with cheers. I do not think Mrs Dev. need be uneasy now. I was horribly lest they should not do what they did for I was sure that he would be shot if he started going round openly. The country could turn into a volcano with very small provocation if they laid hands on him it would begin to get going.

Best love

Au-.

Undated letter sent by Máire Comerford to her mother Eva from Cork, where she was organizing the county for the 1923 election. Polling day was 27 August. The 'Dorothy' referred to is the author and Republican activist Dorothy Macardle.

Green Park Hotel,
New York,
4th December 1923.

My dear Mother. I hope you got my cablegram, sent on Sunday last, and my
letter of Monday. I have of course nothing from you yet but suppose it is too
soon to hope. You will write me every scrap of news won't you? Very little
seems to be received over here and we must try to remedy that. Will you ask
that all propaganda should be forwarded to me personally as well as wherever else
it goes. We are completely boycotted by the Press here. I have hardly met
anyone so far, not more than half a dozen, they persist in declaring that I need
a rest (after doing nothing for three weeks''') There is a great meeting in
some theatre being worked up for me on the 16th and after that there will be
lots to do. A tour is being arranged for the New Year. Linda and I are
going to the Hearns for Christmas. They are the best people in America I am
told and great friends of Mary Mac's. We seem to have great workers every
where and they gave Loyd George a hot reception. There is no definite news of
the end of the hungerstrike beyond that of two deaths. I do think we should
be sent a cable pretty frequently. There is a thing the call a night letter
that gives you quite a lot for 12/-. If it was not stopped but I suppose
that's the trouble. The sky scrapers are wonderful. They seem to build them
inside a month. The streets are very dirty, much worse than Dublin, and
everything is a fiendish price. By the way did you ever think of going to the
Crock of Gold to try on my dress for me. I am writing them by this mail to
ask them to consider whether it would make a nice evening Irish costume. They
are to let you know when they are ready to fit. I never got the dresses I
left behind that time. If you sent them on to the address in London I gave
you it will be alright, I expect that they are on their way. If you have not
sent them will you do so now, in separate parcels I think so as possibly to
escape customs. I wrote to Dimp today too asking her to go back to you, If
she must go somewhere it would be better for her here because people for that
work get extravagent wages here. I wish Sandy could see the University
students working their way through college by doing waiters in resturants
during the evenings. I am dying to get out in the country to see what it is
like. I stupidly left all the letters of introduction I had in London but
I expect I will have them in a day or so and be able to go and see some people.
The weather here is wonderfully mild and I am going round with less clothes
than in London but I suppose there will be a surprise some morning soon,
Ask Ruth is the head of her college Miss Dudley. I knocked across her in a
curious way and made friends with her but she doesn't know who I am or that I
am not English. She asked me to go and see her which I will do. I wonder
will she be shocked when she finds me out in going under a wrong name. How is
Teddy. I was awfully sorry she got so bad the time I was leaving and hope she
is alright again by now. Will you tell propaganda people to look up an
article in the English Review either for this or last month "A Chicago gunman".
Would you get Molly's address of the place that sends paper cuttings I think I
will have to get them as there seems to be no certainty of getting anything.
Now about Brug? Dimpy told me she had a place for her so I hope that's alright.
Will you let me know if not and I will send you something for her as soon as I get
my accounts fixed up.
    I think that's all for the present. I do hope that you are alright and
enjoying life. I don't think you would enjoy this place. By the way I got my
photograph taken this morning. I am certain that it will be wonderful. If its
really good looking I will send you one.
            Best love from your fond
                    Mary.

*Letter home from New York, sent by Máire to her mother in December 1923
shortly after her arrival in the US. The 'Linda' referred to in the earlier part of the
letter is Linda Kearns, later Kearns MacWhinney. 'Dimp' and 'Sandy' reference
Máire's sister and youngest brother, and 'Mary Mac' is Mary MacSwiney.
Teddy and Brug are family dogs.*

[xxiii]

"UP THE REPUBLIC"

MISS MARY COMERFORD

GREAT WEST SIDE

MASS MEETING

UNDER THE AUSPICES OF

Shields and Boru Councils

A. A. R. I. R.

LAWNDALE HALL

Ogden and Trumbull Avenues

Tuesday, April 29th, 1924, 8 p. m.

Miss Mary Comerford, Irish Dispatch Bearer and Hunger Striker will give a talk on present conditions in Ireland.

Captain Owen Moore of the Irish Republican Army will give an address on conditions in Ulster. He will tell of the capture of Dundalk and the release of 500 Republican prisoners. Come and hear. See and meet these patriotic visitors.

GOOD ENTERTAINMENT   **ADMISSION FREE**

CLOHESEY & CO., PRINTERS, 127 N. WELLS ST., CHICAGO

Poster for a mass meeting with Máire as speaker, held in Chicago in April 1924.

the job by fixing him up with a Union card; we all waited and watched while he walked out into the street, and away.

I chanced going back to the Hamman. Cathal Brugha was sitting alone on the low steps that were between the front and back levels of the hotel at street level. His extreme fatigue was evident. 'What about a cup of tea,' I suggested, very quietly. He accepted without protest. Art O'Connor TD,[*] who described himself as a non-combatant, was doing his duty in the kitchen. In contrast to the position in the Four Courts, we were fairly well off for food in the well-stocked hotel. There was meat cut into portions, which we boiled until each bit looked like a walnut; there were tins of pears and peaches, and plenty of eggs – these we boiled hard, and brought them around; there was an abundance of Jacob's two-penny sponge cakes but I do not remember any bread.

I took down the names of the seventeen men who were now prepared for their last stand. They stood behind the narrow openings between sandbags in the windows on the first floor. Their eyes were tired from watching out over the then quiet-looking and empty O'Connell Street. Dr Dorothy Price, and, if I remember correctly, Dr Kathleen Lynn, had a first-aid post, perhaps over Hickey's shop. One of them gave me an injection, and I slept there.

The next day Art O'Connor gave me Cathal Brugha's dinner, and I went looking for him until I came to the roof. It was a beautiful day, with the sun beaming. When Cathal came to the skylight, he invited me to come out and rest awhile, in the valley between two roofs. The sunshine was lovely but the talk was spoiled because his attention was divided between his job and the certainty he felt that I would mortally endanger myself by putting my head up, if he took his eye off me for a moment. Cathal gave me a dispatch, which, he said, needed a reply.

---

[*] Art O'Connor (1888–1950) was an Irish politician, barrister and judge. O'Connor was elected for Sinn Féin in 1918 and was briefly Minister for Agriculture in the Second Dáil. He took the anti-Treaty side and lost his Dáil seat in 1923. He subsequently had a successful legal career, eventually appointed as a Circuit Court judge for Cork.

He explained that he could no longer spare a man to watch the back exit of the hotel; that being so, I would have to return at a fixed time – either 7 pm that evening, or 7 am the following morning, whichever suited.

Before leaving I went to the adjoining roof where Countess Markievicz was positioned for sniping. She was in her usual state of being alert with a rifle poised; her particular enemy was a soldier on Elvery's roof, and the shooting was in full swing. I admit to being somewhat repelled by the sniping, which I didn't like. I gave Con a meal and left, without expressing my thoughts. I would not have liked to be lying on a roof trying to kill someone, but this seemed to be what they were at.

I went out onto the street without incident. Towards evening that day Seán T. O'Kelly gave me a verbal message in reply for Cathal. I cannot be sure that I remember the exact words but the sense of it was that they had confidence that Cathal Brugha would not unnecessarily endanger the lives of the men under his command. This happened in 23 Suffolk Street, and I waited there for 7 pm. Caitlin Brugha, Cathal's wife, came in and we chatted together. I told her everything I knew of the situation. She was worried about my safety and suggested that we change clothes, and we did this.

Almost at the moment when I should have left, someone came running with exciting news – the fire brigade had taken Cathal Brugha, and the remaining men, out on O'Connell Street. Dublin Fire Brigade were popular heroes at that time and when they were mentioned nothing was impossible. Seven o'clock went past while I waited for more information to make my decision whether or not to go back to the Hamman. Why go there if there was no one in it? Waiting for 7 am, I went to sleep under a table outside the first-floor office in Suffolk Street.

To have been sleepy so often seems extraordinary when I look back and remember nobody else sleeping at all. This time I was roused by a Cumann na mBan comrade, Maura O'Connell. She had an urgent message for the men of the Dublin Brigade; Railway Street, near Amiens Street, was full of armoured cars and they seemed to be unguarded. She urged me to bring this news to Frank Henderson, Captain of F company, Dublin Brigade, who, Maura suggested might capture the armoured cars and use them to relieve the Hamman (by this time we knew it had not been cleared earlier in the evening). It seemed to be important news. I told her that I had to return to the Hamman with my message for Cathal at 7 am. Maura insisted that there was time for both things. It was the dead of night. And, while I peevishly wondered why Maura didn't bloody well deliver the message herself, I nonetheless determined that I should take the information, which seemed important, to Henderson.

I knew that it was too dangerous to bicycle down O'Connell Street, for fear of being shot. I decided my best chance was walking out in the street, in full view of both sides, at least in as far as the amount of light would enable any of them to make out a solitary pedestrian on the lonely streets. I was extremely tired and every street landmark became the target of a separate effort. Frank Henderson was in Murray's in Home Farm Road, Drumcondra; When I finally got there, Mrs Murray, a member of my own branch of Cumann na mBan, was on sentry and she woke Frank for me. He informed me that his men had been sent home to sleep and he could do nothing until they returned, but that would not be until some hours later. Frank insisted that I stay where I was, listened to my message for Cathal, and promised that I would be called in time to deliver it for 7 am.

I was asleep in Murray's during the last stage of the fight in the Hamman. The next time I saw Cathal Brugha it was his dead body, when Cumann na mBan mounted a guard of honour over it in the Mater Hospital. I did my best to stand motionless, just at the corner of his shoulder. I remember watching flies moving on his face, before someone, noticing that I was about to collapse from exhaustion, called me out of the guard. Linda Kearns told me afterwards that Cathal had watched for me at 7 pm, and feared that I might have been hurt. Linda and Kathleen Barry* were there until the very end, and saw him fall.

---

* Kathleen Barry (1896–1969) was the sister of Kevin Barry, the IRA Volunteer executed by the British in 1920. She worked for the Dáil in the Department of Home
  Affairs and as a judge in the Republican Courts. In 1922, at the behest of Éamon
  de Valera, Kathleen travelled to the USA, with other prominent Republicans, on
  a fundraising tour. She took part in the Civil War and was with Máire Comerford
  in the Hamman Hotel. After 1922 she was actively involved with the Republican
  Prisoners' Dependents' Fund. During the course of distributing aid, Kathleen
  Barry was arrested and imprisoned in Cork, where she went on hunger strike.

Driving and Dodging

AFTER THE Battle of the Four Courts and defeat at the Hamman Hotel, I was exhausted and broken-hearted. I went down the country, far away from Dublin, where all I really wanted to do was rest and sleep. But as often happens when there is unfinished business, I became quickly restless again. The war was still on and there was work that I could do to keep the struggle for a Republic of Ireland alive. But I felt very despondent during that long summer of 1922 when the Republican army was breaking up everywhere into smaller and less effective units. It looked like we would be worn down piecemeal, even though the men seemed to think that we could carry out much the same tactics as we had used against the British.

In late summer I was sent to Cork with a message for Éamon de Valera and was all over the county, going from place to place, looking for him. On 22 August 1922 I delivered a dispatch at the fall of dusk to a pasture field in County Cork, where the gorse had encroached from the hedges; there were more IRA men in arms than I had seen since the Four Courts. Afterwards, I was escorted to a neighbouring house and was left there to rest and sleep. I had not gone far the next morning when I came to a crossroads, where some women were grouped together talking. As I passed, I was surprised to be hailed by name. 'Hello Miss Comerford. What has you here,' asked Mrs Richards, who I recognized as a farmer's wife from Ardamine in County Wexford; before her marriage, she had been a teacher in Riverchapel Church of Ireland National School. 'Did you know that Michael Collins was shot down the road last night,' she asked me. At the time I did not know anything belonging to our recent history that was in Collins's favour, mainly because death had been so busy. No message of sorrow came to me from the graves of my comrades. I went on my way without great feeling of either sadness or joy. On my journey to Cork city I crossed Éamon de Valera's party at Fermoy. Later, Margaret Looby of Fethard told me that de Valera was with them when the news that Michael Collins had died arrived there the next day. 'Two big tears ran down under his glasses,' she said.

The Barton home at Annamoe continued to be a stopping place on the underground way from the south to Dublin. It was a mansion of large and impressive proportions, and the home of my old friend Dulcibella Barton and her brother Robert (Bob), a former Minister for Agriculture in the Second Dáil, and reluctant signee of the Treaty in December 1921. Bob later rejected the Treaty and remained firmly committed to the Irish Republic. Glendalough House functioned again as a safe house in the days around the funeral of Michael Collins. Dulcibella Barton was hostess in charge, as she had been for the three years of Dáil Éireann, the Black and Tans, Partition, the Truce, the Treaty – and now the aftermath. Éamon de Valera was waiting there and it was my job to guide and escort him to Dublin over the next two days. He was on the run. We walked, me pushing my bicycle, and travelled the mountain roads. I left him in a safe house in Enniskerry. Cumann na mBan worked night and day in those times. The second night we walked to Glencree and from there along the Feather Bed where Mrs Gordon met us as an additional guide.

There was no part of Ireland now where a column of twenty or thirty men might shelter safely, yet there had been dozens of columns twice and three times that size in the Tan War, fifteen months before. Now big columns of men were a risk and became difficult to feed. Of the half dozen houses in any one neighbourhood where our men might have found shelter in the past, now perhaps only one remained open to them. And, such houses were well watched and spied upon. A column was now four men, short of ammunition, usually hiding in a dripping dugout. The temptation to cease operations, to give up and go home, was obvious. I was operating as a courier, trying to maintain links between these crumbling groups. Sometimes I would return to a place to find that the unit was no longer there. The Republican army was disintegrating like snow on a sunny day. But the days were far from sunny; September, October and November 1922 were not my best months.

One cold and bleak winter's night in that same sad year, Erskine Childers, who, despite being part of the delegation for the Treaty negotiations, had taken the anti-Treaty side, arrived at the Barton home when I was passing through. Erskine Childers was twice the Bartons' cousin, because both their parents were cousins. He was very tired and sick when he arrived at Glendalough House, and was given a hot bath, fed and put to bed. He was a much hunted and wanted man by the Free State. I was driving a Republican car at the time and more in the IRA than out of it. I left Glendalough House to drive back to Dublin. When I arrived there Éamon de Valera was very anxious about Erskine Childers's health and asked me to try and find a nice and safe place where he could rest and recuperate.

I had in mind a priest, a hot Republican from another part of Wicklow, and planned to get his help for Erskine. I set off to where I might find him, across the mountain from Annamoe. I had a small allowance to run our poor little car, which had a big end knock and carbonized cylinders. We always expected too much of it. Normally the reverse gear did as well as a brake. But if the car could not climb a steep hill, I had little or nothing except luck to prevent her from running backward, losing hard-won ground. I often brought Maeve Phelan of Cumann na mBan to help me in this contingency. She was a very small person with immense courage, who was only occasionally required to jump out and put the rock we carried under whichever wheel she could get to.

We made our arrangements for Erskine but then got word to travel to the Headquarters of the Second Southern Division. By the time I returned to Annamoe, I found that Erskine had been arrested at Glendalough House. Normally it would have been very difficult to surprise Dulcibella Barton, but the man who led the raid knew the secrets of the old house and had the advantage of surprise. The leader of the raid also knew that the dairymaid went out early in the morning, and when she did, he brought his men in, effectively through an open door. Erskine, husband of my good friend Molly, had a gun when he was arrested – a small revolver that had been given to him as a souvenir by none other than Michael Collins. Nonetheless, he was sentenced to death and shot at dawn by order of the Free State on 24 November 1922. Erskine was to be one of seventy-seven Republican soldiers executed during the Civil War.

General Liam Lynch was the next, and I think the last of the men from Cork to come to Dublin via Glendalough House. I called there for him and a comrade but the car stopped suddenly in Appian Way in Dublin. I felt considerable tension from the back of the car when a soldier in Free State uniform crossed the road to assist me. I don't know how I would have got along without that kind of help, but it was a new experience for my passengers!

The same kind of experience was repeated the next day in daylight. I had returned to Glendalough for Liam's arms and papers. As the car refused to do any more hill-climbing, I was taking the chance of the main Bray Road. The car jerked to stop at Cornellscourt, outside what I thought was a garage owned by my comrade Andy McDonnell's brother. But instead, out came four civic guards, who explained that the place was now a barracks. They showed the usual sympathy when

I said that the car would not go for me. I have an indelible memory of the number because when they opened up the engine, I had time to wonder what would happen next as I contemplated the headless bodies of two kind men on each side of the engine.

At this time the Free State had already executed several of our Volunteers, some with the formality of a court martial, others out of hand. Following the IRA shooting of Seán Hales and Pádraic Ó Máille, two Free State TDs on their way to the Dáil (Hales was killed, Ó Máille badly wounded), the reprisals came fast and furious. Four Republican prisoners were chosen by the Free State for execution – Joe McKelvey, Dick Barrett, Rory O'Connor and Liam Mellows, my fighting comrades, imprisoned following the Battle of the Four Courts. The four men were executed on 8 December 1922.

In January 1923 I was involved, along with Paddy McGrath, in a plot to kidnap William Cosgrave, who had become Prime Minister of the Free State (following the deaths of Michael Collins and Arthur Griffith* in August 1922). The IRA planned to abduct Cosgrave and hold him in a bid to prevent further executions taking place. We had been promised a safe house for the purpose and set out on a dark January night to inspect it. Out at Loughlinstown our car, nicknamed 'Cupid', stopped suddenly and we could not get it going again. We decided that we would have to abandon the car and flagged down a taxi. The taxi was already filled, and one of those passengers was Mrs Richard Mulcahy, or Min Ryan, as she had been prior to her marriage. Min was a former member of Cumann na mBan and so recognized me, although she pretended not to know me. The taxi was crowded and I had no idea she was amongst the passengers until it was too late. The passengers said that they were going somewhere else; you know, polite excuses. But at the first police post Min came to, she informed about us. In the meantime, I had returned to Dublin to obtain another car. My comrade Paddy McGrath was arrested where I had left him and when I returned there, I was arrested too.

---

* Arthur Griffith died as a result of a cerebral haemorrhage on 12 August 1922, ten days before the assassination of Michael Collins on 22 August.

I was brought to Mountjoy Prison, where I joined my Cumann na mBan comrade Sighle Humphreys* and many other women. Sighle had been arrested following the capture of Ernie O'Malley at her house in November 1922. I remember that we were defiant and began our protest against the harsh conditions and overcrowding in the prison almost immediately; as a consequence, I received three months' hard labour and was removed to the 'criminal' section of the jail. Along with a number of other women I decided to go on hunger strike as a protest against our treatment.

While I was in Mountjoy a Free State soldier fired at me and shot me in the leg; I had been waving at other women prisoners in the exercise yard and that was forbidden. In April I was transferred to the North Dublin Union (NDU), but I didn't go quietly. I received three stitches to my head when I objected to and resisted being searched. The NDU was a great barracks of a place, which was then being used as a prison camp. I only had to take one look at the set up there to see that I could easily escape. The Free State didn't know how to make barbed-wire entanglements at that time; they were still beginners at the machinery of oppression. I noted that poles – strong poles – had been erected into the ground, at a distance out from the wall. From the top of the wall rigid barbed wire was stretched down the poles.

---

* Sighle Humphreys (1899–1994) joined Cumann na mBan in 1919 and served, at different times, as director of publicity, secretary and national vice-president of the organization. Her uncle The O'Rahilly and her teenage brother Dick fought together in the GPO in the 1916 Rising; The O'Rahilly was injured in the fighting and died. Following the Rising, Sighle was on the committee of the Irish Volunteers' Dependants' Fund, and during the War of Independence she and her mother, Nell Humphreys, worked to find and provide safe houses for men on the run. The Humphreys home was a known Republican house and during the Civil War raids, then carried out by the Free State Army, were regular occurrences.

During one of these raids, in November 1922, following a shoot-out, leading IRA man Ernie O'Malley was wounded and arrested. Sighle later admitted to playing a part in the shoot-out, but denied that she was responsible for firing the shot that killed the Free State soldier. Sighle, Nell and her aunt Áine were arrested; Sighle went on hunger strike in protest at being detained in solitary confinement and again during another period in prison at the end of the Civil War. She continued her support for Republican ideals, organizations and prisoners' rights throughout her long life. Sighle Humphreys and Máire Comerford remained lifelong friends.

There were also other poles, which had wires all around them. A keen eye could see that that our jailers had actually constructed a kind of ladder for us and, in fact, there was no way I could climb the wall to freedom without all this barbed wire to help me. It was so tempting that I took a long time to do anything about it. I was sure that there had to be a snare or a trap somewhere in the construction.

My city comrades were very reluctant to give it a go but I was country bred. When we were children, if you couldn't climb a fence someone invariably threw your hat across and you had to climb over to retrieve it; if you didn't come home with your hat there would have been hell to pay. My childhood adventures were the perfect training for escape and, when I went for it one night, I got over the wall quite handily. A number of other women followed me into the darkness. But I remained free for only about a month. Going out from the flat where I was hiding out in Nassau Street, I was spotted; it may have been my slouching country walk! On that occasion being country bred might not have been to my advantage. I was taken to Kilmainham Jail, where I went on hunger strike once more. I would not eat, I said, until I was released. Eventually they let me go. After twenty-seven days I was carried out on a stretcher by four soldiers and brought to a nursing home in Synge Street run by my old comrade Josephine (Joe) O'Donel.

Some weeks after my release, an August election was announced. Enormous numbers of our people were in jail – about eleven thousand Republicans. Sinn Féin simply had no machine to fight the election; the Free State, as represented now by Cumann na nGaedheal (formerly pro-Treaty Sinn Féin), was riding high and sure of victory. But our fighting spirit remained somewhat intact and we began to organize to contest the election. I was given a motorbike and the whole of Cork County (minus Cork city) to coordinate. It was a herculean task. Only one of our TDs in Cork, Dáithí Ceannt, was at liberty; he lived in the wilds of East Cork and survived only by staying out of sight. I had the greatest difficulty making contact with him. My motorbike was unable to reach places like Castletownbere in the far west of the county because of the high wind. Nationwide, nearly all of our thirty-six TDs who were not in prison were on the run. The financial deposits required for candidates in the election – a hundred pounds each – had to be collected secretly, and then held in a safe location. Otherwise, the Free State could have seized the money as illegal funds. Cash was transported to Cork and Kerry from Dublin, where it had been lodged in a bank under a private name.

On election day there was mass intimidation. Dozens of our people manning polling booths were arrested, leaving our booths with no supervision from our side of the count. So, all in all, it was extraordinary how well Sinn Féin actually did in that election. We increased our seats, from thirty-six to forty-four. I was pleased with this result, and grateful that some of the people, despite all the horrors of Civil War, remained wedded to the Republican cause.

The great hunger strike started in the jails in October 1923, quickly spreading until 7000 prisoners were refusing food. Without any release in sight for Republican prisoners and the Civil War all but extinguished, the Catholic hierarchy released a statement declaring their opposition to the IRA, and calling for the excommunication of its members. But by then I was already on the high seas, under the guise of 'Edith Lewis', artist, carrying my false passport across the Atlantic.

The Final Chapter

DE VALERA had sent word that I was to travel to America to raise funds for, and to propagate, the Republican cause. I was given twenty-five pounds to disguise myself, travel to London, pick up a fake passport and get myself to America. I had no new outfits since the war started. I went to Switzers department store and bought myself a grand rig of clothes. I arrived at Dun Laoghaire and boarded the mailboat for the first leg of my journey to England. I was there well before departure time, thinking that I could lie low somewhere on board. But I was rooted out and told that I must go up on deck to buy a ticket. Then, being at least partly on the run, I found a seat in a corner of the dining room with my back to everyone. Suddenly, I heard this cheery voice: 'Look there is Máire Comerford, let us go over and talk to her.' As it happened, my departure date was the same morning that James MacNeill, Free State High Commissioner in London, married Josephine Aherne, formerly of Cumann na mBan. Newly married Josephine and her recent husband James made a great fuss of me and insisted that I should travel with them. It was no love match I can assure you, but I could find no way to escape their attentions. I tried to flee at Holyhead when we docked, but once we boarded the connecting train, James MacNeill was sent searching for me. It ended up that I had to accompany the happy couple in their first-class compartment on the train to London. It was an extraordinary turn of events; here was I, a Republican fugitive on a secret mission to America, with thousands of my comrades in jail or dead, sharing the private compartment of the High Commissioner of the Free State and his bride.

I had about seven pounds left in my pocket in London a week or so later when I was told that my passport was ready, except for the required visa. I was informed, much to my dismay, that I must get the visa myself. In reply to my terrified question, wondering if five pounds would be enough to secure the visa, I was told that a ten-shilling bribe was the absolute limit! I was instructed to give it to some random fellow in a tourist office. It was one of the worst days of my life when I tramped from office to office as I tried to key myself to bribe. But the job was done in fewer seconds than the hours I had spent trying to prepare for it. One second my hand was on a counter, and the ten-shilling note under it; the next second the note was gone and a man told me to come back in the morning for the visa.

A woman going to America, even for a visit, had to have American guarantors and be claimed on arrival. This was arranged for me in Dublin before departure. I was told to cable the name on my forged passport from London, and everything would be arranged on the other side. I boarded the ship bound for New York. The voyage was bad enough because my fake identity held me back from any carefree human interaction. I was tormented too by the fact that my back was turned now to Ireland, where my comrades were on the biggest of all hunger strikes, involving some thousands of political prisoners in internment camps and jails.

As the ship came in to port, passengers were brought under discipline. 'Citizens this way. Subjects that way.' I could only sit tight and wait to be claimed. By degree the passengers melted away, the women's names called as each one was welcomed by friends on the dockside. Presently, I heard my own name called – 'Miss Máire Comerford, Miss Máire Comerford,' up and down the waiting lounge. My heart stood still. As I was now Miss Edith Lewis I could do nothing but shake my head as the staff looked at me, the only remaining woman passenger. There was a sad-looking male passenger there also, but I did not know his story. It was clear that Ellis Island was facing us both.

Eventually I was called before the immigration officer. He found no fault with my passport, or my answers to his questions; then he turned to my list of American citizens waiting to welcome me, but for some extraordinary reason not present. 'I was to cable, and did so, but something must have gone wrong,' I suggested. One glance at the list led to a complete change in his manner. 'I know this gentleman,' he said, pointing to a name on the list. 'He is the governor of Sing Sing Prison and would certainly have met you or made some arrangement. I will get you an escort and bring you to him.'

He called a woman wearing the uniform of Travellers' Aid and requested that she should bring me to the prison governor's house. As we set out a page boy was still calling 'Miss Máire Comerford' in the lounge behind me. I cannot say that it was a relief to step on deck again, after the long hours of tension below. Even the fact that I was heading straight for a new jail did not prevent me from looking around with interest now that I was entering America. Then joy, oh joy, a screech came from the bottom of the gangway. There, laughing, waving, shouting at me was Linda Kearns. I tried to thank my escort politely and explain that my friend had arrived. I have no idea what she thought, or whether the name of the governor of Sing Sing had impressed her to such an extent that she had no suspicion in her mind, when me and Linda ran off as fast as my luggage would allow. Linda had been in America on a Republican mission similar to my own for some time. She knew of my arrival but had not been told about the arrangement for my pickup, or of my new identity. Although cables had been sent, at some stage the essential details were missed.

I was sent to America in November 1923 as a messenger bringing documents from Éamon de Valera to Seán O Ceallaigh (Scelig), the official representative of the Republic in the States. Then, I was to remain under Scelig's direction as a member of his team of speakers, especially concerned with fundraising for the rehabilitation of prisoners back home – when the jail gates would open, and there would be need to set them up in the world again. Mrs Tom Clarke came to America around the same time as I did. Linda Kearns who met me, Father Michael O'Flanagan, Hanna Sheehy-Skeffington and Muriel MacSwiney were all there before me. Mrs Pearse, mother of Padraig and Willie, both executed following the 1916 Rising, came later.

I was in America for nine months, and although I should have enjoyed the experience, I was homesick for every day of the mission. I travelled to all the usual East Coast cities including New York, Boston, Washington, Chicago and Detroit, speaking in halls and trying to raise money for a fund to help the prisoners back home. One thing I do recall with humour and fascination was the American love of chewing-gum. I remember speaking at a hall in Boston to a sea of jaws opening and closing in perpetual chewing motion. I could tell when I made a popular point, which resonated with the audience, because all the jaws before me would suddenly shut simultaneously. However, from a fundraising point of view the mission was not very successful. We did manage to raise a few thousand pounds, but that was only a drop in the ocean for the objectives we had in mind.

I was happy when eventually I set sail for home again. I had left many of my friends on hunger strike and I longed to know how they were. As we neared the coast of my beloved country, the dawn light was stealing over the hilltops of Donegal. I rushed down the gangplank at Moville, where customs men were waiting for us. I can still recall how I left that quayside with a great sense of relief. I boarded the train to make my way to the Sinn Féin headquarters in Suffolk Street in Dublin with a load of guns, which my American friends had insisted on stuffing into my luggage. But my arms booty was the last thing my comrades wanted to see. The Civil War was well and truly over and all the IRA arms dumped. I found on my arrival home that Sinn Féin had begun the process of cleansing itself of its military wing, trying to forget, trying to be 'political'.

This was a time of terrible poverty. In the aftermath of the struggle there was sickness and hunger. Republicans were boycotted for employment. Even professional people – doctors, teachers, and lawyers – could not find or get back their former employment. Many were forced to emigrate through economic necessity. Thousands went with vengeance in their hearts, walking the bitter walk, up gangplanks to board ships bound for foreign shores, many never to return. They, their children and their children's children, were destined to become those who continued to support the IRA in the decades to come. Some who opted to stay in Ireland were forced to eke out a living by working piecemeal; many of my former comrades barely managed to survive financially.

When Fianna Fáil left Sinn Féin in 1926, I was placed on the executive of what was now a greatly weakened organization, and one that then, as a result of inertia, gathered speed downhill. I was unable to contribute much to it. For me life was unbearably hard. I was in poor form, living alone on the top of a hill in County Wexford, endeavouring to run my own poultry farm at Mount St Benedict. Each week it was an adventure to try to make ends meet. I had about five shillings to live on, and believe me it was tight. What helped me survive such a terrible dreary spell was that I was able to avail of credit in shops. I had belonged to people who were able to run up bills and this past association was very useful to me, because only for that I could not have managed.

For years I knew little about passing events. I was unable to afford a daily newspaper. I had a motorbike, and whenever I could scrape fifteen shillings together, I would ride from Gorey to Dublin for a weekend with some of my old friends. It was a tonic to be in the city again and to get away from my harsh and lonely life in the countryside. When you are down, you are down, and it is extraordinarily difficult to rise up again.

It was not until Fianna Fáil came to power in 1932 that some Republicans received long arrears of pay. The cynical might say that this was the beginning of Fianna Fáil bribery but it was an overdue instalment of justice too. The lesser fry were promised pensions, pittances of five shillings a week upwards, but just enough to win hard pressed ex-Volunteers away from radicalism. Under Fianna Fáil's two main schemes – the 1932 and 1934 Military Pensions Acts – more than 60,000 people made applications. Only a small proportion eventually got their pensions approved, but the mere fact that so many applied suborned tens of thousands, who otherwise might have stayed Republican. It only goes to show that as a modern state grows up, it becomes very difficult to avoid being enmeshed by it.

Fianna Fáil under Éamon de Valera were not going to bring us nearer to our ideal of James Connolly's Republic, but they were at least able to move the scenery. They were clever with words too. In an interview in 1926 de Valera had said, 'The Irish people will support a reasonable programme based on the exiting conditions. There is a place in Fianna Fáil for all who believe with Padraig Pearse in one Irish nation and that free.' Fair words for everybody, but so open-ended that it has since become meaningless. Could anyone truly imagine Padraig Pearse policing the Irish border, accompanied by units of the British army?

In 1926, on one of my rare excursions to Dublin, I was sentenced to nine months for trying to influence a jury. I had the bright idea of reminding jurors of their 'patriotic duty' in cases involving Republicans. I was in Mountjoy again over Christmas and on into 1927. When I came out most of the Sinn Féin Cumanns in County Wexford had been bamboozled into joining Fianna Fáil. In preparation for the election that year the IRA tried to bring Sinn Féin and Fianna Fáil together on an agreed policy; this failed primarily because Fianna Fáil did not want to agree anything with Sinn Féin. But I have to admit that despite our differences none of us foresaw that Éamon de Valera and his new party would finally falter and agree to take the despised Oath. However much Fianna Fáil obfuscated and obscured the reality of that decision, it came as a bitter blow to those of us who still held onto the Republican dream.

It became known that I voted in the Free State June election in 1927, which was forbidden by Sinn Féin. The issue came up at an Ard Fheis and I was drummed out. My ejection from Sinn Féin in the summer of 1927, as I ended my thirty-third year on earth, seems like a good place to conclude the narrative of this period of my life.

In writing this memoir I would not be at all happy if this flow of memory came across as an account of old historical wrongs; for truth be told, much of England's hypocrisy consists of acknowledging 'past wrongs' while keeping the present wrongs going. People refer to the independence of Ireland as if freedom has been won. But think of it this way – if someone is handcuffed to another person, are they free? The partition of our island has made it impossible for our nation to grow and mature, as modern democratic states should be free to do. My earnest wish, that the partition of Ireland will end, remains intact. Everything I have observed in Ireland since 1923, north and south, only strengthens this belief.

The task assigned to us by the men of the Rising, which those who accepted took up as their life's devotion, was no small one. We had to uphold the nation at the status then so beautifully redefined for us; we had to reverse the military and political conquest of many centuries, and to restore what the feudal system had overturned – the rights of the common people of Ireland. Massive physical strength was on one side, and only a small nation's will on the other.

I have given my evidence concerning what happened in Ireland. I was near the centre when important events happened, and there were times when I was able to lend a hand when more significant people were hard pressed. Being completely new in the Irish Republican movement, when I joined after the Rising, I inherited no personal or political prejudices. Only now have I leisure to ponder over the events where I was a participant in hot blood, while still in the prime of my life. It was interesting to test everything; what my comrades and I hoped to achieve; what we in fact did, or did not, achieve; who stopped us, and how they did it. This memoir is not history per se; it is merely my own narrative and my personal reconstruction of what happened.

Among my new Republican friends, in our lovely world of revolt, there were many who had no more personal grievance against life than I did. We were from various strata of society but we were rank-and-file Republicans in love with the new freedom we hoped to make secure. I have written the story of our efforts as I knew them and to explain how, in the end, we were driven underground, pushed down by the pressure of a soul-destroying political defeat, which followed the forcible partition of our island all those years ago.

I do not suggest that we were unique in our times, or in history. If I could travel in spirit around the world today, with the ghosts from Mountjoy, Arbour Hill and Kilmainham jails, the sun would not set on the bleak prisons where we would find comrades belonging to the undefeatable humans of every colour and creed, who battle against injustice and oppression. The fight goes on.

What Máire Did Next

FOLLOWING THE LATE 1920S when this memoir concludes, Máire Comerford remained wedded to the Republican cause, right up to her death in December 1982, aged eighty-nine. Throughout her long life, her focus stayed firmly on what she called the counter-revolution in the Free State, when the Republican ideals, so dear to her and her fellow revolutionaries, were set aside. She continued to lament and oppose the ongoing tragedy of the partition of Ireland, albeit in a non-military capacity. Máire positioned herself as an able keeper of her own history, and as champion for the many women who, like herself, found themselves excluded from the historical canon of the period. Her extensive archive is testament to a determination to leave her version of Irish history behind.

Máire Comerford was a revolutionary woman in every sense of the word. In the bleak period referred to at the end of this memoir, she eked out a precarious livelihood on a poultry farm, living in a cottage on a small parcel of land loaned to her by her friend, Father Sweetman, at the Mount near Gorey. The school was long closed by the Catholic church authorities, although Father Sweetman, and his loyal school matron, Aileen K'Eogh, spent the remainder of their days there. Father Sweetman never gave up his fight to re-open the school, as can be seen from the fascinating archive of correspondence over many years held at Glenstal Abbey Archives in County Limerick. All three comrades, Máire Comerford, Father Sweetman and Aileen K'Eogh are buried side by side in a plot overlooking the former school.

Máire's salvation from a life of poverty was the offer of a job at the de Valera-controlled *Irish Press* in 1935, which came via her old Cumann na mBan friend, Anna 'Fitz' Kelly. Miss Comerford, as she was known to colleagues, became women's editor at the newspaper. The articles she wrote over a thirty-year journalism career are often charming, sometimes witty, always insightful. As the years progressed, it is difficult to pinpoint the exact nature of Máire's attitude to Éamon de Valera – the *Irish Press* founder, leader of Fianna Fáil, Taoiseach, and eventually President of Ireland – or, indeed, his towards her. But de Valera must have known of Máire's poor circumstances and may well have played some part in affording her the means to make a reasonable living through the *Irish Press*. The job, and the financial security it brought, allowed Máire to buy a house, St Nessan's, in Sandyford Village, South County Dublin, and to bring her beloved mother, Eva, to live there with her (until Eva's death in 1949). It was the first secure home for both of them since Ardavon in Rathdrum, decades previously.

Máire fashioned life in St Nessan's to the tune of her own inimitable style, with touches of grandeur and stark facilities, a library of books and pamphlets, a small stable out back with room for horses, and a garden with chickens, beehives and dogs. St Nessan's was also a place of refuge and shelter for republicans in trouble. All kinds of people passed through Máire's home – politicians, Republican comrades and former enemies, artists, relatives, establishment figures, historians, researchers, film-makers, journalists, broadcasters, Marxists and conservatives, feminists, writers, activists, men and women on the run. The filmmaker Joe Comerford, her cherished nephew, was a frequent visitor, who cared for Máire in her home in the final months of her life. The Special Branch, occasionally parked outside St Nessan's, watched all the comings and goings, and stayed until the very end to observe her coffin, and the mourners, as Máire left St Nessan's for the final time in December 1982. Máire Comerford was given a traditional Republican send-off, and a graveside oration by Danny Morrison.*

History, and particularly the history of the revolutionary period, was her passion. Máire's archive contains a wealth of memorabilia from the 1920s to the 1980s; her extensive writing and articles; historical research; correspondence (1916–1982), which details her involvement in Republican and civil rights campaigns, including the Anti Partition League, the Wolfe Tone Society, the restoration of Tailors' Hall, prisoner's rights from the 1930s to the 1970s, and the political and social situation in Northern Ireland.

When Máire retired from the *Irish Press* in 1964, she did not fade away. If anything, she increased her public profile. She wrote *The First Dáil*, published in 1969, and continued her historical research. She may well have been the most prolific letter-writer to newspapers in her day. Most of her perspicacious missiles were published, often inciting a chain of responses and lively debate. Sometimes wry, the content of her writing was always astute and wise, with keen attention to historical detail. Máire saw this outlet as her way to keep her gracious yet razor-sharp voice in the mix of national debates.

In the 1960s, 70s and early 80s, Máire was interviewed for films and books about the revolutionary period and was the subject of a

---

* Danny Morrison is a writer and journalist who lives in West Belfast. He has published four novels and three non-fiction books, and is a short-story writer, reviewer and journalist. Morrison was formerly the national director of publicity for Sinn Féin (1979–90) and served time as a Republican prisoner. During the 1981 hunger strike he was a spokesperson for Bobby Sands, who died on hunger strike, along with nine of his IRA comrades. Later in 1981, during a debate at the Sinn Féin Ard Fheis, Morrison called for a dual strategy of 'an Armalite in one hand and a ballot box in the other' as the way forward for the Republican movement. He retired from Republican activism to concentrate on writing and is presently secretary of the Bobby Sands Trust.

number of newspaper and magazine profiles. She also took part in several radio and television programmes, perhaps most notably in the film and book *Curious Journey*,[*] a series of interviews with veterans of the War of Independence and the Civil War. In 1971 her imposing reputation ruffled feathers behind the scenes of the popular RTÉ live programme *The Late Late Show*, when she was a panellist on a special about Michael Collins. Her friend, historian Diarmond Brennan, relayed the backstory of her appearance in a letter to Máire.[†] According to Brennan, Margery Forester, the writer of a recently published biography on Collins, 'was very nervous' about Máire's presence on the panel. In the lead-up to the show, others, including Éamon de Valera, worked clandestinely behind the scenes in order to control the content of the discussion. In a letter responding to Brennan's information, Máire declared herself flabbergasted at the convoluted plan to thwart her.[‡] But in typical fashion she was also encouraged by the shenanigans – 'Fancy', she wrote, 'being so formidable that a crowd found it necessary to gang up against me and come in with supporters.'

While Máire kept her Republican faith intact, she was not an uncritical supporter of Sinn Féin and other Republican movements, although she was firm in her conviction that Ireland should be united. She never stopped believing in the Republican ideal and became an influential figure in debates within Republican movements, as they worked to chart a way forward in the 1970s and early 80s.

Women like Máire Comerford, some well known and others lost to history, were central to the fight for Irish freedom from 700 years of British colonial rule in the period 1916–23. They, like the men they fought with side by side, were brave and idealistic. They joined the

---

[*] A film and book featuring interviews with nine IRA men and women, veterans of the revolutionary period, then in their eighties, including Máire Comerford. The film was made in 1976 by Welsh filmmaker Kenneth Griffith. The book *Curious Journey: Oral History of Ireland's Unfinished Revolution* by Kenneth Griffith and Timothy E. O'Grady was published in 1982.

[†] Diarmond Brennan letter to Máire Comerford, 3 June 1971.

[‡] Máire Comerford letter to Diarmond Brennan, 8 June 1971.

revolution to create a free and fair independent country, and were willing to put themselves in grave danger, and their lives on the line, to achieve their goal. Máire wanted her narrative of to be part of that story, yet in her lifetime she failed in her attempts to have this memoir published. It is my very great pleasure to right this wrong now, almost forty years after her death.

Máire Comerford was the daring young dispatch cyclist, pedalling furiously through bullet-ridden streets in Dublin, who became the grand old dame of Republicanism, always committed to the political ideals forged in revolutionary times; fighting the good fight for the country she loved to the end of her days. And, as the concluding line of this memoir attests, the fight goes on.

Hilary Dully

ACKNOWLEDGMENTS

MÍLE BUÍOCHAS MÁIRE COMERFORD, for devoting so much of the latter part of her life to writing this unique memoir, wherever her spirit now roams.

I would like to acknowledge the input of the late Margaret MacCurtain and especially Fintan Vallely, who helped Máire to organize and edit her memoir writings prior to her death in 1982. Fintan Vallely, who worked to try to bring Máire's memoir to publication at that time, was also an early reader of this edited version and I thank him for his comments and encouragement. Other early readers gave valued feedback and spurred me on. A big thanks to Lelia Doolan, Margaret Dillon, Jimmy Carroll, Marie Redmond, Sean Carroll, and Bob Quinn. And thumbs up for the magic email Bob, which got the show on the road!

To the team at the Lilliput Press – publisher extraordinaire Antony Farrell and the super-efficient Ruth Hallinan and Dana Halliday – my greatest appreciation to you all for your guidance and commitment. I would also like to acknowledge the contribution of Professor

ACKNOWLEDGMENTS

David Dickson, who recognized the historical value of this memoir, which helped to move it towards publication. Copy editors are to my mind the unsung heroes of publishing, and a big thank you to Djinn von Noorden for her invaluable work, and also to Bridget Farrell, who took us over the final hurdles. Thanks are also due to Professor William Murphy for his comprehensive historical review of the mem-' oir and notes.

Many others helped along the way, directly and indirectly, at various different stages of bringing this memoir to publication, including Professor Daniel Carey of NUI Galway and, at the research stage, Professor Diarmaid Ferriter, Kate Manning of UCD Archives and Father Henry O'Shea, Monastery Archivist Glenstal Abbey.

I am delighted that Dr Margaret Ward has written an appreciation of Máire Comerford, serving as the introduction to this memoir. Margaret's ground-breaking research on Irish women in the revolutionary period is quite simply exemplary.

For her support, and her example of resilience and courage, I thank my mother, Mary Dully. Thanks also to my wider family, in particular Majella Dully, Martin Dully and Fidelma Clarke. To Marie Louise Kenny, Jenny Roche, Margaret Curran, Máirín Kelly, Kathleen McNamara, Ann Carroll, Susan Liddy, all our friends in East Clare and further afield, and most especially Siobhán Huxley, my heartfelt appreciation for their inspiration and greatly valued friendship. The encouragement and banter from my adult children, Cassie, Danny and Tom Comerford, the future keepers of the flame, was, as always, magnificent.

And finally, I would like to acknowledge Máire's nephew and my husband, Joe Comerford, who afforded me the privilege of editing this memoir for publication with unbridled access to Maire's extensive archive, where I spent many months pleasurably lost in history. My thanks to him for this, and for everything else that makes life so abundant.

Hilary Dully, Editor.

APPENDIX
Newspaper Articles on Máire Comerford, 1923

The Daily Mail, 10 January 1923:

WOMEN REPUBLICANS

The Exploits of Mary Comerford

The government is apparently awakening to the great part women are playing as supporters of the Republican cause and are constrained to take drastic measures against them. A few days ago I stated the fact that it was among the women of Southern Ireland that the Republicans obtained their greatest support and encouragement and were heartened to further efforts when by every rule they should seek for easy terms of peace. It was announced this morning that a Republican woman named Mary Comerford had been captured by the National forces. The official announcement reads –

> Troops proceeded on Sunday to Loughlinstown, County Dublin, where three men found in charge of a motor car on the roadside were arrested. A fourth man and a woman, Miss Comerford, who came from the city in a second car and were about to join the party,

were taken into military custody. Miss Comerford had a revolver in her possession. While being removed to Dublin Miss Comerford made an unsuccessful attempt to escape by jumping out of the car.

OUTWITTED AUXILIARIES

It is no secret that this Miss Comerford is what may be described as the Jeanne d'Arc of the Republican cause. It is probably impossible to disclose anything to the authorities that they do not already know about her. For many years her name has been famous as that of probably the most daring woman working for the Republican cause. Some indication of what she has done will show what many women are doing to-day for the Republicans.

The daughter of an old county family and a relative of Sir Thomas Esmond, she has been well described as an 'outdoor girl', just the kind you would expect to find on an English golf course. She was the girl who defied the British soldiers and outwitted the Auxiliaries when as Michael Collins's messenger and confidante in the days which are known here as 'the terror', she carried despatches and ran arms from one end of Ireland to the other. An expert motorist, she made her way where men accounted brave refused to go, and when the war broke out last June she allied herself with the Republicans.

AT THE FOUR COURTS

It is now common knowledge that it was she and one or two chosen spirits of her own sex who went with Rory O'Connor and his comrades into the Four Courts and also assisted many members of that garrison to escape. She was in Sackville Street during the fighting and with the Republicans inside the Hamman Hotel when it was burning; while it now transpires that she was the amazing cyclist who, when the firing was at its hottest from both sides of the road, coolly cycled down Sackville Street to the chagrin of a cinematograph operator who, at extreme personal risk had been filming the fighting. 'That girl,' he declared, 'has ruined my picture. I've risked my life for nothing for no one will believe that serious fighting is taking place if a girl cycles through the thick of it.'

*

The Westminster Gazette, 23 January 1923:

IRISH WOMAN LEADER
Miss Mary Comerford in Gaol Revolt

ARREST WITH ARMS
Her Daring Exploits in the Rebel Cause

From our own correspondent, Dublin, Monday

Miss Mary Comerford is one of the new women Republicans whose aggressive methods have overshadowed women like Miss MacSwiney and her sister. She believes not only in preaching war against the Free State, like her comrades of Cumann na mBan [Society of Women] but in practising it on her own account.

When arrested with a party of Irregulars engaged with burning railway stations, she was armed with a revolver. Interned in Mountjoy Gaol, Miss Comerford promptly organised a revolt of the other women imprisoned for political offences, smashing fittings wholesale and wrecking a good deal of government property. At present, she is in solitary confinement.

Court Martial Rumours
There have been rumours that she is to be court-martialled for carry-ing a revolver without authority – an offence punishable with death. So far no evidence is forthcoming to support these rumours. It is highly improbable that the government has any intention of taking drastic action against women Republicans, well knowing that to do so would not only give stimulus to the Cumann na mBan, but would have a disastrous reaction on public opinion.

Certainly Miss Comerford would probably desire nothing more ardently than the opportunity of crowning her Republican activities by martyrdom. She is the sincerest of enthusiasts, but she shuns the picturesque sensationalism so dear to the heart of colleagues like the Countess Markievicz.

No one who has met her can imagine Miss Comerford kissing the butt of her revolver before surrendering it. Dublin knows her as a nondescript figure who, though still in her twenties, looks almost middle-aged in a short black frock that seems like a relic of the Victorian era.

A Magnetic Personality

Hopelessly unfashionable, as she pedalled through the streets on her bicycle, glancing neither to right nor left, one would take her for a devoted parish mother rather than a dare-devil revolutionist.

She can put her case effectively, though she is demure, not flamboyant. Unlike most of her fellows, she is not fond of airing her principles in general company,

Yet she has the power of galvanising apathetic Republicans into active fighters, and few did as much as she to keep disheartened flying columns in the field. 'We must cultivate the offensive spirit' was her favourite phrase during the last few months.

Legends have begun to cluster around her name. A good many are pure inventions. Miss Comerford had not a few wild adventures, and more than once bullets have missed her by inches.

Her real service to her cause lay less in her contribution to the fighting than in her gift of inspiring young people of both sexes with the spirit of resistance. She was a very close friend of Erskine Childers and his wife, and it is the Childers tradition which she has done her best to maintain.

*

The Manchester Guardian, 3 February 1923:

A rumour has found its way into the newspapers that Mary Comerford is on hunger strike in a Dublin Gaol. As the Comerfords do not figure among the five families to whom the Irish government, following the precedent of Miss McSwiney's case, have extended the privilege of release under such circumstances, the report, if it be true, is a serious one. In the mind of one reader at least it has awakened some dormant memories of the girl who has quite usurped Mme de Markievicz's place as the Republican Jeanne d'Arc. These memories, (he writes) extend back to the early days of the Great War, when the pistol shot at Sarajevo was reverberating even amid the distant hills of Wexford. A scene in a remote railway station recurs to the mind, and one remembers a short-skirted, wild-eyed girl, the niece of Sir Thomas Grattan Esmonde and therefore a person of no small importance, standing on a platform, her eyes even brighter than usual, waiting for the Dublin train, that she might hand to her brother the long envelope, which had arrived during his absence, and which she now fingered with conscious pride, knowing it contained his Majesty's commission.

Other memoires jostle one another (adds our correspondent) of meals and meetings, of runs with the hounds and of sheltering men on the run. And of a cyclist as reckless in the streets of Dublin as was the horsewoman over the hedges of Wexford. The last scene is again in Wexford. It was during the period between the Truce with England, with its attendant 'split', and the election, that the most indefatigable of the Republican despatch-riders snatched a nights rest at a house in her native county. The next day she must be gone to Enniscorthy; her errand would brook no delay; to stay to lunch was out of the question. Mounting her bicycle, she rode furiously away. Halfway down the avenue she was checked by a familiar sound. In a moment the lawn would be alive with hounds and riders – all the pageantry of the hunt. The hounds were calling to her now; the old life was claiming one little day. After all, Enniscorthy and its Commandant General would still be there tomorrow. Before the hounds had made their appearance the stables resounded to eager cries for the saddling of a 'nag', and as the hunt passed up the hill at the back of the house one could see from the windows a horse and rider – one in unexpected joy – galloping in pursuit. Soon she caught up on them, and they disappeared over the crest of the hill together – those hard hunting men and women brooding over happier days and the young huntress who rejecting their life, had taken her stand with those who were destroying the little world in which these people lived. It was a strange company indeed, and now each day that passes adds something of significance and poignancy to that well-remembered scene.

*

The Irish Republic, Chicago, Illinois, 21 July 1923:

The British Empire has achieved a notable victory, it seems. On Irish soil, through an army of Irishmen 'with an economy of British lives', it has destroyed the Republic which withstood its terror for seven incredible years. Cathal Brugha, Erskine Childers, Rory, Liam, and a hundred others, 'bright candles of the Gael', are dead; the men who remain, as the English boast, are in prison or hunted in the hills. It seems almost that Ireland might enjoy the Pax Britannica again.

Out of Kilmainham Prison, that proud fortress of the Republic, a single desperate challenge rings in spite of the 'Collapse of the revolt,' in spite of the 'Government' that would let hunger strikes die, in spite of the triumphing Empire, Mary Comerford is hunger striking for release.

'It is like her!' that was one's first thought; the second, 'They will let her die,' and the third, bitter and sorrowful, 'Ireland needed this.'

Has a lethargy so deep fallen upon the people that Ireland may be bought and sold, betrayed, enslaved, dishonoured, before they wake? Like the curse of Macha, the 'Kesh' of the Red Branch heroes, this terrible sleep takes the people now and again. While it is over them they will delude themselves with any childish fantasy, believe any coward lies that gives them peace. It is the crack of the rifles of the firing squad only, the sight of their champions lying dead, that can rouse them again to life. And they have become satiated with blood – sacrifice at last – so many loved them well enough to die, so many in all the centuries, so many in the nineteen sixteen, so many this autumn and winter and bitter spring. They have learned to shut their hearts against even the execution of brave men. 'Maybe they'll begin to understand,' girls say wistfully in prison, 'when a woman dies in jail.'

'The logic of unjust tyranny is brutality and more brutality,' a writer in Erie said when Mary Comerford and Sighle Humphries were on hunger strike in Mountjoy. It is true; that is why Mary is on hunger strike in Kilmainham now. Tyranny should be resisted no matter what suffering resistance costs – that has always been her creed. To her mind, every arrest by the usurpers was illegal: It was not her own wish that made her last January accept the status of a prisoner of war – that status she accepted, but she resisted all attempts to infringe it without counting the cost, although she knew, as every prisoner helpless among ruthless enemies knows, that resistance brings only punishment and further punishment again, until the ultimate weapon, hunger strike, wins victory for the prisoner, or death. She resisted overcrowding and was removed, with Sighle Humphries, to the criminal wing. They resisted, by hunger strike, the enforced association with criminals; while they were hunger striking, Mary, for waving her hand to us, was shot by a sentry through the leg. Then came an unsuccessful effort to escape and the punishment – solitary confinement for a certain number of days. For the specified days they submitted; after that they demanded the regulation exercise and association again, and day after day they were dragged by soldiers, struggling, to their cells.

When on 26 March the prisoners were to be transferred to the North Dublin Union, and coarse, drunken women were called in to search the girls. Mary Comerford resisted personal search. Five women attacked her, armed with sticks, and she received a cut on the head, which had to have three stitches, and took long to heal.

But it takes more than a battered head and a wounded leg to keep Mary in jail. In the North Dublin Union she planned an escape so perilous that only the writer's knowledge of her stubborn spirit kept her from imploring her to give up the attempt. Over the wall, in daylight, where sentries swarmed – men who were forever firing, threatening they would 'shoot to kill'. But she had thought of everything. She was the first to go over the top. She got herself over the wall and away.

Then while she was living concealed, impatient, hungry for work in Dublin, came the order to our army to dump arms – our military campaign was at an end. Not so, however, the 'Free' State military campaign. It continued with impunity to the perpetrators, that was the only difference. They continued to hunt down the unarmed men and women whose faith might help to keep the flame alight. They recaptured Mary Comerford on 1 June.

She went on hunger strike at once. She meant to fight her battle herself. She let no one know. For twelve days her mother could not find out the truth. Ireland knows it now. Though our guns are silent, the Republican fight goes on; unarmed we still can resist. She is proving this. She challenged the 'Free' State Government's cynical resolution to let uncharged prisoners die. She has challenged their presumption to continue war-making now that we have laid down arms. She has challenged the might of the Empire to destroy the Republic of the people's will.

The people of Ireland who have given up their will, miserably, have let these things happen. The 'Free' State soldiers who, shame-faced and heavy-hearted, do these things, what are they but the victims of a monstrous lie – that the treaty is freedom, sovereignty, and peace?

The logic of this unjust treaty is 'brutality and more brutality'. Mary Comerford is proving that – proving it for the people of Ireland, on her own body, bruised and wounded and starved. How soon will the people of Ireland understand? Do they need her death?

INDEX

Abbey Theatre (Dublin), 175

Abbey Theatre Company, 26, 27n

Ackerman, Carl, 174

Act of Union (1801), 5, 19

Adavoyle, 208

Aeriocht (Courtown), 70–71

Africa, 14, 146, 173

Aherlow (river), 151

Albert, Fr, xvi, 232, 266, 267

Allgood, Sara, 26, 27

America. *see* United States

Amiens Street Station (Dublin),
44, 203

Ancient Order of Hibernians of
America, 157

Anderson, R. A., 111

Anglo-Irish, xiii, 23n, 28, 40n, 217

Anglo-Irish Trade Agreement
(1938), 212n

Anglo-Irish Treaty. *see* Treaty (1921)

Anglo-Irish Truce. *see* Truce (1921)

Annals of Ulster, 111

Annamoe, 13, 17, 163, 276, 277, 278

Anti Partition League, 293

Antrim, 146, 148

Aonach na Nollag, 126–27, 227

Aranmore Island, 256n

Arbitration Courts, 124n

Arbour Hill Prison, 60, 290

Ardagh Chalice, 52

Ardamine, 50, 106, 276

Ardavon (Rathdrum), 10, 13–14, 292

Ardilaun Gardens, 110

Arklow, 84, 164

Arklow Urban Council, 164

Armagh, 7n, 202, 247

Armistice Day 1919, 122

Arms Order (1918), 86

'Articles of Agreement.' *see* Treaty (1921)

Asgard (yacht), 42, 43, 195

Ashe, Thomas, 72–74

Ashford, 162

Asquith, H.H., 45n, 142

Asquith, Margo, 142, 143

Astor, Lady, 43

Athlone, 22, 55

Atlantic, 282

Australia, 231

Auxiliaries, 129n, 153, 155, 166–67, 171, 199, 253, 300

Avondale, xii, 3–9, 15

Aylesbury Prison, 66

Back Lane Parliament (1792), 9

Balbriggan, 158, 159, 188

Ballinakill, 6

Ballinkeele, 19, 48

Ballsbridge, 194

Ballycourcey (Enniscorthy), 17–21, 60, 177, 194

Ballydavid, 151, 152

Ballygarrett, 249

Ballykillavane (Glenealy), 162, 163

Ballymoney, 211

Ballyowen, 127

Ballyseedy, 263n

Bank of Ireland, 234

Banna Strand, 43n

Banogue Bridge, 50

Bansha, 151

Barrett, Dick, 259, 279

Barrington, Jonah, *The Rise and Fall of the Irish Nation*, 4, 5

Barry, Kathleen, 274

Barry, Kevin, 131, 212, 274n

Barry's Hotel (Dublin), 261, 268

Barry, Tom, 171n, 172, 173

Barton, Daisy, 13, 17

Barton, Dulcibella ('Daa'), 13–14, 17, 35, 163–64, 195, 276, 278

Barton family (Annamoe), 276, 277

Barton, Robert (Bob), 13, 103–4, 163, 210, 220, 276

Bean na hÉireann, 64n

Béaslaí, Piaras, 104, 120, 201

Beatty, Admiral David, 34

Behan, Peter, 121–22

Belfast, 5n, 7, 78, 103, 104, 124, 176, 183, 200, 205, 208, 217, 224, 228, 235, 293n

   pogroms, 86–87, 147, 188, 216–17, 229

   refugees, xvi, 217, 252

   Twelfth July (1920), 146–47

Belfast Boycott, 123

Belfast Jail, 104

Belgium, 37, 42, 44, 45

Bell, Alan, xiv, 168, 169

Benedictines, 14, 18, 37. *see also* Sweetman, Fr J.F.

Benedict XV, Pope, 221–22

Bennett, Louie, 66

Bergin, Osborn, 111

Best, Dr Richard Irvine, 107–8, 111

Bewley, Mr, 57

Bewley's Café (Dublin), 57, 240

Birkenhead, Lord (F.E. Smith), 45

Birmingham Jail, 234n

Black and Tans, 43, 111, 112n, 137, 141n, 142, 144, 153, 154, 155, 158n, 180, 184n, 186, 189, 193, 199, 204, 210, 218, 220, 221, 253, 276

'Black Justice' (coalman), 116

Blackrock, xiii, 53, 206

Bloody Sunday (1920), 170–71, 207n, 268n

Bloxham, Elizabeth, 83, 84

Blythe, Ernest, 100

Bodenstown commemorations, 104, 144–46, 200, 207

Boer War, 14, 218

Boland, Angela, 180

Boland, Harry, 102, 246, 248, 254

Bonar Law, Andrew, 225, 228, 256

Book of Kells, 52

Boston, 286

Bóthar Cualain, 50

Boundary Commission, 224, 235, 236, 256

Boyne, battle of (1690), 7n

Brady, Maggie, 19–20, 21

Brady, Tommy, 21

Breen, Dan, 115, 150, 154

Breen, Jack, 249

Brehon Laws, 68

Brennan, Diarmond, 294

Brennan, Dr. Joseph, 267–68

Brennan, Robert (Bob), 94, 112, 140, 167–68, 244

Brennan Whitmore, W. J., 67

Bridewell Prison, 126

Brighton, 3

Britain, 79, 85, 137, 141, 142, 174, 200, 224

British and Irish Millers Convention (1886), 11

British army, 7, 14, 23, 67, 121, 127, 131n, 133, 142, 144, 159–60, 175, 208, 216, 233, 256n, 288
 Curragh 'Incident' (1914), 247n–248n

and Easter Rising, 53, 54, 59–60

martial law, 178–79

transfers of barracks (1922), 240–41

World War I, 40–46; conscription crisis (1918), 83–87; Reservists, 42–43; Ulster Division, 44

British Commonwealth, xv, 172, 174, 228n, 234, 247

British Empire, 24, 31, 46, 172, 173, 247, 255, 304

British ex-servicewomen, 241

British forces (Crown forces), 122, 133, 141n, 142, 150, 166–67, 178–79, 187, 188, 209, 228. *see also* Auxiliaries; Black and Tans; British army
 murder gangs, 138, 139–40, 151–56, 188
 and Truce, 210–11

British Government, 89, 90n, 101, 121, 139, 172, 210, 211, 216, 224, 248, 255, 260. *see also* Dublin Castle; Lloyd George, David; Treaty (1921) proscription of Dáil, 102, 119

British Local Government Board, 164–65

British parliament. *see* House of Commons; Westminster

Brixton Prison, 137

Broadstone, 257

Brodrick, Albinia (Gobnait Ní Bhruadair), 78–82, 210, 232

Brodrick, William St John. *see* Midleton, Lord

Brooke, George, 19

Brown Bread Shop (Dublin), 234–35

Browne, Dr Robert, Bishop of Cloyne, 184

Bruges, 7

Brugha, Caitlin, 272

Brugha, Cathal, 99, 103, 211, 232, 304
    and Civil War, 268, 269, 270, 271,
        272, 273
    death and funeral, xvi, 273–74

Bunclody, 204–5

Burke, Peter, 158n

Burke's Peerage, 6

Burke, Thomas, 145n

Burmese War, 7

Burrow (river), 70

Bushy Park (Dublin), 167, 195, 226

Buttevant Barracks, 187

Butt, Isaac, 25n

Byrne, Christy, 162, 163–64

Byrne, Mrs, 163

Byrne, Myles, 69

Byrne, Paddy, 85

Cadogan Gardens (London), 223

Caherdaniel (Co. Kerry), 79, 81

Cambridge University, 4

Camolin band, 95

Campbell, Gordon (Lord Glenavy),
    112

Carlow, 41, 103

Carolan, (Professor), 150–51

Carson, Sir Edward, xiii, 28, 28n–29n,
    45, 100, 147, 172, 200, 203, 228,
    253n, 255

Casement, Roger, 43, 45n, 69, 86,
    90n, 100n, 105, 132, 139, 146, 147

Casement, Tom, 132–33, 146, 147–48

'Castle Catholics,' 7, 38

Castletown (Co. Wicklow), 84, 211

Castletownbere, 281

'Cathleen Ni Houlihan,' 69

Cathleen Ni Houlihan (Yeats), xiii, 26,
    145n

Catholic Church, 185, 282, 292

Catholic clergy, 74, 84, 95, 185,
    231–32

Catholic Committee, 9n

Catholic Emancipation, 81n, 82

Catholics, 4, 6, 7, 10, 32, 73, 82, 97,
    147, 188, 200, 216

Catholic Truth Society, 56

Cavendish, Lord Frederick, 145n

Ceannt, Áine (Mary Francis), 62n, 63,
    124, 175, 203, 219, 223, 252–53

Ceannt, Dáithí, 281

Ceannt, Éamon, 39, 62, 124

Celtic Renaissance, 23

Chamberlain, Austen, 230

Chartres, Anna Vivanti, 161

Chartres, John, 161

Chicago, 286

Childers, Erskine, 42–43, 111, 140,
    167, 195, 219, 277–78, 302, 304
execution, 196

Childers family, 175, 177, 229

Childers, Molly, xv, 111, 156, 195–96,
    226, 238, 278

China, 80, 173

Christian Brothers, 68

Christy, Mrs, 157

Churchill, Winston, 253, 255, 260

Churchmount, 15

Church of Ireland, 79

Church of The Three Patrons
    (Dublin), 53

City Hall (Dublin), 74

Civil War, ix, xvi, 13, 50, 80, 160n,
    168, 171n, 193n, 236, 244n, 253,
    255–82, 286, 294

combatants. *see* Free State army;
  Republican IRA
ending of, 286–87
executions and reprisals, 193n,
  196, 246n, 254n, 279; assassina-
  tion of Collins, 276, 279
Four Courts battle, 255–66.
  see also Four Courts
prisoners' hunger strike (1923),
  282
Clancy, George, 139–40
Clancy, Peadar, 129, 170n, 268n
Clanwilliam House, 54
Clara, Vale of, 10
Clare (county), 215
Clarke, Joe ('Duck the Bullet'), 116,
  118, 119
Clarke, Kathleen (née Daly), 63, 64n,
  118, 228, 286
Clarke, Tom, 39, 63, 64, 193n, 228
Clemenceau, Georges, 100n
Clifford, Madge, 258, 265
Clohamon, 14
Clonskeagh, 252, 257
Clontarf, 81n, 82
Clune, Conor, 170n, 268n
Clune, Patrick, archbishop of Perth,
  173, 181, 182
Clyne, Bridie, 258, 264
Coalisland, 244n
Cole (Alderman), 201
Colivet, Michael, 199
College of Surgeons (Dublin), 56, 109
Collins, Michael, 27, 54, 72n, 90, 102,
  102n, 112, 114, 127, 134, 140, 173,
  174, 176, 179n, 194, 201, 205, 207,
  242, 251, 253, 260, 278, 294, 300
  and 1921 elections, 202, 216

and 1922 elections, 248; Pact with
  de Valera, 247–48
assassination, 276, 279
and Childers, 196
and Dublin Castle mails, 121–22
and Four Courts siege, 255–56
and Provisional Government, 255;
  Dublin Castle transfer, 240
'restless ghost' of, 248
and Treaty (1921), 161, 228, 229,
  230–31; negotiations, 219, 221,
  223, 224; ratification, 235–36;
  pro-Treaty meetings (1922),
  241; implementation, 247–48
and War of Independence:
  escapades, 118–19, 120, 122;
  safe houses, 112n; Special
  Squad. *see* 'Squad'
and Wilson assassination, 247–48,
  255, 256
Colthurst, Captain Bowen, 88
Colum, Mary (née Maguire), 89
Comerford, Bill (uncle of Máire), 4, 13
Comerford, Dimpy (sister of Máire),
  226
Comerford, Eva (née Esmonde)
  (mother of Máire), xii, xiii, 5, 6, 7,
  8–9, 11, 17–18, 22, 27–28, 47–48,
  57, 65, 77, 91, 177–78, 184, 204,
  217, 292
  'aunt' to Collins, 194
  and Belfast refugees, 252
  girls' school, 37–38, 41, 167
Comerford family, xii–xiii, 6, 10–13,
  22, 48
Comerford, James ('Mr Thorne')
  (father of Máire), xii, xiii, 4–5, 9,
  10–11

death of, 17

Comerford, Joe (nephew of Máire), vii, 293

Comerford, Máire (Mary)
appreciation, xi–xvii
childhood and early years, vii, xii–xiii; Avondale, 1–8; Ardavon (Rathdrum), 10–16; cycling, 15–16; Ballycourcey (Enniscorthy), 17–21; mother's family (Esmondes), 18–21; riding and hunting, 20–21; education (Athlone and England), xiii, 22–24; London (1912), 25–31; secretarial school, xiii, 27–31
and co-operative movement, 33–36
Cumann na mBan (Republican activism), xii, xvi, xvii, 62, 104, 114, 124, 198–99, 299–306; Wexford, 83, 84–85, 89–91, 177–79; Dublin, 125–31; Bodenstown, 145–46, 207; Leitrim, 148–49; Tipperary, 150–57; prison visits, 180–81; Convention (1921), 222–23; Treaty (1921), 226–32, 233–37, 238–42; anti-Treaty electioneering (1922), 243–45, 249–50; post office raids, 244–45; Four Courts, xvi, 257, 258–66, 300; Hammam Hotel operations, xvi, 267–74, 300; later operations, 267–79; imprisonment and hunger strike, xvi–xvii, 279–81, 301, 302, 304, 305, 306

Cushendun holiday, 146–48
Dáil lecture committee, work for, xv–xvi, 167–68, 218
and de Valera, xvii, 292
driving lessons, 261n
and feminism. see women's rights/feminism
The First Dáil, 293
later period, 291–95; expulsion from Sinn Féin, xvii, 289; Irish Press women's editor, 292, 293; St Nessans (Sandyford home), vii, 292–93; writings and interviews, ix, vii–viii, 293–94; death and funeral (1982), 293
memoir and archive, vii–viii, ix, 215n, 259n, 269n, 291, 293
and Michael Hayes, 259n
newspaper articles on, 299–306
politicization, viii, xi–xiii
Republican idealism, vii, 212, 288, 291, 294–95
Republican memorabilia, vii
and Stopford Green, work with. see Stopford Green, Alice
and United Irishwomen/ICA, 34–35
US propaganda mission (alias Edith Lewis), xvii, 282, 283–86
White Cross work. see White Cross
and World War I, 40–46

Comerford, Sandy (brother of Máire), 14, 74, 198

Comerford, Tom (brother of Máire), 14, 42, 44

Congested Districts Board, 81n

Congo, 43n

Connaught, 184

Connolly, Captain , 128

Connolly, James, 62, 64n, 65, 66, 69, 113, 176, 196, 212, 239n, 249, 288

Connolly, Peter, 43

Connolly, Seán, 128

Conscription Crisis (1918), 83–87

Conservative Party, 202, 225

Constitution of Irish Free State. *see* Free State Constitution

Contemporary Ireland (Paul-Dubois), 30

co-operative movement, 33–36, 112, 188

Cope, Alfred, 216, 255

Corcoran, John, 209

Cork, 78, 79, 103, 112, 136, 137, 138, 172, 186, 187, 218, 222, 248, 259, 275, 276, 278, 281, 282

burning of city, 188

Cork Corporation, 136, 137

Cornelscourt, 278

Cosgrave, Mrs, 235

Cosgrave, William T., 100n, 165, 193, 213, 254n, 279

Cotter, Lily, 180

Cotter, Madge, 180

Courtney, Jack, 199

'Courtney's Anvil' (Kilmashogue), 199

Courtown, 41, 69, 102, 103, 105–6, 211

Aeriocht, 70–71

Courtown, earl of, 36–37

Courtown Harbour, 36, 37

oyster bed, 60–61

Courtown Harbour Sinn Féin Club, 70

Cousins, Margaret, 63n

Coyle, Eithne, 179

Craig, Sir James, 28n, 208, 215

Crimean War, 7

Crimes Act, 168

Croghan Kinsella, 103

Croghan Mountain, 106

Croke Park killings. *see* Bloody Sunday (1920)

Cromwell, Oliver, 49

Cronecribbon, 85

Cross Guns Bridge (Dublin), 128

Cross of Cong, 52

Crowley, Kate, 180

Crown forces. *see* British forces

Cuchulainn, 210

Cuffe, Peg, 204

Cullen (RIC Sergeant), 41

Cullenswood House (Ranelagh), 39n, 159–60

Cumann Leigheacht an Phobail, 218

Cumann na mBan, xii, xiv, xvi, 26n, 27, 62, 63n, 64n, 83, 84, 88–92, 104, 109, 114, 120, 124, 126, 128, 129n, 130, 148, 151, 153, 163, 168n, 177, 192n, 198, 203, 204, 214, 222, 229, 252, 272, 273, 276, 278, 279, 280, 283, 292, 301

aims of, 35n

and Aonach na Nollag (1919), 127

Bodenstown commemorations, 145, 207

Central Branch, 125, 127

Conventions: 88, 90–91, 158, 239

and Easter Rising, 207n

and feminist cause, xv, 35, 89, 90

Flag Day, 125–26

and Four Courts siege, 258–66

Heads Up (news leaflet), 240–41

and IRA and IRB, 89–90, 149; spy inquiry (1920), 158–60

Máire and. *see* Comerford, Máire
publicity department, 240–41
and Treaty (1921), 233–34,
  238–39; resignations of pro-
  Treaty members, 89, 239–40
Ulster work, 251
Cumann na nGaedheal, 108n,
  259n, 281
Curious Journey (film and book), 294
Curragh camp, 144, 146, 208n
mutiny (1914), 248n
Curraghduff, 155
Curran, John, 164
Curran, Maria, xv, 164, 165
Cusdendall Regatta, 147–48
Cushendun, 146–48
Custom House (Dublin), 134n,
  205, 257

Dáil Cabinet, 174–75
Dáil Éireann, xii, xiv, 13, 144, 150,
  164, 167, 168, 170, 174, 175, 176,
  188, 196, 210, 211, 212, 213, 222,
  224, 229, 231, 241, 242, 259, 262,
  276, 279
  elections (1921), 200–202
  financing of civil service, 122–23
  First Dáil, 13, 27, 43, 46n, 49, 64n,
    69, 76n, 98–104, 108, 109, 113,
    114, 115, 116, 121, 128, 199n,
    227; proscription, 102, 119
  lecture committee, xv, 218
  loan, 116, 122–23, 139
  offices. *see* Harcourt Street
  Publicity Department, xiv,
    138–39, 151, 188, 218, 238
  Second Dáil, 69, 213, 216, 225,
    226, 247, 254, 276

third anniversary, 201
Third Dáil, 246–47, 251–56;
  meeting with Provisional
  Government, 254
  and Treaty (1921): debates,
    228–29, 233–34, 235–36;
    elections (1922), 243–50,
    251–52; Peace Committee
    (1922), 246; factions, 246,
    253–54; ratification, 235–36,
    243n
  and War of Independence:
    meetings during, 216
Daily Mail, 269, 299–300
Dalton, Charles, *With the Dublin
  Brigade,* 89–90
Dalton, Emmet, 216, 255
Daly, Paddy (aka O'Daly), 263
Dante, 227
Dardanelles, 44, 116
'Dardanelles' (Wexford Street),
  114–15
Davis, Brigid, 66
Davis, Thomas, 239
Dawson Street (Dublin), 114, 126–27,
  179n. *see also* Mansion House
Dease, Charlotte, 56
Debrett's Peerage and Baronetage, 6
Defence of the Realm Act (DORA),
  41, 67
Dempsey, Frank, 186–87
Department of Finance, 122–23
Department of Home Affairs, 123
Department of Labour, 124
Derry, 65, 103, 147, 148, 202, 205,
  235, 247
Derrynane, 81–82

Despard, Charlotte, xvi, 77–78, 142, 156, 157, 252

Detroit, 286

de Valera, Éamon, xv. 27, 97, 100, 104, 113n, 121, 135, 140, 148, 176, 195, 196, 205, 206, 207, 213, 223, 227, 241, 242, 246–47, 254, 288, 292, 294. *see also* Fianna Fáil
    and 1921 elections, 202, 216; pact with Devlin, 200–201
    Cabinet changes, 174–75
    and Civil War, 259, 267, 275, 276, 277
    escape from Lincoln Jail, 102, 103
    London talks (July 1921), 208; Mansion House speech, 215
    and Treaty (1921), xv, 228, 229–31, 236, 237, 238; Document No. 2, 228, 231, 232; telegram to Pope, 221–22
    and USA, 193n, 283, 286; return from, 173, 174

Devereux (Glen of Downs), 162

Devlin, Joseph, xvi, 201

Devlin's pub (Dublin), 127

Dillon, Geraldine (Gerry) (née Plunkett), 184

Dillon, James, 95–96

Dillon, John, 95n, 96, 97

Dillon, Tommy, 184

Dineen, Fr Patrick, *Irish Dictionary*, 109

Dixon, Robert (Bob), 260–61

Dominic, Fr, 232

Donegal, 50, 179, 187–88, 252, 286

Donnelly, Eamon, 244

Donnelly, Simon, 170–71

Donnybrook, 54, 189, 206

Donoghue, Joseph, 140

Dorrins, Ned, 205

Dorset Regiment, 178

Douglas, James, 111, 156, 218

Down (county), 202, 215, 216, 247

Downing Street, 255

Downing Street (London), 202, 221, 223

Downpatrick, 235

Downside Abbey, 14, 18

Doyle, Chrissie, 239

Doyle, Seamus, 60, 205, 251

Doyne, Robert, 33

Drumcondra, 150, 273

Dublin (city), 6, 7, 11, 19, 52–53, 67, 69, 73, 76, 78, 83, 85, 91, 97, 98, 102, 107, 109, 125, 126, 129, 132, 140, 141, 143, 144, 145, 146, 149, 150, 156, 159, 161, 168, 175, 176, 177, 184, 187, 190, 194, 199, 204, 205, 206, 207, 209, 211, 216, 217, 222, 223, 226, 228, 234, 235, 240, 243, 245, 248, 249, 252, 260, 261, 275, 276, 277, 278, 279, 282, 284, 286, 287, 288, 295. *see also* Glasnevin Cemetery; GPO; Liberty Hall; Mansion House
    British administration, seat of. *see* Dublin Castle
    children's games, xiv, 169
    Civil War, 245, 246. *see also* Four Courts; Hammam Hotel
    and Easter Rising, 57–65. *see also* Easter Rising (1916)
    funeral of Thomas Ashe (1917), 74
    home of Stopford Green. *see* St Stephen's Green

lord mayor. *see* O'Neill, Laurence

Máire's 'half-mile radius,' 114–17

Provost Marshal, 85–86

Republican northside, 127–28

royal visit (1911), 239

streets and squares, 120, 125,
126, 240, 241, 261, 266, 269,
270, 271, 272, 273, 281. *see also*
Harcourt Street; Morehampton
Road; Parnell Square; St
Stephen's Green; Suffolk Street;
Wexford Street

Union Jacks, flying of, 233–35

War of Independence, 150–51;
safe houses, 190–97

Dublin Brigade IRA, 129n, 134n,
192n, 205, 246n, 268, 273

Dublin Castle, 8, 32, 49, 52, 54, 66,
90n, 111, 119, 128, 129, 129n, 168,
199, 201, 204

Bloody Sunday killings, 268n

G Men, 119

and Sinn Féin activists, 120–22

transfer to Provisional
Government (1922), 240–41

Dublin Corporation, 128, 239n

Dublin Fire Brigade, 272

Dublin Lockout (1913), 38, 64n, 66

Dublin Metropolitan Police (DMP),
120, 121, 134, 231, 263n

Dublin press, 215

Dublin University. *see* Trinity College
Dublin

Duggan, Eamonn, 211

Dumont, F.T.F., 114, 141, 177

Dumont, Mrs. ('Little Dear'), 141, 177

Dun Emer Guild, 196, 196n

Dun Emer Industries, 196n–197n

Dun Laoghaire, 219, 227, 283

Dunne, Reggie, 248n, 256, 259

Dunsany Castle, 40n

Dunsany, Lord (Edward Plunkett), 40

Dwyer, Edward, 151, 152

Dwyer, Frank, 151, 152

Dwyer, Kate, 152

Dwyer, Mrs, 152

Dwyer, Tom, 249

Earlsfort Terrace. *see* University
College Dublin

Easter Rising (1916), xiii–xiv, 20,
26n, 27n, 41, 43n, 46n, 49, 52–58,
53, 54, 55, 56, 59–64, 60, 68, 70n,
73–74, 76, 88, 94, 99n, 108, 109,
119, 129n, 146, 193, 199n, 207n,
211, 212, 214n, 221, 227, 228, 251,
259n, 263n, 286, 289

battles: Mount Street Bridge, 108,
115, 116; North King St atrocity,
59–60

Commemorations (1917), 64–65,
67, 76

Cork mobilisation, 136n

court-martials and executions, 49,
61–62, 64n, 65n

Fingal battalion, 72n

garrisons: Boland's Mills, 62n,
97n, 134n, 159n; Four Courts,
107n; GPO, 53, 56, 61, 62,
64n, 65, 265n, 270n, 280n;
St Stephen's Green, xiii–xiv,
54–55, 56

Northern Volunteers, 244n

prisoners: escapes, 102, 103–4;
release of, 69–70, 102–3

Proclamation, 62, 65–67, 88, 101

Egypt, 191
elections: (1918), 93–97, 250, 253n;
    (1921), 201, 202, 203; (1922),
    243–50, 251; Pact, 247–48, 249–50,
    260; (1923), 281–82
Elizabeth II, Queen, 239n
Ellis Island (New York), 285
Ellis, Mr (hangman), 131
Elvery's store, 272
Emmet, Robert, 53, 98
England, xiii, 5, 14, 24, 69, 102,
    103, 141, 153, 156, 172, 187,
    209, 210, 220, 221, 224, 226,
    247, 255, 283, 289
Enniscorthy, 14, 18, 19, 48, 49, 60,
    84, 245, 249, 266, 303
Cumann na mBan, 177–78
Enniscorthy Echo, 48–49, 70
Enniskerry, 276
Ennis, Thomas (Tom), 205, 257
Errington, Lady, 59–60
Esmonde, Dr (1792), 9
Esmonde, Eva. *see* Comerford, Eva
Esmonde family, 6–7, 18–21
Esmonde, Laurence, 33
Esmonde, Millie (aunt of Máire), 8,
    15, 19, 21, 33–34, 177
Esmonde, Matilda (grandmother of
    Máire), 7, 8, 19, 77, 177
Esmonde, Sir Thomas (cousin of
    Máire), xiii, 18–19, 25, 33, 49, 85,
    94, 300
Esmonde, Lt. Col. Thomas, VC
    (grandfather of Máire), xii–xiii, 7
Esmonde, Tommy (uncle), 18, 20,
    35–36, 48, 60, 77, 302
Esmonde, Zephie (aunt of Máire), 8,
    19, 20–21, 177

Etchingham, Seán (Johnny), xiv,
    36–37, 46, 47–51, 60, 69, 70,
    114–15, 162, 174, 175, 190, 192,
    204, 211, 234–35, 249, 251, 261n
    death and burial place, 50, 51
    'Mr Quinn,' 193–94
    'Patsy Patrick,' 48–49
    release from prison, 102–3
Ethics of Sinn Féin, The, 132
Europe, 82, 109, 138
Executive Forces (anti-Treaty), 246, 256

Fabian Society, 155
Fagan, Brian, 120
Famine, 4, 55
Farnborough school (Hampshire),
    23–24
Featherbed Mountain, 192n, 276
'Felons of our Land' (song), 71, 73
feminism. *see* women's rights
Fenians, 6, 38n, 39, 55, 68
Fermanagh, 202, 205, 246, 247
Fermoy, 276
Fermoy Barracks, 187
Ferns, diocese of, 95
Fethard (Co. Tipperary), 276
ffrench, Lord and Lady, 112
ffrench-Mullen, Madeleine, 66n
Fianna, 160
Fianna Éireann, Na, 44n, 76n,
    193n, 261
Fianna Fáil, 129n, 270n, 287,
    288–89, 292
Fine Gael, 95n, 108n, 259n
Fisher, J.R., 236n
FitzAlan, Lord, 240, 253
Fitzgerald, Desmond, 108, 112,
    134, 140

Fitzgerald family, 234
Fitzgerald, Mabel, 239, 240
Fitzsimmons, Anna. *see* Kelly, Anna
Flanagan, Captain Paddy, 205
Flanders, 42, 67, 86
Flannery (RIC Sergeant), 189
Fleming, Patrick J., 104, 135
Flower, Robin, 111
Fogarty, Charlie, 85
Ford, John, 27n
Forester, Margery, 294
Four Courts (Dublin), 107n, 171n,
    192n, 193n
    occupation (1922), xvi, 243, 246,
        252, 255, 271; battle, 255–57,
        258–66, 275, 279, 300
Four Courts Hotel, 261–62, 263
France, 77, 83
franchise, 82, 222, 241–42
Franco-Prussian War, 7–8
Freeman's Journal, 130
Free State (Saorstát Éireann), 100n,
    116n, 196, 226, 236n, 246, 262
Free State army, 80, 257n
    and Civil War, 270, 277, 278–79,
        280, 282, 283, 284, 289, 291;
        Four Courts siege, 260, 261; in
        Kerry, 263n; prisoners, 269–70;
        raids by, 280n
Free State Constitution, 249, 250,
    253, 254
Free Staters, 239, 245, 270
French, Colonel , 60
French, Lord, 77–78, 83, 121, 150
Friargate (mare), 48
Frongoch camp, 263n
Furry Park (Killester), 112n

Gaelic Athletic Association (GAA),
    27, 93
Gaelic League, xiii, 21n, 23, 36,
    67–68, 95n, 99n, 234n, 244n
Gaelic Revival, 36, 68
'Gaelic Sunday' (1918), 93n
Gaiety Theatre (Dublin), 26
Gallagher, Frank, 112, 129–30,
    140, 175
Galtee Mountains, 151
Galway, 6, 184
Galway Express, 184n
Galway IRA, 184n
Galway Jail, 184
Galway University, 184
Gandhi, Mahatma, 191, 260
'Gap of Danger,' 202, 205, 216
Garda Siochána, 231n
Garda Special Branch, 293
Gavan Duffy, George, 162
Gavan Duffy, Louise, 175, 192, 239
general elections. *see* elections
George V, King, 208, 221, 223–24, 249
    oath to. *see* Oath of Allegiance
    visit to Ireland (1911), 239
'German plot,' 90
German troops, 41, 42, 44, 45, 54
Gibbet Hill (Clohamon), 14, 68
Gibraltar, 174
Gilmartin, Dr Thomas, archbishop
    of Tuam, 184–85
Gilmore, George, 44
Gladstone, William Ewart, 80, 219
Glanmire, 180
Glanmore Castle, 159n
Glasgow, 65, 187
Glasnevin Cemetery, 3, 18, 72n,
    74, 127

Gleeson, Evelyn, 197n

Gleeson family (Moher), 154

Gleeson, John, 154

Gleeson, Mary Agnes, 154

Gleeson, Tom, 154

Gleeson, Willie ('Black Willie'), 154,
155–56

Glenart Wood, 209

Glencree, 276

Glendalough House (Annamoe),
13–14, 163, 276, 277, 278

Glen of the Downs, 162

Glens of Antrim, 148

Glenstal Abbey Archives, 292

Gloucester Jail, 104

G Men (Dublin Castle), 119

Gogarty, Oliver St John, *A Serious
Thing*, 175

Gonne, Maud. *see* MacBride, Maud
Gonne

Gordon, Patrick, 214n

Gordon, Winnifred (Una) (née
Cassidy, later Stack), 214, 276

Gorey, 8, 14, 50, 59, 61, 67, 68, 74,
77, 85, 91, 102, 211, 250, 261,
287, 291
    Cumann na mBan, 204
    election meeting (1918), 95–96

Government of Ireland Act (1920)
('Partition Act'), 173, 198, 200,
205, 224

GPO (Dublin), 65, 67, 73
    Easter Week garrison. *see* Easter
        Rising (1916)
    IRA intelligence agents, 122n

Gradwell, Miss, 28–29

Grand National, 21

Grattan, Henry, 18–19, 52

Great War. *see* World War I

Green, Alice Stopford. *see* Stopford
Green, Alice

Green family, 81

Green, John Richard, *Short History of
the English People,* 105

Green, Rev William Spotswood, 81

Gregory, Lady Augusta, 26n

Gresham Hotel (Dublin), 133, 216

Greystones Golf Club, 194

Griffith, Arthur, 100, 104, 112,
118, 145, 147n, 173, 174, 181,
182, 205, 247, 251, 253, 254,
255, 256, 260
    and 1921 elections, 202, 216
    death of, 279
    founding of Sinn Féin, 113n
    and franchise law, 241–42
    and provisional administration,
        238–39
    and Treaty (1921), 230–31;
        meetings and speeches (1922),
        241, 246; negotiations, 219,
        224; ratification, 235–36

Griffith, Kenneth, 294n

Guildford, 78

Hackett, Rosie, 66

Hales, Seán, 279

Hamman Hotel (Dublin), xvi, 266,
267–74, 275, 300

Hans Place (London), xvi, 221, 223

Harcourt Street (Dublin), 114, 116,
156, 211. *see also* Standard Hotel
    British raids, 171
    Sinn Féin and Dáil offices
        (Nos. 6 and 76), 118–22, 123,
        129n, 167

Harcourt Street Station, 77
Hayes, Michael (Professor), 259
Head, Dan, 205
Heads Up, 240–41
Hearst papers (New York), 120
Hegarty, Brede, 120
Henderson, Frank, 273
Henderson, Leo, 257
Henry, Augustine (Professor), 105, 111
Henry, Mrs Augustine, 105, 108, 111
Hickey's shop (Dublin), 271
Hoey, Patricia, 120–21
Hogan, Patrick, 246
Hogan, Seán, 150
Holloway Prison, 27n
Hollyfort Hill, 8
Holyhead, 283
Home Rule, viii, 3n, 21n, 25, 32–33,
    38, 45–46, 47, 55, 78, 80n, 91n,
    139, 147, 172, 174, 185, 219n. *see
    also* Irish Parliamentary Party
Home Rule Bill (1912), 25n, 26, 28n,
    32, 45
Home Rule League, 25n
Houlihan, Garry, 269
House of Commons, 19, 25–26, 29n,
    80, 199n
House of Lords, 80
Howard, Ralph Francis, 7th Earl of
    Wicklow, 11, 15
How Green Was My Valley (film), 27n
Howth gun-running (1914), 42, 99n,
    109, 195
Hoyne, Mary, 164
Hoyne's Hotel (Arklow), 164
Humphreys, Dick, 214n, 280n
Humphreys, Mary Ellen (Nell) (née
    O'Rahilly), 214, 223

Humphreys, Nell, 280n
Humphreys, Sighle, 280, 305

Independent, 130
India, 78, 173, 191, 260
influenza epidemic (1918), 91
Inghinidhe na hÉireann, 26–27,
    64n, 76n
IRA, 43, 44n, 64n, 133, 142, 153,
    154, 158n, 162, 163, 168, 183, 184,
    184n, 187, 204, 205, 209, 217,
    242, 245, 248, 275, 277, 279, 282,
    287, 288. *see also* Dublin Brigade
    IRA; Northern Divisions; War of
    Independence
  army council, 234n
  assassination of Sir Henry Wilson
    (1922), 248n
  and Belfast refugees, 217
  bombing campaign in England
    (1938–9), 160n
  and Cumann na mBan, 149,
    158–60
  and Dublin Castle transfer
    (1922), 240
  oath. *see* Republican Oath
  training courses, 216
  and Treaty (1921): anti-Treaty
    forces. *see* Republican IRA;
    pro-and anti-Treaty factions,
    246
  and Truce, 211, 216
  Volunteers, 144, 145, 152, 153,
    165, 170, 174, 190, 192, 195,
    198, 204, 205, 235, 242, 257,
    265, 279, 288
IRB, 21n, 27, 38n, 39, 46n, 48, 62n,
    64n, 65n, 67, 72n, 99n, 100n,

102n, 113n, 127, 145n, 207, 210, 223, 245
  and Cumann na mBan, 89–90
  and Treaty, 229, 230
Irish Agricultural Organisation Society, 33n
Irish Anti-Conscription Committee, 83n
Irish Bulletin, 167
Irish Bulletin, The, 108, 129n, 140
Irish Citizen Army, 64, 65, 66, 69, 77n
Irish Convention, 78
Irish Countrywomen's Association (ICA), xiii, 34–35
Irish Dames of Ypres, 37
Irish Freedom, 64n
Irish Free State. *see* Free State
Irish Guards, 256n
Irish Home Rule Party, 3n
Irish-Ireland Movement, 36, 68
Irish language, 22–23. *see also* Gaelic League
Irish National Invincibles, 145
Irish National Land League. *see* Land League
Irish Parliamentary Party, 3n, 19n, 25n, 26, 45, 94, 95n, 96, 97, 100, 185, 200, 201n
Irish Press, 129n, 292, 293
Irish Republic (Chicago), 304–6
Irish Republican Army. *see* IRA; Republican IRA (anti-Treaty forces)
Irish Republican Brotherhood. *see* IRB
Irish Times, 19, 20, 171, 172
Irish Unionist Alliance, 78n
Irish Unionist Parliamentary Party, 28n
Irish Volunteers, viii, 21, 35n, 36, 43, 46, 47, 49, 68, 74, 83–84, 86, 99n,

104, 119, 123, 130, 135, 140. *see also* Easter Rising (1916); IRA; War of Independence
  gun-running. *see* Howth gun-running (1914)
  Kerry Brigade, 100n
  Third Tipperary Brigade, 103n
  War of Independence. *see* IRA
  Wexford Brigade, 94n
  women's auxiliary. *see* Cumann na mBan
Irish Volunteers' Dependents' Fund, 280n
Irish White Cross. *see* White Cross
Irish Women's Franchise League, 63n
Iveagh Gardens (Dublin), 167

Jacob, Rosamond, 89, 156
James II, King, 7n
'John Bull,' 212
Johnston, Col. W. E., 121
Joyce, James, 69
Just Peggy (film), 27n
Jutland, battle of (1916), 34n

Kavanagh, Margaret, 85
Kavanagh, Mary, 179, 209
Kearns, Linda, 179–80, 273–74, 285, 286
Kellet's shop (Dublin), 169
Kelly, Anna (née Fitzsimmons) (Fitz), 120, 129–30, 292
Kelly, David, 119–20
Kelly, Eithne, 218
Kelly, Frank, 129n
Kelly, John, 84n
'Kelly the Boy from Killane' (song), 84
Kenmare, 79, 263n

Kenmare Bay, 79

Kennedy, Dr Henry, 111

Kennedy, Louie (Margaret/Lou), 159, 234

Kenny family, 204

Kenny, Mrs, 165

K'Eogh, Aileen ('The Matron'), xiv, 73–74, 96, 101, 127, 182, 292
    arrest and imprisonment, 178, 179, 180, 181–82

Kerry, 79, 80–81, 232, 263n, 282

Kerry Brigade (Irish Volunteers), 100n

Kettle, T.M., 30

Kiernan, Kitty, 102n

Kilbride (Co. Carlow), 73

Kilcoole, 46

Kildare, 145

Kildare Street Club, 217

Kilfeacle Cemetery, 151

Kilkelly, Mrs, 190

Kilkenny (city), 6

Killane, 84, 204

Killarney, 79

Kilmainham Jail, 43, 62n, 63n, 122, 159n, 170, 281, 290, 304

Kilmashogue, 199

Kilmichael ambush (1920), 171n

Kingsbridge railway station, 144, 153, 155

Kinnane family, 154–55

Kinnane, James, 155

Kinnane, Jerome, 155

Kirwan's pub (Dublin), 127

Knocklong, 150

Labour Party, 48, 249, 250, 251–52

Labour Party (Britain), 155

Ladies Club (London), 28

Ladies' Land League, 90

Lá na mBan (Women's Day, 1918), 91

Lancers (British army), 53

Land Bank, 163

Land Commission, 18

Land League, 8, 90n, 91n

Land War, 18

Larkin, James, 69

Lascelles, Lady Mary (Mrs Doyne), 33

Late Late Show, 294

Lawlor's (Heytesbury Street), 115

Lee, Mrs, 85

Leinster, 198, 201

Leinster House, 253, 254

Leinster, RMS (shipwreck), 18

Leitrim, 148, 149, 258

Leitrim Volunteers, 149

Lemass, Noel, 192

Le Matin (Paris), 141

Leo XIII, Pope, 99n

Lett, Mrs Harold, 34

Liberal Party, 19, 26, 142

Liberties (Dublin), 139

Liberty Hall (Dublin), 65, 66, 76–77

Liffey (river), 256

Liffey Dock Yard (Dublin), 133–34

Limerick, 112, 138, 139–40, 199, 206

Limerick Junction, 151, 155, 186, 206

Lincoln Jail, 27, 102, 121

Llewelyn Davies, Compton, 112

Llewelyn Davies, Moya (née O'Connor), 112

Lloyd George, David, 78, 142, 143, 144n, 173, 174, 175, 181, 200, 201, 202, 228, 235–36, 253, 254, 260
    and Four Courts battle, 255–56
    London peace talks (July 1921), 208

and Treaty negotiations, 221,
224–25
and Truce, 210
London, 34, 50, 111, 138, 139,
142–43, 146, 156, 161, 174, 181,
196, 200, 201, 212, 215, 226, 227,
230, 236, 247, 248, 259, 283, 284
July talks (1921), 208
Máire in (1912), xiii, 25–31
Treaty negotiations (1921), 62,
219, 220–24
London Battalion IRA, 256n
London Cumann na mBan, 27, 109
Londonderry House (London), 29
Londonderry, Lord, 29
London GPO, 112
Looby, Margaret, 276
Loughlinstown, 279
Loughrea, 184
Lynch, Kate (née Ryan), 151
Lynch, Liam, 278
Lynn, Dr Kathleen, 66, 271

Macardle, Dorothy, 141–43
The Irish Republic, 142
MacBride, Major John, 27n, 39,
209n
MacBride, Maud Gonne, vii, xvi,
27, 78, 141–42, 175, 209n, 252
MacBride, Seán, 209
McCann, Piaras, 104
McCarthy, Dan, 244
McCarthy's (Thurles), 153
MacCurtain, Tomás, 136, 137, 138
MacDermott, Seán, 64n
McDermott, Sorcha, 27
McDonagh, Joseph (Joe), 174, 175
McDonagh, Thomas, 26n, 56

McDonnell, Andrew (Andy), 134,
199, 237, 278
MacDonnells, 52n
McElroy, Margaret, 207
McEntee, Seán, 270
McGarry, Seán, 69, 103
McGrane, Eileen, 114, 179
McGrath, Paddy, 160, 279
McGrath, Seán ('Bainc ar
Siubhall'), 123
McKee, Dick, 170n, 268
McKelvey, Joe, 279
Macmine Castle, 37
MacNeill, Eoin, 70, 86, 106, 111,
140, 181, 182, 202, 216, 218,
236n, 242, 247
MacNeill, James, 283–84
MacNeill, Josephine (née Aherne), 283
Macready, Sir Cecil Frederick Nevil,
144, 211, 255
MacSwiney, Annie, 112
MacSwiney, Mary (Máire Nic
Suibhne), 112, 222–23, 228, 230,
245, 254, 301, 302
MacSwiney, Muriel, 269, 286
MacSwiney, Terence, 72, 100, 137,
138, 159, 212, 222, 232, 269
MacWhorter, Mary, 157
Maghera, xvi, 203
Mahaffy, Dr John Pentland, 74
Maher, George, 48
Maher, Matt, 48
Mahon, Sir Bryan, 67
Mallow, 186–87
Mallow Military Barracks, 187
Mallow Urban Council, 186
Malone, Brigid, 115n
Malone, Michael, 115

Manchester Guardian, 302–4

Manchester Jail, 104, 129n

Manners, J. Hartley, *Peg O'My Heart*, 27n

Mansfield, Maude (cousin of Máire), 53, 55

Mansion House (Dublin), 72–73, 83, 98, 100, 115, 122, 228, 247

   Aonach na Nollag (1921), 227

   Dáil meetings. *see* Dáil Éireann

   Peace Conference (1921), 211, 215

   President's office, 213

   rooms: Oak Room, 101, 121; Round Room, 98–99, 126, 183; Supper Room, 101, 126

   White Cross launch (1921), 183

Markievicz, Countess Constance, vii, xiii, xiv, xvi, 55, 76, 77, 100, 104, 124, 134–35, 174, 175, 179, 180, 214n, 222, 272, 301, 303

Marne, battle of, 43

Marsh's Library (Dublin), 107

Martial Law, 198

Martin, Hugh, 140–41

Maryborough Jail, 135

Mary, Princess, 33

Mary, Queen, 239n

Masonic Order, 217

Mater Hospital (Dublin), 128, 205, 268, 273

Mayo, 97

Meath, 28

Meath estates (Wicklow), 10

Meath, Lord, 10

Mechanics Institute Building, 262

Mellows, Barney, 120

Mellows, Liam, xv, 193, 194, 206, 211, 243, 248, 252, 304

Four Courts battle (1922), 260, 262, 264, 265, 266

   execution, 279

Middle East, 153

Midleton, Lord (William St John Brodrick), 78, 210

Military Pensions Acts, 288

Milory, Seán (Ó Muirthile), 207

Milroy, Seán, 120, 202, 242

Mitchell, John, 149

Moher, 153

Moloney, Helena, 64, 66–67, 89

Monaseed, 69

Mons, battle of, 42

Moore, Col Maurice, 33

Moran, Mary, 177–78

Moran's Hotel (Dublin), 268

Morehampton Road (Dublin), 257

   safe house, 190, 191–92, 194

Morning Post, 236n

Morrin, Paddy, 65

Morrison, Danny, 293

Mountjoy Prison, 73, 103, 107n, 127–29, 179, 180–82, 222, 257, 265, 290

   escapes, 104, 135, 182, 191

   executions, 130–31

   Máire Comerford in, 280, 288, 301, 305

   Republican hunger strike, 129–30, 305

   visiting justices, 180

Mount Nebo (Wexford), 8, 14

Mount St Benedict school (Gorey), 14, 37, 38, 39, 73, 74–75, 95, 127, 208, 209, 287, 291–92

   British raid, 178

Moville, 286

Moynihan, Patrick, 122
'Mr Thorne' (jockey). *see* Comerford, James
Mulcahy, Min (née Ryan), xvii, 239, 279
Mulcahy, Richard, 190, 211, 279
Mulvoy, Seán, 103
Munster, 198, 201
Munster Division (British army), 44
Murphy, Charlie, 69, 116, 119
Murphy, Fintan, 27
Murphy, Greg, 46
Murphy, Seamus, 184
Murray family (Drumcondra), 273
Murray, Mrs, 273
Murray, Willie, 120

National Agricultural and Industrial Development Association (NAIDA), 127
'National Aid,' 62
National Army, 107n. *see also* Free State army
Nationality, 116, 118
National Library (Dublin), 107–8
National Literary Society, 191
National Museum of Ireland, 165
National Union of Women's Suffrage Societies, 155
National University of Ireland, 110, 259n
National Volunteers, 33, 127
Nation, The, 46n
Neil-Watson, H. C., 156
Nenagh, 188–89
Nevinson, Henry, 140
Newtownmountkennedy, 162–63
New York, 120, 193n, 284–85, 286

Ní Bhruadair, Gobnait. *see* Brodrick, Albinia
Nic Shiubhlaigh, Máire (Mary Walker), 26–27
Nic Suibhne, Máire. *see* MacSwiney, Mary
Ní Riain, Eilís, 207
Nolan, Dr, 91
Nolan, Seán, 264
North Dublin Union (NDU) barracks, 280–81, 305
Northern Catholics, 203, 216–17
Northern Divisions (IRA), 86, 216, 229
Northern Ireland, 200, 228–29, 246, 293
Northern Ireland Parliament, 200–203
  official opening, 208, 223–24
Northern Irish Volunteers, 244n
Northern nationalists, 200–201, 235, 236
Northern Protestants, 203
North Sea, 42, 43
Nugent, Larry, 117
Nugent, Mrs, 117

Oakley Road (Ceannt home), 124, 219, 252–53
Oath for the Republic. *see* Republican Oath
Oath of Allegiance, 201, 223, 225, 226, 249, 253
O'Brennan, Áine. *see* Ceannt, Áine (Mary Francis)
O'Brennan, Elizabeth (Lily), 62, 124, 190, 214, 219–20, 223
O'Brien, Art, 27
O'Brien, Kate, xiii

O'Brien, Paddy, 256, 257, 265–66

O'Callaghan, Kate, 112, 138–39, 222, 241

O'Callaghan, Michael, 112, 138–39, 140

Ó Ceallaigh, Seán (Sceilg) (J.J. O'Kelly), 174, 286

Ó Ceallaigh, Seán T. see O'Kelly

Ó Conaire, Pádraic, 126

O'Connell, Daniel (the Liberator), 81–82

O'Connell, Jeremiah Joseph ('Ginger'), 257, 262, 265

O'Connell, John, 82

O'Connell, Maura, 272–73

O'Connell, Miss, 82

O'Connor, Art, 174, 271

O'Connor, Batt, 120, 134

O'Connor, Fergus, 134

O'Connor, Mary Elizabeth. see Llewelyn Davies, Moya

O'Connor, Rory, 227–28, 243, 254, 254n, 264, 266, 279, 300, 304

O'Donel family, 127, 175

O'Donel, Gerry, 127, 258, 261, 262

O'Donel, Josephine (Joe), 127, 281

O'Donel, Lile, 127

Ó Donnchadha, Dáithí, 116, 122–23, 139–40

O'Donnell, Peadar, 256

O'Donovan, D. J., 122

O'Donovan Rossa, Jeremiah, 38–39

O'Dwyer, Seamus (James), 246

O'Flanagan, Fr Michael, 95, 99, 203, 286

O'Hanrahan, Michael, 128

O'Hanrahan sisters, 128

O'Hegarty, P.S., 111, 218
    Victory of Sinn Féin (1924), 229–30

O'hÉigeartuigh (O'Hegarty), Diarmuid, xv, 210

O'Higgins, Brian, 234–35

O'Higgins, Kevin, 254–55, 254n, 255, 256, 259

O'Kane, Mr, 148

O'Keefe, Fr John, 84

O'Keefe, Páidín, 119, 124, 203, 244

O'Kelly, J.J. (Sceilg). see Ó Ceallaigh, Seán

O'Kelly (Ó Ceallaigh), Seán T., 46, 70, 212, 245, 272

Omagh, 228

O'Mahony, John, 246

O'Mahony, Mr, 202, 205

Ó Máille, Pádraic, 279

O'Malley, Ernie, 170–71, 265, 280

Ó Muirthuile, Seán. see Milroy, Seán

Ó Murchada, Colm, 107

O'Neill, Joseph, 37

O'Neill, Laurence, 83n, 116, 121, 122, 129

O'Neill, Shane, 52

Oola (Limerick), 186

O'Rahilly (Rahilly), Anna, 63–64

O'Rahilly, The, 39, 63n, 214n, 280n

Orange Free State, 218n

Orange ladies, 148

Orange Order, 7n, 100n, 204, 224, 260

Orange pogroms, 86–87

Orange riots, 7

O'Reilly, Patrick, 205

O'Reilly, Stephen, 205

O'Shea, Katherine, 3n

O'Shea-Leamy, Mrs, 239

O'Shea, William, 3n

O'Sullivan, Joe, 248n, 256, 259
O'Sullivan, Mary, 116, 121
Our Lady's Bower (Athlone), 22–23

Palestine, 175
Paris, 45
Paris Peace Conference (1919–20),
  100–101, 173n, 221
Parkhurst prison, 163
parliamentary elections. see elections
parliamentary franchise. see franchise
Parliament House (College Green),
  241, 253
Parnell, Anna, xiii, 91n
Parnell, Charles Stewart, xii, 3, 4–5, 8n,
  18, 19, 25n, 74, 90, 91n, 185, 219
Parnell, Delia Stewart, xii, 4, 5–6
Parnell, Fanny, 5
Parnell, Sir John, 5
Parnell Square (Dublin), 62, 124,
  125, 127, 268
Parry, Gertrude (née Bannister),
  146, 147, 148
Parry, Sydney, 146, 147, 148
Partition, xvi, 200, 201, 236n,
  276, 289
Partition Act. see Government of
  Ireland Act (1920)
Patrick, Saint, 111, 136
Paul-Dubois, Louis, *Contemporary
  Ireland*, 30, 33
Payne-Townshend, Charles Frances
  (Mrs George Bernard Shaw), 66
Peace Committee (1922), 246
Pearse, Margaret, 286
Pearse, Padraig, 38n, 39, 56, 60, 62,
  64, 68, 86, 113, 159, 160, 176, 196,
  207n, 212, 249, 286, 288

Pearse, Willie, 286
Peel, Robert, 119
Peg O'My Heart, 27n
Pembroke Republican Court, 124
Pembroke UDC, 214n
Penal Laws, 6, 82n
Pentonville Jail, 43n, 69
Perolz, Marie (Mary/Máire), xiii, 77
Perth, archbishop of. see Clune, Patrick
Phelan family, 116, 175
Phelan, Maeve, 278
Phelan, Mrs, 114
Phoenix Park, 255
Phoenix Park killings (1882), 145n
Pilkington, Ellice (née Esmonde)
  (cousin of Máire), xiii, 34, 67, 94
Pitt, William, 5n
Plunkett, Count, 99, 100, 174, 175,
  207n, 227, 265n
Plunkett, Edward John, Lord
  Dunsany, 40
Plunkett family, 175, 227
Plunkett, Fiona, 207
Plunkett, George (Seoirse), 265
Plunkett, Sir Horace, 33, 34, 36n, 111
'Plunkett House people,' 36
Plunkett, Joseph, 57, 67, 99n, 184,
  207n, 265n
Plunkett, Josephine, 207n
Plunkett, Mimi, 67
Poblacht na hÉireann (War News), 259
Portadown, 44
Portland Prison, 210
Portobello Barracks, 88
Price, Dr Dorothy, 271
prisoners. see Republican prisoners
Proportional Representation Society
  of Ireland, 147n

Protestants, 4, 8, 19, 30–31, 32, 50, 87, 97, 147, 200
Provisional Government, 240, 241, 253, 255, 260
    joint meeting with Dáil, 254
Provisional parliament. *see* Southern Ireland parliament
Punch, 48, 212n

Quakers, 156
Quinn, Máire T., 27
Quisling, Vidkun, 119

Railway Hotel (Limerick), 139
Railway Men's Union, 186
Ram's Arms Hotel (Gorey), 95
Ranelagh, 124, 203, 214n
Rathdrum, xii, 3, 4, 6, 10–16, 17, 22, 48, 292
Rathfarnham, 39n, 159
Rathgar, xiii, 53, 55
Rathkeale Jail, 199n
Rathmines Republican Court, 124
Reading Jail, 193n
Rebellion of 1798, 5, 9n, 26n, 50n, 69, 84, 162
Red Cross, 80, 183–84, 261, 266
Redmond, James, 106
Redmond, John, 19, 25n, 26, 33, 42, 45–46, 82, 85, 220
Red Scare, 260
Repeal Association, 81n
Republican Courts, 116, 124, 155, 234n, 274n
Republican government, xv
Republican IRA (anti-Treaty forces), 238, 239, 244n, 251, 254, 255–66, 275, 277, 278, 279, 281, 282, 283, 284, 285, 288, 289, 290, 291, 292, 293, 294. *see also* Civil War; Four Courts
    dumping of arms (1923), 287
    Hammam Hotel, operations from, 267–74
Republican Oath, 166, 176, 246
Republican police, 170–71, 231, 241
Republican prisoners, 127–31, 178–82, 184, 199, 234n
    escapes, 135, 182, 191, 193n
    hunger strikes, 73, 129, 130n, 138, 274n, 280, 281, 282, 284, 286, 302, 304, 305, 306
    (1922–23), 280–82, 284, 286;
    executions, 246n, 254n, 279
Republican Prisoners' Dependents' Fund, 66, 110, 207n, 274n
Republicans, 20, 35, 50, 63, 68, 76, 78, 84, 85, 96, 100, 112–13, 114, 115, 116n, 118, 119, 120, 121, 123, 126, 127, 130, 140, 144, 147, 148, 151, 153, 156, 166, 168, 176, 178, 179, 184, 185, 189, 190, 195, 201, 207, 210, 211, 214, 216, 219, 220, 224, 234. *see also* IRA; IRB
    and 1922 elections, 243, 244, 245, 246
    anti-Treaty forces (1922–23). *see* Republican IRA
    boycotting of, 287
    intransigents, exclusion of, 174–75
    women activists. *see* Cumann na mBan; Republican women
Republican women, vii–viii, xv, 88–92, 254, 258–59, 269n, 299–300. *see also* Cumann na mBan

Republic, the, 119, 144, 164, 174, 175, 177, 203, 206, 207, 215, 218, 219, 221, 226, 227, 229, 230, 236, 238, 239, 245, 246, 247, 249, 275, 276, 286, 288
flag of, 241
Restoration of Order Ireland Act (1920), 41n
RIC. *see* Royal Irish Constabulary (RIC)
Richards, Mrs, 276
Richmond Barracks, 134n, 159n, 214n
Rigney, Máire, 120, 179, 180, 239
Riverchapel band, 95, 102–3
Riverchapel Schoolhouse, 96, 276
Robinson, David, 43
Robinson, Seamus, 150
Rock of Cashel, 151
Roebuck House, xvi
Rooney, Willie, 145
Roscommon, 179, 191
Ross, 204
Rowantree, Mother, 24
Royal Court Theatre (London), xiii, 26, 27
Royal Dublin Society, 253
Royal Hussars, 208n
Royal Irish Academy, 107, 109
Royal Irish Constabulary (RIC), 7, 41, 50, 84, 90n, 103n, 158n, 189, 214n
Royal Munster Fusiliers, 256n
Russell, George (Æ), 111, 218
Russell Hotel (Dublin), 55, 116
Russian Revolution, 212, 260
Ryan, Alice and Kate, 151
Ryan, Michael, 155
Ryan, Min. *see* Mulcahy, Min

St Catherine's Church (Thomas St, Dublin), 53
St Enda's School. *see* Scoil Éanna
St Nessans (Sandyford), vii, 292–93
St Patrick's Cathedral (Dublin), 134
St Scholastica's school (Courtown Harbour), 37–38
St Stephen's Green (Dublin), 133, 141–42, 168–69, 171, 192, 229
    Easter Week garrison, xiii–xiv, 54–55, 56
    home of Stopford Green (No. 90). *see* Stopford Green, Alice
    Máire's 'half-mile radius' from, xiv, 114–17
St Ultan's Hospital for Infants (Dublin), 66n
Sallins (Co. Kildare), 145
Sands, Bobby, 293n
Sandyford Village, vii, 292
Sandy Row (Belfast), 146–47, 252
Sarsfield, Patrick, 55
Scanlon ('Big Scanlon'), 96
School of Irish Learning (York St, Dublin), 107
Scoil Bhríde (Dublin), 192n
Scoil Éanna (St Enda's School), 39, 159, 160
Scoil Íte (Cork), 222
Scotland, 148
Screen, 250
Sea of Moyle, 148
Shannon, Mrs, 66
Shaughnessy, Hannah, 85
Shaw, Charlotte Frances (née Payne-Townshend), 66
Shaw, George Bernard, 66n
Sheehan, Cis, 27

Sheehan, Paddy, 159

Sheehy-Skeffington, Francis, 63n, 88

Sheehy-Skeffington, Hanna, 63–64,
88–89, 156, 286

Shelbourne Hotel (Dublin), 56,
114, 141

'Shinners,' 216–17

Simon, Sir John, 139, 168

Sing Sing Prison, 285

Sinn Féin, xii, xiv, 19, 21n, 30, 46n,
62n, 63n, 64n, 88, 95, 96, 113, 114,
119, 124, 129, 145, 147n, 162, 163,
164, 200, 234, 252, 281, 282, 286,
293n, 294
   Ard Craobh, 120
   ard fheiseanna: (1917), 113n;
     (1921), 223; (1922), 240,
     247, 289
   Courtown Harbour club, 70
   elections. see elections
   Ethics of Sinn Féin, 132
   and Fianna Fáil, 287, 288
   and First Dáil. see Dáil Éireann
   founding of, 113n
   and 'German plot,' 90n
   headquarters. see Harcourt Street
     (Dublin)
   and Treaty (1921), 247;
     anti-Treaty organisation,
     243–50, 244–45, 286;
     election Pact (1922).
     see elections; pro-Treaty
     organisation, 251; split, 243n

Sinn Féin Bank, 119

Sinn Féiners, 36

Skerries College, 118

Skinnider, Margaret, 252

Slaney Lodge (Enniscorthy), 18

Slattery, Miss, 19

Sligo, 179, 191

Snowden, Ethel, 155–56

'Soldier's Song, The,' 73

Soloheadbeg Ambush (1919), 103,
115n, 150

South Africa, 132, 218, 228

Southampton, 7

South Dublin Brigade (IRA), 134n

Southern Ireland parliament, 201,
208, 238–39, 240, 253, 254

Southern Unionists, 176, 230

Squad ('Twelve Apostles'), 64n, 90,
170n, 236–37, 263n

Stack, Austin, 100, 104, 123, 159,
214n

Stack, Winnifred (Una) (née
Cassidy), 214, 276

Staigue Fort, 82

Standard Hotel (Dublin), 122,
156–57

Stanley, Joe, 67

Stanley Street, 268

Star Chamber, 168

State, Department of, 240

Stephens, James, 111

Stewart, Delia. see Parnell,
Delia Stewart

Stockley, Germaine, 112, 136,
137, 138

Stockley, W. P. (Professor), 112,
136–38

Stopford, Dr Dorothy (later Stopford
Price), 168

Stopford Green, Alice, xii, 27, 114,
116, 135, 136, 138, 139, 140, 159,
161, 166, 167–69, 171–73, 177,
179, 222

Dublin home (90 St Stephen's
Green), xiv, 106, 108, 110–13,
114, 168–69, 171, 217–18; raid
on, 133, 166–67; visitors, 133,
134, 135, 136–38, 140–41, 161,
167–68, 210, 218
letters of, 172
Máire Comerford and, xv,
172–73, 218; Cushendun
holiday (1920), 146–49;
secretary and researcher, xiv, xv,
105–13; Tipperary assignments
(1920), 151–56
publications, 105, 111, 112
and Tom Casement, 132–33
and Truce (1921), 210
and White Cross, 188, 189
Strangeways Jail, 104
Suffolk Street (Dublin), 243, 272, 286
Swan, the (Athy), 135
Sweetman, Fr J.F., xiv, xvii, 14, 37–39,
73, 74–75, 85, 96, 127, 178, 179,
181–82, 208–9, 291–92
Switzerland, 42
Switzers, 283
Swords, 162
Synge, Alexander Hamilton, 159n
Synge, Doreen Hamilton, 159
Synx (racehorse), 19

Tailors' Hall (Dublin), 9, 293
'Tan War.' see War of Independence
Tara, 50, 68
Taylor, Mr, 167
Teeling, Frank, 170–71
Thames (river), 111
Third Tipperary Brigade, 103n
Thurles, 153, 154

Times (London), 80, 161
Tipperary, 103, 206
War of Independence, 151–56
White Cross work, 186–87
Tipperary Brigade IRA, 150, 171n
Tivoli (Cork), 136, 137
Tobin, Paddy, 249
Tone, Theobald Wolfe, 9, 104, 200,
204, 212. see also Bodenstown
commemorations
Tories, 173–74
Trade Union Congress (TUC), 38
Transvaal, 218n
Travellers' Aid, 285
Traynor, Oscar, 134, 205, 268
Traynor, Thomas, 131
Treacy, Seán, 150–51, 152
Treaty (1921), 116n, 138, 144n, 185,
192n, 231, 232, 236, 239, 240,
241, 242, 245, 246, 247, 248, 250,
251, 253, 254, 255, 256, 259, 262,
276, 277, 281. see also Boundary
Commission
Dáil debates, 228–29, 233–34,
235–36
Dáil ratification, 235–36, 243n
negotiations, 45n, 62, 161, 219,
220–24; Irish delegation, xvi,
62n, 104n, 220–21, 222
opponents of, 193n, 222n,
227–30, 237, 238, 248, 251,
277; and 1922 election,
243–44; anti-Treaty forces. see
Civil War; Republican IRA
and partition, 173n
signing of, 64n, 224–25, 226
split, 226–32
Treaty of Limerick (1691), 55, 82n

Trinity College Dublin, 28n, 52n, 54, 73, 74, 107, 253, 253n
Truce (1921), 127, 206–12, 213, 215, 217, 228, 233, 241, 276
    Gresham Hotel offices, 216
    terms of, xv, 210–11
Tuam, 184
Tyrone, 202, 205, 247

Uisneach, Hill of, 16
Ulster, 97, 174, 200, 201n, 203, 216, 252. *see also* 'Gap of Danger'; Northern Ireland
    provisional government, 29, 45
    religious Civil War, 203
Ulster Covenant, xiii, 28, 45n
Ulster Division (British army), 44
Ulster Protestants, 87
Ulster Unionist Council, 29
Ulster Unionists, 28n, 173n
Ulster Volunteers, 21n, 29–30, 45, 86
Unionists, 26, 28, 78, 97, 100, 162, 176, 202, 230, 236n, 255, 256. *see also* Carson, Sir Edward; Southern Unionists; Ulster Unionists
Union Jack (flag), 133–34, 146–47, 148, 200, 233–34, 235
United Irishman, 145n
United Irishmen, 9n, 34–35, 55, 69n, 200
United Irishwomen, xiii, 34–35, 36
United States, 6, 21, 39, 63n, 88–89, 95n, 101, 102n, 104, 141, 156, 157, 173, 174, 193, 220, 222, 260, 274n
    Máire in, xvii, 283, 284–86
University College Dublin (UCD), 106, 259

Treaty debates (Earlsfort Terrace), 231–32, 233–34
University College Dublin Archives, viii
Upperchurch, 154

Valentine, Emily, 207
Vale of Clara (Wicklow), 10
Vane-Tempest-Stewart, 6th Marquess of Londonderry, 29
Vatican, 59
Vaughan's Hotel (Dublin), 127
Veney, Charlotte, 204
Veney, Mrs, 204
Versailles, 101, 221
Victoria Cross, 7
Victoria, Queen, 7
Volunteers (1778–82), 5
Volunteers (1913–19). *see* Irish Volunteers

Walker, Mary (Máire Nic Shiubhlaigh), 26–27
Walsh, D. P., 83
Walshe family, 6
Walsh, J. J., 104
Wandsworth Prison, 256n
War of Independence, viii, 13, 27n, 43, 47, 89, 107, 115n, 116–17, 144–45, 150–57, 165, 168, 170–76, 184, 187, 209, 216, 244, 246n, 263n, 265n, 277, 294
    American and English visitors, 156–57; journalists, 140–41
    Bloody Sunday (1920), 170–71
    British terror campaign, xiv–xv, 151–56, 188, 199–200. *see also* Black and Tans; martial law,

198, 201, 207; murder gangs, 138, 139–40

casualties, 165, 204, 205, 208

fear and bravery, 209–10

IRA actions, 170; Adavoyle ambush (1921), 208; Custom House, 204; female spy inquiry, 158–59; flying columns, 103, 123, 123n; intelligence agents, 122n; Kilmichael ambush, 171n

Republican prisoners, 127–31; arrests and escapes, 177–82

safe houses, 112n, 162–63, 190–97, 214. *see also* Woods, Mrs (Maa)

Special Squad. *see* Squad

spies, 158–61

Truce (1921), 206–11

Washington, 286

Waterford, 179

Webb, J. H., 156

West Britons, 18, 23, 29, 233

Westcove House (Kerry), 81n

Westmeath, 140

Westminster, 111

Westminster (parliament), 45, 46, 76n, 153, 201n, 242. *see also* House of Commons

Westminster Gazette, 301–2

West, Mr, 65, 67

Wexford, 14, 35, 36, 48, 59, 60, 64, 81, 104, 106, 116, 167, 184, 194, 204, 208, 211, 261n, 269, 287, 303. *see also* Courtown; Enniscorthy; Gorey Cumann na mBan, xii, xiv, 83, 84–85, 89–91, 177–79, 204 elections (1922), 251; anti-Treaty electioneering, 243–45, 249–50

Máire's family, xii–xiii, 6–7, 10–13, 18–21, 32–34

political controversy, 32–33

Rebellion (1798), 69n

War of Independence, 204; martial law, 178

and WWI, 41–42

Wexford Street (Dublin), 114–15

Wexford Volunteers, 46, 83

White Cross, xii, xiii–xiv, 124, 183–89, 204

White, Jack, 162

White, Mrs, 120

Wicklow, 162–65, 209, 277

Wicklow County Council, 163

Wicklow Gap, 209

Wicklow, Lord, 11, 15

Wild Geese, 55, 82

William III, King, 7n

Wilson, Sir Henry, 247–48, 255, 256, 259

Wilson, Lea, 70, 96

Wilson, Woodrow, 88, 100n, 109, 121

Wolfe Tone Society, 293

women activists, xv, 88–92. *see also* Cumann na mBan; Republican women; women's rights

Women's Alliance of the Ancient Order of Hibernians of America, 157

Women's League for Peace and Freedom, 157

women's rights/feminism, xiii, xv, 9, 35, 241–42, 292 Cumann na mBan and, xv, 35, 89, 90

Women's Workers Union, 66

Woodenbridge, 45, 46, 208

Woods family, 175, 206, 211, 257

Woods, Mrs (Maa), xv, 189, 190–92, 193, 194, 256–57
Woods, Tony, 190, 257
Workers' Republic, The, 66
World Court, 221
World War I, viii, 34n, 37, 39, 40–46, 100n, 159n, 193n, 212, 256n
World War II, 25
'Wrap the Green Flag' (song), 103
Wyse Power, Jenny (O'Toole), 90–91, 239

Wyse Power, Nancy, 90–91

Yeats, Elizabeth and Susan, 197n
Yeats, Jack, xiv, 105, 197n
Yeats, Mrs, 105
Yeats, William Butler, 27n, 197n
    Cathleen Ni Houlihan, xiii, 26, 145n
Yeo, Captain, 178
Yeomanry, 50
Yorkshire, 80
Young Irelanders, 55